Praise for
IMPLEMENTING U.S. HUMAN RIGHTS POLICY

"*Implementing U.S. Human Rights Policy* turns the spotlight on the United States' mixed record of promoting human rights throughout the world. The cases explored in this volume will prompt sober reflection and perhaps some regret for missed opportunities. However, they also will inspire pride in America's abiding commitment to the cause of human rights and hope that the United States can play a robust role as a champion of freedom even more effectively in the future."

JIMMY CARTER
President of the United States, 1977–81

"Over the past quarter-century, human rights have become a major concern in U.S. foreign policy, but rarely is that concern implemented in a coherent and compelling fashion. Students, scholars, activists, and policymakers seeking to understand why will find no better guide than this outstanding collection. With detailed and accessible case studies by an exceptional group of country specialists, *Implementing U.S. Human Rights Policy* analyzes the possibilities, contradictions, and constraints in U.S. foreign policy and, most crucially, the conditions for making human rights count in widely varying contexts. Timely, constructive, and informative, this book should be read by anyone who cares about improving human rights around the world."

LARRY DIAMOND
Senior Fellow at the Hoover Institution, Stanford University

"The stated objective of American foreign policy is to help make the 21st Century the Century of Democracy and Human Dignity. How realistic is that aim? How effective will those opponents be whose power is thereby threatened and who will resist that objective? How determined and consistent will we be as we face those who resist and retaliate with violence? This volume should help us understand where we are on the way to our goal and what obstacles still lie in our way."

MAX M. KAMPELMAN
Ambassador and Former Head of the U.S. Delegation to the Conference on Security and Cooperation in Europe; Chairman Emeritus, Freedom House

"This volume offers a unique and extensive analysis of the evolution of U.S. human rights policy in fourteen key countries and places that policy evolution thoughtfully within the broader frame of U.S. foreign policy and bilateral relations. A most useful volume—one that I will consult frequently in my own work."

HAROLD KOH
Gerard C. and Bernice Latrobe Smith Professor of International Law, Yale Law School

"This thought-provoking book offers readers a unique perspective by connecting academic study and policy work in its examination of the United States' role in protecting and enforcing human rights policies. This important contribution allows us to move away from simple slogans and old formulations and instead look critically at what works in the pursuit of human rights today."

WILLIAM F. SCHULZ
Executive Director, Amnesty International USA

"In a world wracked by conflict and terrorism, the promotion of human rights has become increasingly important to international security. This useful volume of essays edited by Debra Liang-Fenton traces the growth of human rights promotion in U.S. foreign policy over the last decade and offers lessons for policymakers drawn from fourteen different country situations. With its practical emphasis on 'what works' and what doesn't, the book offers valuable insights into the interplay between human rights and other competing—and often dominant—interests in foreign policy."

JOHN SHATTUCK
CEO, John F. Kennedy Library Foundation; Former Assistant Secretary of State for Democracy, Human Rights, and Labor

Implementing U.S. Human Rights Policy

Implementing U.S. Human Rights Policy

Agendas, Policies, and Practices

EDITED BY DEBRA LIANG-FENTON

UNITED STATES INSTITUTE OF PEACE PRESS
Washington, D.C.

The views expressed in this book are those of the authors alone. They do not necessarily reflect views of the United States Institute of Peace.

UNITED STATES INSTITUTE OF PEACE
1200 17th Street NW, Suite 200
Washington, DC 20036-3011

First published 2004

Printed in the United States of America

The paper used in this publication meets the minimum requirements of American National Standards for Information Science—Permanence of Paper for Printed Library Materials, ANSI Z39.48-1984.

Library of Congress Cataloging-in-Publication Data
Implementing U.S. human rights policy : agendas, policies, and practices /
    edited by Debra Liang-Fenton.
        p. cm.
    Includes bibliographical references and index.
    ISBN 1-929223-49-8 (cloth) — ISBN 1-929223-48-X (pbk.)
    1. Human rights—Case studies. 2. Human rights—Government policy—
United States—Case studies. 3. United States—Foreign relations—20th
century—Case studies. I. Title: Implementing US human rights policy. II. Liang-
Fenton, Debra. III. United States Institute of Peace.

JC571.I475 2004
323'.0973—dc22   2004066335

Contents

PART V The Middle East

PART VI Conclusion

Foreword

President Jimmy Carter's decision to make the promotion of human rights a key aspect of his administration's foreign policy was a dramatic but risky innovation. President Reagan was later to show that human rights could be a powerful force for change in adversary states such as the Soviet Union, but Carter's initiative held dangers —as proponents of realpolitik were quick to point out—because it constrained America's ability to pursue core national interests such as the maintenance of vital security relationships and the development of foreign trade and investment. Many of the geostrategically important countries with which the United States had close ties were run by repressive regimes. Would the United States put those ties at risk for the sake of denouncing human rights abuses? Carter's decision was also risky because it opened up the United States to accusations of moral deceit and hypocrisy. Public proclamations from the White House of a national commitment to the cause of human rights would ring embarrassingly hollow when, as was inevitable, the United States would find it either inexpedient or impossible to insist that all of its client states and allies forsake their rights-abusing ways. Also, and somewhat contradictorily, experience has shown that our government tends to apply human rights standards selectively, demanding more of friendly states than of adversaries.

These risks associated with human rights promotion were real, and remain so. Indeed, they have been amplified by the declaration of the war on terrorism, which has been presented as a fight not only for U.S. national security but also for the human dignity of the peoples held captive by repressive regimes that breed and support terrorists. Countries such as Saudi Arabia and Pakistan, with their high geostrategic importance and poor human rights records, illustrate the near impossibility of waging a fight on both these fronts simultaneously. Furthermore, these dilemmas can exact a significant price in terms of the coherence of, and support for, U.S. foreign policy objectives. For instance, the erosion of international sympathy and support for the United States since the attacks of 9/11 is fueled in part by a widespread perception that U.S. declarations of high moral purpose in its war on terrorism are hypocritical and self-serving.

How should the United States deal with this dilemma? Should it abandon its commitment to human rights? To do so would be to turn America's back on the considerable advances made over the past fifty years in international acceptance of the notion of inalienable individual rights. To do so would be to deny the long-term advantages to U.S. security and prosperity that accrue from the global spread of democracy and of the human rights that democracy sustains. More profoundly, to do so would stifle the American sense of mission, the self-perception of our country as a society whose values have universal resonance, whose greatness lies not in its economic or military prowess but in the freedoms and liberties that inspire people around the world.

The problem of balancing ethical and practical objectives cannot be solved by summarily abandoning the human rights component of U.S. foreign policy. Rather, as several contributors to this volume argue, the solution is less spectacular and more complex, less dramatic and more demanding. It is to fashion a foreign policy of coherence and consistency by encouraging policymakers to match goals with means, to remember the practical challenges of policy implementation during the process of policy formulation.

In pursuit of this goal, *Implementing U.S. Human Rights* makes a significant contribution. The volume brings a unique breadth and depth of perspective to our understanding of how stated U.S. human rights objectives have been translated or mistranslated into practice or ignored. Examining no fewer than fourteen countries, the authors of this impressive volume explore the evolution of U.S. policy over recent decades. They underline the complex interplay of differing goals, competing interests, and shifting circumstances in the process of policy implementation. Not only do they evaluate results but they also seek to disentangle the contributions to those outcomes made by a large cast of actors—ranging from the White House to Congress, from human rights activists to U.S. ambassadors. The cases covered include both successes (South Africa is probably the greatest cause for celebration) and failures (Rwanda is surely one of the darkest chapters). In most instances, however, the impact of U.S. policies on local respect for human rights is shown to have been mixed. Throughout, as the volume's editor, Debra Liang-Fenton, emphasizes in her introduction and conclusion, the contributors seek to answer one overarching question: When it comes to implementing U.S. human rights policy, what works?

This concern with the practical as well as the analytical dimensions of U.S. foreign policy was central to the United States Institute of Peace's Human Rights Implementation Project, from which this book emerged. Launched in 1999, the project sought to critically examine human rights policies promoted by the U.S. government in order to identify ways in which they might be improved. Like many other initiatives undertaken by the Institute, the project brought together highly respected figures from a variety of fields to exchange ideas and build a body of knowledge informed by multiple perspectives. Policymakers, diplomats, academics, and human rights activists met together in a spirit of constructive and critical assessment. Their aim was not to defend or damn the U.S. record on human rights, but to calmly assess past policies and to carefully tease from the experience of their application lessons for future practice. Given the passions that the subject of human rights regularly and understandably inflames, this goal was far from modest. Fortunately, however, the participants in the project succeeded admirably, and this volume testifies to their impressive ability to steer clear of denunciations and obfuscations while still offering forthright and revealing critiques of U.S. policy.

We at the Institute would like to think that tackling sensitive subjects candidly but not censoriously has become a hallmark of much of our work. Other organizations have ideological or institutional imperatives that lead them to defend particular views and to denounce others. The Institute, in contrast, has been charged by Congress with examining international conflicts from a nonpartisan vantage point and with improving the conduct of U.S. foreign policy. Its mission is to expand, not to narrow, understanding of the ways of preventing, managing, and resolving conflict. In practice, this means spotlighting issues that are almost inevitably highly charged politically, issues that elicit strong reactions not only from the parties directly involved in conflicts abroad but also, often, from their supporters here in the United States. In such situations, our commitment to an unflinching but evenhanded treatment of sensitive but important subjects, and to clear-sighted and cool-headed analysis, stands us in good stead.

Implementing U.S. Human Rights Policy admirably sustains this tradition. It tackles a challenging subject that always sparks strong feelings on all sides, and it does so without shying away from incendiary issues. If Americans both inside and outside government heed the lessons elaborated in this volume, it may help policymakers avoid the dangers inherent in promoting human rights while gaining for the country the benefits of doing so.

Richard H. Solomon, President
United States Institute of Peace

Acknowledgments

I AM GRATEFUL TO THE UNITED STATES INSTITUTE OF PEACE for providing me with the opportunity to conduct this study, and in particular to Richard H. Solomon, the president of the Institute, whose support and vision made the project possible. Patrick Cronin, former director of the Research and Studies program, provided guidance and wise counsel, and Paul Stares, the program's current director, was helpful in bringing the project to fruition. I would like to thank the entire staff of the Institute for their willingness to share their views about the project with me and for numerous other forms of support: Margarita Studemeister was particularly helpful on the Latin America cases; and Jodi Koviach, Donna Ramsey Marshall, Christina Zechman Brown, Elise Murphy, and Erin Bair gave a wide range of assistance. The Institute's publications staff under the directorship of Dan Snodderly were wonderful colleagues to work with. I am especially thankful for the editorial efforts of Nigel Quinney, who lent the book much greater clarity and cohesion than it might otherwise have had.

The project assigned to each case study a working group of leading experts in their fields who helped inform the content. This distinguished cast included a wide range of policymakers, diplomats, and other government officials, academics, NGO activists, and some members of the business community. While it is not possible to name every participant, they know who they are, and this volume has benefited substantially from their many contributions. I would like to thank Catharin Dalpino, who played an essential role as adviser and sounding board. Holly Burkhalter gave generously of her time and guidance, especially with respect to the Africa studies. I am also grateful to Mark Palmer, Harold Hongju Koh, George Lopez, Yvonne Thayer, Christine

Morfit, Kati Suominen, Ashley Barr, Maureen Greenwood, Joe Stork, and the late Mike Jendrzejczyk for their contributions.

This project could not, of course, have come to fruition without the contributions of the case study authors. I am indebted to all of them for their hard work, insightful analyses, and patience. I am particularly grateful to Jack Donnelly, who not only co-wrote the introduction to this volume but also developed an initial analytical framework that helped to shape the project as a whole.

I benefited greatly from the advice and encouragement of many other colleagues and friends: Marc Plattner, Larry Diamond, Louisa Coan Greve, John Gould, and Phil Costopoulos, to name only a few. Last, I thank my husband, Daniel, for his constant support and good humor and my daughter, Isabel, for displaying patience beyond her years.

Contributors

Debra Liang-Fenton is executive director of the U.S. Committee for Human Rights in North Korea. From 1988 to 2002, she directed the Human Rights Implementation initiative at the United States Institute of Peace. Before joining the Institute, she was project officer of the International Forum for Democratic Studies at the National Endowment for Democracy. She has also served as an editor of the *Journal of Democracy*. Liang-Fenton is the author of "The Golden Triangle: Burma, Laos, and Thailand," in *The International Handbook on Drug Control*, and several special reports published by the United States Institute of Peace on U.S. human rights policy. She testifies regularly before Congress, and in April 2003 was the keynote presenter at Amnesty International's annual general meeting.

• • •

Pauline H. Baker is president of The Fund for Peace, a nonprofit organization that works to prevent war through research, education, and action. Baker is also an adjunct professor at the Graduate School of Foreign Service at Georgetown University and a distinguished professor in residence at American University. She has previously held positions with the Carnegie Endowment for International Peace, the Aspen Institute, and the Senate Foreign Relations Committee.

Joel D. Barkan is professor of political science at the University of Iowa. A specialist on electoral processes and democratization in Africa, he served as the first regional democracy and governance adviser for eastern and southern Africa at the U.S. Agency for International Development in 1992 and 1993.

Henri J. Barkey is the Bernard L. and Bertha F. Cohen Professor in International Relations and chair of the Department of International Relations at Lehigh University. He served as a member of the U.S. State Department from 1998 to 2000, working primarily on issues related to the Middle East and the Eastern Mediterranean.

Harry G. Barnes, Jr., is senior advisor to the Asia Society and a member of the advisory committee on Asia of Human Rights Watch. During his career as a Foreign Service officer, he served as U.S. ambassador to Romania, India, and Chile. Subsequently, he directed the human rights and conflict resolution programs at The Carter Center.

Susan Diane Burgerman is associate director of the Center for Democracy and Election Management, Office of International Affairs, American University. She was formerly adjunct professor of international affairs at Columbia University's School of International and Public Affairs, where she also served as associate director of the Institute of Latin American Studies.

Alison Des Forges, senior adviser to the Africa Division, directs Central African research for Human Rights Watch. Author of *Leave None to Tell the Story: Genocide in Rwanda,* she testified before the International Criminal Tribunal in Rwanda, in national courts, and at the UN, OAU, French, and Belgian investigations into the genocide.

Jack Donnelly is Andrew W. Mellon Professor at the Graduate School of International Studies at the University of Denver. He has lectured widely within the United States and in other countries on human rights issues. His numerous publications include two recent books, *International Human Rights* and *Universal Human Rights in Theory and Practice.*

Merle Goldman is professor of Chinese history emerita at Boston University and associate of the Fairbank Center at Harvard. Her recent books are *Sowing the Seeds of Democracy in China* (1994) and, with John K. Fairbank, the new enlarged edition of *China: A New History* (1998). She was a member of the U.S. delegation to the UN Commission on Human Rights in 1993–94.

Jack F. Matlock, Jr., had a long and distinguished career in the American Foreign Service, culminating with his appointment as ambassador to the Soviet Union from 1987 to 1991. After returning to the United States, he was a professor at Columbia University, New York City, and then at the Institute for Advanced Study in Princeton. He is currently visiting professor of public and international affairs at Princeton University.

Paula R. Newberg is an adviser to the United Nations and the author of a number of books, articles, and monographs on international human rights and on politics in South Asia, including *Judging the State: Courts and Constitutional Politics in Pakistan* and *Double Betrayal: Human Rights and Insurgency in Kashmir.* She has taught at Columbia and Johns Hopkins Universities and led human rights investigation and observation missions on behalf of U.S.-based and international organizations.

Michael Shifter is vice president for policy at the Inter-American Dialogue. He talks and writes widely on Latin American politics and U.S.–Latin American relations. He has lectured at universities throughout the Western Hemisphere and has been an adjunct professor at Georgetown University's School of Foreign Service since 1993. Since 1996, he has testified on eight occasions before Congress about U.S. policy toward Latin America.

David I. Steinberg is Distinguished Professor and director of Asian Studies at Georgetown University, School of Foreign Service, and was previously Distinguished Professor of Korean Studies. He has been president of the Mansfield Center for Pacific Studies, a representative of the Asia Foundation in Korea, Burma, Hong Kong, and Washington, and a member of the Senior Foreign Service, AID, Department of State.

Jennifer Stillerman is a graduate of Harvard Law School, where she served as an editor of the *Harvard Law Review*. She has been a junior fellow at the Carnegie Endowment for International Peace and a program associate at the Inter-American Dialogue in Washington, D.C.

Denis J. Sullivan is director of the Cronin International Center and chair of International Studies at Bentley College. He also is an affiliate in research at Harvard's Center for Middle Eastern Studies.

Jon Western is Five College Assistant Professor of International Relations at Mount Holyoke College. He served as the coordinator of the Dayton Upgrade Project at the United States Institute of Peace. From 1990 to 1993, he was an East European specialist at the U.S. Department of State. He holds a Ph.D. in political science from Columbia University.

Implementing U.S. Human Rights Policy

Introduction

JACK DONNELLY AND DEBRA LIANG-FENTON

HUMAN RIGHTS HAVE LONG BEEN A CONCERN of U.S. foreign policy, reflecting not only deeply held American values but also responses to both domestic developments (such as the movements for the abolition of slavery, women's suffrage, and civil rights) and international events (such as the Holocaust and the Vietnam War). In the mid- and late 1970s, however, a qualitative change in the level, frequency, and intensity of U.S. interest and action in human rights occurred. International human rights law was strengthened by developments such as the Helsinki Accords of 1975 and the entry into force of the International Human Rights Covenants in 1976. The number of nongovernmental organizations (NGOs) devoted to human rights began to increase, as did their prominence when Amnesty International won the Nobel Peace Prize in 1977. And in October 1977, human rights finally found a permanent and formal institutional place in the U.S. foreign policy bureaucracy when President Jimmy Carter established the Bureau of Human Rights and Humanitarian Affairs (now called the Bureau of Democracy, Human Rights, and Labor).[1] Since then, ordinary citizens and policymakers alike have devoted growing and increasingly consistent attention to human rights issues in U.S. foreign policy.

This volume examines U.S. efforts to implement its human rights objectives and policies since the mid-1970s. Growing out of a United States Institute of Peace working group composed of prominent policymakers, activists, business leaders, and academics, this book brings

3

together leading experts from the policymaking, NGO, and academic communities to examine a diverse set of case studies about the process of implementing U.S. international human rights policies. Our shared aim is to develop knowledge that is of interest to scholars and the public, is useful to human rights advocates, and, most important, provides practical advice to policymakers who are considering new human rights initiatives and improving old human rights formulas.

The fourteen countries examined in this volume illustrate the diversity of problems and issues faced by those charged with implementing U.S. international human rights policy. Because these case studies reflect the diversity of regions, regime types, history, and patterns of U.S. interests—as well as the varied experiences and perspectives of the authors—no rigid methodological framework has been imposed on any chapter. The geographic range of the cases spans the globe from China, Pakistan, and South Korea to Rwanda, Kenya, and South Africa; from Chile, Colombia, El Salvador, and Guatemala to Bosnia, the USSR, Egypt, and Turkey. The combination of cases has been chosen not only to chronicle the most commonly known examples but also to shed light on those examples that have escaped front-page headlines. In this way, we hope to see a well-rounded picture of U.S. human rights policy implementation. All cases focus on what works in implementing international human rights policies, how policymakers use the tools available to them, and how policymakers respond to the myriad challenges they face.

This project was conceptualized with the implicit knowledge that human rights in foreign policy should be driven not solely by what is effective but, more important, by what is right. The case studies attempt to describe and explain the motivations behind action, or inaction, while always cognizant of the moral component behind human rights policy. But it should be noted that the central focus of this volume remains the methods used to impact human rights practices.

The volume offers no simple, or even single, model of the determinants of success. Nearly every case examined, however, points to a need for improved integration of human rights with other foreign policy concerns. U.S. international human rights policies, when they are not completely subordinated to competing security concerns, too often are impeded by a recurrent pattern of ad hoc, and thus too often incoherent, implementation. As long as U.S. international human rights policy continues to be rooted in reactions to immediate, short-run challenges and events, and until human rights concerns are more coherently articulated with other foreign policy objectives, the promise and aspirations of U.S. human rights policies will be compromised by inefficiency and incoherence in their implementation.

WHAT WORKS? AIMS, OPPORTUNITIES, AND IMPACTS

This volume seeks to answer a deceptively simple question about U.S. international human rights policy: What works? This requires asking what was intended, what was possible, and what was achieved. But each piece of the picture—aims, opportunities, and impacts—is itself complex, making "success" a surprisingly elusive notion.

Foreign policy is often the semiplanned outcome of the interaction of numerous actors who have multiple, conflicting objectives. Consider, for example, the complex and shifting interests and forces that produced U.S. policy toward China in the days, months, and years following the Tiananmen Square massacre. Especially in lower-profile cases, "policy" most often emerges incrementally in response to particular events. Describing "U.S. policy" often requires teasing out an implicit logic for a series of actions undertaken on the basis of ad hoc, reactive judgments.

Beyond examining official statements and other verbal expressions of intent, we should look at the evidence of nonverbal behavior, which is also essential to determining aims. Despite the philosophical and methodological problems of deducing motives from behavior, we can reasonably infer intent from action. A complementary body of information can be provided by tracing which actors, interests, and intentions helped shape policy and its implementation.

In assessing impact, we see that no less important than what was intended and what was achieved is what was possible. The configuration of forces in the target country regularly facilitates or frustrates initiatives on behalf of human rights (or any other policy objective). For example, after Tiananmen, however much the United States wanted to foster China's democracy movement, the best that could be hoped for was ameliorating the conditions of some victims of the crackdown and imposing some modest costs on the Chinese authorities for their disregard of international human rights standards.

Constraints and opportunities within the United States are also important in determining what is "possible." Consider Kosovo. After the United States decided to intervene militarily, its strategy and tactics seem to have been dictated as much by the domestic political logic of minimizing American casualties as by the international humanitarian logic of minimizing the suffering of innocent civilians on whose behalf the United States was intervening.

U.S. policy also faces international and global constraints. For example, a more global and interdependent economy alters the impact of bilateral, multilateral, and transnational actors on the economic and social rights in other countries. The spread of democracy as a widely endorsed international norm enables some kinds of initiatives but constrains others.

Finally, it is important to explore the impact of the full range of U.S. foreign policy behavior on international human rights practices, not just those initiatives that explicitly address human rights. The case studies, therefore, broadly examine the place of human rights concerns and initiatives in the full range of U.S. foreign policy toward the country in question. They address

- how human rights have (or have not) become an active concern of U.S. foreign policy practice in particular concrete cases;
- what means were considered, rejected, and employed to pursue both declared and implicit U.S. human rights objectives;
- how human rights objectives interacted with other foreign policy objectives and the means adopted to implement them; and
- what impact the full range of U.S. foreign policy practice toward a country has had on respect for or violation of internationally recognized human rights.

U.S. INTERESTS AND OBJECTIVES

U.S. national interests cover a vast range of qualitatively different concerns. Because these interests and concerns are in constant flux, there is considerable confusion, semantic and otherwise, about the precise nature of U.S. aims, goals, objectives, and policies, and what they are intended to achieve. However, for analytical and practical purposes, three questions help to focus discussion of the implementation process in the case studies:

- Were word and deed consistent? In every case considered, there was substantial inconsistency from the U.S. government. In some cases—for example, China during the Cold War, Egypt since Camp David, and Pakistan since September 11—broad U.S. pronouncements of human rights commitments had almost no effect on policy. More typical, however, are cases such as Kenya, El Salvador, and China since Tiananmen, where stated human rights concerns neither simply triumphed over other interests nor were simply subordinated. The relationship between word and deed seems to be complex and shifting to the point that it defies most generalizations.

- Did the policy declared in Washington govern practice in the field? Joel Barkan emphasizes the special influence of the U.S. ambassador in implementing U.S. policy in Kenya and the impact a "rogue ambassador" can have on human rights. In the case of Chile, Harry Barnes points to the ambassador's role in explaining U.S. policy and the ways in which shifts in policy can sometimes create both hope in grassroots organizations and tension in the U.S. relationship with a host government.

- Both in Washington and "in country," was policy made on the basis of a synoptic vision and an integrated assessment of goals and objectives, or incrementally, in response to particular events, opportunities, and constraints? Here the evidence of the case studies largely suggests ad hoc incrementalism as the norm. And when there has been an overarching policy vision, it has been one that largely excludes human rights from the picture, as in pre-Tiananmen China and post–Camp David Egypt.

Most chapters also undertake a similar analysis of relevant U.S. security and economic interests (as well as other relevant foreign policy concerns). Some chapters highlight interests that are especially relevant to the particular country. This is perhaps clearest in the case of the war against illegal narcotics in Colombia. And special attention has been given to determining what happened when human rights concerns came into conflict with other objectives and initiatives.

The case studies provide examples that range across the entire spectrum of possible outcomes. Sometimes human rights have been completely subordinated to competing national security and economic objectives. For example, Jon Western argues that for most of the Bosnian conflict U.S. policy was dominated by geostrategic interests that not merely kept it from ameliorating the human rights situation but even unintentionally contributed to abuses. Denis Sullivan's answer to the question of the role of human rights issues in U.S. foreign policy toward Egypt is "almost certainly none." He suggests that the two governments even work hard to avoid discussing the topic.

In a few instances, however, human rights concerns have competed at least equally with economic interests. This was clearly the case not only in the initial responses to Tiananmen but also in the surprisingly long and robust duration of U.S. sanctions and the substantial influence of human rights advocates in Congress right through the mid-1990s. Such a prominent place for human rights is especially striking because of the scope of economic benefits and the presence of important strategic interests (which even during the heyday of sanctions the Bush administration found formal and informal ways to pursue, sometimes even in direct contradiction to stated American policy).

Often human rights have taken priority over concerns lying in the vast residual category of "other" interests. For example, as Pauline Baker describes in the case of South Africa, after much protracted and bitter debate between Reagan administration officials and Congress about how to deal with the apartheid regime, human rights issues supported by a comprehensive package of sanctions eventually were given primacy over the notion that strategic and economic concerns supersede all. But, as Michael Shifter and Jennifer Stillerman point out, Colombia dramatically illustrates that other interests can just as readily trump human rights.

Some cases involve fascinating, complex interactions between different objectives and initiatives in which interests are reshaped and policies are redefined. For example, Jon Western suggests that the dramatic nature of the massacres in Srebrenica and Zepa caused the United States not merely to restate its humanitarian interests but to redefine their relation to strategic concerns; the very meaning of avoiding intervention in Bosnia changed. And Joel Barkan suggests that U.S. policy not only toward Kenya but more broadly toward Africa reflects a creative interaction of concerns for regional order (threatened by "failed states" and humanitarian crises), democratization, and free-market reforms. In this context, human rights have become infused with strategic and economic concerns, which have themselves been reshaped by the post–Cold War emphasis on democracy and human rights.

Individual human rights objectives may also conflict with one another. For example, punitive actions in response to past abuses may not be the most effective way to prevent future violations. Debate over Cold War–era involvement with rights-abusive regimes often focused on this issue, especially when the question was raised of undoing the consequences of past abuses that were sanctioned, or at least tolerated, by the United States. This question tended to be posed with special vigor when the United States had a role in overthrowing a democratically elected government, as in the cases of Arbenz in Guatemala and Allende in Chile.

This problem reflects the conflict between short-term and long-term objectives. In this regard, one of the key challenges facing policymakers, as illustrated in the case studies, is the tension between the closely related interests of human rights promotion and democracy building. Denis Sullivan points out that because the United States views Egypt as pivotal to stability in the region, neither human rights nor democracy has figured prominently in the foreign policy equation, and this ultimately has implications for long-term prospects for peace in the region. Paula Newberg describes a similar scenario in the case of Pakistan, where (even historically) its strategic role in efforts to combat the threat of Soviet communism and, more recently, terrorism has superseded concern for human rights or democracy. In the case of Rwanda, Alison Des Forges notes that democracy promotion without a human rights framework can jeopardize prospects for a democratic transition and, in this case, contribute to a humanitarian disaster.

Means

The means available to realize human rights improvements, as with other foreign policy objectives, range from privately hoping for change to declaring war and seeking unconditional surrender. The typology produced by the Sanctions Working Group of the State Department Advisory Committee on International Economic Policy has had considerable circulation within the State Department. This schema, with illustrative policy instruments, is reproduced in table 1 and lists the full complement of U.S. foreign policy tools and the categories under which each tool falls. Although useful, the schema does not fit the purposes of this study, as its breadth and extensive nature do not lend themselves to the parameters of this volume. However, it does provide a useful outline of specific mechanisms that apply more directly to each case.

The case studies in this volume suggest that seven tools have been most commonly employed:

- *Private diplomacy:* confidential representations between government officials.

- *Public diplomacy:* statements made in the target country, the United States, and international forums by officials of varying seniority that praise, condemn, or otherwise address human rights practices.

- *Cultural, scholarly, and other exchanges and contacts:* increasing or decreasing the range or frequency of sponsored, encouraged, or permitted formal or informal transnational interaction between citizens and private organizations of the United States and the target country.

- *Economic and political sanctions and incentives:* restricting, extending, or threatening to alter access to U.S. resources and official contacts, including diplomatic, political, or military contacts, foreign assistance, debt servicing, investment insurance, trade, and arms sales.

- *Democracy promotion:* strengthening civil society and political parties in the target country.

- *Country Reports on Human Rights Practices:* a congressionally mandated annual report (running to 3,095 pages in 2003), produced by the Department of State, that examines national human rights practices, with special attention to violations or deficiencies and changes in behavior, in more than 190 countries.

- *Congressional action:* hearings, legislation, and nonbinding resolutions that encourage or require the executive branch to act in a particular way.

The strengths and drawbacks of each of these tools are discussed in the first section of the conclusion.

While the toolbox is large and the tools within it are varied, we must be aware that sometimes none are employed. Often the key foreign policy action of the United States is the decision not to act. For example, as Alison Des Forges suggests, the U.S. decision not to act in the face of growing abuses in Rwanda helped to enable genocide in that country. More broadly, any analysis of the impact of U.S. foreign policy on international human rights must be open to the possibility of the United States being part of the problem rather than the solution. Thus, Susan Burgerman suggests that Washington's greatest contribution to improved human rights practices in El Salvador and Guatemala was the loss of U.S. interest in supporting repressive regimes.

CONSTRUCTIVE ENGAGEMENT, OPPORTUNITY COSTS, AND UNINTENDED CONSEQUENCES

Whatever the particular instruments, policymakers face a recurrent strategic question: Isolate or engage? For example, Susan Burgerman argues that isolating Guatemala in the 1980s reduced U.S. leverage, whereas engaging El Salvador created an avenue through which the U.S. government could influence behavior by using the right combination of sanctions and incentives. Is this more generally true? Do the benefits of associating closely with a grossly repressive regime outweigh the costs? Our case studies do not provide a clear answer to these questions. But they do help to clarify the character of the issues.

Constructive engagement—engaging rights-abusive regimes in order to develop relationships and dependencies that increase U.S. leverage—was, for example, a central issue in discussions of U.S. policy toward South Africa in the 1980s and China in the 1990s.

Table 1. U.S. Foreign Policy Tools: An Illustrative Matrix of Selected Options

	Friendly, Persuasive	Hostile, Coercive
Diplomatic (Executive)	• Embassy: Open/Expand • Ambassador: Accredit • Visas: Liberalize • Landing Rights: Extend/Expand • Intl Orgs: Support Membership/Position • Intl Confs: Support Sponsorship/Participation • Communiqué: Friendly • State Visits: Support • Senior Officials Exchange: Support • Hostile Neighbors/Opposition: Minimize Contacts	• Embassy: Reduce Staff • Ambassador: Recall for Consultations • Visas: Restrict to Targeted Group • Landing Rights: Restrict • Binational Commissions: Pare Back • Intl Orgs: Oppose Membership/Participation • Intl Confs: Oppose Sponsorship/Participation • Communiqué: Hostile • State Visit: Oppose • Senior Officials Exchange: Restrict • Embassy: Close • Ambassador: Withdraw • Visas: Suspend • Landing Rights: Suspend • Binational Commissions: Suspend • Intl Orgs: Urge Exclusion • Intl Confs: Urge Exclusion • State Visit: Cancel • Senior Officials Exchange: Cancel • Hostile Neighbors/Opposition: Expand Contacts
Political (Executive and Legislative)	LEGISLATIVE • Resolutions: Friendly • CODELS: Increase • NBD: Increase Funding • Intl Parliamentary Orgs: Support Partic./Position • Opposition: Minimize Contacts • Arms Transactions: Support EXECUTIVE • Proclamation: Friendly • State/Local Exchanges: Sister City Agreements, • State Offices, Overseas: Support	LEGISLATIVE • Resolutions: Hostile • CODELS: Fact-Finding Missions • NBD: Restrict Funding • Intl Parliamentary Orgs: Oppose • Opposition: Increase Contacts • Arms: Cancel Trans./Boycott EXECUTIVE • Proclamation: Hostile • Opposition: Host Visit

Cultural (Executive and Legislative)	• Aggressive Broadcasts: Decrease/Suspend • Academic Exchange: Establish,' Expand • Intl Athletic Events: Support Participation/Sponsorship • Entertainment/Cultural Tours: Support Participation/ Sponsorship	• Peace Corps: Expand • Public Exchange: Establish/ Expand • Intl Cultural Orgs: Support Membership • Scientific Cooperation: Establish/Expand • Internet Sites: Expand	• Aggressive Broadcasts: Increase • Academic Exchange: Restrict • Intl Athletic Events: Oppose Participation/Sponsorship • Entertainment/ Cultural Tours: Oppose Partic./Sponsorship • Peace Corps: Restrict • Publication Exchange: Restrict • Intl Cultural Orgs: Oppose Membership • Scientific Cooperation: Restrict	• Academic Exchange: Suspend • Intl Athletic Events: Urge Exclusion • Entertain./Cultural Tours: Ban from US/Urge Exclusion • Peace Corps: Suspend • Publication Exchange: Suspend • Intl Cultural Orgs: Urge Suspension • Scientific Cooperation: Suspend
Economic (Executive and Legislative)	• Debt Rescheduling: Permit/Liberalize Terms • Preferential Tariff Treatment: Expand • Regional Trade Agreements: Permit Participation • Trade Credits: Expand • Investment: Expand Promotion • Business Contacts: Encourage • Trade Missions: Expand • OPIC/EXIM/TDA: Open/ Expand	• Trade Controls: Liberalize Terms • Double Tax Agreement: Negotiate • IFIs: Support Membership/ Position • Financial Controls: Relax • Assts: Release • Postal Cooperation: Expand • Aid/Technical Assistance: Increase	• Debt: Tighten Terms • Investment: Restrict Promotion • Business Contacts: Discourage • Trade Missions: Pare • OPIC/EXIM/TDA: Restrict on Targeted Basis • Trade Controls: Limited (commodity/product-based) • IFIs: Oppose Membership/ Participation • Financial Controls: Increase • Aid/Technical Assistance: Restrict	• Debt: Suspend • Preferential Tariff Treatment: Suspend • Regional Trade Agreements: Suspend Participation • Trade Credits: Restrict • Investment: Ban • Trade Missions: Suspend • OPIC/EXIM/TDA: Suspend • Trade Controls: Expand • Trade Embargo • Double Tax Agreement: Suspend • Tax Treaty: Suspend • IFIs: Urge Exclusion • Assets: Freeze • Postal Cooperation: Suspend • Aid/Technical Assistance: Suspend • G7 Sanctions Group: Activate

continued

Table 1. U.S. Foreign Policy Tools: An Illustrative Matrix of Selected Options (*cont.*)

	Friendly, Persuasive	Hostile, Coercive
Military (Executive; Legislative Consultation)	• Training (IMET/E-IMET): Increase • Officer Exchange: Increase • Military Cooperation (joint exercises/training/technical cooperation): Increase • Port Visits: Increase • Confidence-Building Measures: Increase • Peacekeeping Forces: Maintain • Coop. w/ Hostile Neighbors/Opposition: Restrict • Local Maneuvers: Restrict	• Training: Restrict • Officer Exchange: Restrict • Military Cooperation: Restrict • Confidence-Building Measures: Restrict • Training: Suspend • Officer Exchange: Suspend • Military Cooperation: Suspend • Confidence-Building Measures: Suspend • Port Visits: Suspend • Peacekeeping: Withdraw • Cooperation w/ Neighbors/Opposition: Increase • Local Maneuvers: Increase • Show of Force • Act of War

Source: Sanctions Working Group, State Department Advisory Committee on International Economic Policy

CODELS = congressional delegation; EXIM = Export-Import Bank; IFI = International Financial Institution; IMET = International Military Education and Training program; OPIC = Overseas Investment Corporation; TDA = Trade and Development Agency

Pauline Baker notes that President Reagan's official constructive engagement policy of offering concrete incentives to Pretoria was met with sustained nonviolent protests, which eventually led Congress to enact a series of comprehensive sanctions that gave human rights concerns primacy over strategic interests. Merle Goldman indicates that constructive engagement in the form of state visits to China reflected the U.S. desire to maintain a stable relationship with a country that holds both strong strategic and economic significance to the United States. She cites National Security Advisor Brent Scowcroft's visit to Beijing soon after the Tiananmen Square massacre. The Most Favored Nation and subsequent Permanent Normal Trading Rights debates over linkage to human rights issues also reflected the view that, while other fora were going to raise human rights with China, when it came to practical implications concerning trade issues, the likelihood was that economic interests would prevail. In the end, it should be noted, the linkage of human rights to China's trade status had little real impact on human rights practices in the country, while the symbolic importance of linking human rights to trade privileges did have positive impact on groups and individuals on the ground.

Another general issue connected with the choice of means arises from the limitations of time, resources, and attention. Taking any particular action requires forgoing other possible actions; that is, among the considerations are what economists call opportunity costs. For example, increased attention to trade or security issues may lead to downgrading the concern for human rights, more through limited attention than by conscious choice. The war on terrorism has in many countries pushed concerns for human rights and democracy into the background, often through inattention rather than design. And among human rights objectives, some are likely to receive special attention (e.g., workers' rights, women's rights, or freedom of religion), which, given a fixed amount of resources and attention, means that attention will be diverted from others.

This suggests the central importance of attending not just to intentions but to unintended consequences, some of which may reinforce U.S. policy but others of which may undermine it. For example, U.S. initiatives to foster market-based trade and financial reforms often have negative consequences for the enjoyment of economic and social rights, especially in the short run. Reducing subsidies on staple foods, to take one common policy prescription in structural adjustment packages, usually harms the nutrition of poor children. Although clearly unintended, such effects are well known and quite predictable. And even when consequences are genuinely unanticipated, they may be crucial to determining the overall impact of U.S. initiatives.

ACTORS

So far we have treated the United States and the target government as unitary rational actors. This common analytical simplification is obviously inappropriate for a study of foreign policy practice, which involves multiple actors with interests that conflict as frequently as they converge.

The most important actor in U.S. international human rights policy has been the president, as is especially clear in Jimmy Carter's role in introducing human rights explicitly into the mainstream of U.S. foreign policy. Even Carter, however, followed and in many ways built on earlier congressional initiatives (especially the legislatively mandated linkage of U.S. foreign aid to the human rights practices of recipient states). In addition, Congress can force changes even in policies of great importance to the administration. As mentioned earlier, South Africa strikes the most prominent example of congressional initiatives creating a shift in the executive's policies. In the case of Chile, the dispute between Congress and the executive over how to address human rights, however, was protracted. When the Kennedy Amendment became law in December 1974, Congress made it more difficult for the administration to grant military aid to that country. One of the results of congressional pressure was that for the first time, the U.S. government voted in favor of a UN resolution condemning Chile's human rights abuses.

Although it does not possess the same independent authority as does Congress, the federal bureaucracy is not simply an extension of the president. Policy changes at the top often do not penetrate very quickly, or sometimes even very far, into the foreign policy bureaucracy. The distinctive bureaucratic interests of different agencies— and even different branches within a single agency—add a further level of complexity and present potential impediments to coherent and effective human rights policy formulation and implementation.

An unwillingness to overcome bureaucratic constraints can be said to have contributed to U.S. inaction in the early stages of the crisis in the former Yugoslavia, according to Jon Western. In the case of Bosnia, pressures that eventually shifted senior-level focus included protracted media attention, congressional and NGO criticism, and the 1995 massacres in Srebrenica. Denis Sullivan points out that Egypt is the largest recipient of USAID-managed assistance in the world, but that according to the USAID and Egyptian human rights officials, there has been little effective activity in human rights promotion. One reason for this gap may be attributed to the lack of coordination between USAID and the Bureau of Democracy, Human Rights, and Labor in the State Department. Most recently, after much criticism from the NGO community and heightened media attention related to the Saad Eddin Ibrahim case, the second Bush administration, in a clear shift in policy, linked human rights performance to economic aid.

Beyond governments, important nonstate actors include organized interest groups of just about every imaginable character, as well as the media and influential elites. And the public includes an incredibly diverse array of "ordinary" citizens, both passive and mobilized. The NGO community and the media play an important role in helping to shift policy at the upper levels of the U.S. government decision-making process. The growing influence of prominent human rights NGOs helps local actors work under difficult circumstances. For example, Henri Barkey notes that in Turkey these NGOs have been useful to U.S. policymakers in providing them with information relevant to their work. In addition, the State Department even included these human rights NGOs, together with manufacturers, in its discussions on the expected Turkish request to purchase attack helicopters.

Finally, all of these actors are themselves complex combinations of individuals and subgroups. For example, Congress is a grouping of 535 strong-willed men and women, plus thousands of staff members and dozens of committees and caucuses (and their staffs). Even the president (and his office) is a complex corporate actor.

It is impossible to generalize about such a complex range of actors. Nonetheless, most of the case studies do demonstrate that the particular configuration of actors and the political forces they represent —not only in the United States, but also in the target countries of U.S. policy—are central to the impact of U.S. international human rights policies. And as Michael Shifter and Jennifer Stillerman argue in their analysis of U.S. policy toward Colombia, the problems posed by multiple actors can be especially severe in the absence of a clear and integrated overarching strategy. In such cases, U.S. policy, or at least a particular segment of it, really does depend on who is occupying the office in question.

ARENAS OF ACTION

The arenas of action are more numerous and varied than is implied by the focus on direct state-to-state relations. In addition to bilateral channels, potentially important multilateral, transnational, and transgovernmental arenas must be considered.

International financial institutions, for example, have been a focus of U.S. human rights initiatives for two decades. Since its inception, the Organization for Security and Cooperation in Europe (OSCE, formerly the Conference on Security and Cooperation in Europe) has been a central arena for U.S. human rights policy toward the countries of Central and Eastern Europe. Conversely, the countries of Southeast Asia have used the Association of Southeast Asian Nations (ASEAN) as a forum to coordinate responses to—and often to attempt to buffer the impact of—U.S. and other international human rights initiatives. Are there lessons to be learned about how the United States could work more effectively in multilateral forums, both global and regional? Jack Matlock indicates that in the case of the Soviet Union, U.S. participation in the Helsinki Final Act of 1975 succeeded in meeting the U.S. objectives of keeping Europe stable while at the same time securing a Soviet commitment to protect specific human rights. From a military standpoint, the combined force of NATO aerial bombings and gains made by Croats and Muslims on the ground in Bosnia compelled the Serbs to sign a cease-fire agreement. This strategy was not without its flaws, however.

Cooperation with foreign governments outside the context of formal organizations must also be considered. Working unilaterally has advantages and disadvantages. The contributors in this volume have attempted to examine the opportunities for and significance of international consensus on human rights values and initiatives. An important issue with respect to improving U.S. human rights implementation is the willingness and ability of the U.S. government to support and enhance the efforts of foreign governments, multilateral institutions, and other actors that share its human rights goals. This is one of the principal lessons Susan Burgerman draws from her examination of El Salvador and Guatemala. One of the lessons she identifies is that U.S. human rights interests were best achieved in Central America when they were "expressed through support for multilateral efforts" such as UN-mediated peace talks and deployment of observer missions.

The importance of transnational interactions—relations across borders between private actors rather than public authorities—may at first sight seem less obvious. In many cases, however, transnational actors and channels may be of great political salience. Consider, for example, pressures from prominent human rights NGOs such as Amnesty International and Human Rights Watch have often helped to shape U.S. policy objectives and initiatives. Or, to take a multilateral example, at the 1993 World Human Rights Conference in Vienna, the United States found Asian human rights NGOs a valuable ally in countering arguments by some Asian governments that they should not be held to universal human rights standards.

Margaret Keck and Kathryn Sikkink have identified another important transnational channel, which they call the boomerang effect.[2] Local human rights advocates whose efforts are blocked by a resistant government often use international colleagues to mobilize their own governments to apply international pressure. This pattern of action was especially evident in the Southern Cone of South America in the 1970s and 1980s. And it alerts us to the broader issue of cooperation (and conflict) between governmental and nongovernmental actors in designing and implementing international human rights policies. This is especially important because of the prominence attached to civil society in many recent U.S. initiatives.

Finally, attention may need to be paid to transgovernmental relations, more or less direct relations between parts of the bureaucracy of one country with counterparts in another country, with little or no direct supervision between central decision makers. For example, relations between Latin American and U.S. military officials during the Carter administration often appeared to reflect interests and objectives that differed from those expressed in high-level policy statements.

TYPES OF EFFECTS

The obvious measure of success is the extent to which human rights practices in the target country changed in response to U.S. initiatives. This is an area, however, in which generalization is especially difficult. For example, U.S. (and other international) initiatives have often brought about the release of individual prisoners of conscience. But international human rights pressures have rarely brought major structural reforms in rights-abusive regimes. In between these two extremes is a broad range of possible effects that vary not only with the means employed but also with the objectives sought and the particular conditions in the country in question.

Many of the effects of international human rights initiatives, however, are indirect or outside the immediate target country. Despite failing to change behavior now, an initiative may reduce the likelihood of an undesirable behavior being repeated in the future. For example, the limited pressures of the Reagan administration on El Salvador, which in the short run had little discernible influence on military violations of human rights, may have had some impact in later months and years. Deterrence may be no less important in human rights policy than in national security policy, and it can either reinforce or operate against other policy objectives toward the immediate target.

Seemingly ineffective U.S. initiatives might also have positive effects by supporting local human rights advocates or delegitimating repressive regimes. By subtly altering the local human rights environment that a rights-abusive regime faces, U.S. policy can have significant long-term effects. This is perhaps the greatest lesson of the Helsinki process in countries such as Czechoslovakia and the Soviet Union. South Africa is another prominent example.

The impact of U.S. policies on the broader normative environment must also be considered. For example, although sanctions imposed in the late 1970s and 1980s on governments in Central and South America usually had little impact on the behavior of the target governments, they were crucial elements in altering international expectations and giving new force to the norms of the Universal Declaration of Human Rights and other international instruments.

Strengthening international norms can easily become an excuse for doing less to stop particular violations. But it is arguable that this is the most important effect of U.S. and other international human rights initiatives over the past quarter century. Individual efforts to support human rights may not always have been successful in the short term, but their long-term cumulative effect has been to strengthen international norms.

It is worth noting that such impacts on the local and international normative environments can strengthen later U.S. human rights initiatives. Only because of the existence of widely endorsed international norms are human rights violations no longer treated entirely as a matter of sovereign prerogative and domestic jurisdiction. And the striking difference between the Cold War and post–Cold War environments for international human rights initiatives owes as much to normative change as to changes in the global balance of power.

We should also consider the possibility of important "internal" effects on the development of U.S. international human rights policy. Doing action a at time t in country x may create precedents that shape future responses to similar violations later or elsewhere. For example, the initial Carter decision to suspend aid to Guatemala in 1977 established a precedent that had immense effects, despite the failure of that initiative to alter the policies of the Guatemalan military regime. Conversely, failing to act in a particular case may create inconsistencies that would reduce the efficacy and credibility of U.S. policy in the future.

International human rights policies may also be undertaken primarily to satisfy powerful constituencies in the United States. There is something troubling in the notion of a "successful" policy that satisfies national political constituencies with no international effects, but if that is what the policy is designed to do, that reality must be acknowledged. For example, periodic changes in U.S. support to the United Nations Fund for Population Activities seem driven more by the abortion debate in the United States than by anything else. And at least some of the supporters of sanctions against South Africa or Burma seem to have been more interested in responding to mobilized domestic constituencies than in bringing about change overseas. In any case, as Joel Barkan emphasizes in his discussion of U.S. human rights initiatives in Kenya, the presence of a mobilized U.S. constituency that follows events in that country often is a powerful determinant of U.S. policy.

We must also note that speaking out and acting against evil may be desirable, even demanded, whether or not there is a reasonable prospect of changing anything anywhere. In personal relations we may appropriately chastise friends, colleagues, or relations over whose behavior we have no substantial influence. We may even be held in disrepute if we silently stand by in the face of their misbehavior. So too in international politics. Our values may demand that we speak and act even when our words and actions have no discernible effect, if only because failing to do so may undermine those values or our own identity and credibility.

Finally, in assessing impact, wherever we might be looking for it, we must remember that the governments whose behavior U.S. foreign policy seeks to influence are not passive recipients of U.S. initiatives. "What works" often is determined by the reaction of target governments to the ends sought, sometimes irrespective of the means applied on their behalf. This is especially true because states rarely engage in serious human rights violations unless there are substantial (political, financial, or other) costs to respecting the rights in question. How U.S. objectives are perceived and valued by the target government, which usually will be largely outside the control of the United States, often is one of the most important determinants of success.

In the case of Turkey, a close ally of the United States, Henri Barkey notes that the Turkish government takes very seriously any criticism from the U.S. government, especially in the form of public statements. U.S. objectives of democracy and human rights in Turkey are seen through the prism of the NATO alliance and so do not engender the same sentiments that guide U.S. policy toward countries that do not enjoy as close a relationship. David Steinberg points out that the United States convinced the Syngman Rhee, Park Chung

Hee, and Chun Doo Hwan governments in South Korea to act on specific points of concern with respect to human rights issues, and they complied. The combined effect of rising nationalism, the Korean public's lingering perception that the United States has historically supported dictatorial regimes in South Korea, and some specific acts of violence committed by U.S. military personnel stationed in South Korea has contributed to the constraints the United States faces in pursuing human rights in that country, however.

THE STRUCTURE OF THIS VOLUME

As stated earlier, this volume seeks to identify what works in U.S. human rights policy. Contributors have attempted to draw out broader implications of their studies. Additional attempts at generalization are offered in the concluding chapter, but no simple solutions are to be found in this volume. The various cases, however, do lay out the specific tools available to policymakers and the challenges confronting these policymakers as they implement their human rights policy agenda.

Alison Des Forges describes in striking detail the events leading up to the 1994 genocide in Rwanda and the U.S. response to these events. Hindsight is 20/20, and the lessons that can be drawn from this case may shed light on preventing future crises of this magnitude.

Clearly articulated but inconsistently applied policy on the transition to democracy and the protection of human rights in Kenya has had mixed results with respect to human rights achievements. Joel Barkan illustrates his case in part by emphasizing the role of the ambassador in affecting the success of U.S. human rights policy and in part by examining U.S. potential and limitations in this regard.

Perhaps South Africa represents the clearest example of how the impact of the right set of tools combined with the right set of environmental circumstances can positively affect human rights conditions on the ground. In her chapter, Pauline Baker illuminates the range of U.S. policy options and the multiple actors that drove the process.

Merle Goldman, in her chapter on U.S. human rights policy toward China, stresses the importance of multilateral institutions in changing Chinese views on human rights. In China, the various tools that have been used to impact human rights practices (and that have been used discretely) have had mixed results. Even so, some lessons may be drawn with respect to the way in which China thinks about and speaks about human rights.

Pakistan presents a case in which strategic concerns have historically dominated the bilateral relationship with the United States. Paula Newberg outlines the problems and challenges that confront policymakers and the consequences of neglecting a human rights and democracy–promoting agenda.

David Steinberg looks at the multiple influences on U.S. policy toward South Korea and the ways in which the bilateral relationship has shaped current perceptions of that policy. He explores the motivations behind U.S. human rights policy and the implications for how Koreans view the United States more generally.

Jon Western presents a case that (from a policy perspective) lays out the challenge of high-level inattention to a growing crisis in Bosnia. Could a more robust preventive diplomacy effort have forestalled the egregious human rights violations in that country?

Jack Matlock covers a thirty-year history in his examination of the Soviet Union. He explores the development and implementation of a U.S. human rights/democracy promotion strategy toward this superpower.

In her comparison of El Salvador and Guatemala, Susan Burgerman considers the impact of U.S. leverage in the form of military assistance as an important contributing factor to influencing regime behavior.

In the case of Chile, Harry Barnes notes the important role of Congress in pressing human rights concerns and the impact this can have on a target country. Shifts in U.S. policy from one administration to another have also meant changes in the way human rights are implemented.

Michael Shifter and Jennifer Stillerman posit that the U.S. government's interest in combating the drug trade in Colombia has overshadowed a clear human rights objective in that country. In their chapter, the authors chart the myriad challenges that U.S. policymakers must address in implementing a realistic human rights policy in a conflict zone.

Turkey presents a case in which an important strategic alliance has been forged to the extent that issues of human rights can be perceived as intrusions on an otherwise stable association. Henri Barkey analyzes this complex relationship through the prism of U.S. human rights policy.

Regional tensions govern the nature of the relationship between Egypt and the United States. Given the primacy of regional stability in U.S. foreign policy calculations, Denis Sullivan explores the ways in which human rights policy has been (and can be) advanced in a pivotal state, where other concerns top the agenda.

The volume is rounded off by a conclusion that seeks to synthesize the analyses and insights offered by the case studies. The first part of the conclusion identifies the range of tools available to U.S. policymakers and practitioners as they seek to translate policy objectives into concrete accomplishments. The discussion examines the strengths and weaknesses of the various tools and assesses the conditions under which they are likely to be most effective. The second part distills a series of six lessons from the case studies. Intended as guidelines rather than as a set of detailed instructions, these lessons offer practical advice to those who craft and execute U.S. human rights policy.

NOTES

1. The State Department had established the position of coordinator for humanitarian affairs on April 21, 1975, in response to growing congressional interest in human rights issues in foreign policy.

2. Margaret E. Keck and Kathryn Sikkink, *Activists beyond Borders: Advocacy Networks in International Politics* (Ithaca, N.Y.: Cornell University Press, 1998), 12–13.

Part I
Africa

1

Learning from Disaster

U.S. Human Rights Policy
in Rwanda

ALISON DES FORGES

T HE ENORMITY OF THE FAILURE of U.S. human rights policy at the
time of the 1994 genocide dwarfs its other failures in Rwanda
but is related to them. It also overshadows those few successes
before and after the catastrophe. The U.S. government can try to
reproduce and expand upon the successes, but such efforts will lack
credibility unless it first deals with its inaction in the face of the systematic slaughter of civilians before, during, and after the genocide.

DEVELOPMENT AND DEMOCRACY

Rwanda, a small, poor state with no apparent natural resources,
attracted little notice in Washington in the years after its independence from Belgium in 1962. Throughout the Cold War, U.S. diplomats valued Rwanda primarily as an ally and were willing to invest
modest amounts of aid in promoting economic development to ensure
its cooperation. After military strongman Juvénal Habyarimana took
power in a coup in 1973, the United States, like other donor nations,

29

approved of his generally effective administration, his execution of development projects, and his success in avoiding the indebtedness that ensnared other African governments. Although Rwanda was then a one-party state that limited civil and political rights, U.S. diplomats treated these limitations as neither surprising nor egregious.[1] The only human rights issue that drew serious U.S. criticism was the sentencing of nearly three hundred Jehovah's Witnesses to long prison terms at Habyarimana's behest in 1986. After a U.S. protest, Habyarimana released most of the prisoners and promised that future church-state conflict would be settled by dialogue. The promise was soon broken, but when subsequent imprisonments became known, Habyarimana passed it off as the fault of subordinates, thus sparing himself further U.S. criticism.

After the Cold War ended, the U.S. government decided to promote democracy and human rights more vigorously in Rwanda, as elsewhere in Africa. The Habyarimana government was then being weakened by a series of economic reverses (a fall in the world price of coffee and tea, the chief Rwandan exports, combined with unfavorable growing conditions) and by a new political opposition that criticized the government's increasing corruption. The ever-adaptable Habyarimana echoed the new concern with human rights in his speeches, played host to international conferences on the issue, and declared his openness to political reforms. Impressed by this rhetoric as well as by the administrative effectiveness of the government, U.S. policymakers selected Rwanda for substantial democratization assistance, including training for personnel of the National Assembly, study tours to the United States for leaders of new political parties, seminars for journalists, and support for human rights organizations and women's associations.

But even as U.S. officials put energy and money into promoting democracy and human rights, they declined to confront Rwandan government discrimination against the Tutsi minority. The government, made up of people from the Hutu majority, excluded Tutsi from schools and government jobs, doing so by a system of population registration and identity cards that indicated ethnic affiliation. In 1991 consultants to the U.S. Agency for International Development (USAID) recommended that the United States make aid for democratization projects conditional upon an end to this practice, but U.S. officials ignored the recommendation.[2] The identity cards remained in use through the genocide, at which time assailants used them to identify Tutsi for slaughter.

INEFFECTUAL RESPONSE TO WARTIME ABUSES

In October 1990 the largely Tutsi Rwandan Patriotic Front (RPF) launched a war aiming both to topple Habyarimana, a Hutu, and to assure that hundreds of thousands of exiled Tutsi could return to Rwanda. The Tutsi, once the ruling elite, had been overthrown by a revolution that began in 1959, and many had followed their king into exile.

Habyarimana saw the attack as an opportunity to rebuild his eroding control over the Hutu majority by rallying them against the RPF and against Tutsi who lived inside the country. After staging a fake assault on the capital to heighten the sense of danger, Habyarimana arrested more than ten thousand persons, including both Tutsi and Hutu who challenged his leadership. Many detainees were beaten or tortured, and they were held in deplorable conditions.

Staff of the U.S. embassy, together with other diplomats, visited the prisons and pressed for a speedy release of the thousands against whom there was no evidence. They succeeded in getting many released, but they did not contest the official line that Tutsi and Hutu opposed to Habyarimana were "accomplices" of the RPF. Thus unchallenged, Habyarimana used the same pretext to justify the detention of thousands more in later months and the arrest of smaller numbers over the next three years. After April 1994 the Rwandan government used this explanation in an attempt to justify the genocide of Tutsi and the slaughter of Hutu dissidents.

Two weeks after the RPF attack, Rwandan authorities organized the first massacre of some three hundred "accomplices." U.S. and other ambassadors intervened quietly, apparently with the effect of cutting short the killing. But here, too, the diplomats accepted the official explanation that the massacre was a spontaneous outburst of popular rage. Not held accountable for the killings, Habyarimana repeatedly used the same tactic of killing and blaming the slaughter on an outraged populace at the ultimate cost of some two thousand lives in the next three years. Similarly, when apprised of the slaughter of three hundred to five hundred Tutsi civilians by Rwandan soldiers, U.S. officials accepted the official explanation that civilians could not be distinguished from enemy soldiers, who often wore civilian clothes.

After a massacre of Tutsi in March 1992, State Department officials conceded that local authorities likely played a role in inciting the killings, but still they hung back from criticizing Habyarimana. They treated the abuses as the inevitable result of war and saw ending the war as the way to end the abuses—as well as the way to restore stability and resume economic development. Hoping to broker a peace deal, they wanted to be perceived as neutral, which meant abstaining from open criticism of the Rwandan government.

During this period, fledgling local human rights groups were gaining increasing credibility with the foreign diplomatic community, benefiting from both financial aid and political protection. They believed, however, that their allegations of government abuses would carry greater weight if backed by international organizations, and they spurred the establishment of an international commission. After an investigation in Rwanda, the commission organized by Human Rights Watch (then Africa Watch) and the International Federation of Human Rights Leagues published a report in March 1993 detailing official abuses, including massacres of Tutsi and human rights violations by the RPF.[3] Several months later, the UN special rapporteur on summary and arbitrary executions confirmed the findings of the commission. After the publication of the commission report, the U.S. government announced that it was "deeply disturbed" and soon after reduced a $19.6 million aid package for Rwanda to $6 million, much of this humanitarian assistance, and warned that further cuts might follow. But U.S. policymakers cited poor economic performance and growing war expenditures as well as human rights abuses as reasons for the cut, thus sending a mixed signal to the Rwandan government. The Belgians, another important donor, protested the abuses more clearly by recalling their ambassador for consultations after the publication of the commission report, which was also extensively debated in the Belgian Senate.

Opponents of Habyarimana, by now part of a coalition government, used the leverage provided by international criticism to force an official apology for the killings and an acknowledgment that officials had failed to control the violence, through either negligence or incompetence. The government removed or transferred some of those implicated, and the massacres ceased for a number of months. But despite this short-term victory, neither Habyarimana nor his immediate supporters felt obliged to give up scapegoating Tutsi, in part because France, their strongest ally since the start of the war, continued its firm support. Some lower-ranking French officials supposedly privately reproached Rwandan authorities, but the French ambassador as well as President Mitterrand himself remained solidly behind Habyarimana.

Seeking an Easy Success

The signing of the Arusha Accords by the Rwandan government and the RPF in August 1993 ended the war, and the United Nations established a peacekeeping force, the United Nations Assistance Mission for Rwanda (UNAMIR), to assist in implementing the treaty. With this development, officials at the U.S. mission to the United Nations and those responsible for peacekeeping operations at the State Department and the National Security Council (NSC) joined State Department Africa Bureau personnel and embassy staff in dealing with Rwanda. At the time, the costs of peacekeeping had mushroomed, the most recent operation in Somalia had failed and cost the lives of eighteen U.S. soldiers, and influential members of Congress were muttering about the futility of such undertakings.[4]

Thus, when U.S. policymakers approved the creation of UNAMIR, they were hoping for a success—and a cheap one, besides. The Rwandan operation, remarkably requested by both parties to the conflict, looked to be it. The U.S. government proposed a force of five hundred soldiers, while the UN staff requested five thousand. The compromise force of twenty-eight hundred was too small to carry out all the tasks originally foreseen, so the mandate of the force was cut from that specified in the Arusha Accords.[5]

In late 1993 and early 1994, U.S. officials realized that both sides were preparing for renewed combat even as they continued pretending to want to implement the accords. The officials also knew of preparations for a different kind of violence, attacks on Tutsi civilians and Hutu opposed to Habyarimana. They knew that extremists were recruiting militia, distributing firearms and disseminating inflammatory propaganda on the radio and in the press. Local and international human rights organizations, members of the clergy, and journalists all denounced these preparations, which were carried out in full view. In addition, U.S. diplomats knew that Hutu refugees from ethnic violence in Burundi were receiving military training in camps located in southern Rwanda.

On January 11, 1994, UNAMIR commander General Romeo Dallaire cabled UN Headquarters that lists had been prepared of Tutsi in Kigali and that militia members were prepared to kill up to one thousand Tutsi in the first twenty minutes after a signal was given. He reported that he was preparing to raid a cache where arms were stored for these attacks.[6]

UN Headquarters immediately ordered that the raid be canceled, a virtually automatic reaction meant to avert a repetition of the Somalia disaster, which had been sparked by a similar operation to recover illegal arms. This refusal, like others to Dallaire's repeated requests for authorization to undertake firm action in the coming months, eventually left the peacekeepers unable to execute their mandate and even put UNAMIR itself at risk.[7]

U.S. officials in Kigali, Washington, and New York knew of the January 11 telegram and of similar pessimistic assessments by their Belgian and French counterparts.[8] In addition, a CIA analysis in late January predicted the possible loss of a half-million lives if combat were to resume.[9] But U.S. officials focused on the risk of another peacekeeping failure and on the need to keep expenses down rather than on a potential widespread slaughter of Rwandans. Thus, when Belgium asked for a broader mandate and more troops for UNAMIR in mid-February, the United States—along with the United Kingdom—rejected this proposal, in part because it would increase the cost of the operation. "In case of any difficulties," they said, they preferred simply to withdraw the peacekeepers.[10]

THE GENOCIDE: PROTECTING PEACEKEEPERS, NOT VICTIMS

On April 6, 1994, an airplane carrying Habyarimana was shot down over Kigali airport. The genocide was launched within hours, and the RPF resumed the war against the Rwandan government soon after that. The U.S. ambassador immediately called Washington to request a stronger mandate and more troops for UNAMIR.[11] To operate effectively, the force would also need new supplies and equipment. Washington decided instead to implement the plan foreseen in case of "difficulties." By late the next day, U.S. representatives at the Security Council opposed strengthening the mandate, and several days later they advocated withdrawing most of the peacekeepers, a position that became complete withdrawal by the end of the week, April 15.[12]

During this same period, information from the field showed that Tutsi were being killed solely because they were Tutsi. Taking this in the context of massacres during the previous three years, the public incitement to violence against Tutsi in the preceding months, and the training and arming of the militia, U.S. policymakers must have understood that a genocide had begun. But they decided that it was both too risky and too costly to use UNAMIR to save the victims. One U.S. diplomat told the Belgian ambassador to the United Nations that it was "unacceptable" to use peacekeepers to avert a "humanitarian drama." To do so risked making other peacekeeping operations "unworkable."[13]

NSC international operations staff moderated this policy several days later, perhaps because of the scale of the slaughter, perhaps because of lobbying by human rights and humanitarian organizations. Representatives of Human Rights Watch and the Association for the Defense of Human Rights and Public Liberties (ADL), a Rwandan human rights organization, for example, appealed to Madeleine Albright, U.S. ambassador to the United Nations, arguing that total withdrawal would mean the annihilation of some twenty-five thousand persons who had placed themselves under UN protection. She gave them a sympathetic hearing and sent them to NSC staffers, who later that day agreed to keep a token force in Rwanda. The Security

Council adopted this position on April 21, leaving in place several hundred soldiers who effectively protected thousands throughout the genocide.[14]

In late April a quarter of a million Hutu fled to Tanzania in twenty-four hours, frightened by the advance of the RPF. U.S. officials feared destabilization of the entire region and also were subjected to growing demands for U.S. action from human rights and humanitarian groups as well as members of Congress, who had remained silent for the first weeks of the genocide. The UN secretary-general, initially compliant with U.S. wishes to reduce the peacekeeping force, and several nonpermanent members of the Security Council had also decided that more UN peacekeepers must be sent to Rwanda.

Under these pressures, U.S. policymakers once more changed position and agreed to return a stronger force, UNAMIR II, to Rwanda. In early May Presidential Decision Directive 25 formalized the guidelines for U.S. involvement in UN peacekeeping operations. Officials, who were already acting informally under these guidelines, followed the new directive rigorously in planning for UNAMIR II, thus delaying final Security Council authorization until mid-May. Because of further delays in finding and equipping troops—this latter attributable to the United States as to others—the force arrived too late to help stop the genocide.

WHISPERED OUTRAGE

Reluctant to use UN peacekeepers, U.S. officials quickly dismissed—if they ever seriously considered—using U.S. troops to halt the slaughter.[15] Nor would they agree to using military capability from a distance to jam the radio that was by this time giving specific directives on where to find Tutsi and how to kill them. Instead, U.S. diplomats sought quietly to end the war, apparently believing—as before the genocide—that ending combat would also end the slaughter of civilians. In continued pursuit of the neutrality needed to serve as broker, they eschewed any strong condemnation of the Rwandan government.

In the first weeks the White House issued two statements, one by National Security Adviser Anthony Lake on April 22, after a visit by representatives of Human Rights Watch and the Rwandan organization, ADL. He called on four Rwandan army officers by name to end the violence against civilians, thus signaling that the White House knew who was responsible for the killings. A week later, in a rare radio message to Rwandans, President Clinton appealed to them "to recognize their common bond of humanity," hardly a statement to strike fear into the heart of genocidal leaders. On May 7 John Shattuck, assistant secretary of state for democracy, human rights, and labor, joined Ugandan president Yoweri Kaguta Museveni in declaring that "Rwandan leaders must end all forms of violence against civilians," but this firmer language counted for less than it would have had it come from Clinton himself.[16]

The United States, like other external actors, did not challenge the legitimacy of the genocidal government nor its right to keep its seat as a nonpermanent member of the UN Security Council. Six weeks into the genocide, however, the U.S. government refused visas to representatives of the genocidal government who wanted to lobby U.S. officials in Washington. This decision may have helped discredit the Rwandan government in diplomatic circles, but it was done so quietly that it had little impact inside Rwanda.

Occasionally U.S. diplomats telephoned Rwandan military leaders directly to protest the genocide or, in one case, to demand an end to threats against Tutsi sheltered at the Hôtel des Mille Collines. France and probably Belgium also intervened quietly to deter attacks on the hotel, which was left largely unmolested throughout the genocide. This small success, achieved with minimal investment of resources, suggests the readiness of Rwandan leaders to listen to important foreign actors, particularly when they spoke together. For the United States to have translated this success onto a larger scale, however, would have required considerably more effort. France continued supporting the genocidal government—its position on the hotel notwithstanding—and even held out the promise of military assistance. The genocidal government heard the U.S. expression of disapproval clearly enough to direct the population to make the slaughter less visible. But as long as U.S. remonstrations remained discreet and intermittent and French support steady and public, the genocidal government felt obliged only to move the slaughter from the roads to the banana groves, not to end it altogether.

Many of the civil society leaders once encouraged by support from the United States were killed at the start of the genocide. Others initially hoped for backing in resisting the genocidal government. When the United States, Belgium, and France remained silent and rapidly evacuated their own citizens, the potential resisters gave in to fear or opportunism. Some dissenters fled, others hid, and others joined the killing campaign.

AVOIDING THE "G" WORD

Midlevel and senior-level officials at the State Department, in touch with representatives of human rights and humanitarian organizations throughout the crisis, conscientiously sought and worked hard to persuade their superiors at State and those in other agencies to act more imaginatively and energetically. The senior director for Africa at the National Security Council similarly showed serious concern, but others in his division and that of international operations showed less urgency about stopping the genocide. Whether on larger policy questions or on the concrete issues of providing equipment to UNAMIR or jamming the genocidal radio, Pentagon officials had no help to offer those seeking to end the slaughter.[17]

When a Human Rights Watch representative asked Lake how to raise concern about the genocide at the White House, he answered: "Make more noise." But those at the White House who wished to minimize the noise directed that the term "genocide" not be used in discussing Rwanda.[18] They may have been correct in assuming that such usage would heighten public demands for action. When asked in a 1994 survey whether "the U.N., *including the U.S.*, should intervene with whatever force is necessary to stop acts of genocide, 65 per cent of the respondents replied either 'always' or 'in most cases.'"[19]

By early June the death toll was in the hundreds of thousands and the UN secretary-general, the pope, and other international leaders were using the term "genocide" without hesitation. Members of Congress, some of whom had first written the White House asking for action in late April, multiplied their calls, both in a congressional hearing and through additional letters. Clinton finally responded to the pressure and directed the administration to increase efforts to get

UNAMIR II to Rwanda.[20] The new force arrived in July after the RPF had defeated the genocidal government and driven it from the country.

ALLOWING SECURITY CONCERNS TO EXCUSE CIVILIAN SLAUGHTER

The former government reorganized to carry on the war from the Zairian side of the border. Soldiers and militia, many of whom were mingled among refugees in large camps, threatened attacks against the new government and the remaining Tutsi. Removing armed elements from among the refugees and moving the camps away from the borders would have minimized this threat. The newly arrived UNAMIR troops could have done this, but the French opposed this proposal and U.S. policymakers were unenthusiastic, so the idea was dropped.

U.S. officials wanted instead to support the new government in its efforts to defend itself. Increasingly aware of their own responsibility in failing to halt the genocide, they wanted to ensure that the Tutsi would be well protected. But they knew that information was surfacing about large-scale killings of Hutu civilians by soldiers of the RPF (officially the Rwandan Patriotic Army [RPA]). If the new government were discredited by such reports, it would have trouble winning the international political and financial support needed to resist attack.

In early September 1994 Robert Gersony, a consultant to the UN High Commissioner for Refugees, delivered an extensive report of RPA massacres to authorities of the new Rwandan government and to representatives of the United Nations in Kigali. When the information was communicated to Washington, the assistant secretary of state for African affairs directed the Africa Bureau officials who had just left Rwanda to return there. They did some preliminary checking but neither confirmed nor disproved Gersony's allegations. Tim Wirth, undersecretary of state for global affairs, arrived in the region soon after. He was briefed by Gersony and found his presentation convincing. He nonetheless rejected Gersony's conclusion that the killings were widespread and systematic and accepted the RPF contention that they were crimes by individual soldiers, many of them spurred by grief or rage.[21]

The UN secretary-general, foreseeing the embarrassment that would result from revelations that UNAMIR II had been unaware of RPA killings, ordered the Gersony report suppressed. U.S. policymakers concurred. In return, the RPF agreed to an investigation. The short-lived commission, which included representatives of UNAMIR, did little and the investigation and the matter were dropped. In the meantime, the United Nations and the United States put heavy but private pressure on the RPA to halt the killings, which did diminish— indicating that the military hierarchy had the capacity to control them.

In subsequent months RPA troops killed small numbers of people in more than a dozen incidents and caused the "disappearance" of hundreds of others. U.S. officials at very high levels raised the issue with Rwandan president Pasteur Bizimungu and with vice president and defense minister General Paul Kagame, but always with a realization of how "delicate" it was. National Security Adviser Lake remembers choosing language very carefully, seeking to avoid any suggestion of equivalence between RPA killings and the genocide.[22] The discreet pressure may have helped limit abuses in the short term and for cases that the Rwandan authorities saw as minimally threatening. But it did not inhibit later slaughter, such as that at the Kibeho displaced persons camp in April 1995, where the RPA killed at least two thousand people whom they saw as a greater threat to their security. There were too many foreign witnesses for the RPF to deny the incident. Instead, it sought to understate the fatalities, claiming there were fewer than four hundred, and agreed to an investigation by an international commission. Confronted with a horror of this magnitude, U.S. officials permitted or directed their representative on the commission to find mitigating circumstances to excuse the crime. The final report assigned no responsibility for the slaughter. U.S. officials further presented an inaccurate account of the massacre in the State Department *Country Report on Human Rights Practices in Rwanda*, contradicting eyewitness testimony by UN observers and representatives of international human rights and humanitarian organizations.

Although several European governments at first strongly condemned the Kibeho massacre and other RPA abuses, most eventually softened their stance in the face of continuing U.S. support for the Rwandan government. One European diplomat complained that the reproaches of his government counted for nothing as long as the United States stood behind Kigali. Being able to rely on steady U.S. backing permitted those within the Rwandan government who favored or condoned violence against civilians to strengthen their position. Those opposed to the violence lacked such powerful external support and were marginalized and eventually removed several months later.

U.S. officials again showed their willingness to tolerate the slaughter of civilians when RPA soldiers killed tens of thousands of refugees in Zaire beginning in October 1996. As early as August 1995, senior Pentagon officials responded to Rwandan security concerns by signaling U.S. readiness to tolerate RPA attacks on the camps in Zaire, thus overruling opposition by the State Department.[23] A year later Kagame visited Washington and indicated that he would attack the camps unless there was international action to end the threat they posed. U.S. policymakers again gave him at least tacit approval for the attack, provided it was a "clean" operation, that is, one with minimal civilian casualties. At the same time, the United States sent soldiers to train Rwandans in small-group tactics, marksmanship, and other skills useful in combat.[24]

Once the RPA launched the attack in Zaire, Rwandan military intelligence kept U.S. officials well briefed, at one point providing updates every four hours. The United States in turn provided the Rwandans with information about refugee movements obtained from satellite surveillance of the area, thus helping them track those who fled the camps.[25] U.S. military or private agents associated with them may have provided other assistance in such areas as communications and logistics. Staff of the U.S. embassy as well as a visiting U.S. general ignored information from UN agencies and nongovernmental organizations about the number of refugees needing protection. By grossly and apparently knowingly underestimating how many needed assistance, they helped quash a planned multinational force to save them.[26]

U.S. embassy staff in Kigali, military officers, and some high-ranking officials at the NSC and State and Defense Departments continued supporting the Rwandan government even when massacres by its troops became widely known. A few dissenting voices at State had little impact. When congressional critics led by Representative Christopher Smith held a hearing on the U.S. role in the Zairian operation in December 1996, high-ranking officials from State and Defense inaccurately depicted both the situation on the ground and the extent of U.S. military assistance to Rwanda.

The slaughter of refugees in Zaire (renamed the Democratic Republic of Congo [DRC]) provoked demands for an international investigation. After the DRC government blocked a first investigatory commission, the United States helped facilitate entry of a second, but it then backed down with the rest of the Security Council before a new refusal to cooperate by DRC authorities. The killings have yet to be investigated.

During 1997 and 1998, U.S. policymakers again confronted RPA slaughter of civilians, this time of those who supposedly supported an insurgency inside Rwanda. As in the previous cases, Rwandan authorities had legitimate security concerns and U.S. policymakers accepted these as an excuse for the killings and "disappearances" of civilians, which were particularly widespread in northwestern Rwanda. By mid-1998 European diplomats in Kigali talked of more than two hundred thousand persons missing, the vast majority of them killed by RPA soldiers. Unwilling to go that far, one NSC official believed that fifty thousand had been slain. Publicly, the United States expressed mild disapproval, but in the annual human rights report on Rwanda for 1997 and 1998, it minimized the number of dead and repeated the official Rwandan explanation that its soldiers had difficulty distinguishing civilians from insurgents, who often wore civilian clothes. David Scheffer, U.S. ambassador for war crimes, visited the Kanama caves soon after a large number—reportedly eight thousand—civilians had been slain there in late 1997. His inconclusive remarks at the time and the U.S. failure to insist on any subsequent establishment of responsibility for the crime reinforced the impression that the U.S. government condoned these killings.

Officials in Kigali and in Washington insist that they frequently remonstrated privately with high-ranking Rwandan authorities about the killings, but the U.S. refusal to condemn the abuses firmly and publicly left unchallenged those who favored brutal repression and left unsupported those opposed to the slaughter.

The U.S. government provided training in human rights and in civilian-military relations, meant to help win the "hearts and minds" of the population. In mid-1998 the RPA transferred significant numbers of reintegrated soldiers, Hutu from the army of the former government, into the northwest. Soon after, with the start of the second Congo war, insurgents in Rwanda were cut off from their rear bases in the DRC and had to reduce their activities and retreat into the forest. By the end of 1998, the number of RPA soldiers in northwestern Rwanda was reduced and the cases of abuses against the civilian population declined markedly. It is unclear how much this improvement resulted from U.S. pressure and training and how much it resulted from the changed military situation on the ground.

JUSTICE

Before 1994 U.S. policymakers showed little concern with bringing officials accused of abuses, even of massacres, to justice. When Habyarimana visited Washington in October 1993, Human Rights Watch pressed Assistant Secretary of State George Moose to raise this issue with him. Moose did not, reportedly because he preferred not to spoil the "positive atmosphere" of the discussions. Nor did U.S. policymakers insist on justice for ethnically based killings that had taken tens of thousands of lives in neighboring Burundi at the end of 1993 and in early 1994. Impunity for slaughter in both these countries encouraged extremists in Rwanda to imagine they could kill Tutsi on an unprecedented scale and escape punishment. During the genocide, they broadcast assurances on the radio that killers would escape justice just as had others in the recent past.[27]

Recognizing finally that justice was essential in breaking the cycle of slaughter, the United States announced before the end of the genocide that it would demand accountability for the perpetrators and it has done so, being one of the most effective supporters of the International Criminal Tribunal for Rwanda (ICTR). After a troubled start, the ICTR has increased both the number and the competence of its staff and is trying those accused of genocide. But it has yet to fulfill the other part of its mandate, prosecuting RPA soldiers for violations of international humanitarian law. Until it does so, its credibility hangs in the balance and its full potential for deterring further massive slaughter remains untested.

The United States also supported justice within Rwanda, contributing more than $20 million to the judicial system in the years after the genocide. The Rwandan government arrested more than 135,000 people, many of whom were detained for years without investigation. By 2003, some eight thousand had been tried and twenty-five thousand others provisionally released. The United States was appropriately patient at the start, given the difficulties of reestablishing the judicial system and the enormity of the task. But as the material and logistical problems have been resolved and the Rwandan courts continue to perform poorly, U.S. officials have set their standards too low and have been reluctant to criticize judicial inadequacies. In July 1996 a high-ranking embassy official remarked that Rwandan courts would be "kangaroo courts, but that they must be credible kangaroo courts," indicating a willingness to accept the appearance for the reality of justice.

U.S. officials generally take pride in the aid given to military justice, which many see as the most substantial contribution by the United States to ending RPA abuses. U.S. training has undoubtedly helped improve the functioning of Rwandan military courts, encouraging investigation and prosecution of abuses that would otherwise have passed unnoticed. But Rwandan judges generally condemn soldiers and junior officers for serious abuses and acquit senior officers or find them guilty of less grave infractions. Colonel Ibingira was tried for having commanded the Kibeho massacre, for example, found guilty only of nonassistance to persons in danger, and sentenced to sixteen months in prison (already served before the trial) and minor court costs. When RPA soldiers or officers are found guilty of killing civilians, the crime is generally attributed to personal motives. Major Bigabiro was condemned to life in prison for having ordered the massacre of some thirty civilians, supposedly because they sought to prevent him from raping a woman. Had the United States forthrightly and publicly criticized inadequate prosecution or inappropriate judgments, Rwandan officers who face the difficult task of bringing the powerful to court might have felt encouraged to administer justice more rigorously.

UN AGENCIES

During the genocide, the United States turned to the human rights agencies of the United Nations to cover its own inaction. It encouraged the newly appointed UN High Commissioner for Human Rights to undertake a mission to Rwanda, but neither in Rwanda nor after his return did the High Commissioner make any significant contribution to ending the killing.[28] The United States also supported an emergency meeting of the UN Human Rights Commission, but it too failed to bring any relief to the victims, although it named a special rapporteur to investigate whether genocide had occurred, thus beginning the process that would lead to the establishment of the ICTR.

After the genocide, the United States did little to help UN agencies seeking to protect Rwandans, whether it was the UN High Commission for Refugees at the time of the Gersony report and the massacres in Zaire or the UN Human Rights Field Operation at the time of Kibeho and the massacres in the northwest. The Field Operation published detailed reports based on eyewitness accounts of killings in northwestern Rwanda in 1997, making it difficult for the Rwandan government and external actors to deny that the killings had taken place. Yet a high-ranking U.S. diplomat often tried to do just that. According to one observer, the U.S. diplomat contested every aspect of the UN human rights report presented at one meeting, acting "like the lawyer for the Rwandan government." When the Rwandan government managed to transform the post of UN special rapporteur into that of a special representative, thus eliminating his responsibility to monitor abuses, and when it refused to permit further monitoring by the Field Operation, thus causing its withdrawal, the U.S. government made no protest.

HUMAN RIGHTS ORGANIZATIONS

Before the genocide, U.S. officials encouraged Rwandan human rights organizations, both by offering some financial assistance and by listening—politely, though at first skeptically—to their reports. As local activists learned to document better their accusations and when international human rights organizations joined them in making the same charges, embassy staff found their reports increasingly credible and passed them on to Washington. From 1994 through 1998 activists critical of the Rwandan government felt shut out of the U.S. embassy and their names were unknown in Washington. In late 1999 USAID was supporting local nongovernmental organizations working in such areas as health but was giving no assistance to human rights groups. After Human Rights Watch representatives questioned this practice, USAID officials began looking into giving such support.

Similarly, representatives of international human rights organizations whose data and analyses were welcomed before, during, and immediately after the genocide found their information rejected after 1995 when it included criticism of RPA abuses. One U.S. official in Kigali advised an agent of a humanitarian organization to suppress information about human rights abuses and another stated that he was forbidden to talk to anyone from Human Rights Watch. When Rwandan authorities declared the representative of Human Rights Watch persona non grata in 1997 and explained that this was because the organization had published a report critical of RPA abuses in the Congo, U.S. embassy staff refused to intervene and wrongly described the incident as the result of a visa problem in the State Department *Country Report on Human Rights Practices in Rwanda*. During the same period, Human Rights Watch shared confidential information with State Department officials, only to find it later in the hands of Rwandan authorities. According to one senior State Department official, he sometimes told Rwandan officials that his protests about abuses were responses to pressure from Human Rights Watch or similar organizations. Hearing this, Rwandans presumably concluded that human rights concerns were not part of his agenda or that of the U.S. government.

LESSONS

When a government is committing grave human rights abuses, the first imperative is to try to stop them. In urgent cases U.S. officials have sometimes succeeded in halting abuses through discreet initiatives, for example, protecting Jehovah's Witnesses from arbitrary arrest in 1986 and Tutsi from similar arrests and torture in 1990 and saving Tutsi targeted for killing in the massacres of 1990 or at the Hôtel des Mille Collines during the genocide. Similarly, U.S. actors apparently succeeded in reducing the level of killings by the RPA in September 1994 and, perhaps, in northwestern Rwanda in 1998.

But without clear, firm, and public condemnation of the abuse, these initiatives produced no long-term reform. Thus, Habyarimana was again harassing Jehovah's Witnesses soon after releasing them from prison and he launched one massacre of Tutsi months after halting another. Under pressure, the genocidal government let Tutsi live at the Hôtel des Mille Collines but continued to slaughter them elsewhere. RPA officers reduced the number of killings by their soldiers in September 1994 but later permitted or ordered the Kibeho massacre, the killings of refugees in Zaire, and the killings of civilians in northwestern Rwanda.

The absence of firm public condemnation of the abuse strengthened abusers and weakened moderates. Thus, the silence of the world in the face of the genocide rapidly discouraged most who might have resisted the killing campaign. After the establishment of the new government, the absence of external criticism of RPA killings convinced moderates that their opposition to such abuses was futile and led some of them to quit the government.

Public condemnation of abuses must be backed by accountability, whether within the international or the national arena. Any form of justice must investigate and prosecute all parties equally. The easy acceptance of justifications (such as the need to ensure security), or excuses (such as that abuses resulted from acts of uncontrollable subordinates), or patently sham investigations (such as that after the Kibeho massacre) undermines any effort at accountability and breeds cynicism about the standards that are purportedly being enforced.

Human rights are best supported by consistent, unified action, whether within a single national framework or between nations. When all external actors protested together about the threatened attack on Hôtel des Mille Collines, the tragedy was averted, but when French authorities received representatives of the genocidal government with honor, this undermined its own earlier position as well as that of the United States in trying to limit the slaughter. Similarly, the strong U.S. support for the RPA made it more difficult for protests by certain European governments to influence Rwandan behavior.

The ultimate longer-term goal of building support for human rights within a local society requires more than financial support or technical assistance. It requires demonstrating real conviction about these ideals. Funding programs for democratization while ignoring official discrimination against the Tutsi minority or training RPA soldiers in human rights law while keeping silent about RPA slaughter of civilians is not only ineffective but counterproductive because it fosters hypocrisy about human rights ideals.

The most effective contribution that U.S. policymakers can make to human rights in Rwanda is to fairly and consistently maintain the standards of human rights, regardless of the ethnic group or political affiliation of perpetrators and victims. They must also apply those same standards to their own behavior. Given the enormous harm done by U.S. inaction in the face of the genocide and by apparent tolerance of RPA killings of civilians, U.S. officials need to examine openly and honestly the decisions made in policy toward Rwanda in the past ten years. Only then might they regain the moral stature necessary to effectively promote human rights in Rwanda or elsewhere.

NOTES

1. See the study by Peter Uvin, *Aiding Violence: The Development Enterprise in Rwanda* (West Hartford, Conn.: Kumarian Press), 1998.

2. Habyarimana himself had promised such a change the year before but had done nothing to implement it.

3. Africa Watch (later Human Rights Watch/Africa), International Federation of Human Rights Leagues, Interafrican Union for Human and Peoples' Rights, and the International Center for Human Rights and Democratic Development, *Report of the International Commission of Investigation on Human Rights Violations in Rwanda since October 1, 1990* (Brussels and New York, March 1993).

4. See Michael N. Barnett, "The UN Security Council, Indifference, and Genocide in Rwanda," *Cultural Anthropology* (1997): 551–578.

5. Sénat de Belgique, Commission d'enquête parlementaire concernant les événements du Rwanda, *Rapport*, December 6, 1997, 394.

6. Alison Des Forges, *Leave None to Tell the Story: Genocide in Rwanda* (New York: Human Rights Watch and the International Federation of Human Rights Leagues, 1999), 150–151.

7. United Nations, "Report of the Independent Inquiry into the Actions of the United Nations during the 1994 Genocide in Rwanda"; and Des Forges, *Leave None to Tell the Story,* 152–154, 157, 160, 162, 167, 169, 170.

8. Sénat de Belgique, *Rapport*, 244.

9. Des Forges, *Leave None to Tell the Story*, 159.

10. Sénat de Belgique, *Rapport*, 394.

11. David Rawson former U.S. ambassador to Rwanda (speech at Southern Illinois University, November 14, 1999). The commander of the peacekeeping force made the same request of his superiors in New York, both immediately and on repeated occasions after, insisting that with reinforcements he could stop the killing.

12. United Nations, "Report of the Independent Inquiry into the Actions of the United Nations during the 1994 Genocide in Rwanda"; Sénat de Belgique, *Rapport*, 519, 531–532; and Des Forges, *Leave None to Tell the Story*, 628–629.

13. Des Forges, *Leave None to Tell the Story*, 631.

14. In fact, the number in Rwanda was about four hundred because Dallaire managed by one device or another to delay their departure.

15. One source claims that a high-level meeting on April 17 discussed the use of U.S. troops but quickly dismissed the idea.

16. Des Forges, *Leave None to Tell the Story*, 640–641; U.S. State Department, "Joint Press Statement by President Museveni of Uganda and U.S. Assistant Secretary of State John Shattuck on the Situation in Rwanda," Kampala, May 7, 1994.

17. See Holly J. Burkhalter, "The Question of Genocide," *World Policy Journal* 11, no. 4 (winter 1994–95): 48.

18. Douglas Jehl, "Officials Told to Avoid Calling Rwanda Killings 'Genocide,'" *New York Times*, June 10, 1994.

19. A study done by the University of Maryland Program on International Policy Attitudes, quoted in Kenneth J. Campbell, "Clausewitz and Genocide: Bosnia, Rwanda, and Strategic Failure," *Civil Wars* 1, no. 2 (summer 1998): 33, emphasis added.

20. Michael R. Gordon, "U.S. Acting More Urgently to End Rwanda Slaughter," *New York Times*, June 16, 1994.

21. Notes taken at a briefing by Tim Wirth, undersecretary of state for global affairs, State Department, October 11, 1994.

22. Anthony Lake, telephone interview by Human Rights Watch, May 4, 1998.

23. Human Rights Watch field notes, Kigali, August 1995.

24. Letter from Representative Christopher Smith to President Clinton, August 28, 1997.

25. UN official, telephone interview by Human Rights Watch, October 14, 1998; Nick Gowing, "New Challenges and Problems for Information Management in Complex Emergencies. Ominous Lessons from the Great Lakes and Eastern Zaire in Late 1996 and Early 1997" (London, May 27, 1998), 60.

26. Filip Reyntjens, *La Guerre des Grands Lacs* (Paris: L'Harmattan, 1999), 75–100.

27. Jean-Pierre Chrétien, *Rwanda, les médias du génocide* (Paris: Karthala, 1995), 318–319.

28. The High Commissioner helped negotiate a plan for the release of hostages from the hotel, but their convoy was attacked by militia and soldiers and they returned to the hotel.

2

U.S. Human Rights Policy and Democratization in Kenya

JOEL D. BARKAN

U.S. HUMAN RIGHTS POLICY toward Kenya has been a derivative of broader U.S. foreign policy objectives worldwide and across Africa. The policy has consequently been closely intertwined with U.S. efforts to promote transitions from authoritarian to democratic rule on the continent after the end of the Cold War. Whereas U.S. policymakers seldom voiced concern about human rights abuses or authoritarian rule before the breakup of the Soviet Union, U.S. policy changed dramatically during the final two years of the first Bush administration. Since 1991, a shifting combination of three basic goals has driven U.S. Africa policy: (1) conflict resolution and the rebuilding of failed states following periods of civil war, (2) democratization, the transition from authoritarian to democratic rule, and (3) macroeconomic reform (i.e., "structural adjustment") leading to the establishment of free-market economies and the reduction of poverty.

These three goals formed the basis of U.S. Africa policy during the Bush and Clinton administrations and the first three years of the second Bush administration. The events of September 11 added a fourth goal that is related to the first three—that Africa, especially failed states such as Somalia, not become a haven for international terrorists. These goals reflect the limited strategic and economic interests of the United States in Africa. The continent is no longer the site of proxy wars between the superpowers, as it was during the 1970s and 1980s—in Angola, Mozambique, and the Horn. Southern Africa is no longer under white rule, a condition that complicated U.S. relations with the rest of the continent. Although U.S. investment in Africa increased greatly during the 1990s,[1] it remains limited, particularly outside South Africa. U.S. investment in Africa accounts for less than 1 percent of U.S. overseas investment worldwide. Africa's share of U.S. trade is likewise very low.[2]

Given these changing realities, the United States adjusted its foreign policy objectives to address its long-term strategic interests and Africa's immediate needs. These are (1) the maintenance or reestablishment of peace and political stability across a continent marked by chronic instability and (2) the desperate need for sustained economic growth and poverty reduction on a continent whose peoples are the poorest in the world. As long as Africa remains an unstable region, the United States is vulnerable to becoming directly or indirectly drawn into humanitarian and/or peacekeeping operations that are potentially costly to the United States, but where American interests are rarely at stake.[3] As long as Africa remains poor, the prospects for maintaining peace and/or political stability are likewise poor. And as long as Africa remains an unstable region with a disproportionately large number of failed and semifailed states—Congo, Somalia, Sudan, Sierra Leone, Liberia—the continent is a potential haven for terrorists, including al Qaeda, intent on attacking the United States. The first of these needs is addressed by a regional foreign policy that emphasizes conflict resolution and democratization; the second, by a policy that emphasizes economic reform and a reduction in corruption. A principal lesson of the first thirty years of Africa's independence is that authoritarian rule failed to provide either peace or abundance. These failures in turn led to widespread abuses of human rights and state decay.

Although U.S. policymakers have articulated the three goals of conflict resolution, democratization, and economic reform throughout the 1990s and into the next decade, U.S. officials have pursued the policy inconsistently because of a shifting emphasis among these goals—by Washington and by American ambassadors in the field. These inconsistencies will persist and become more pronounced as the United States expands the war on terrorism.

U.S. human rights and democratization policy toward Kenya is an example of these inconsistencies. The Kenyan experience is also instructive regarding the potentialities and limitations of Washington's ability to improve human rights conditions and promote democratization abroad.

This chapter makes six arguments about U.S. human rights and democratization policy in Africa through a consideration of the Kenyan case:

- U.S. human rights policy in general and toward Kenya in particular underwent several changes following the end of the Cold War.
- Although senior U.S. officials, including the president and the secretary of state, have been unambiguous in their articulation of U.S. policy goals on human rights and democratization, the translation of these goals into American policy toward individual states has often been ambiguous and/or contradictory.
- Notwithstanding the conventional wisdom that foreign policy is made in Washington and carried out faithfully abroad, the U.S. ambassador's intellectual perspective and personal diplomatic style profoundly affects the implementation of U.S. human rights and democratization policy. Put simply, the ambassador counts.
- The United States is the key player in the international community when it comes to human rights and support for democratic transitions. When the United States takes a strong diplomatic position to protect human rights and support democratization, other Western democracies are more likely to do the same.
- The United States and the rest of the international community have limited means and power to protect human rights and/or support democratization abroad. They can, at best, facilitate and nurture a process that is driven mainly by domestic forces in each country to which the policy is applied. They cannot unilaterally guarantee the respect for human rights or the emergence of democracy.

- An effective foreign policy to protect human rights and advance democratization in Africa is a project of ten to thirty years' duration because it is a project of building new political institutions supported by a new political culture.

U.S. HUMAN RIGHTS AND DEMOCRATIZATION POLICY AFTER THE COLD WAR

U.S. foreign policy on human rights and democratization underwent two (possibly three) changes during the early 1990s. First, U.S. concerns about human rights were no longer subordinated to the policy of containment that had dominated American policy throughout the Cold War. Human rights policy became a more visible and central component of a new foreign policy that sought to advance international peace and security by placing greater emphasis on resolving internal conflicts and reducing the causes of internal conflict, especially in multiethnic societies.[4] This emphasis on conflict resolution, and the end to proxy wars in Africa between the United States and the former Soviet Union, was the principal focus of U.S. Africa policy during the first Bush administration when Herman Cohen was assistant secretary of state for African affairs.

Second, U.S. efforts to protect human rights became intertwined with American efforts to promote transitions from authoritarian to democratic rule. Rather than view the protection of human rights as an objective that should or could be pursued independently from a policy that supported democratization, the United States closely linked support for human rights to support for democratization over the long term. Indeed, democratization was increasingly viewed as the most effective long-term guarantor of human rights.

Third, though not explicitly, U.S. policy evolved from defining human rights exclusively in terms of civil liberties and political rights for individuals—the so-called first-generation human rights—to recognizing but not fully articulating the importance of economic and social rights, environmental rights, gender rights, and so on—rights that the scholarly and legal literature refers to as second- and third-generation human rights.[5] Whereas during the Cold War U.S. policy focused solely on the advancement and protection of individual political and

civil rights, the promotion of human rights from the early 1990s on-
ward encompassed a broader set of goals. The linkage, or "bundling," of
these different types of human rights paralleled the linkage of democratization with the development of free-market economies. As political reform became linked to macroeconomic reform and vice versa,
political rights became linked to economic and social rights.[6] Similarly, a previous emphasis on the rights of individuals gave way to the
recognition that both individual *and* group rights required protection
and promotion.

VARIATIONS ON A THEME: U.S. HUMAN RIGHTS POLICY ACROSS AFRICA

Although the advancement of human rights and democratization has
long been one of the stated goals of American foreign policy, it did
not feature prominently in day-to-day policy until after the end of the
Cold War. Despite the goal's prominence, especially in the official
rhetoric of the Clinton administration, U.S. human rights and democratization policy has been fraught with ambiguity when translated into
a series of bilateral policies toward individual states. While some tension between principle and practice is inevitable, the gap has widened
in respect to U.S. support for human rights and democratization across
Africa and especially in eastern Africa and the Horn.

During the 1990s U.S. bilateral policies in support of democratization and human rights across Africa ebbed and flowed as a function
of four variables: (1) the "historical experience" of each country in
the region, (2) whether the country in question had been aggressive
in pursuing macroeconomic reform, (3) the existence of a U.S. constituency that follows events in the country, and (4) whether the
country is vulnerable to donor pressure as a result of its dependency
on foreign aid.

The United States has been less vigorous and less rigorous in
articulating the desirability of democratization in countries emerging
from periods of civil war or countries that have experienced genocide
than in countries that have escaped such traumas. In postconflict societies, the United States has delinked the defense of human rights from
the promotion of democracy. Where human rights abuses are modest

or substantially fewer than previous violations, democratization has not been a primary foreign policy goal. The justification for this "softer treatment," or uncoupling of U.S. rights policy from its democratization policy, is that the leaders of war-torn countries need time—and hence diplomatic breathing space—to rebuild their political systems before being held to universal democratic standards.[7] If, for example, a country such as Uganda has greatly reduced the incidence of human rights abuse and increased civil liberties, it receives a "pass" or "discount" on democratization despite the fact that for all intents and purposes it is still a one-party state.[8] A similar sliding standard has been applied to Rwanda, Eritrea, and Ethiopia—but *not* to Kenya, which fortunately has not endured periods of civil war.

The same is true for countries that have embraced macroeconomic reform and have aggressively established or reestablished free-market economies. Countries that have followed International Monetary Fund (IMF) and World Bank guidelines for economic reform, such as Ethiopia and Uganda, also receive a pass or discount on democratization. Ghana would be another example during the first half of the 1990s—but again, not Kenya, where the commitment to macroeconomic reform has been consistently weak.

The presence or absence of a domestic U.S. constituency that follows events in a foreign country and that sometimes seeks to influence U.S. diplomacy toward that country is a third factor that gives rise to inconsistencies in U.S. human rights and democratization policy toward individual African states. Whereas few Americans can identify more than two or three African countries by name, Kenya, together with South Africa and Nigeria, is usually among that select group. Several reasons explain Kenya's saliency in the minds of some Americans: Kenya's tourist attractions; Kenya's history, particularly the rise and legacy of its white settler community as depicted in the writings of Karen Blixen and Robert Ruark and in films such as *Born Free*, *Out of Africa*, and *White Mischief*; the longtime presence (since the 1920s) of American missionaries and the more recent presence (since the 1960s) of Peace Corps volunteers. Nearly five thousand U.S. citizens currently reside in Kenya, one of the largest U.S. communities in sub-Saharan Africa. More than ten thousand Kenyans are permanent residents in the United States. There has also been a continuous flow of Kenyan students to U.S. colleges and universities since the 1960s, and a similar though much smaller counterflow of American students to Kenya.

Two private organizations with access to U.S. policymakers, the National Democratic Institute and the Robert Kennedy Foundation, have tracked political developments and human rights in Kenya since the late 1980s and have disseminated their findings to interested members of Congress. The International Republican Institute has also operated programs in the country. Amnesty International and Human Rights Watch have long monitored human rights in Kenya and disseminated their findings. In sum, a diverse constituency of Americans who follow or are periodically made aware of events in Kenya is second or third in size only to the number of Americans who follow events in Nigeria and South Africa. While it is impossible to determine the precise size of the "Kenya constituency" in the United States, its numbers and voice have been sufficiently large to make itself heard—at the State Department and particularly among the small group of congressional leaders interested in African affairs. Kenya's human rights record and protracted transition to democracy are well known—to those outside government who track U.S. policy on human rights and democratization, and to those within. As human rights abuses in Kenya rose during the late 1980s and as the regime of President Daniel arap Moi became increasingly authoritarian and corrupt in its rule, the government of Kenya drew heavy criticism from Americans familiar with the country.[9]

The extent of a country's dependency on foreign aid appears to make that country both more *and* less vulnerable to international pressure on the issues of human rights and democratization. In the case of failed or war-torn states seeking to rebuild their political and economic systems after periods of civil war, the desperate need for donor assistance may in fact forestall pressure on human rights and democratization, provided the country moves decisively to implement needed macroeconomic reforms. As noted earlier, Ethiopia, Ghana, Rwanda, and Uganda all appear to be beneficiaries of this tendency. Where, however, the leadership of an African country perfected the combination of poor macroeconomic policies and authoritarian rule during the late 1980s, as in Kenya under Daniel arap Moi, in Cameroon under Paul Biya, in the former Zaire under Mobutu Sese Seko, and in Zambia under Kenneth Kaunda, the donor community has suspended and conditioned aid to force reform. In the case of Kenya, assistance was suspended in November 1991 and again in July 1997 and December 2000 after being resumed in 1994 and July 2000. A more extensive discussion of the impact of aid suspension and aid conditionality in Kenya follows, showing that the efficacy of the policy to achieve either economic reform or democratization has been mixed.

THE AMBASSADOR COUNTS: INCONSISTENCY OVER TIME

Although it is widely believed that policy is made in Washington and implemented faithfully in the field, the experience of Kenya illustrates the extent to which U.S. policy can vary with the personality, policy interests, and experience of the U.S. ambassador. The ambassador is the key actor in determining how U.S. human rights and democratization policy is articulated in the country to which he or she is accredited. However, the ambassador often faces several trade-offs when articulating the policy—between U.S. strategic interests and specific human rights and democratization concerns, between short-term and long-term objectives, between public and private diplomacy, between coercive and cooperative approaches, and between unilateral and multilateral approaches. How the ambassador weighs these trade-offs is a function of his or her assessment of the realities on the ground, which are in turn a function of his or her approach to these issues. U.S. ambassadors in Nairobi have faced each of these trade-offs. One American ambassador also believed that a trade-off existed between the pursuit of a forceful policy to encourage democratization and support for Kenya's economic development.

The trade-off between U.S. strategic concerns and U.S. concerns for human rights and democratization was particularly great during the 1970s and 1980s, when Kenya was an island of political stability and relative prosperity in a turbulent region and when U.S. foreign policy was preoccupied with the Cold War. During this period, all of Kenya's neighbors except Tanzania were embroiled in civil strife. The collapse of Uganda under the regimes of Idi Amin and

Milton Obote from 1972 to 1987, the thirty-year civil war in southern Sudan, the Soviet-backed regime of Mengistu Haile Mariam in
Ethiopia from 1974 to 1991, and the collapse of the Said Barre regime
in Somalia—all enhanced Kenya's strategic importance to the United
States. Notable components of Kenya's regional importance were its
geographic position as "the hub" of East Africa, its status as the most
developed country of the region, and the amenities of Nairobi. Kenya's
economy is also more than the joint product of Tanzania and Uganda,
its two principal neighbors.[10]

This combination of factors led U.S. policymakers to view Kenya
as one of the "anchor" states of Africa. Kenya became a platform for
a wide range of U.S. activities in eastern Africa and the Horn. The
U.S. embassy in Nairobi expanded to become the largest American
outpost in sub-Saharan Africa.[11]

Throughout his tenure as the president of Kenya, from August
1978 through December 2002, Daniel arap Moi took advantage of his
country's regional position to obtain support from the United States.
In 1979, soon after Moi came to power, Kenya entered into an agreement with the United States that permitted the U.S. Air Force to
land military aircraft at Kenya's international airports in Nairobi and
Mombasa on twenty-four-hour notice.[12] The U.S. Navy was likewise
accorded the use of the port of Mombasa as a rest-and-recreation
facility for its Indian Ocean fleet. Kenya usually supported the U.S.
position at the United Nations and other international fora. In return, the United States dredged the harbor at Mombasa and length-
ened the runway at the Mombasa airport, enhancing the commercial
and military importance of these facilities. The United States also
provided military assistance to the Kenyan air force by selling Kenya
a squadron of F-5 jets on favorable terms and training its pilots and
crews. By 1991 U.S. development assistance to Kenya had risen to
$60 million a year, one of the highest figures for U.S. support to an
African country.

Kenya's regional position and Moi's cooperation with the United
States gave the president a certain license to govern as he pleased.
During the 1980s economic growth in Kenya slowed and the Moi
regime became increasingly authoritarian and kleptocratic. Corruption soared while the Kenyan government's ability to deliver social

services to its people sharply declined. Although a succession of U.S. ambassadors reported Kenya's decline, they refrained from public comment. As human rights violations mounted, the United States expended little diplomatic effort to reverse them. However, at the end of the Cold War, U.S. diplomacy toward Kenya shifted nearly 180 degrees. For Moi and his closest associates in the Kenyan government, this shift was viewed as a betrayal by a country they had long supported and regarded as "a good friend of Kenya." The rancor of the shift still lingers among Moi and his associates.

Between 1986 and 2003, five ambassadors represented the United States in Kenya: Elinor Constable (1986–89), Smith Hempstone (1989–93), Aurelia Brazeal (1993–96), Prudence Bushnell (1996–99), and Johnnie Carson (1999–July 2003). All but Hempstone are career Foreign Service officers. Each had a somewhat different approach toward implementing U.S. policy.

Elinor Constable

Elinor Constable served as the U.S. ambassador to Kenya during the final three years of the Cold War. Her approach to human rights and democratization issues reflected the subordination of human rights to the strategy of containment during this period. As human rights abuses mounted in Kenya, including the detention and torture of opponents of President Moi, Constable remained publicly silent, though she later claimed that she had engaged in private diplomacy on human rights with the Kenyan government. Neither Constable nor the Department of State expressed public concern about the replacement of the secret ballot with "queue voting" for the 1988 parliamentary elections— arguably the most grievous violation of political rights since independence. Although Kenya had been a one-party state since 1964, when the ruling Kenya African National Union (KANU) merged with the principal opposition party,[13] parliamentary elections had continued to be genuine contests similar to primary elections in the United States. Kenyans did not have the opportunity to change the head of government, but they did have the regular opportunity to change their representatives to the national legislature—and did so until 1988.[14] However, the introduction of queue voting, a procedure that required voters to line up in public behind the agent of their preferred candidate, intimidated the electorate and laid bare the declining legitimacy of the Moi regime. Less than a quarter of the eligible electorate went to the polls, the lowest turnout since independence.

Smith Hempstone

An ex-marine, career journalist, and former editor in chief of the *Washington Times*, Smith Hempstone was a political appointee of the first Bush administration. His tenure as U.S. ambassador coincided with the beginning of the new U.S. human rights and democratization policy of the post–Cold War era, and with the emergence of widespread demands in Kenya for the end of one-party rule.

Although he was initially skeptical of the new policy, Hempstone soon embraced it with an enthusiasm and bluntness that gave pause to some at the State Department.[15] When Hempstone had first visited Kenya, in the 1950s, he had been captivated by the country's beauty, its wildlife, and the legacy of its settler era. Subsequently, he had also been impressed by Kenya's accomplishments during its first two decades of independence. Thus, he was deeply troubled by the country's economic and political decline during the second half of the 1980s. The assassination of Kenya's foreign minister, Robert Ouku, in February 1990, widely attributed to Moi and his closest associates, also troubled him.[16]

Although Hempstone had sought to develop a close personal relationship with Moi during his first year as ambassador, he was unusually forceful in articulating the evolving U.S. position on the need for political reform. In a speech to the Rotary Club of Nairobi on May 3, 1990, he observed that the Kenyan government would soon find itself "behind the curve" in respect to U.S. Africa policy if it did not embark on a program of political reform (i.e., an end to human rights abuses and a reduction in corruption) and ultimately democratization. He also stressed the need for Kenya to pursue economic reform.

The reaction by the Kenyan government was swift. The government-controlled press rebuked Hempstone for "interfering" in the internal affairs of a sovereign state. The ambassador stood his ground, stating that his intent was not to criticize but rather "to inform" Kenyans about the new directions of U.S. Africa policy. U.S.-Kenyan relations became so strained that then assistant secretary of state for Africa Herman Cohen felt it necessary to fly out to Nairobi to soothe Moi and prevent Hempstone's expulsion. The State Department, however, stood by Hempstone, and Cohen subsequently sent a cable to all posts in mid-1992 in which he stated that tensions would inevitably arise between the United States and African authoritarian regimes as the United States pursued its new policy. U.S. diplomatic personnel should therefore prepare themselves for this eventuality and get on with the job. Notwithstanding these tensions, Moi and his government continued to support other U.S. objectives in the region (e.g., the stabilization of Somalia, support to southern Sudan).

Hempstone's utterances were especially challenging to the Kenyan government because they reflected the changing mood *within* Kenya as well as the changing view of other Western countries toward authoritarian regimes. As the economy declined and the Moi government resorted to increasingly repressive measures to subdue its opponents, various individuals within Kenya, particularly among the clergy and the legal profession, began to question the utility of one-party rule. On the same day as Hempstone's Rotary Club speech (though unbeknownst to the ambassador until after his talk), two former cabinet ministers who had been expelled from the government, Kenneth Matiba and Charles Rubia, called a press conference to demand an end to one-party rule and the legalization of opposition parties. They were later detained, on July 4, 1990, after attending the annual Independence Day celebration at the ambassador's residence. The detentions were followed by widespread rioting in Nairobi and across Kenya that resulted in twenty deaths but laid bare the issue of whether Kenya would continue as a one-party regime of personal rule or embark on political reform. The interplay between Kenyan domestic politics and U.S. foreign policy had reshaped the terms of Kenyan politics for the decade.

Hempstone's boldness, however, also revealed the dilemmas facing the United States in its efforts to define and implement a new human rights and democratization policy toward Africa. First, to be credible in the minds of local political leaders, both government and opposition, it was necessary that the new policy be clearly *and publicly* articulated across the continent from one country to the next. Such a policy could not be initiated, nor could it attain credibility, solely through private diplomacy with the host government, for who outside government—whether the general public or elites demanding democratic change—would know what the new U.S. policy entailed? Hempstone was widely criticized within the State Department for resorting to public utterances, but even his critics acknowledged that he had made the U.S. position clear and changed the terms of diplomatic discourse in the region. Other ambassadors, most notably those of Germany and the Scandinavian countries, soon followed his lead by publicly expressing their own concerns about the necessity of political reform. The British high commissioner to Kenya, who disdained public diplomacy and regarded Hempstone as something of "an American cowboy," did not.

Hempstone's resort to public diplomacy helped change the parameters of Kenya's domestic debate about the country's future. Whereas before his utterances and the detentions of Matiba and Rubia, the Kenya government had simply harassed and/or jailed those who called for an end to human rights abuses or the return to multiparty politics, President Moi now felt compelled to justify the status quo by questioning the wisdom of a return to multiparty politics. He typically argued that those calling for democratization were promoting "disunity" and conflict, because multiparty politics would inevitably result in the emergence of parties that reflected constituencies defined on ethnic lines. The ambassador's statements had nevertheless emboldened Kenya's nascent opposition to press on for democratic change. Certainly the Kenya government thought so. By mid-1991 opposition elements had coalesced into an amorphous movement known as the Forum for the Restoration of Democracy (FORD). Although Moi ultimately succeeded in splitting the movement, opposition politics in Kenya had become a fact of political life for the first time in more than twenty years.

Hempstone's tenure also coincided with the coalescence of the donor community on the need for political reform and the willingness by the United States and other "like-minded" donors to suspend aid, particularly nonproject assistance such as cash disbursements, if reform was not forthcoming.[17] By the end of 1991, the members of the donor community had become increasingly concerned about continued violations of human rights and mounting corruption by senior officials in the Kenyan government. Notwithstanding the resort to public diplomacy supplemented by repeated expressions of concern through normal diplomatic channels, there was little sign of reform from the Moi government.

The first to suspend aid was Norway, after it broke relations with Kenya in October 1990. The rest of the donor community, including the United States, had also made it clear at the annual meeting of the Consultative Group (CG) for Kenya in November 1990 that a suspension of aid was possible if the government did not put its house in order. Actual suspension, however, did not occur until the next meeting of the CG, in Paris on November 25 and 26, 1991. After reviewing the lack of any significant progress over the preceding year, the donors announced a halt of more than $250 million pending an end to human rights abuses, a significant reduction in corruption, and the pursuit of sound macroeconomic policy.[18]

Although a principal objective of the donors was a measure of political liberalization in Kenya, it is important to remember that they did *not* call for democratization defined in terms of ending one-party rule and holding multiparty elections. President Moi nevertheless interpreted the donors' conditionalities in these terms. He announced in December that he would ask the Kenya National Assembly to repeal section 2a of the Kenyan constitution, which mandated Kenya a one-party state, thus legalizing the return of multiparty politics.[19] The repeal of 2a and the passage of supplementary legislation set the stage for the registration of opposition parties and the holding—on December 29, 1992—of general elections on a multiparty basis for the first time in twenty-six years. The elections returned Moi and his ruling party, KANU, to power with a third of the vote following the splintering of the opposition into three principal parties and nearly a dozen small ones.[20]

The return to multiparty politics was marked by increased violence and human rights abuses of a new form known as "ethnic clashes." The clashes occurred first in the Rift Valley soon after the repeal of section 2a and continued throughout the first half of 1992. "Warriors" of unknown origin attacked members of the ethnic groups known to support opposition parties. Victims believe that Moi perpetrated the clashes to demonstrate—as a self-fulfilling prophecy—that the return of multiparty politics would bring disunity to Kenya. The clashes resumed briefly in January 1993 immediately after the elections. More than fifteen hundred died in these conflicts and upward of a quarter-million people were driven from their homes. The diplomatic community, including the United States, reacted vigorously to these developments, which were widely reported in the Kenya press. Moi also condemned the violence, but his government frustrated subsequent efforts by the United Nations Development Program to provide assistance to clash victims.

Hempstone's ambassadorship also oversaw the initiation of modest programs by the United States Agency for International Development (USAID) and other donors to support human rights and democratization in Kenya and in other African countries. The United States began its program in Kenya in 1990 with a series of small grants (i.e., from $15,000 to $25,000 each) to several civil society organizations, including the Human Rights Commission of Kenya and the Law Society of Kenya. It expanded the program in 1992 by providing support to the electoral process from the African Regional Election Assistance Fund (AREAF). This included more than $100,000 in grants to the National Election Monitoring Unit, a consortium of Kenyan NGOs that ultimately trained and posted observers to roughly half of the six thousand polling stations established for the elections. The United States also funded a delegation of fifty-five international observers organized by the International Republican Institute, part of the more than three hundred foreign observers who traveled to Kenya for the elections. The United States and Canada were the lead players in the establishment of the Donor Democracy and Governance Group (DDGG), a multidonor forum that coordinated assistance for the elections and that continues to coordinate donor assistance for democratization as the Like-Minded Governance Group, eleven years after its formation. The European Union, Germany, the Scandinavian countries, and the Netherlands were also active in providing assistance to ensure that the 1992 elections would be "free and fair." Although the United Kingdom eventually joined the DDGG, it did so only after the other donors moved more aggressively in pressing for open elections.[21]

All of these efforts were facilitated by the sustained commitment of the ambassador, Deputy Chief of Mission E. Michael Southwick (later U.S. ambassador to Uganda), and the director and deputy director of the USAID mission to Kenya. Throughout this period of transition, U.S. human rights and democratization policy toward Kenya was clear and unambiguous while the groundwork was laid for future efforts. Though Moi and KANU retained power and did little to further political reform after the election, the period was nonetheless a watershed in Kenyan politics.

Aurelia Brazeal

Aurelia Brazeal became U.S. ambassador to Kenya in August 1993, more than six months after Hempstone's departure at the onset of the Clinton administration. A career Foreign Service officer, she went to Nairobi after serving as the U.S. ambassador to Micronesia and minister counselor for economic affairs at the U.S. embassy in Japan. Her instructions were to reduce the tensions that had built up between the United States and Kenya during Hempstone's tenure while continuing to articulate U.S. concerns regarding the need for political and economic reform. Her approach was to begin her term as her predecessors had done, by seeking to establish a cordial working relationship with President Moi and other key officials in the Kenyan government. Her understanding of the relationship between economic development and democratization in the context of the "East Asian Miracle" led Brazeal to believe that economic development in Africa had to *precede* rather than follow democratization. The new ambassador also made it clear to all that she was "not Hempstone" and that a new approach to U.S. objectives was the modus operandi in Nairobi. She was also more concerned than her predecessor, as was the Clinton administration, about enlisting Kenyan support for U.S. initiatives to secure peace in Sudan and the Horn.

Unfortunately, both the Moi government and leading members of the opposition and Kenyan civil society viewed this stance as a retreat by the United States from the more explicit approach to human rights and democratization of the early 1990s. President Moi's approach to governance was to continue to run the country as if it were still a one-party state. Dialogue with opposition leaders over issues of policy was nonexistent—indeed actively discouraged—while the president and his closest associates sought to woo and/or bribe members of the opposition to defect to the ruling party. Given these developments and in the absence of any overt support from the U.S. embassy, opposition leaders concluded that they could no longer count on the United States to vigorously defend their disparate elements against harassment by the Moi regime. Leaders of civil society organizations were also unsure of where the United States stood on the next stage of democratization and whether the U.S. embassy would defend their right to pursue their programs as in the past.

Brazeal's view that economics came first led her to support the resumption of quick-disbursing aid by the Consultative Group to Kenya in 1994. Although little movement had occurred in respect to political reform or corruption following the 1992 elections, Kenya did take several significant, though limited, steps toward economic reform. These included the end of fixed and overvalued exchange rates for the Kenya shilling, the liberalization of trade licensing, and a modest reduction in the budget deficit. The World Bank also resumed assistance by providing $80 million in budget support.

Brazeal's tenure can be summarized as a period of drift in respect to promoting human rights and democratization while placing much greater emphasis on economics and issues of regional stability—the two other goals of U.S. post–Cold War policy. USAID programs to support democratization also assumed a lower profile as the mission devoted its entire democracy and governance program to the strengthening of civil society organizations and backed away from an opportunity to strengthen the National Assembly. This may have been a prudent adjustment to local realities. A major lesson of the early 1990s was that multiparty elections alone, even if free and fair, do not necessarily lead in the short run to a democratic transition. With no general election likely until 1997, the time had come to focus on strengthening other democratic institutions.

Prudence Bushnell

Prudence Bushnell came to Nairobi after serving as deputy assistant secretary of state for African affairs. Her tenure, which lasted from August 1996 to June 1999, spanned the run-up to Kenya's second multiparty elections, in 1997, and the beginning of the next inter-election period. This was a period of increasing fluidity and violence in Kenyan politics. It was also a period of renewed economic decline as the government drew back from the reforms adopted in 1993–94 while corruption continued.

Bushnell's approach differed from her predecessor's and resembled Hempstone's, though with a softer touch. Unlike Brazeal, she understood that in the context of a neopatrimonial (i.e., "big man") system such as Kenya's, political and economic reform are inextricably linked and that economic reform is contingent on political reform, not the other way around. The government resisted economic liberalization— especially downsizing its bloated civil service and privatizing bankrupt state-owned enterprises—because liberalization pared away at the patronage base of the Moi regime. Under Bushnell, and with concurrence from Washington, the pendulum of U.S. policy swung back to a renewed emphasis on political reform. Bushnell was also willing to speak out publicly when human rights were violated and the forces of political reform needed diplomatic support.

During the run-up to the 1997 elections, Bushnell and the United States took a more proactive approach to sustain the reform process. First, the United States supported the suspension of approximately $350 million in quick-disbursing aid by the IMF and the World Bank in July 1997 in response to Kenya's failure to implement its agreed-on program of economic reform. The suspension of aid was similar to the suspension of 1991, though much less bilateral assistance was halted by this suspension than in 1991, because the United States and other donors (excluding Japan) had not resumed quick-disbursing aid in 1994.

Second, the United States, together with the other Western democracies, reacted forcefully to episodes of political violence by condemning the resumption of "ethnic clashes" in the coastal town of Likoni in August 1997. Although the clashes had more or less ceased during the interelection period, their renewal five months before the 1997 elections sent a signal that Kenya's second round of multiparty elections could be as bloody as the first. Between two hundred and three hundred people were reported to have died in the Likoni clashes and several thousand to have been left homeless. The public outcry within Kenya was instantaneous, as was the condemnation by the diplomatic community. The Moi government was once again chastised and the violence ceased with the exception of a sharp conflict in Laikipia district in January 1998, after the elections.[22]

Third, the United States and other like-minded donors renewed funding for civil society organizations seeking to monitor the elections, particularly a consortium of the Institute for Education and Democracy, the National Council of Churches of Kenya, and the Peace and Justice Commission of the Catholic Church. Better organized than its predecessor in 1992, the consortium trained and posted more than twenty-four thousand observers to nearly all of Kenya's 12,700 polling stations —a dramatic achievement that institutionalized the role of domestic monitors in Kenyan elections. The participation of the church also meant that the mobilization of Kenyan citizens across the rural areas reached a new high, one of the positive outcomes of the elections.

The 1997 elections were a replay of 1992—President Moi and KANU won reelection because the opposition failed again to unite behind a single slate of candidates. However, the elections produced several significant outcomes that indicated democratization was proceeding, albeit in fits and starts.[23] In the wake of the clashes and suspension of aid, the opposition succeeded in obtaining modest but important amendments to Kenya's constitution by threatening to boycott the elections. Moi and his associates had overreached by procrastinating on economic reform and allowing the renewal of ethnic clashes. They were now backed into a corner by a combination of the domestic opposition and the international community, forced to make concessions to ensure that the elections—which they knew would return them to power—would go forward.

In the context of the 1990s, both the Kenyan public and the international community would have regarded any nonelectoral outcome as illegitimate. Suspension of the elections was therefore not an option for Moi. The amendments to the constitution included a provision that the president would no longer appoint twelve members of his own choosing to the National Assembly. Instead, he would appoint the additional members on a proportional basis from all parties that won seats in the National Assembly and do so by accepting their nominees. Because KANU had won a narrow 107- to 103-seat majority in the parliamentary elections, the ruling party thus ended up with a total of 113 seats to 109 for the opposition. This resulted in the periodic defeat of the ruling party in votes on legislation it proposed to the National Assembly. Moreover, the ruling party could not always block legislation proposed by the opposition, as it had always done before.

Most significant in this regard was the passage in 1999 of a constitutional amendment that reestablished the legislature as an independent branch of government. KANU's narrow majority also meant that the party was no longer able to amend the constitution on its own, a tactic that it had previously used to stack the electoral law in its favor. The "mini-reforms" of 1997 also required the minister of local government to select appointed members of local councils on a proportional basis, thereby preventing the minister from creating artificial KANU majorities on councils where opposition parties had won a majority of the elected seats. Last but not least, the reforms contained an agreement to establish a constitutional review commission after the elections to pave the way for a broader overhaul of the Kenyan political system.

As for the elections themselves, a new generation of parliamentarians swept into office. Although the distribution of seats among the major parties was similar to that in 1992, roughly half of those elected had not served in the previous parliament. The composition of the KANU parliamentary party was markedly changed as younger, better-educated, and more independent-minded MPs took the seats of their predecessors. This group consistently reached out to members of the opposition and created a coalition for reform within the National Assembly that the president could not control. The coalition was responsible for the passage of the Parliamentary Service Commission amendment in 1999 and other reforms—including a new structure of parliamentary committees—to give the National Assembly the capacity to exercise meaningful oversight of the executive.[24] The United States and the other members of the "like-minded" group have looked with favor on these reforms. Following an analysis of the potential for effective assistance to the National Assembly in April 1999, USAID announced that it would begin a three-year program to strengthen the legislature. The program commenced in the fall of 2000 and has been well received by the Speaker and other leaders of the National Assembly.[25]

Despite these achievements, Bushnell's tenure as U.S. ambassador will be remembered for the bombing of the U.S. embassy in Nairobi on August 7, 1998, by operatives of Osama bin Laden and al Qaeda.

Twelve Americans and more than two hundred Kenyans died in the blast. More than five thousand bystanders, most of whom were Kenyans, were injured. The embassy itself was rendered useless and ultimately torn down. The ambassador, who was in a building next door at the time of the blast, escaped injury. Though the bombing occurred three years before the attacks of September 11, it was a harbinger of the war on terrorism and Kenya's unfolding importance in subsequent efforts by the United States to deny al Qaeda a haven in East Africa.[26] As Bushnell ended her term, she was increasingly preoccupied by security issues, though she never retreated from her firm support of U.S. efforts to promote human rights and continued democratization in Kenya. U.S. concerns about terrorism had yet to trump other policy goals.

Johnnie Carson

A career diplomat who previously served as U.S. ambassador to Uganda and Zimbabwe and as the principal deputy assistant secretary of state for African affairs, Johnnie Carson is probably the most knowledgeable observer of Kenyan politics that the United States has sent to Nairobi. Kenyans sometimes construed his strong preference for quiet diplomacy, however, as an indication that defending human rights and advancing democratization had become lower priorities for the United States.

Carson arrived in Nairobi in September 1999 and served until July 2003. It was one of the most turbulent periods in Kenyan politics since independence, but it culminated with the end of the twenty-four-year regime of Daniel arap Moi on December 30, 2002, and the auspicious beginning of a new government headed by Mwai Kibaki. During this period Kenya completed the first phase of its protracted transition to democratic rule. On December 27, 2002, Kenya held its third election since the resumption of multiparty politics 1992. Although more than a hundred thousand voters of an electorate of eleven million were inexplicably dropped from the voter registers, the elections were better administered than in 1997 and resulted in a sweeping defeat of the ruling party and the first alternation of government since independence. Kibaki, who had won 31 percent of the vote in the 1997 elections, when he was the leading challenger to

Moi, won decisively with 62 percent of the vote after the opposition united behind him and a single slate of parliamentary candidates under the banner of the National Rainbow Coalition (NARC). Whereas the opposition had been the victims of state harassment and an unlevel playing field in 1992 and 1997, it had mainly beat itself by failing to unite. This time it succeeded after negotiations that lasted more than two years and that were not concluded until two months before the elections.

Space does not permit a detailed review of the run-up to the election, but the main points are as follows.[27] Following his reelection in 1997, President Moi faced four dilemmas. The first was that because Kenya's constitution barred him from seeking a third elected term as Kenya's president, he was required to dissolve the National Assembly and schedule new elections to determine his successor and for a new parliament no later than the end of 2002.[28] The question was would he honor the constitution and retire, or seek to change it. Although he remained silent on the issue for more than three years, KANU did not have sufficient votes in the National Assembly to amend the constitution. Nor, as indicated earlier, could the president count on the loyalty of all parliamentarians of his own party. By early 2001 the president more or less acknowledged that he would step down at the end of his term.

The second question was who would succeed the president, and to what lengths Moi would go to determine his successor and ensure his election by fair means or foul. By the end of 2000 the prospect of Moi's retirement had generated a half-dozen announced and unannounced contenders for his job. This resulted in an endless shifting of alliances among secondary leaders, especially MPs who sought to become part of the winning coalition in the next elections. It was a process akin to "musical chairs." The game did not fully start (or end) until the music stopped—in this case when the president declared his intentions.

Moi began by stating that although he would probably step down at the end of his term, he would continue to be the chairman of KANU and remain active in political life; that is, he would continue to be the power behind the throne. By the end of 2001 he had made it clear that if the time had come for him to relinquish the presidency, his successor should be someone who "did not have gray hairs" and who would therefore not be a member of the current leadership of KANU, including his vice president, George Saitoti. The strategy, which played itself out from November 2001 to October 2002, orchestrated the selection of Uhuru Kenyatta, the forty-three-year-old son of Kenya's first president, Jomo Kenyatta, as the KANU nominee and Kenya's next president. Its main purpose was to enhance the prospects for a KANU victory and to ensure Moi's influence following the elections. Moi was particularly concerned that he and his closest associates be protected from prosecution for corruption and human rights abuses, including the ethnic clashes, during their tenure in office.[29] The possibility of a future trial and retribution, even on a delayed basis, as in Chile, was not lost on Moi and his entourage.

A third question that was closely related to the second was whether to allow a repeat of the ethnic clashes that preceded the 1992 and 1997 elections to intimidate the opposition. Though "deplored" by Moi at the time, the clashes could not have occurred without his assent, if not his direct instigation. The prospect of renewed clashes worried the diplomatic community, including the United States, and with good cause. As the clashes unfolded in 1997, especially just after the elections, it was clear that the victims were prepared to arm themselves and fight back, precipitating an escalation of ethnic conflict and perhaps even civil war. Although the clashes had ended in 1998, sporadic outbreaks of ethnic violence began to recur in 2001, suggesting that the regime might go to any lengths to ensure the electoral outcome it desired.

Finally, there was the question of whether Kenya would move forward, as the government and opposition had agreed before the 1997 elections, to establish a process for writing a new constitution—one that would probably result in a substantial reduction of presidential power and the devolution of authority from the central government to the provinces or districts. The demand for a new constitution became a rallying issue for the opposition. Not surprisingly, Moi attempted to stall the process indefinitely.

Throughout this period the position of the United States was clear: President Moi should abide by the constitution by holding its next round of presidential and parliamentary elections on schedule, and he should not seek to run for another term. Although Moi never had the votes in the National Assembly to amend the constitution, the U.S. position was conveyed through quiet diplomacy and by several public statements made by Secretary of State Colin Powell during the course of his visit to Africa in May 2001. While the secretary's public statements did not mention Moi by name and were directed primarily at Zimbabwean president Robert Mugabe, the implication of remarks made while he was in South Africa could not have been lost on the Kenyan president.

The United States and Ambassador Carson were more explicit and public in their statements regarding the prospect of renewed violence. As the election year approached, and outbreaks of violence occurred in 2001 in the northern Rift Valley between Turkana and Pokots, the embassy expressed its concerns about the problem of violence. It also jawboned the government quietly, including the Kenyan military, on the dangers of politically related violence. At the same time, USAID supported efforts by a group of civil society organizations to monitor and report incidents of political violence around the country.

Although Johnnie Carson was never fully persuaded of the need for a new constitution,[30] he did join eighteen other ambassadors in April 2001 to urge Moi to end delays in establishing the Constitution of Kenya Review Commission (CKRC) and to let the commission begin its work. The CKRC ultimately published a draft constitution on September 27, 2002, that called for a substantial reduction of presidential powers and the creation of the position of prime minister. However, under the elaborate procedures agreed to by Moi and the opposition to establish the review commission, the draft needed to be first deliberated, amended, and ratified by a National Constitutional Conference (NCC) and then passed again by parliament in a vote of at least 65 percent of all members before it replaced the old constitution. Although these steps might have been completed before the end of 2002, and hence *before* the elections, both Moi and the opposition decided to contest the elections under the existing constitution. For Moi, the issue was simple. He wanted no reduction of presidential power on the assumption that Uhuru Kenyatta would succeed him in office. For the opposition, the issue was more complex. Although it was committed to the enactment of a new constitution, it also had some disagreements with the proposed draft. Most important, by the middle of October Kibaki and other opposition leaders believed that the opposition would win the elections by a wide margin. They felt that it was better to proceed with the elections on schedule and emerge victorious than to get bogged down in the NCC and risk that the elections would be postponed. As a result, the NCC was postponed until after the elections.[31]

The primary objectives of the United States in respect to human rights and democratization were thus two: that Moi proceed with the elections before the end of 2002 and retire from public life and that the run-up to the elections be free of violence and contested on a level playing field. To this end the embassy engaged in a protracted campaign of quiet diplomacy with President Moi that included meetings with Secretary of State Colin Powell in Nairobi in May 2001, during the secretary's African tour, and with Vice President Dick Cheney in Washington in November, at which meeting Moi pledged to hold the elections by the end of 2002. The United States stuck to these priorities throughout 2002; the embassy made few public statements on the election campaign other than to express the hope that it be nonviolent and free and fair.

In March Moi orchestrated a merger of KANU with Raila Odinga's National Development Party and the election of a new slate of officers for KANU. The idea was to broaden the party's base for the coming elections, but it backfired when Moi threw his weight behind Kenyatta and announced in July that Kenyatta would be KANU's presidential nominee. While KANU was beginning to fragment, the opposition started to unite. In August three of the four largest opposition parties, including Mwai Kibaki's Democratic Party, came together to form the National Alliance of Kenya (NAK). The alliance was the first major step toward unity, but it fell short of representing a clear majority of the Kenyan population. NAK was basically a coalition of leaders from three of Kenya's largest ethnic groups—the Kikuyu and related groups, who constitute 30 percent of the population; the Luhya, 14 percent; and the Kamba, 12 percent—but KANU also claimed support within these communities. Moi's insistence that KANU nominate Uhuru Kenyatta (himself a Kikuyu) continued through September, during which time he castigated those in KANU who opposed his choice. Kenyatta's nomination was formalized at the party's nominating convention, held during the second week of October, but it was a

hollow victory. More than fifty KANU MPs, including three prominent cabinet ministers—former vice president George Saitoti, Raila
Odinga, and Kalonzo Musyoka—quit the party. Within a few weeks,
they negotiated a deal with NAK to create the broader National Rainbow Coalition. In return for an unspecified number of positions in the
cabinet, they agreed to support Mwai Kibaki for president and nominate a single slate of parliamentary candidates.[32] The defectors consoli-
dated the opposition's support among the Kikuyu, Luhya, and Kamba
and broadened its base to include the Luo of Nyanza province, who
make up 12 percent of Kenya's population. NARC also made inroads
into KANU areas of the Rift Valley Province and in Coast Province.
Assuming the elections would be held on schedule, the likelihood of
NARC victory was now clear.

To raise the prospects for honest elections, the United States,
through USAID, provided assistance to the Election Commission of
Kenya and to several civil society organizations to conduct voter education before the elections. As it did before the elections of 1992 and
1997, USAID also joined with other donors to fund a coalition of
church and civil society organizations to monitor the elections. Approximately thirty thousand observers were trained and deployed by
this effort; observers were present at nearly every polling place and the
vote was accurately reported.[33] Most important, the domestic monitoring of elections in Kenya is now an accepted fact of political life.
USAID also funded a delegation of approximately twenty international observers organized by the Carter Center. The U.S. embassy,
however, emphasized domestic rather than international observation
because the former provided the greatest coverage and a more enduring impact on Kenya's electoral process.

To assure a smooth endgame and transition, the embassy arranged
a valedictory visit by Moi to Washington three weeks before the elections, on December 3–5, to meet Vice President Cheney again and
to meet President Bush at the White House, a meeting Moi craved.
During the course of these meetings, Moi reaffirmed his pledge to
hold the elections on schedule and to work closely with the United
States on the war on terrorism. In response, President Bush commended the Kenyan president on his statesmanship and wished him
well in his approaching retirement. The same message was conveyed in

meetings with lesser officials, including several members of Congress, and at the Council on Foreign Relations, where Moi made a presentation on the future of Africa. Ambassador Carson accompanied Moi throughout the visit.

Realizing at last that KANU would probably lose the election, Moi justified the praise by visiting Mwai Kibaki at a London hospital en route home to Kenya. Kibaki had been hospitalized after an auto accident and did not return to Kenya until two weeks before the elections. Moi also facilitated a speedy transfer of power on December 30, barely three days after the poll. Kenya had come a long way since the one-party era of the late 1980s.

LESSONS LEARNED: IMPLICATIONS FOR U.S. POLICY IN KENYA

The United States has pursued its human rights and democratization policy inconsistently in Kenya yet achieved significant results when the policy has been firmly articulated and backed by a willingness to exert pressure, both financial and diplomatic, on the Kenyan government. The experience of the 1990s also demonstrates five additional lessons about the pursuit of human rights and democratization in a country where the transition to democratic rule is protracted and where a kleptocratic regime clings to power. The first and most important lesson is that democratization is a long-term and difficult project. Beginning in the 1970s with the transitions to democracy in Portugal and Spain and continuing with the transitions of the 1980s in Latin America and Eastern Europe, American foreign policy makers have viewed the holding of multiparty elections as the essence of democratization. The African experience, including Kenya, however, teaches us that while elections are a necessary condition for democratic rule, they are not sufficient. Indeed, as Fareed Zakaria notes, elections alone may merely create "illiberal" democracy—political systems in which parties compete for office, but where vestiges of human rights abuses remain and there is little tolerance or bargaining between government and opposition.[34]

The Kenyan experience also demonstrates that a *series of* elections, as distinguished from a single founding election, can open up significant political space—by affording new opportunities for civil society to organize and by facilitating the regular circulation of secondary elites and the emergence of a new political generation that might someday control the executive branch. Kenya is a very different and more open polity today than it was in November 1991 before the return of multiparty politics, but the sea change of its political system has been incremental and taken a dozen years. Like the democratic transition in Mexico, the Kenyan transition has moved forward incrementally despite concerted attempts by those in power to block its advance. The point of this lesson is that if the United States is serious about nurturing democratization, it must be patient as well as consistent and stay the course.

The second lesson is that the United States and the rest of the international community have limited but significant leverage over human rights and the prospects for democratization. The improvement of human rights conditions and the pace of democratization are determined more by evolving domestic factors than by the wishes or pressure of the world community. The mixed impact of aid conditionality provides the clearest illustration of limited international leverage. Kenya's embrace of economic and political reform during the 1990s ebbed and flowed as a function of the government's dependence on donor assistance to carry it through its periodic budget crises. Corruption was particularly impervious to outside pressure—elites that are intent on theft will continue to steal. That said, the international community and particularly the United States have periodically opened up space for domestic political actors while their aid programs have strengthened civil society and may yet strengthen key political institutions such as the National Assembly.

Third, it is impossible to measure with precision the impact of U.S. human rights and democratization policy in countries such as Kenya, or to disentangle the impact of U.S. efforts from those of the other Western democracies. These programs do make a difference, albeit at the margin. If this were not the case, then domestic actors, both government and opposition, would not seek assistance from the international community or resist its programs that promote reform. But it is the totality and consistency of that effort that counts.

Fourth, the United States is the key player, but not the only important player in any international effort to promote human rights and democratization. The impact of U.S. efforts is much greater when the United States joins forces with other international actors rather than going it alone. The emergence of such coalitions, however, is usually accelerated when the United States makes a clear commitment to support the reform process. The experience of Kenya demonstrates that when the United States commits both diplomatic and development assistance to supporting political reform, other countries are more inclined to do the same. Conversely, when the United States hangs back, as it did from 1994 to 1996, the international effort slows. The United States must also encourage the IMF and the World Bank to pursue lending programs that are consistent with supporting democratization and limiting human rights abuse while recognizing that neither of these institutions bases its lending on these criteria. The international financial institutions are usually the largest donors. If their programs prop up authoritarian regimes, the task of nurturing democratization is more difficult.

Finally, there is no viable alternative to a foreign policy that supports democratization that is in the U.S. interest. While some observers argue that a forceful human rights and democratization policy is a "moralist approach" that does not address the U.S. interest, this is not the case in Africa, where U.S. economic interests are small but our vulnerability to being drawn into civil conflict is high. It is one thing to shun peacekeeping and/or humanitarian interventions. It is another to expend far less in time and resources to prevent the need for such interventions. Moreover, as noted earlier, Africa's, and Kenya's, integration into the global economy depends on the establishment of free-market economies grounded in the rule of law. In the context of Africa, these conditions have not developed in the absence of democratization and human rights. Put simply, a realist foreign policy toward Africa contains elements of the so-called moralist approach. These are not mutually exclusive approaches but different sides of the same coin. As the second Bush administration faces the task of rebuilding Iraq on a democratic basis, the complementarity between U.S. security interests and democracy promotion is increasingly acknowledged by those who once held that the two were not linked.

NOTES

The author wishes to thank former assistant secretary of state Herman J. Cohen and Ambassadors Smith Hempstone and E. Michael Southwick for their assistance in clarifying events discussed in this paper.

1. David Gordon, David Miller, and Howard Wolpe estimate that U.S. investment in sub-Saharan Africa increased between 1990 and 1994 from $876 million to $2,987 million, or by 340 percent. The amount of U.S. investment was more than three times larger than U.S. government aid to Africa, though most investment was concentrated on extractive industries such as mining and oil. David F. Gordon, David C. Miller, and Howard Wolpe, *The United States and Africa* (New York: W. W. Norton, 1998), 38.

2. Although trade has increased between the United States and Africa, Africa is not a significant market for the United States, nor is Africa a significant source of imports for the United States, with the notable exception of oil.

3. Following the deaths of eighteen marine peacekeepers in Somalia in 1993, the United States has refused to send troops to quell internal conflicts in Africa and has been hesitant to provide financial or logistical support to peacekeepers of other nations. The failure of the United States to respond to the 1994 genocide in Rwanda is a case in point, as is limited U.S. support for UN peacekeepers in Sierra Leone. In response to the criticism that it was avoiding its responsibilities in Africa, the United States established the African Crisis Response Initiative (ACRI), a program of assistance to African militaries to provide the continent with its own peacekeepers.

4. It should be noted that the Carter administration signaled the importance of human rights when it appointed Patricia Derian as the first assistant secretary of state for human rights. However, from the beginning of the Reagan administration until 1991—the final decade of the Cold War—U.S. concern for human rights was again subordinated to the strategy of containment.

5. Burns H. Weston, "Human Rights," in *Human Rights in the World Community*, 2d ed., ed. Richard Pierre Claude and Burns H. Weston (Philadelphia: University of Pennsylvania Press, 1992).

6. Beginning with the UN covenants on human rights and continuing throughout the Cold War, the former Soviet Union and its allies articulated the concern for economic and social rights, viewing the covenant on economic rights as tantamount to the right to socialism. Since the end of the Cold War, economic and social rights have been defined as the right to certain minimum material standards of living, standards that are most likely to be achieved (though not exclusively achieved) through the higher rates of growth found in free-market economies. In other words, from an operational standpoint, economic rights are now equated with the right to capitalism.

7. Robert Dahl has summarized these standards in *Democracy and Its Critics* (New Haven, Conn.: Yale University Press, 1989), 221.

8. In March 2003 President Yoweri Museveni of Uganda announced that his country would transform its "Movement" system into a full-blown multiparty system before the next elections, scheduled for 2006.

9. A succession of events evoked expressions of concern that resonated with key members of the House subcommittee on African affairs, particularly its then chair, Howard Wolpe.

10. Kenya's position as "the hub" of East Africa was not an accident, but the result of British colonial policy. During the colonial period, the development of Kenya was systematically emphasized over the development of Tanzania and Uganda, the two other territories that made up British East Africa.

11. In addition to the normal complement of diplomatic personnel, the embassy housed the regional security office, a regional military attaché, and the regional office of the U.S. Department of Agriculture. Nairobi also became the site of a regional office of the Library of Congress.

12. Sometimes notice was indeed short. In August 1992 the United States notified the Kenyan government that it would be landing C-130 and C-141 aircraft to provide food relief to Somalia, but it did not do so until after the planes had departed from the United States. While this clearly tested Kenya's friendship, Moi let the mission go forward. Moi also accommodated the United States on more delicate missions. In February 1991 the government of Kenya permitted the United States to evacuate ninety anti-Gadhafi Libyan guerrillas to Kenya and let them remain there for ninety days until a safe haven could be found in another country.

13. KANU won two multiparty elections held before independence, in 1961 and 1963, and was the ruling party through 2002.

14. Kenya held both presidential and parliamentary elections in 1966, 1969, 1974, 1979, and 1983. These elections were essentially referendums on the abilities of incumbent members of parliament to foster economic development in their constituencies. On average, roughly 55 percent to 60 percent of incumbents lost their seats, resulting in a considerable turnover in the composition of the National Assembly.

15. The new emphasis on human rights and democratization in U.S. policy toward Africa was laid out by the assistant secretary of state for Africa, Herman J. Cohen, at the annual chiefs of mission meeting for U.S. ambassadors held in Washington in the spring of 1990. In the discussion that followed, Hempstone expressed doubts whether such a policy could be effective.

16. In his memoir of his tenure in Nairobi, Hempstone attributed the murder to Nicholas Biwott, formerly minister of East African affairs in the Kenyan government. See Smith Hempstone, *Rogue Ambassador: An African Memoir* (Sewanee, Tenn.: University of the South Press, 1998).

17. Nonproject assistance, or "quick-disbursing" aid, is grants or loans provided to cover balance-of-payments deficits and/or budgetary deficits to ease shocks to ordinary citizens caused by deep cuts to government programs or the end of fixed and overvalued exchange rates. The most significant providers of quick-disbursing aid are the IMF and the World Bank, which curtailed their programs under pressure from Kenya's bilateral donors.

18. It is important to remember that by suspending quick-disbursing aid, the donors were not suspending typical development assistance projects in such areas as agriculture, education, and health. World Bank, "Communiqué on the Consultative Group for Kenya," Paris, November 26, 1991.

19. While U.S. policy had emphasized the desirability of democratization, the United States never insisted on multiparty elections. However, once Moi declared that Kenya would no longer be a one-party state, the United States insisted that the forthcoming elections be contested on a level playing field.

20. Joel D. Barkan, "Kenya: Lessons from a Flawed Election," *Journal of Democracy* (July 1993); and David W. Throup and Charles Hornsby, *Multi-Party Politics in Kenya* (Oxford: James Currey, 1997).

21. The United Kingdom was less enthusiastic about donor coordination in support of the elections, preferring instead to support efforts by the Commonwealth and to provide its assistance directly to the Kenyan government on a bilateral basis. During the second half of the 1990s, the United Kingdom became an active participant in the Like-Minded Group.

22. It is reported that Moi asked the Kenyan army to put down the Likoni clashes, but that the army refused to do so, telling the president to rein in the rogue elements among his supporters. The clashes also had a long-term impact on the Kenyan economy, crippling tourism along the Kenya coast. The clashes in Laikipia were notable in that the intended victims acquired guns and killed several dozen of their attackers. The United States sent special envoy Jesse Jackson to the region to demonstrate its concern.

23. Joel D. Barkan and Njuguna Ng'ethe, "Kenya Tries Again," *Journal of Democracy* (March 1998).

24. The amendment de-linked the National Assembly from the Office of the President by establishing an independent scheme of service for legislators and the staff of the assembly.

25. This program is being implemented by the State University of New York, which currently has a full-time staff member in Nairobi. Other donors, including Canada, the European Union, the United Kingdom, and the World Bank, are also supporting the strengthening of the National Assembly.

26. The bombing of the embassy in Nairobi and the U.S. embassy in Dar es Salaam in Tanzania was ultimately attributed to Osama bin Laden and to one of his closest associates, Ayman al-Zawahiri, who planned the attack.

27. For a more detailed discussion, see the article by Stephen Ndegwa in *Journal of Democracy* 14, no. 3 (July 2003).

28. Before the repeal of section 2a in 1991, which provided for the resumption of multiparty politics and thus multiparty elections, Kenya's president was not directly elected but was simply the leader of the ruling party. Beginning in 1992, the president was directly elected and permitted to serve two terms. Moi thus served a total of five terms—three under the constitution of the one-party era and two under the revised constitution.

29. The strategy is attributed to Moi's son and business partner, Gideon, who was a high school classmate of the young Kenyatta. Just as Moi had protected the Kenyatta family against allegations of corruption following his ascension to the presidency in 1978, Kenyatta would now protect Moi.

30. It was Carson's belief that Kenya's existing constitution could be significantly improved through the amendment process and that the basic problem of governance was not the text of the existing constitution but the lack of political will on the part of Moi and his associates to abide by the document. While Carson's assessment was valid, he missed the importance that the opposition and broad elements of civil society, including the church, placed on the need for a new basic law.

31. The National Constitutional Conference convened on April 28, 2003, but had yet to complete its deliberations at the time this chapter went to press.

32. The details of the deal are murky, though they were supposedly formalized in a memorandum of understanding. The defectors claim that they were supposed to get half of the cabinet positions in the new government. The representatives of NAK deny that this was the understanding.

33. A major improvement for the 2002 elections was the decision by the Electoral Commission to count ballots at the polling place rather than transporting all ballot boxes to a central place within each constituency.

34. Fareed Zakaria, "The Rise of Illiberal Democracy," *Foreign Affairs* 76, no. 6 (November-December 1997): 22–43.

BIBLIOGRAPHY

Barkan, Joel D. "Kenya: Lessons from a Flawed Election." *Journal of Democracy* 4, no. 3 (July 1993): 85–99.

Barkan, Joel D., and David Gordon. "Democracy in Africa: Don't Forsake It." *Foreign Affairs* 77, no. 4 (August-September 1998): 107–111.

Barkan, Joel D., and Njuguna Ng'ethe. "Kenya Tries Again." *Journal of Democracy* 9, no. 2 (March 1998): 32–48.

Carothers, Thomas. *Aiding Democracy Abroad*. Washington, D.C.: Carnegie Endowment for International Peace, 2000.

Dahl, Robert. *Democracy and Its Critics*. New Haven, Conn.: Yale University Press, 1989.

Gordon, David F., David C. Miller, and Howard Wolpe. *The United States and Africa*. New York: W. W. Norton, 1998.

Hempstone, Smith. *Rogue Ambassador: An African Memoir*. Sewanee, Tenn.: University of the South Press, 1997.

Ndegwa, Stephen. "Kenya: Third Time Lucky." *Journal of Democracy* 14, no. 3 (July 2003):

Rice, Condoleezza. "Promoting the National Interest." *Foreign Affairs* 79, no. 1 (January-February 2000): 45–62.

Throup, David W., and Charles Hornsby. *Multi-Party Politics in Kenya*. Oxford: James Currey, 1997.

United States Institute of Peace. "Special Report: The Role of the Ambassador in Promoting U.S. Human Rights Policy Abroad." Washington, D.C.: United States Institute of Peace, August 30, 2000.

Weston, Burns H. "Human Rights." In *Human Rights in the World Community*, 2d ed., ed. Richard Pierre Claude and Burns H. Weston. Philadelphia: University of Pennsylvania Press, 1992.

World Bank. "Communiqué on the Consultative Group for Kenya." Paris, November 26, 1991.

Zakaria, Fareed. "The Rise of Illiberal Democracy." *Foreign Affairs* 76, no. 6 (November-December 1997): 22–43.

Zoellick, Robert. "A Republican Foreign Policy." *Foreign Affairs* 79, no. 1 (January-February 2000): 63–79.

3

Getting It Right

U.S. Policy in South Africa

Pauline H. Baker

THE RESPONSIBILITY FOR MOVING SOUTH AFRICA from apartheid to democracy lies primarily with the people of South Africa, but the United States was an important and, in many ways, critical actor in the transition. In the 1980s and early 1990s, the United States strengthened internal forces that were moving the country from a decades-old system of racial oppression to a democratic transition, a role that catapulted the United States into being the single most important bilateral supporter of the first black-majority government in the country.

Following a long and acrimonious debate, the U.S. government shifted from a policy of constructive engagement and quiet diplomacy that gave priority to strategic objectives in the region to a hybrid policy in which both incentives and punishments were adopted to promote human rights. This new policy deepened U.S. engagement with the antiapartheid opposition while leaving the door open to work with Pretoria on regional diplomacy. Surprisingly, the policy turned out to be a stunning success. Rarely has a U.S. human rights policy had such an unambiguously positive outcome, one in which human rights goals and strategic objectives in the region were achieved.

85

In examining the transferability of lessons learned, however, we need to recognize the importance of specific conditions in South Africa that made the policy effective. These conditions may or may not appear elsewhere. Analysts and policymakers should have a clear understanding of these factors before making similar recommendations for other countries. Nonetheless, South Africa is not as sui generis as many assume. A retrospective examination of how U.S. policy worked in South Africa yields useful insights relevant for other human rights predicaments.

POLITICAL INTRACTABILITY

Perhaps the most striking observation of a retrospective analysis is how wrong predictions were at the time about the feasibility of a peaceful resolution of the South African conflict. The assumption of political insolubility was widespread, just as it is today in many divided societies. Yet, as South Africa shows , even decades- or centuries-old conflicts are not static. They must be continuously reassessed in light of generational and political changes.

In the 1980s the international community viewed South Africa as one of three intractable disputes worldwide (the others were Ireland and the Middle East). Each was seen as a conflict in which opposing peoples were locked, like scorpions in a bottle, in an interminable fight. The South African conflict, it was feared, would ultimately lead to a race war—a plausible scenario given the steadily growing resistance to white-minority rule since 1912, when the African National Congress (ANC) was formed, the overwhelming military superiority of the apartheid regime, the adamant refusal of whites to give up political power, and the willingness of the ruling National Party to ruthlessly suppress the black population, irrespective of international public opinion.

Yet this conflict was resolved through a negotiated settlement that resulted in a power-sharing formula, a new constitution, and majority rule.[1] The U.S. government acted in South Africa just as internal forces for democratic change were mounting an unprecedented protest and the ruling regime's resistance to change was beginning to erode. Considerable violence accompanied the transition, but the doomsday scenario did not occur.

This underscores the importance of questioning outdated assumptions that perpetuate pessimistic beliefs about the intractability of "ancient tribal rivalries," including those in places such as Kosovo, East Timor, Afghanistan, and Iraq. Generational changes can transform a long-simmering situation that once was immovable into a fluid situation that is "ripe for resolution."[2]

In South Africa both blacks and whites had changed by the 1980s. There was far more ferment in the country than most people assumed. The majority of the rural-based white Afrikaner population had become urbanized, sophisticated, and business oriented. They shared a strong interest with English-speaking whites in preserving the economy, ending their country's pariah status, and finding a way out of apartheid, which was breaking down through widespread violations of the influx control laws and other restrictions.

By the same token, a new generation of resistance leaders emerged under the banner of the United Democratic Front (UDF), a collection of some six hundred associations that opposed attempts by the government to modernize, rather than abolish, apartheid. Affiliated with the African National Congress, the UDF gave the resistance, whose leaders had been jailed, banned, or exiled, an internal face with a new spirit and organizational presence. They tapped into the surging energy of the "youth bulge" in the black population, youngsters who had grown up under rigid apartheid and faced a grim future in a deteriorating economy in which they were marginalized. Impatient with the docility of their parents and disdainful of the inferior black educational system, they confronted authorities as no other generation had during months of unrest that made the black townships "ungovernable."

Notwithstanding increased militancy, the leadership of the black resistance was still committed to negotiations. Nelson Mandela's personal journey was a marker of that commitment. After twenty-seven years in prison, he had evolved from being a fiery leader of the youth wing of the African National Congress to a voice of racial reconciliation. In addition, a new cadre of skilled managers and negotiators from both sides of the racial divide came on the scene, assuming the responsibility of working out a settlement. Cyril Ramaphosa, a black labor union activist, and Roelf Meyer, an Afrikaner from the ruling National Party, symbolized these new elites. As Patti Waldmeir notes, they became the "Siamese twins of the revolution . . . who did the hardest work of negotiating a South African peace."[3]

TIMING

Like military or diplomatic offensives, human rights initiatives should be strategically timed or their impact will be limited. In the South African case, external actions did not have a visible political impact until the 1980s, when an antiapartheid opposition was exploding into an open, violent revolt; splits were occurring in the ruling party; the global and regional climate was shifting; and the U.S. antiapartheid movement was coalescing into a grassroots network of activists pressing for action. Nelson Mandela's towering stature and unbreakable fortitude provided a personal focal point for internal and external activism, much of which focused on pressuring the South African government to set him free.

The international media was also spotlighting South Africa. Over a period of fourteen months, from September 1984, when the black protests began, to November 1985, when the South African government banned television cameras, Americans followed events through day-to-day reports of racial conflict. These reports struck a deep chord in the American psyche and fueled domestic protests.

Interaction was a two-way street, however. Rightly or wrongly, the United States and South Africa saw each other as mirror images of themselves, and they were keenly aware of the reactions of reciprocal publics. Black South Africans stepped up their lobbying for U.S. action when the media saturated the townships with cameras, documenting "Trojan horse" tactics of police brutality. Americans were fixated on the drama unfolding thousands of miles away, which they saw as a descendant of their own civil rights movement. Despite different demographics, history, culture, and laws, there was a sense of common purpose through racial struggle. The moral clarity that apartheid engendered made it relatively easy for activists to mobilize public support for sanctions and send a message of solidarity with blacks.

Should action have been taken sooner? It is impossible to tell whether the measures adopted by the U.S. government in the 1980s would have been as successful had they been adopted, say, in the 1960s. UN arms and oil embargoes were imposed in the 1960s, resulting in higher oil prices for South Africa and a heightened sense of vulnerability. However, Pretoria cushioned the effect of these measures by sustaining a three-year petroleum stockpile, buying oil on the spot market, investing in oil-from-coal technology, and starting an indigenous arms-manufacturing industry.

Ironically, mandatory multilateral oil and arms embargoes were not as effective as the unilateral economic actions taken later by the United States. Instead, South Africa dug in its heels in the sixties. All the major antiapartheid groups were banned, dissent was suppressed, and odious racial laws were extended.

By the eighties things were different. Various U.S. players had been mobilized. The administration continued to defend constructive engagement, Congress was split largely along partisan lines, nongovernmental organizations coalesced for effective lobbying, corporations faced shareholder resolutions, and universities experienced student demonstrations. Churches, unions, local and state governments, and professional associations were confronted with demands for divestment. Gradually, these protests coalesced into enormous domestic political pressure on Capitol Hill. In October 1986, when the U.S. Congress decided by an overwhelming vote to overturn the veto of President Ronald Reagan and impose economic sanctions, South Africa was dealt the strongest psychological and economic blow it had ever received from the international community. Nonetheless, although U.S. antiapartheid activists had called for stronger measures, the sanctions enacted were mild in comparison to the harsher embargoes that the U.S. government has inflicted against adversaries, such as Cuba, Iraq, and North Korea. The law (the Comprehensive Anti-Apartheid Act of 1986, or CAAA) terminated direct air flights between the United States and South Africa and prohibited new investment in South Africa, except in black-owned firms. It also banned loans to the private sector and to the South African government, except for housing and educational and humanitarian purposes. It limited South African imports, terminated the bilateral tax treaty that avoided double taxation for U.S. companies operating in South Africa, and required U.S. firms to apply fair labor standards based on the Sullivan Principles, a voluntary code of conduct launched in 1977 by the Reverend Leon H. Sullivan, pastor of the Zion Baptist Church in Philadelphia and a member of General Motors' board of directors.[4] The law spelled out new terms of engagement designed to promote negotiations and included a well-defined road map specifying the conditions that would lead to the lifting of the restrictions.[5] Guidelines were provided for deepening U.S. engagement with the South African black population, including providing economic and educational support that strengthened civil society and black leadership.

There was no breaking of diplomatic relations, cultural or sports boycotts, or compulsory corporate divestment. Instead, corporations were encouraged to adopt the Sullivan Principles, educational and cultural exchanges continued, and the Reagan administration was encouraged to continue working with Pretoria to move toward meaningful political negotiations with authentic black leaders and to pursue regional settlements.[6]

The existence of a viable opposition was another factor that made the timing of these initiatives effective. An alternative future government existed that was plausible and legitimate. Interestingly, the importance of this point was not lost on Mandela. When Nigerian opposition forces supporting multilateral sanctions against the dictatorial regime of Sani Abacha approached Mandela as president of South Africa, he declined to back them on the grounds that there was no alternative government ready to take over. He advised the opposition figures to work harder to unite the opposition before calling for international action.

HUMAN RIGHTS VERSUS STRATEGIC AND ECONOMIC INTERESTS

The South African case was a notable exception to the common assumption that the U.S. government cannot effectively pursue human rights interests simultaneously with larger strategic and economic interests. If there is a clash between these contending interests, human rights invariably are downgraded in importance. Tensions between human rights and other U.S. interests exist in a range of countries today, including China, Russia, Saudi Arabia, Turkey, and Pakistan. Overriding strategic or economic interests in these states have often taken priority.

In the 1980s South Africa was also considered a strategic ally for whom human rights considerations were of secondary importance. Successive administrations had opposed apartheid and urged peaceful political change in South Africa, but all had rejected broad economic sanctions as a means of pressuring the government. Some presidents spoke more openly in favor of political change, such as John F. Kennedy and Jimmy Carter, but strategic and economic interests tended to override human rights in the larger scheme of things.

President Ronald Reagan, like President Richard Nixon in his South African policy, tilted strongly in the direction of strategic and economic considerations. Reagan warmly recalled that Pretoria was an ally in World War II, pointed out its role as a supplier of strategic minerals, and lauded its staunch anticommunist record. In addition, the administration feared that pressuring South Africa on black political rights would discourage Pretoria from relinquishing control of Namibia, which it had administered since World War II. The U.S. government linked the independence of Namibia to the removal of Cuban troops from Angola.

Instead of discouraging change, as many assumed, sanctions ultimately had the opposite effect. The main political breakthroughs on strategic and regional goals were achieved *after* the United States moved against South Africa on human rights. This is not to suggest that sanctions induced South Africa to compromise on regional issues, but merely to note that sanctions did not obstruct progress on these issues. South Africa calculated that it was in its interest to strike deals with the Reagan administration before it left office, noting that the terms might be even worse with the next administration.

The Reagan administration had presented itself as the friendliest that Pretoria could hope to have in Washington. Its opposition to corporate divestment and other economic pressures called for by antiapartheid protesters was the incentive it used to induce South Africa to cooperate. But there were also real U.S. economic interests at stake that the administration wanted to protect. There were 284 U.S. corporations in South Africa in 1984, many of which were resisting shareholder resolutions designed to get them to pull out of South Africa. Billions were also invested in mutual funds and other South African securities.

Tension between strategic/economic interests and human rights concerns was at the heart of the domestic policy debate, which erupted when public protests were mounted in front of the South African embassy in Washington, D.C., in 1984. The demonstrations were as much against Reagan's policy of constructive engagement (the official policy of offering concrete incentives to Pretoria) as they were against apartheid. Sustained for two years, along with similar nonviolent protests across the country, the protests did not end until sanctions legislation was enacted.

The CAAA turned U.S. policy on its head. Human rights concerns were given primacy over geopolitical and economic interests for the first time in U.S. history. Unsurprisingly, U.S.-South African relations cooled for a few months, but regional negotiations were revived shortly thereafter. Former assistant secretary of state Chester Crocker, an ardent opponent of sanctions and an equally tenacious advocate of regional diplomacy, mounted an intensive campaign of shuttle diplomacy in the last year of the Reagan administration. He succeeded in shepherding a sanctioned South Africa and other regional actors to agree to two U.S.-mediated treaties that provided for the removal of some fifty thousand Cuban troops from Angola and the independence of Namibia. He received widespread praise for his efforts.

By 1990 Nelson Mandela and Namibia had won their freedom, a dual success for U.S. policy. A year later, apartheid laws were repealed, political exiles were given amnesty, and the government and opposition groups signed a National Peace Accord,[7] fulfilling the conditions for the lifting of economic sanctions. South Africa continued its march toward a negotiated revolution, culminating in the 1994 election of Nelson Mandela as president.

This positive outcome suggests that, in some cases at least, it is possible to make progress on human rights and strategic or economic goals if the U.S. government makes its goals clear and is willing to exert appropriate pressure on recalcitrant regimes. In the South African experience, domestic political change went hand in hand with regional political change. The more oppressive South Africa was with regard to its own population, the more aggressive it became in the region. Its domestic and foreign policies were based on a single goal: to make the area safe for white rule.

Linkage between external change and internal change, and knowing how to balance them, is critical in such situations. The Reagan administration understood the connection but had a sequential view of events, rejecting the strategy of vigorously pursuing multiple U.S. interests simultaneously. Instead, government officials concluded that a robust human rights policy would jeopardize regional priorities. This proved to be a false assumption, a lesson that ought to be taken into account in other situations in which human rights take a backseat to competing U.S. interests.

The costs of being overly cautious can be high. The refusal of the U.S. government to exert meaningful pressure on South Africa early in the Reagan administration's first term gave Pretoria a free hand to act with impunity, both domestically and internationally, without facing the consequences of its intransigence. Though it promised action, Pretoria neither granted meaningful political rights to blacks nor cooperated in good faith on regional and strategic initiatives. It reneged, for example, on the U.S.-mediated 1984 Nkomati Agreement, a nonaggression pact in which Pretoria agreed to stop supplying Mozambican rebels with arms in return for Mozambique's agreeing to deny the ANC military bases. Pretoria also launched repeated cross-border attacks on its neighbors that even the Reagan administration later recognized as having gone beyond legitimate defense needs. South Africa had developed a nuclear weapons capability, launched assassination raids on ANC leaders, conducted chemical and biological weapons research, inspired black-on-black violence, and inflicted extensive damage on civilians in its policy of destabilization of the region, all of which were inimical to U.S. policy.

Only when a price was exacted for South Africa's recalcitrance was a policy balance restored and South Africa restrained. By that time, the situation had worsened and the violence had escalated.

Eventually, the United States got it right, but not right from the beginning.

QUIET DIPLOMACY

Another lesson of the South African case pertains to the utility of quiet diplomacy in pressing for human rights. Although activists refute this contention, conventional wisdom among government officials holds that U.S. human rights policies must be pressed quietly to be effective. By this measure, U.S. policy should have failed in South Africa, for it stimulated the longest and most bitter nationwide foreign policy debate in the United States since the Vietnam War.

South Africa divided the country, split party ranks, pitted the executive and congressional branches of government against each other, attracted major media attention, and galvanized a broad array of church leaders, students, labor and civil rights groups, intellectuals, and corporations to take a stand. Residual bitterness over sanctions also fueled congressional battles over U.S. policy toward other states in southern Africa, spawned controversy over the appointment of a new black U.S. ambassador to South Africa, fueled shareholder activism that resulted in significant financial losses for South Africa, stimulated state and local government antiapartheid legislation, and provoked boycotts and demonstrations that continued up until the time Nelson Mandela was released. Yet, paradoxically, this controversy contributed to an effective policy.

There is no question that U.S. policy toward South Africa underwent a difficult labor and a messy delivery. Far from being well thought out and carefully planned, the struggle was prolonged and left deep scars, racial resentment, and a high domestic political cost. It was also an extraordinarily emotional debate, contrasting sharply with other foreign policy dilemmas, from the 1991 Persian Gulf War to the 1994 Rwandan genocide, which ended either in broad consensus (support for the war against Saddam Hussein) or in paralysis (failure to intervene to prevent the genocide). The South African debate produced a hybrid policy that operated simultaneously to exert pressure on Pretoria for internal change while remaining open for strategic negotiations.

POLICY PHASES

Constructive Engagement (1981–84)

Quiet diplomacy was the primary policy instrument employed by Assistant Secretary of State for Africa Chester Crocker, Reagan's top Africa aide, when he launched Reagan's new approach. Crocker had a unique political advantage in that he was in virtual control of U.S. Africa policy for nearly eight years, enjoying the confidence of Secretaries of State George Shultz and Alexander Haig. As the longest-serving head of the African affairs regional bureau, he provided continuity and consistency, features that also made the policy an easy target of criticism when it came under attack from liberal opponents in Congress and right-wing elements within the administration.

Crocker viewed the government of South African president P. W. Botha as a modernizing regime and his military as a lobby of reforming patriots. The best way to effect change internally, he argued, was to work with the white power structure and take account of white fears. Constructive engagement was a policy that precluded him from publicly criticizing the regime for human rights abuses and that openly rejected economic sanctions.

However, Crocker had a nuanced view of the Soviet threat. He dismissed Pretoria's theory of "total onslaught" based on an alliance of communism and black nationalism, a belief widely shared by Pretoria's governing elite and the military that made it easy for them to dismiss black claims for political rights as a communist ruse. But the Reagan administration gave minimum attention to black politics and to black leaders in South Africa. A small scholarship program for black South Africans was started in 1980, and this was later significantly expanded by Congress to include funds for the promotion of human rights and black leadership. In this regard, the administration's emphasis was on "black economic empowerment," not "black political liberation."

The aid program became a subject of intense controversy. Blacks in South Africa saw the aid program as illegitimate because it was linked to a policy that they felt supported the apartheid regime. Some groups refused to accept U.S. aid at all. A debate ensued in the U.S. government between those who wanted aid to be directed through official apartheid institutions and those who wanted to direct it to antiapartheid nongovernmental groups. The latter group won in Congress, which gave approval for the first U.S. aid program to be openly political in nature and to bypass the host government. The program had to make a sharp shift toward supporting black groups, a move that was later denounced by conservative groups as racist. The aid program, though hotly debated in Congress, was not central to the Reagan administration's goals. Its emphasis continued to be on the achievement of regional and geopolitical objectives by working with the South African government.

Opposition to Constructive Engagement (1984–86)

Sustained criticism of constructive engagement began in 1982, but it did not rise to the level of a national debate until two years later. The "trigger" that exploded events was the attempt by the South African government in 1983 to implement a new constitution creating a racially segregated legislature with three unequal chambers, each of which would represent a racial group of whites (with the most powers), Coloureds (mixed-race people), and Indians. The proposed constitution gave no political rights to blacks, who represented 75 percent of the population. In essence, South Africa was trying to co-opt minorities as junior partners in apartheid, hoping to make racial domination more palatable to the outside world and domestic protesters by showing that it was ending white exclusivity.

The gamut backfired badly, sparking spontaneous opposition. Security forces cracked down brutally in black townships, a pattern of abuse that was broadcast on nightly television. Cameras also documented the mass public funerals, the gruesome "necklace" killings (in which individuals were set ablaze with burning tires flung around their necks) by angry mobs taking vengeance on suspected state collaborators, and waves of South African youth "toyi-toying" (dancing) through the townships in defiant protest. Meanwhile, South Africa continued to mount military attacks on its neighbors, to increase its aid to UNITA, the Angola rebel movement, and to support Renamo, the Mozambican rebel forces.

Four years after constructive engagement was introduced, it came under intense fire at home for tilting in favor of whites without meaningful outcomes. In the United States, black leaders, labor leaders, students, supporters of the divestment campaign, the Congressional Black Caucus, state and municipal governments, corporations, and universities all jumped into the debate, agreeing to be "arrested" in peaceful protests and selling shares in U.S. firms invested in South Africa. In 1985 Chase Manhattan Bank, followed by other creditors, suddenly announced that it would not roll over outstanding loans to Pretoria, a decision that sent the South African stock market into free fall. Continuing South African brutalities fed U.S. activism, spawning a move in Congress for a comprehensive antiapartheid act that included more aid, sanctions, and an opening to black leaders. With public opinion turning against him, President Reagan proposed milder sanctions of his own and vetoed the sanctions legislation. However, in a stunning reversal for the extremely popular president, his veto was overridden by a bipartisan majority vote in both houses of Congress, even though the Senate was then in Republican hands. It was a massive foreign policy defeat for the administration and a reversal of fortune for South Africa, which had been counting on the Reagan administration to protect it from sanctions.

Synthesis (1987–89)

The CAAA was a watershed in U.S. policy. South Africa now had to pay a price for denying blacks their political rights. It put Congress at the center of the policy process and gave South Africa only two ways out: either Congress could lift sanctions with an act of both houses (an unlikely event) or Pretoria could fulfill the specific conditions set down in the law. Moreover, while sanctions were imposed unilaterally, the law encouraged other international allies to follow suit.

The administration treated sanctions as an unwanted add-on to existing policy, but constructive engagement was, for all practical purposes, over. The term was not used to describe the policy any longer. The U.S. ambassador was changed to signal the shift in policy, meetings with black leaders occurred at higher levels, speeches had more explicit human rights goals, and relations with black states improved. Pretoria's relations with Washington became more distant and, indeed, many thought that U.S. diplomacy had reached an impasse, especially in light of Angola's parallel decision in 1986 to break off negotiations with the United States following the Reagan administration's decision to arm UNITA.

Not all sanctions supporters had the same goals: some wanted to make a political statement by putting the United States on the right side; some believed that sanctions would have an impact, but that it would be a long and drawn-out affair; and some wanted to act in support of domestic constituencies. Few believed that there would be an immediate impact. Even the law's most ardent supporters pointed out that there was no precedent for a ruling elite relinquishing power without force and that sanctions rarely are enough to dislodge a regime that is militarily secure.[8] Opponents felt that the sanctions would be counterproductive, hurt blacks more than whites, make whites more intransigent, and kill regional negotiations.

These fears proved to be exaggerated. In March 1987, less than six months after economic sanctions against South Africa were enacted, diplomatic activity resumed in a complex series of messages and meetings that went through many twists and turns, across several continents, and finally to the finish line at the United Nations twenty months later. It was the beginning of the end of the Cold War, and the Soviet Union cooperated, wanting to be relieved of overseas commitments. With barely a month of President Reagan's final term left, interlocking accords were signed by Angola, Cuba, and South Africa that resulted in the mutual withdrawals of Cuba from Angola and South Africa from Namibia.

The triumphant conclusion of these complex negotiations was due to several factors: changes in the U.S.-Soviet relationship, a shift in the regional balance of power from aggressive Cuban military activities that had caused South African casualties, and rising economic and political costs for all the warring parties. A year after the agreements were signed, Mandela was freed. It took four more years before the South African transition to majority rule was complete, but public clamor in the United States had died down by the time the first Bush administration took office and the negotiations for a new election based on a universal franchise were well under way.

Aftermath

In 1993 Nelson Mandela and F. W. de Klerk, the last white leader, who released Mandela from prison and negotiated the transition to democracy, shared the Nobel Peace Prize. In 1994 Mandela was elected the first black president of South Africa. U.S. policy goals shifted from supporting a democratic transition to consolidating democratic gains and promoting economic development. The Clinton administration identified South Africa as one of "top ten emerging markets," a U.S.–South Africa binational commission was established to symbolize the importance of that country, and an aid program of roughly $80 million a year was approved.

President Mandela's priority was racial reconciliation. He succeeded masterfully. In 1999 Thabo Mbeki was elected the second post-apartheid black president of South Africa. His challenges—from wiping out poverty to eliminating crime and dealing with the world's fastest-growing HIV/AIDS crisis—were quite different, having less to do with securing human rights for blacks than with consolidating the democratic transition and making human rights meaningful in economic and social terms.

In the post-liberation phase, the relationship between the United States and South Africa changed once again. South Africa was disappointed in the level of economic assistance it received from the United States, which fell far short of expectations relative to the rhetoric that the U.S. government used to describe the importance of the South African "miracle." Mandela described the U.S. package as "peanuts." In addition, the level of foreign investment from U.S. corporations was disappointing. Those that had pulled out of South Africa during the 1980s either did not come back (some had lost their markets) or did so through shareholder stakes or joint ventures, rather than equity investments in job-producing manufacturing operations. The total value of foreign investment in South Africa from 1994 to 2000 was about $12.5 billion, of which approximately one-third came from the United States. This roughly equals the amount of capital that was estimated to have left South Africa by the end of the 1980s. Thus, in the first six years after apartheid, South Africa had managed to bring itself up to the levels of capital investment that it had in the 1980s, but not to exceed them. Between 1994 and 2000 South Africa was also estimated to have lost seven hundred thousand jobs.[9]

The South African market opened up in an international business environment in which, after the fall of communism, there was a

host of newly emerging alternative markets. Having dropped its socialist ideology and adopted free-market capitalism, the ruling ANC found
it hard to make the case for investment solely on economic grounds,
when the moral imperative no longer applied. South Africa had to pass
the same bottom-line scrutiny as any other country, with investors wary
of the powerful labor unions, high crime rates, taxes, and an HIV/AIDS
infection rate that rivaled that of any other country. Mbeki's regressive
HIV/AIDS policy, allegations of ANC corruption, and the adoption of
a policy of constructive engagement toward Zimbabwe after Robert
Mugabe's rigged elections and lawless seizure of white farmland plunged
that country into crisis have tarnished the image of South Africa as a
government wedded to human rights and good governance.

Despite these problems, South Africa overall remains the most
developed and hopeful country on the African continent at the beginning of the twenty-first century. Its democratic roots are institutionalized; witness the independence of the South African Constitutional
Court, which has ruled against the government and vigorously defended human rights. The South African government adheres to constitutional processes, boasts a vibrant free press, has a strong civil society, and sustains an energetic private sector that is expanding beyond
its own borders. While postapartheid problems exist, the country masterfully handled an enormously difficult political transition that could
have easily turned sour.

Unlike many other societies in conflict, South Africa experienced a successful transition in part because it did not actually collapse as a state. Its institutions stayed intact, though the personnel
and legal framework within which they operate has changed radically.
The police, civil service, military, and judicial systems all continued
to function. This established a level of continuity and stability that
did not force South Africa to build from the ground up.

POLICY TOOLS

The intensity, duration, and scope of the policy debate in the United
States, and the broad-based social activism it stimulated among di-
verse groups, were distinctive characteristics not frequently found in
U.S. human rights policy challenges. Few countries spawn protracted

public debate of the sort provoked by South Africa. A racial issue that penetrated corporate boardrooms, university campuses, churches, municipal and local governments, labor unions, and the African American community, it gave rise to a broad-based social activism that began in the 1970s and culminated in the 1980s as a major instrument of policy change.

Social activism was, however, a mixed blessing. On the positive side, it generated mass public action for a common purpose that led to concrete legislation. However, it also contributed to partisan wrangling, strained race relations, and poisoned legislative-executive relations.

Social activism over South Africa left a legacy that continues to be used as a standard-bearer for human rights activism. Shareholder resolutions and pressure at state and local government levels have challenged executive branch control of foreign policy. For example, based on the antiapartheid movement, activists drafted legislation enacted in Massachusetts to penalize companies doing business in Burma, triggering a new battle on the constitutional limits of state governments to make foreign policy that was challenged in the Supreme Court. The measure also brought complaints by the European Union and Japan that Massachusetts was violating World Trade Organization rules. The Supreme Court struck down the right of states to challenge foreign policy decisions, but on a narrow technical point (namely, that sanctions were already in place in the case of Burma), leaving open the question of the legality of state and local government boycotts on human rights grounds. In these legal contests, South Africa has consistently been used as the reference point.

South Africa is also a good example of how sanctions and aid were used together as effective policy instruments. History will continue to debate the scope and nature of the impact, but it is indisputable that embargoes had both psychological and economic effects, especially financial sanctions that deprived the economy of much needed capital. Guidance was given in the sanctions legislation on the steps U.S. policymakers ought to take toward a variety of other issues, such as the black-controlled states in the region, aid to South African black education and labor unions, the U.S. attitude toward "necklacing" (mob lynching), and the beliefs and tactics of the opposition parties, especially the South African Communist Party.

Of these, the least controversial instrument, on the surface, was aid to South Africa. However, it too eventually became embroiled in controversy. Initiated in 1980 with an $8 million scholarship fund organized by Rep. Stephen Solarz (D-N.Y.), then chairman of the House of Representatives Subcommittee on Africa, the aid program grew to $25 million in 1986 during the times of heightened congressional pressure for sanctions. To some, the aid program was a politically acceptable alternative to sanctions and it enjoyed bipartisan support early on. However, a behind-the-scenes struggle erupted between House and Senate aides over the kinds of projects and organizations that should be supported.

The House of Representatives wanted the funds to go to groups that were "credible" in the black community and that were not white dominated or controlled by the state. The Senate wanted the money to go to established institutions, even if the South African government ran them, and proposed that the funds should not be used for purposes that were inconsistent with constructive engagement. Senate aides also argued that the money should go for "black empowerment," whereas House aides supported projects that would lead to "black liberation." The U.S. Agency for International Development (USAID) distanced itself from constructive engagement and accepted the House criteria, channeling up to $91 million in assistance during the Reagan years to nonracial, grassroots projects that had no connection with the South African government. This was the first USAID program that was openly presented as an effort to promote democracy rather than economic development, and the first to be spent only in the nongovernment sector. After 1994 U.S. aid shifted again, this time toward a normal developmental program. However, it was criticized for abruptly leaving civic organizations that the United States had supported without adequate financial support or training to make the transition. In addition, the U.S. government did not have a sufficient package of tax incentives, loans, risk insurance, and joint-venture promotion to promote more U.S. investment. To secure the human rights gains that were won in South Africa, the economy must grow and poverty alleviation must assume a top priority.

While the domestic political costs were high, the efficacy of U.S. policy instruments was nonetheless high as measured by the outcomes the instruments helped produce: a successful transition in South Africa that led to the abolition of apartheid and the transition to democracy. U.S. geopolitical and regional policy objectives were also achieved due to the tenacity of the administration and a fortuitous set of conditions. The heated debate educated the U.S. public, displayed the moral tenets of U.S. foreign policy, gave greater visibility to Africa, and guaranteed that the public would view South Africa overwhelmingly in human rights terms for years to come.

TACTICAL LESSONS

In the 1980s most Americans did not fully appreciate what they were dealing with in South Africa. Besides oppressing blacks, the white South African government had been sponsoring international terrorism, developing chemical and biological weapons, and building a nuclear weapons capability. While there were allegations of such activities, they had not been publicly confirmed until Prime Minister de Klerk announced the voluntary abolition of South Africa's weapons of mass destruction programs months before the transition to majority rule.[10] Had the existence of such programs been known earlier, the U.S. government would have been compelled to put South Africa on the list of states with emerging weapons of mass destruction, along with Iraq, Iran, and North Korea. The U.S. public would have demanded greater isolation and punishment of the regime, the domestic debate in the United States would have been further enflamed, and the geopolitical and regional policy outcomes might have turned out differently. In essence, the U.S. government was confronting a hideous threat: a racist nuclear state that supported terrorism and sponsored race-based biological and chemical weapons research. Only after apartheid collapsed was the world made fully aware of the real danger that South Africa presented. In light of these considerations, the success of the U.S. human rights policy is even more significant and the tactical lessons that can be learned are of even greater import.

The most critical factors that accounted for the success of U.S. human rights policy were the following:

- *Timing.* Internal events and forces in South Africa guided the policy process. International influence was important, mainly through many points of contact aimed at bringing people together, putting out brushfires, and educating constituencies. U.S. policy, however, lagged behind the actions of civil society. U.S. human rights policy was formulated in response to these and other trends and did not become forward looking until Congress imposed a new policy on the administration. However—and this is a vital point—this new approach was designed not to overthrow the regime but rather to strengthen antiapartheid forces and level the playing field for negotiations between internal democratic forces and the apartheid regime. Fortunately, South Africa was "ripe for resolution," making the approach effective.

- *Waning of the Cold War.* The Soviets wanted cooperation with the West as the Cold War drew to a close, allowing regional diplomacy to move forward. After Namibia became independent, the Soviet threat dissolved in the eyes of the South Africans, diminishing the perceived threat of "total onslaught." This meant that black rights had to be looked at, not as a foil for communist expansion, but as a legitimate demand.

- *Role of civil society.* In South Africa and the United States, public activism played an essential role in shaping trends. Not many countries have mass-based activism, but for those that do, the most effective U.S. policies will be those that are in sync with public sentiments as expressed through legitimate public dissent and authentic popular leaders.

- *Existence of a visible and viable opposition.* The existence of the ANC, the most popular black political opposition group, and the quality of leadership in Nelson Mandela and other top ANC officials meant that there was a legitimate future government capable of managing negotiations, a transition, a free and fair election, and a democratic political system. Such leadership does not always appear in divided, conflict-ridden societies.

- *U.S. public support.* In the end, bipartisan support for the CAAA became widespread, with the central objective being to distance the United States from a racist government. When the legislation passed, the U.S. government spoke with one resounding voice, which was overwhelmingly supported by the public.

Only when this became apparent did Pretoria begin to take seriously the primacy of human rights in U.S. policy.

- *Split within the ruling party.* The de Kerk faction of the National Party challenged P. W. Botha, exposing rifts within the power structure that broke the myth of the white monolith. Eventually, the de Klerk faction took over, released Mandela, and led the negotiations toward majority rule.

- *The CAAA, though it included sanctions, did not totally isolate South Africa.* Indeed, it deepened engagement with the opposition and with civil society. These were "smart sanctions," carefully targeted to deprive the government of funds, an important pillar of a capital-importing economy, and they impacted white attitudes. They did not isolate South Africa but rather reengaged the U.S. government on different terms.

- *The law provided a road map for lifting sanctions.* Providing a road map was an important feature because it suggested a future relationship that could be resumed, once basic steps were taken. That meant that the U.S. government could continue to exert influence on South Africa. Blanket sanctions, with no guidelines for lifting them, would have slammed the door shut on bilateral relations. Sanctions were lifted in 1991, five years after the legislation was enacted, as soon as the five conditions spelled out in the law were satisfied. The apartheid government was still in place.

- *Sanctions were imposed by law, not by executive action.* The importance of this feature is that it removed an "escape hatch" for the South African government, which would likely have tried to gain waivers from a sympathetic executive branch. This was no longer possible. Congress was the main player with regard to sanctions. In many cases, congressionally imposed sanctions can be unduly rigid, but the CAAA established clear conditions for the lifting of sanctions. This occurred as soon as South Africa complied with the necessary conditions.

- *TV coverage.* For months, television images of South African security forces brutalizing antiapartheid activists fueled the domestic debate in the United States. This was a vital link that made it possible for antiapartheid activists in the United States to mobilize mass public support. Divestment activists had been laboring for a decade to get more support. Only when South Africa became a major story in the media did that movement join forces with others for a successful push for sanctions.

- *Elites cared about the economy.* Sanctions hurt whites and shaped their perceptions. After the economic measures were imposed, the feeling in the white community was that there was no turning back. It would be only a matter of time before other countries would follow suit. In a sense, by loosening white attitudes, sanctions gave de Klerk the constituency he needed to move forward. Whites were concerned that holding out too long would result in a wasteland, in which whites as well as blacks would suffer.

- *Sanctions delayed, but did not stop, regional diplomacy.* The U.S.–South Africa relationship cooled, but national interests took precedence in South Africa. Agreements were reached at the end of the Reagan administration while sanctions were still in place, partly because South Africa wanted to get the best deal possible before a Democratic administration took over.

POLICY RISKS

Success was not a foregone conclusion. Many things could have gone wrong. Among the biggest risks were the following:

- *Bitterness of the domestic debate.* The debate sent mixed signals to South Africa, raising questions about the direction and commitment of the U.S. government toward human rights, and sending U.S. policy reeling from one approach to another. Some concluded U.S. policy had become a "morality play"; others criticized it as being "racist." Some have argued that these dissident voices in the United States were beneficial because they kept the government off balance. However, until sanctions were enacted, the U.S. government was not speaking with one voice. This raised questions over the credibility of the United States, undermined its influence, and enflamed racial tensions in American society.

- *Recalcitrant leadership in South Africa.* Had P. W. Botha stayed in power, South Africa may not have agreed to political negotiations and the country could have spun out of control. Continuing violence under hard-line National Party leadership could have resulted in a nightmare scenario of full-scale race war.

- *Complete boycott with no chance of lifting sanctions.* Had there been a complete boycott of South Africa and had a political road map detailing the way out not been provided in the law for removing sanctions, engagement with South Africa would likely have stopped altogether. U.S. policymakers would not have been able to provide assistance to antiapartheid groups, regional diplomacy would have ground to a halt, and all U.S. corporations would have withdrawn, with little prospect of coming back. That would have worsened the South African situation and diminished the chances for a peaceful settlement.

- *No sanctions at all.* Failure to make a midcourse correction in U.S. policy to impose some penalties would have given the South African government a "free ride." Pretoria was manipulating Washington to its own advantage and Washington's leverage was declining. Sanctions created new political leverage. This does not imply that all sanctions increase U.S. influence; on the contrary, sanctions often end U.S. influence if not designed correctly. Each country must be looked at on its own terms to decide what is effective. In this case, sanctions affected white attitudes to the extent that the de Klerk government was able to take a new course.

TRANSFERABILITY

There is a temptation, especially since September 11 and the launching of the war on terrorism, to downgrade human rights in favor of strategic security objectives. While every country is different, it would be folly, and often counterproductive, to push aside human rights concerns as was done in the early stages of the Reagan administration's policy toward South Africa. Indeed, if the U.S. government seriously reduced its pressure on human rights, it would invite repression, foster instability, and invite more terrorism from groups that resent that policy and accuse us of double standards. We need not be so timid. South Africa shows that even when we apply significant pressure to protest human rights violations, repressive states may still cooperate with the United States on critical strategic and regional matters when it is in their self-interest to do so.

South Africa also shows that we should not give up on trying to advance human rights in conflicts deemed to be "intractable." Conditions change, leaders change, and generations change. No situation is static. South Africa and Ireland, considered intractable conflicts in the 1960s, eventually entered into negotiations leading to peaceful political settlements. The trick is to know how and when to move conflicted or repressive societies forward and having the political will to apply multiple approaches in a credible and targeted way.

This means paying attention to the timing and tools of policy implementation. Public statements that support democratic forces help to liberalize repressive societies, because they bring hope to the powerless, add a measure of international protection to their leaders, and show that they are not forgotten. More coercive instruments, such as economic sanctions, are most likely to be effective when internal forces mount a serious challenge to established authority and show that they have the skills to be a responsible alternative government. Repressive regimes then must confront internal and external pressures simultaneously. Internal forces also are best positioned to take advantage of external pressures when they present themselves as a plausible and legitimate party capable of upholding constitutional safeguards of human rights.

Many states, of course, do not have the advantage of coherent and cohesive oppositions ready to take over. Moreover, economic sanctions can have a limited effect in situations of gross human rights violations, such as in Kosovo during the Milosevic regime or in Iraq during Saddam Hussein's regime. Then the crisis becomes so critical as to prompt military intervention for either humanitarian or security reasons. States that have experienced military intervention must be allowed time to develop the political infrastructure and state institutions that are necessary to protect human rights. In Afghanistan, for example, international human rights policies are intimately connected to postconflict political rehabilitation and state-building strategies; the lack of such human rights protections favors warlords and drug deal-ers. The same is true in post-war Iraq, where lawlessness immediately followed U.S. military victory.

South Africa was not invaded by an outside power and did not descend into full-scale internal war, but it underwent a political trans-formation from apartheid to democracy that was every bit as radical as that of Afghanistan after the Taliban and that of Iraq after Hussein. The South African state could have collapsed but did not. It thus pres-ents a rare instance of regime change—indeed, it was a system change —that resulted in a dramatic improvement of human rights. Critical external intervention was applied successfully and in a timely way, without the use of military force.

Policy tools to foster human rights range from open condemna-tion (which provides important moral backing for human rights ad-vocates) to targeted economic, diplomatic, and military sanctions against political elites (preferably multilateral but, if necessary, unilat-eral, with others encouraged to follow suit) and substantial aid to civil society (to strengthen the internal economic and political capacities of human rights activists). It is important to recognize that while South Africa had a reprehensible racist system of oppression, U.S. policy did not, in the end, adopt total isolation or total embrace. In other situations of this kind, U.S. policy should likewise pursue issue-specific policies, with terms of engagement that advance democratic and human rights policies while working collaboratively, if possible, on other policy issues.

How hard should the U.S. government press for human rights compliance? That depends on a number of factors:

- Is there a capable state, or a capable opposition, with compe-tent and pragmatic leadership? If not, how do we foster such leadership?

- Do we know what motivates the political elites and popular con-stituencies in the targeted state? (For example, South African white elites cared about the economy and therefore were vulner-able to economic sanctions.)

- Can we sustain the policy by carefully calibrating pressure and rewards, timing them to internal events, or is our attention span too short to stay with the policy and reassess its impact as conditions change?

- Do we have the diplomatic skill and political courage to manage incentives and disincentives so that they are not counterproductive, politically divisive, or short of the mark?

- In ongoing conflicts, can we devise a road map that is more than symbolic or merely hopeful—one that lays down specific steps to be taken by the targeted leadership and specific implications if such steps are not taken? A road map shows polarized leaders and communities that there is a way out and clarifies U.S. policies, spelling out what actions must be adopted, what the consequences are for noncompliance, and what positive benefits come with compliance.

The Middle East conflict is one hot spot in which some of these lessons may apply, although the situation, admittedly, is quite different. Significant effort has gone into resolving the conflict by several administrations, but different human rights principles, and violations of those principles, are competing for international legitimacy. Which should be condemned more—Israeli occupation and settlement of conquered territory or Palestinian terrorist attacks? Which right takes precedence—the right of Israeli self-defense or the right of Palestinians to self-determination? Which comes first—the recognition of Israel's right to exist or the right of Palestinians to return to land taken from them? Can the road map offered be implemented and is the United States willing to spell out, and implement, the consequences of noncompliance?

Unlike South Africa, where the moral clarity of the conflict was evident, the Middle East is full of moral ambiguities and contradictions. Unlike South Africa, where the question was how different racial and ethnic groups can have their rights and security protected within one state, the issue in the Middle East is how groups can have their rights and security protected in two states.

However, one similarity between South Africa and the Middle East stands out. It is that the continuing violence and power imbalances in both conflicts were fundamentally a result of unresolved human rights issues. U.S. policies cannot be based, therefore, simply on redrawing territorial borders, forging alliances based on counter-terrorism, or introducing compromises that do not address the fundamental problems. U.S. policy must contain a long-term strategy for respecting international human rights for all aggrieved parties, with a road map that presents a vision of how two states can live in peace, side by side, in the Middle East. That road map has been published, but as of this writing, it is not certain that sufficient political will and resources exist to apply the necessary pressures, as was done in the case of South Africa in the 1980s.

Indeed, from the Middle East to Pakistan to China, where U.S. relations are also very complex, there needs to be a fundamental understanding that Washington will not drop its concerns about human rights to advance other interests. On the contrary, it should press them harder precisely because the rule of law advances U.S. security, political, and commercial interests and is consistent with U.S. values, even in an age of terrorism. It is increasingly clear that, in the post–Cold War world, "any administration that fails to take human rights into account . . . risks loss of credibility and a political backlash against that policy at home."[11] It also risks a further rise in violent anti-Americanism abroad.

NOTES

1. For an excellent summary of the negotiations, see Patti Waldmeir, *Anatomy of a Miracle: The End of Apartheid and the Birth of the New South Africa* (New York and London: W. W. Norton, 1997).

2. This is a term that William Zartman has coined to describe propitious times for intervention.

3. Waldmeir, *Anatomy of a Miracle*, 125.

4. For further information, see S. Prakesh Sethi and Oliver F. Williams, "Creating and Implementing Global Codes of Conduct: An Assessment of the Sullivan Principles as a Role Model for Development of International Codes of Conduct—Lessons Learned and Unlearned," *Business and Society Review* 105, no. 2 (summer 2000): 169–200; and S. Prakesh Sethi, *Setting Global Standards: Guidelines for Creating Codes of Conduct in Multinational Corporations* (Hoboken, N.J.: John Wiley and Sons, 2003).

5. These included (1) the release of Nelson Mandela and all political prisoners, (2) the repeal of the state of emergency that gave South African police more powers of detention, (3) the unbanning of political parties, (4) the repeal of two key apartheid laws: the Group Areas and Population Registration Acts, and (5) the agreement to enter into good-faith negotiations with truly representative members of the black majority without preconditions.

6. See Princeton Lyman, *Partner to History: The U.S. Role in South Africa's Transition to Democracy* (Washington, D.C.: United States Institute of Peace Press, 2002).

7. For an inside view of how the National Peace Accord worked on the ground with grassroots workers committed to stopping the violence, see Susan Collin Marks, *Watching the Wind: Conflict Resolution during South Africa's Transition to Democracy* (Washington, D.C.: United States Institute of Peace Press, 2000).

8. Former congressman Steve Solarz restated these beliefs at a meeting held at the United States Institute of Peace, Washington, D.C., on March 22, 2000.

9. "South Africans Who Fought for Sanctions Now Scrap for Investors but They Find Luring Back Capital Is a Lot Harder Than Was Chasing It Out," *Wall Street Journal*, February 11, 2000, 1.

10. See "Lethal Legacy: Bioweapons for Sale," *Washington Post*, April 20, 2003, 1; and "Biotoxins Fall into Private Hands," April 21, 2003, 1. In 1993, the South African government declared that it had dismantled its nuclear, biological, and chemical weapons programs and destroyed all the weapons and pathogens. However, the expertise and bacterial strains supposedly destroyed remain on the market, and law enforcement authorities are concerned that they could end up in the hands of extremist groups or hostile foreign governments.

11. See my analysis of the policy of U.S. engagement in South Africa, "The United States and South Africa: Persuasion and Coercion," in *Honey and Vinegar: Incentives, Sanctions, and Foreign Policy*, ed. Richard Haass (Washington, D.C.: Brookings Institution Press, 2000), 114; and *The United States and South Africa: The Reagan Years* (New York: Ford Foundation and Foreign Policy Association, 1989).

Part II
Asia

4

Monitoring Human Rights in China

MERLE GOLDMAN

S INCE THE END OF WORLD WAR II and especially since the Carter presidency (1977–81), concern for human rights has been an integral part of U.S. foreign policy. Following the military crackdown on protesters in Tiananmen Square on June 4, 1989, televised worldwide, and the collapse of the Soviet Union in 1991, U.S. human rights policy has increasingly focused on China. Still, the issue of human rights in Washington's foreign policy toward China ranks below maintenance of the military balance in East Asia, preservation of Taiwan's autonomy, control of arms proliferation, and expansion of U.S. trade and investment in China. And after September 11, 2001, China was allowed more latitude in silencing dissenters and particularly separatist ethnic groups, such as the Muslim Uighurs in northwest China, in the name of assisting the U.S. policy against terrorism. Nevertheless, the issue of human rights continues to be an important and contentious element in the U.S. relationship with China. Even when human rights issues clash with other U.S. interests in China, U.S. criticism of China's human rights abuses persists, primarily because of China's continuing human rights abuses and pressure from the U.S. public, NGOs, and Congress.

On the executive level, however, human rights issues have been of secondary importance to other issues in U.S.-China relations.

115

When President Richard Nixon's visit to China in 1972 opened relations with China during the later years of the Mao era (1949–76),
China was in the midst of the Cultural Revolution (1966–76), one of
the worst periods of political persecution in Chinese history. Yet the
U.S. government refrained from criticism, or offered only the most
perfunctory criticisms, of China's human rights abuses because it
wanted China's cooperation in a tacit alliance against the Soviet
Union. Most likely, no matter how loudly or persistently the United
States might have denounced China's egregious human rights abuses
during the Mao years, it would have had little impact because Mao
did not care what the outside world thought of his policies.

Only during the post-Mao regimes of Deng Xiaoping (1978–89)
and his successors, Jiang Zemin (1989–2002) and Hu Jintao (2002–),
has the People's Republic cared about its international status and
sought to be considered a responsible member of the world community.
Consequently, China's post-Mao regimes have been more willing to
acknowledge the concept of universal human rights and to make
some symbolic concessions on human rights issues, however grudgingly. The regimes have directed such concessions primarily toward
improving relations with Western nations in order to acquire the technological and scientific know-how, foreign investment and markets,
and membership in international organizations they so desire.

China's more conciliatory approach toward human rights issues
has also reflected internal changes in post-Mao China. As China has
moved from a state-controlled to a market economy and has become
engaged with the outside world, it also has shifted away from the totalitarian rule of the Maoist era to a form of soft authoritarianism.[1] While
China's post-Mao leaders still do not tolerate any public political criticism of themselves or the Communist Party, they have ended the
massive, violent campaigns against supposed political dissidents of
the Mao years. The Deng-Jiang-Hu governments have also relaxed
the party's controls over the personal lives of most Chinese. The rights
to choose one's employment and residence and to travel and explore
new ideas and cultures, as long as one does not touch on political
issues, are now permissible. Moreover, the Administrative Litigation
Law, put into effect in 1990, has made possible the right of any citizen
to bring suit against local government officials for abuses of power.

Minxin Pei found that in 1994 the general percentage of favorable court settlements for the plaintiffs was about 35.7 percent and in 1995 about 37.5 percent,[2] though he also found that that percentage declined to 27.7 percent in 2000.[3]

Elections for leaders at the village level and for village councils began in 1987 and by the late 1990s had spread to more than 70 percent of China's villages.[4] Starting in the mid-1980s the National People's Congress (NPC), China's hitherto rubber-stamp parliament, became increasingly assertive vis-à-vis the party-state leadership. Though it has yet to reject a party policy, it has been able to delay, revise, or send back for more work a number of party directives.[5] Moreover, NPC votes on important issues, and appointments are no longer unanimous. Also significant, as Andrew Nathan has pointed out, is that while all of China's constitutions, whether under the monarchy, the Nationalists, or the communists, granted a common core of political rights consisting of freedom of speech, publication, assembly, and association,[6] the 1982 revision of the constitution placed the section on rights near the front of the text, which was officially interpreted as symbolically giving higher priority to rights than in the past.[7]

These domestic reforms have made China since the 1980s a relatively more accommodating international player. The loosening of internal controls and opening to the outside world have been reflected in China's greater participation in international organizations, even with respect to issues of human rights, as seen in China's actions in the UN Human Rights Commission.

MULTILATERAL APPROACH TO MONITORING CHINA'S HUMAN RIGHTS PRACTICES: THE UN COMMISSION ON HUMAN RIGHTS

The most effective means for dealing with China's human rights abuses have been through multinational organizations. In her book *China, the United Nations, and Human Rights: The Limits of Compliance*, Ann Kent traces in well-documented detail the history of China's participation in UN activities since 1949.[8] She points out that even though the Chinese People's Republic assumed Taiwan's seat in the UN Security Council in 1971, it did not participate in the UN

Commission on Human Rights (HRC) until after Deng Xiaoping had come to power in late 1978. Throughout the Mao era, China regarded the concept of national sovereignty as the core of all issues in international law and thus denounced intervention by a state in another state's internal affairs. Moreover, as China became an advocate for the interests of the developing countries at UN forums, its representatives asserted that because of their colonial histories, relative economic backwardness, and different values, the priority in developing countries should be given to sovereignty and economic rights rather than to political and civil rights, as emphasized by the Western nations. They argued that developing countries cannot be concerned with political and civil rights until their citizens have enough to eat. Therefore, a country must reach a certain level of socioeconomic development, China's representatives asserted, before citizens can seek political and civil rights.

The devastating experience of China's Cultural Revolution, however, ignited Chinese interest in the issue of human rights early on in the Deng era among China's party leaders, intellectuals, and urban dwellers who had been brutally persecuted by Mao. They sought to prevent a recurrence of the large-scale persecution and deprivation of rights that they had suffered during the Mao era. The Democracy Wall movement of ex–Red Guards and workers, calling for human rights among other things, exploded in late 1978–79 in Beijing and spread to most of China's large cities. Although Deng suppressed this movement from below as destabilizing, members of his government and a number of intellectuals embarked on a learning process on how to prevent a recurrence of human rights abuses. One aspect of that process was China's participation in the HRC, which began in 1979 when China sent observer delegates to the annual meeting of the HRC in Geneva and also to the meetings of its Subcommission on the Prevention of Discrimination and Protection of Minorities. In 1981 China became a permanent member of the HRC and its subcommission.

Gradually, during the last two decades of the twentieth century, China moved toward recognizing the norms of universal human rights and their integral role in the international order. Although at times China's leaders and its representatives at the HRC argued that historically such norms, specifically civil and political rights, were alien to China, in fact, Chinese reformers had adopted the term for human rights, *ren quan*, in the late nineteenth century from Japan. Marina Svensson, in her books on this subject, points out that Chinese reformers used the concept in their criticisms of the Manchu Qing dynasty.[9] And in the early decades of the twentieth century, they used the term to attack the Confucian system, even though some of its proponents found resonances of the concept of human rights in Confucianism, such as that people had the moral right to criticize and even overthrow a ruler who abused his power and abandoned moral values. The concept was also used to fight for political rights, first against the warlords, then by the Communists against the Nationalist government of the Guomindang under Chiang Kai-Shek (1928–49), and then by the Guomindang against the Chinese Communists. In addition, a number of organizations and publications were established in the 1930s and 1940s to work for human rights. A study by Sumner Twiss reveals that China's representative to the United Nations in 1947–48, P. C. Chang, had played a significant role in the final formulation of the UN Universal Declaration of Human Rights in 1948.[10] Representing the pre-1949 Chinese Nationalist government, Chang had inserted into the final formulation several Confucian ideas on the need for a moral and a communitarian outlook.

Despite these pre-1949 individual and group efforts, however, it was not until China became a member of the HRC that the People's Republic officially recognized the Universal Declaration of Human Rights, which stipulates that political and civil as well as economic and social rights are universal. In September 1988 China's foreign minister declared at the UN General Assembly that "despite its historical limitations, the Declaration has exerted a far-reaching influence on the development of the post-war international human rights activities and played a positive role in this regard."[11] China also implicitly affirmed the UN Covenant on Civil and Political Rights when, in 1985, it voted for a UN General Assembly resolution entitled The Indivisibility and Interdependence of Economic, Social, Cultural, Civil, and Political Rights, which implied recognition of civil and political rights. At an August 1996 meeting of the HRC in Geneva, Wu Jianmin, the head of the China delegation, spoke positively about civil and political rights. Although he repeated the standard

Chinese view that "the right to survive and develop is the most fundamental human right for the Chinese people," Wu asserted that "China also attaches importance to ensuring that its people enjoy civil and political rights according to law."[12] In a speech before the UN General Assembly in 1986, China's foreign minister observed that "the Two Covenants have played a positive role in realizing the purposes and principles of the UN Charter concerning respect for human rights. The Chinese government has consistently supported these purposes and principles."[13]

As befitting an increasingly influential powerful and permanent member of the UN Security Council, China also assumed a more assertive role in the HRC. It began to participate actively in debates and, on occasion, even contradicted its emphasis on sovereignty by voting in favor of intervention in countries charged with abuse of human rights. In 1984, for example, China supported the appointment of a rapporteur to examine the human rights situation in Afghanistan after the Soviet invasion, despite Soviet protests against interference in its internal affairs. And China approved of sanctions against governments that severely infringed on human rights, such as the former apartheid regime of South Africa.[14]

Another reason why China may have been willing to recognize political and civil rights in the 1980s was that for most of that decade, as the U.S. government set aside ideological differences with China for the sake of a tacit alliance against the former Soviet Union, Washington expressed relatively little concern about Beijing's human rights abuses, though U.S. NGOs continued to do so. It was only in the aftermath of China's violent crackdown on June 4, 1989, occurring in the same year as the dismantling of the Berlin Wall and the withdrawal of the Soviet Union from Eastern Europe, that the United States and most UN members condemned China for its human rights violations. The HRC subcommission passed a resolution in August 1989 strongly condemning the Tiananmen crackdown. The resolution won virtually unanimous support from most of the Third World and the Soviet bloc as well as the Western nations. The hundreds of international NGOs that regularly attend the HRC's annual meetings also supported the resolution. For the first time, a permanent member of the Security Council was singled out for wide-scale abuse of human rights.

It is impossible to gauge the impact on China of the 1989 sub-commission's resolution, along with the worldwide condemnation of the crackdown. To what degree, if any, did international censure re-strain or curtail the Chinese leadership from expanding its repression and imposing even harsher punishment on the demonstrators and their supporters after June 4, 1989? There is no way of knowing how much worse the crackdown might have been without the subcommission's resolution, the worldwide media focus, and the threat of further sanc-tions. Most of the twenty-one student leaders of the Tiananmen demonstration and what the Chinese government called their "behind-the-scenes backers," as well as leaders of demonstrations in other Chi-nese cities, were imprisoned for a number of years. Hundreds of worker participants were sentenced to even longer sentences and several were executed. But compared with Mao's nationwide campaigns of repres-sion, such as the 1957 campaign against "rightists," when a half-million intellectuals were silenced for almost twenty years, and the Cultural Revolution, when millions were persecuted and killed, the June 4 re-pression was relatively mild. Most other student leaders and their intel-lectual supporters were released after brief periods of detention, and many of those imprisoned were released before their terms ended.

The violent June 4 crackdown marked the end of China's im-munity from international criticism. In its aftermath, there was not much the United States could do to revive the democratic movement in China of the late 1980s. At best, it could offer asylum to some of the demonstrators and temporarily suspend contacts with high-level Chinese officials. It also sought to work with its allies in the HRC to pass yearly resolutions critical of China's human rights abuses. Because of the negative impact of the June 4 crackdown, the Chinese govern-ment was even more sensitive about its image in the world community and sought to do whatever it could to prevent further "loss of face" internationally. On the one hand, it went to great lengths to prevent passage of another critical resolution at the annual meetings of the HRC; on the other hand, it gradually became more responsive to multilateral international pressures to bring its domestic views and practices into line with international standards. Thus, the worldwide condemnation of the June 4 crackdown did not completely interrupt the gradual learning process and the acceptance of international norms begun in the 1980s. While China defended itself vigorously at the 1989 subcommission discussions by denying the applicability of human rights norms to China and by rejecting any interference in its state sovereignty, it did not deny the validity of the political and civil norms themselves, even though it strongly stressed that development and sovereignty supersede human rights.[15]

Rising nationalism in China in the post–June 4 period and increasing Chinese resentment of what Chinese officials called U.S. "hegemonism," "unilateralism," and efforts to contain China caused China's leaders to regard condemnation from the international community, as expressed in the HRC, as carrying more weight than the condemnation from any one country, specifically the United States and its Congress. China used both the carrot and the stick to derail any censure at the annual HRC meetings. In the months preceding the HRC's spring meetings in Geneva, the Chinese government engaged in extensive lobbying, expenditure of money, and diplomatic activity, particularly with the developing countries, to win their support against any critical resolution. To a certain degree, such efforts proved successful in preventing passage of further resolutions against China in the HRC. The unity achieved on the subcommission resolution in August 1989 could not be sustained. It had worked only in the immediate aftermath of June 4 as a temporary expedient to punish China for that violent crackdown rather than as a deterrent for future human rights abuses.

In 1990 China sent a delegation of more than forty diplomats to the spring HRC meetings to lobby against any resolution.[16] The final draft resolution of that session was mildly worded, as would be all draft resolutions critical of China henceforth. It expressed concern over continuing violations of human rights and fundamental freedoms and called on the Chinese government to take measures to ensure observance of human rights norms and to cooperate with special rapporteurs. It also voiced concern over China's repression of religious worshipers in Tibet and in Muslim areas. Though the resolution had solid Western sponsorship, China used a procedure that it would continue to use thereafter to deal with critical resolutions: It called for a no-action vote on the resolution in place of a vote and discussion on the resolution itself.

This procedure succeeded by a narrow margin in the 1990s, except in 1995, when Geraldine Ferraro, former Democratic nominee for U.S. vice president, headed the U.S. delegation to the HRC. For almost six weeks before the Geneva meeting, Ferraro lobbied Latin American delegates to vote in favor of the actual resolution. Other U.S. officials lobbied the African delegates. Meanwhile, President Bill Clinton turned from denouncing China's human rights record, as he did in his 1992 political campaign, to boosting U.S. trade with China. This sudden burst of energy was related to the plan to delink China's Most Favored Nation (MFN) status in May 1994 from its human rights record in exchange for the release from prison of the two major leaders of the 1989 Tiananmen demonstration. Such intense U.S. lobbying was intended to convince human rights NGOs and the U.S. Congress to work through the HRC, rather than to threaten U.S. trade sanctions as the means for limiting China's human rights abuses and to refocus international attention on UN mechanisms to deal with China's abuses.[17] Despite the unprecedented success of the rejection of the no-action motion in 1995, the vote on the actual resolution lost by one vote. Although Russia had voted with the United States to reject the no-action motion, it then voted against the resolution itself.

As China's expansion of its regional and international economic clout accelerated in the late 1990s, the United States was not able to garner enough support to get another vote on the resolution itself in the HRC. In addition to China's increasing economic clout, months before the HRC spring meetings Chinese officials continued to travel to developing countries and disperse generous donations to ensure that a critical resolution did not come to a vote. And in 2001 the United States could get no other Western country to join it in co-sponsoring a resolution critical of China's human rights abuses. In fact, in 2002 China, in cooperation with other countries that resented the Bush administration's "unilateralism," was instrumental in getting the United States voted off the HRC, if only for a year. Although the United States resumed its position on the HRC in 2003 and China's human rights abuses had not significantly abated, the United States did not sponsor a resolution critical of China's human rights practices because of the George W. Bush administration's overriding concern to win China's cooperation in the war against terrorism and help in opposing North Korea's resumption of nuclear weapons production.

At the same time, using its traditional policies of divide and rule as well as carrot and stick, China was able to drive a wedge between the United States and European countries on the HRC resolution. In 1996 it finalized a China–European Union Airbus sale, to the dismay of the U.S. company Boeing and threatened the European nations with loss of trade if they were to vote for the resolution. In addition to increasing its economic leverage, China offered to engage in bilateral human rights dialogues and to sign the two UN human rights covenants if the Western countries did not vote for the resolution. This approach proved successful in dividing the Western alliance. In 1997, for the first time, members of the alliance—Australia, Canada, France, Germany, Italy, Spain, and Japan—did not cosponsor a human rights resolution critical of China with the United States, though they did vote against the no-action motion. China threatened Denmark, which cosponsored the resolution with the United States in that year, with economic consequences. Nevertheless, in October 1997 China signed the Covenant on Economic, Cultural, and Social Rights, which China had promised it would do if those Western nations did not cosponsor the resolution. The United States then joined the other Western countries that had not sponsored the resolution in 1997 in not cosponsoring the resolution in 1998. In return, China signed the Covenant on Civil and Political Rights in October 1998. Thus, the trade-off for not cosponsoring the resolutions in 1997 and 1998 was China's promise to sign the two UN covenants.

The Chinese government claimed that the two covenants were inoperable until ratified by the National People's Congress. The Covenant on Economic, Cultural, and Social Rights was ratified in 1998, but with the deletion of the clause on the right to form independent labor unions, which the Chinese government regards as a direct threat to its authority. By the beginning of the twenty-first century, the NPC had not yet ratified the Covenant on Civil and Political Rights, which the Chinese government regards as an even greater challenge to its authority. Nevertheless, the fact that the government signed the two covenants had an important domestic impact. Chinese citizens cited China's signature on the two covenants to justify attempts to achieve political and civil as well as economic rights. For example, members of the China Democracy Party, formed in 1998, cited the Covenant on Civil and Political Rights to justify their efforts to establish the first opposition party in the People's Republic; the Buddhist-Daoist Falun Gong and other meditation groups similarly cited the covenant in their demands for official recognition. Workers, protesting the loss of their wages, pensions, and health benefits following the privatization of state-owned industries, refer to both covenants to justify their protests. Therefore, despite the failure to pass a resolution critical of China's human rights abuses after 1989, such efforts in the HRC have not been totally ineffective. In order to avoid censure, China has responded to international pressure by acknowledging important human rights concepts, specifically the UN covenants, which Chinese citizens cite as justification for asserting their political and economic rights.

While the yearly threat of a critical resolution in Geneva exerted a positive form of pressure in the 1990s, prompting the Chinese government to comply with some human rights norms, even if only formally, it also has exerted a negative form of pressure. Around the time of the yearly Geneva meetings of the HRC, China generally restrained its repression so as not to mobilize the international community to condemn its human rights abuses. It also usually released a small number of well-known political prisoners, conducted negotiations with the International Committee of the Red Cross on allowing regular prison visits, opened Tibet to visits by foreign journalists and human rights groups, and in 1998 invited the new UN High Commissioner for Human Rights, Mary Robinson, to visit China later in the year. In March 2000 Robinson led a workshop for Asian countries on human rights in Beijing.

Because of China's participation in the HRC and its signature on the UN covenants, China's leaders could no longer criticize the Western nations for imposing alien values on China. Despite its rhetoric about noninterference in the domestic affairs of other countries, China's actions acknowledge that it cannot be protected by the principle of absolute sovereignty. Therefore, even though the resolutions critical of China at the annual meetings of the HRC have been defeated, the yearly ritual in the 1990s of presenting the resolution has been effective in focusing international attention on China's human rights abuses to the point that China has been willing to make some concessions in order to avoid public censure. As Kent observes, the HRC has en-meshed China in a global human rights environment that involves an acceptance of norms and procedures that can be repudiated only at the cost of isolation.[18] She shows that from the early 1980s on, China has accepted the right of the international community to monitor the po-litical and civil rights of member-states, despite its objections to being made a target of criticism. China's experience in the HRC reveals that, because its leaders wish China to be regarded as a responsible member of the international community, it has gradually conformed to the views and regulations of international organizations.

THE EFFECTS OF CHINA'S MEMBERSHIP IN THE WORLD TRADE ORGANIZATION

Even an economically oriented organization such as the World Trade Organization (WTO), which China entered in 2002, may act as a restraint on China's human rights abuses. The threat of public shaming can be used in the WTO, as it has been used in the HRC, to bring China's domestic conditions more into conformity with international standards. Participation in the WTO requires following norms of behavior, such as transparency and legal procedures in doing business, though they are not directly related to human rights. In addition, the greater access of the new information technologies to China's mar-kets may indirectly foster the cause of human rights in China. The technologies—computers, the Internet, faxes, cellular phones, pagers, and phone messaging—have already made it more difficult to suppress groups attempting to organize efforts to assert their rights. One reason why the Chinese government had such difficulty in repressing the meditation group the Falun Gong, which it calls "an evil cult," was that its members used these new technologies to organize protests, spread information, and maintain contacts with their colleagues abroad as well as in China. Membership in the WTO will make available even more advanced technologies and organizational tools to those Chi-nese seeking to assert their political and religious rights. Also, China's increasing role in the twenty-first century as the "factory of the world" may lead in time to better treatment of its workers. Although most international businesses have not brought pressure on China to improve work conditions in the factories making their products, a few have set an example, such as Nike and Reebok. In the late 1990s these corporations, in meeting their own standards and bending to pressure from their U.S. customers, began to monitor the safety and treatment of workers in the Chinese plants.

U.S. Monitoring of China's Human Rights Abuses

Monitoring through MFN Treatment

Although China is less responsive to U.S. monitoring of its human rights abuses than to monitoring by multilateral organizations, that does not mean that unilateral pressure is totally ineffective. As was the case with the Soviet Union, the U.S. threat to remove China's MFN trading status if it did not improve its human rights record was the most conspicuous domestic effort to influence China's human rights conditions. The threat waxed and waned not only in relation to China's rights abuses but also because of U.S. domestic politics. The first Bush administration attempted to stabilize U.S.-Sino relations shortly after June 4 by sending high-level officials to meet with Chinese leaders. This conciliatory mission became a campaign issue in the 1992 presidential campaign, as Clinton condemned Bush's policy of "coddling dictators." Consequently, Clinton came into office committed to a policy of promoting human rights in China, which included reemphasis on linking renewal of MFN to China's human rights record. Although midway through his first term Clinton shifted his emphasis to improving economic relations with China, initially the Clinton administration appeared to be interested primarily in civil and political rights, especially the freedoms of speech, religion, and association.

As it did before the yearly meetings of the HRC, China would time the release of some well-known political prisoners around the impending annual congressional vote on MFN renewal on that portentous date of June 3. China's release in spring 1994 of the two major "black hands" behind the 1989 Tiananmen demonstration was timed around the MFN debate in Congress as well as the HRC meeting. But other than the release of well-known political prisoners, the linkage of MFN to China's human rights record had little impact on China's overall human rights behavior. At the same time, the MFN issue evoked a powerful U.S. business lobby working to delink MFN status from China's human rights record. Despite his campaign rhetoric, great pressure from the business community and the release of political prisoners led Clinton to delink human rights issues from MFN renewal. Nevertheless, with the support of a broad bipartisan right-to-left coalition in Congress, from Republican Jesse Helms in the Senate to Democratic Nancy Pelosi in the House of Representatives, the yearly debates on MFN continued, but they became a ritual without substance, what the Chinese would call a "paper tiger." Finally in 2000, owing to persistent pressure from the executive branch and the business community, China was granted Permanent Normal Trading Rights.

A different mechanism, therefore, was needed to replace the MFN yearly review of China's human rights practices. In place of the annual MFN debate, Congress established the U.S. Commission on China, which was to hold hearings and direct attention to the various human rights reports on China, issued during the year by the State Department and by various commissions and NGOs. Unlike with the annual MFN debate, the focus was directly on the issue of human rights, which also included China's labor and environmental abuses. The commission had its own staff and budget devoted exclusively to investigating and monitoring China's human rights abuses and bringing these abuses to public attention. It could also exert some economic pressure by urging that the World Bank and the International Monetary Fund condition loans on improvement of China's human rights record. Congress also established the U.S. Commission on International Religious Freedom. One of the commission's major tasks was to focus on China, specifically the persecution of Christians as well as meditation sects such as the Falun Gong. It also issued an annual report.

Another method for U.S.-China human rights interaction has been the establishment of formal mechanisms for bilateral dialogue between the U.S. State Department and China's Foreign Ministry. Though interrupted early in 2001 by the U.S. downing of a Chinese fighter plane, the dialogue resumed in December 2002 when the U.S.

assistant secretary of state for democracy, human rights, and labor visited China. Beijing announced that it would allow three UN human rights experts to report on the state of torture, arbitrary arrests, and religious freedom in China and committed itself to respond to their findings. Although a Tibetan activist in Sichuan was summarily executed, supposedly for a series of bomb blasts, shortly after that visit, the continuance of the bilateral dialogue demonstrated that the Chinese government has not been totally unresponsive to U.S. pressure on domestic human rights issues.

Use of State Visits

Presidential visits between China and the United States have been another way of eliciting human rights concessions and influencing China's views and actions on human rights. Before Jiang Zemin's visit to the United States in October 1997, the Clinton administration sought to exact pledges from China to improve its human rights performance. During the visit Jiang made several statements that acknowledged the interconnection between economic rights and political rights. At a luncheon on October 30, 1997, hosted by the National Committee on U.S.-China Relations, the Council on Foreign Relations, and the Asia Society, Jiang talked about China's traditional respect for humane values: "Nothing holds more value and is more dignified in the universe than human beings. These ideas advocated by ancient sages have deep-seated influence in Chinese society." He repeated the Chinese political mantra that the Chinese people at present have never had such extensive human rights, which he defined as sovereign, economic, and cultural rights, and that China's human rights will evolve with the nation's economic and cultural development. Nevertheless, he concluded that "the seeds of human rights and democracy can be found in the classics over 2,000 years ago. 'A ruler prospers when he has popular support, perishes without it.' These ideas as well as Western ideas of human rights and democracy have helped develop contemporary Chinese people's ideas of human rights and values. China respects the Universal Declaration of Human Rights."[19] Immediately after Jiang's return to China, the most outspoken leader of the Democracy Wall movement of 1978–79, Wei Jingsheng, was released from prison and exiled to the United States.

Then, just before Clinton's visit to China in June 1998, Wang Dan, the coleader of the Tiananmen demonstrations, was released from prison and exiled to the United States. At Beijing University, Clinton talked about human rights in a speech that was translated and televised nationally on China's state television station, CCTV. In that speech, Clinton praised the great accomplishment of the Chinese people on acquiring economic rights, but he cautioned that such rights could not be sustained without political rights. In an impromptu press conference also broadcast on national television, Clinton urged Jiang to engage in dialogue with the Dalai Lama. Clinton's visit was also a factor in getting China's signature on the UN Covenant on Civil and Political Rights, which China signed in October 1998. In 2002, after Jiang Zemin's visit to George W. Bush's ranch in Crawford, Texas, China released Xu Wenli, a Democracy Wall and China Democracy Party leader. Xu had spent sixteen years in prison and was the first prisoner to be released who had been convicted of "endangering state security." He went into exile in the United States.

Thus, both U.S. and Chinese presidents have used their official visits to win concessions and state publicly their positions on human rights to each other's populations.

NGOs AND INTEREST GROUPS

Human rights NGOs, business lobbies, labor unions, and academia are also major actors helping to shape U.S. policy on China's human rights. NGOs in the United States have formed around various issues of human rights: Human Rights Watch/Asia, for example, focuses on a broad range of human rights issues, including political dissent, labor exploitation, and environmental damage. Amnesty International is also active in calling attention to human rights abuses in China, as it did in November 2002 when it listed the names of thirty-three cyber-dissidents who had been arrested for using the Internet to spread their political views. A unit of the AFL-CIO publishes a newsletter that focuses on labor abuses in China. Other NGOs have formed around specific areas such as religious freedom, legal reform, Tibet, Xinjiang, and forced sterilization and abortion.

Steven Teles points out that while public opinion may be shaped by interest groups, public opinion also shapes the environment in which these groups operate.[20] To counter the institutional interests of the executive branch of government, business groups and think tanks concerned with trade and strategic-military issues, human rights groups, and labor unions, primarily the AFL-CIO, have mobilized and maintained a high level of public concern on China's human rights abuses and labor exploitation. These groups lobby Congress and keep the issues alive in the media and in public forums. But it was not until the closing days of the Cold War and the televised crackdown on the Tiananmen demonstrators on June 4, 1989, that human rights NGOs attracted the attention of the media, which gave priority to condemnation of China's human rights abuses by human rights groups and by Chinese human rights advocates in exile in the United States.

The impact of NGOs and the televised June 4 crackdown is revealed in the results of Gallup polls. One poll taken in early 1989 showed that 72 percent of the U.S. public had a favorable attitude toward China; but in August 1989, 58 percent of Americans held unfavorable views. Such hostility has moderated slightly since 1989, but as of June 1997, 50 percent of Americans still held an unfavorable opinion of China and viewed China as a potential "threat" to the United States. In December 1993, 65 percent of Americans wanted China to improve its human rights record in order to continue trading with the United States. In 1997, 67 percent supported linkage between trade and human rights.[21] Teles concludes that the post–June 4 hostile view of China set the limits within which policymakers could operate. Moreover, China is given more attention than countries with even worse human rights records, such as Burma and Nigeria, because China is a more significant global player.

Thus, U.S. media concerned with human rights issues, the rhetorical skills of human rights advocates and exiled Chinese dissidents, and the effect of public opinion on Congress mean that there is pressure from below for monitoring and criticizing China's human rights abuses.[22] Since the September 11, 2001, terrorist attack on the United States, however, it appears that general U.S. hostility toward China has moderated because of the greater fear in the United States of Islamic radicalism. Moreover, soon after September 11, the United States and China joined together to fight terrorism. In fact, the United States in 2002 acknowledged that China has a legitimate right to crack down

on a group of Uighurs in northwest China, whom the Chinese consider to be Islamic separatists and accuse of engaging in terrorism.

Unlike U.S. NGOs, China's NGOs, which must be attached to
a governmental institution and registered with the Ministry of Civil
Affairs, primarily reinforce Chinese government policies. Consequently, Westerners call them GONGOs (government NGOs). As with
the social groups that formed in China in the late nineteenth and early
twentieth centuries, Chinese citizens in the late twentieth century
formed voluntary organizations to deal with social needs that either are
not funded or are ignored by the state, such as protecting the environment, improving rural education, and helping battered women.[23]
Unlike the East European and Soviet NGOs in the 1980s that explicitly challenged the Leninist party state, the Chinese NGOs generally
cooperate with the state and conform to Chinese government policy.

The Chinese government has established a number of GONGOs
to deal with the issue of human rights. Unlike with Western human
rights NGOs, their mandate is not to monitor the human rights situation in their county but rather to defend their government's view on
human rights and engage in official human rights dialogues with Western countries and academics. One of the first and most important of
these groups is the Chinese Society for the Study of Human Rights, established in 1993 and headed by Zhu Muzhi, the retired former director
of the Xinhua News Agency and a former official of the Communist
Party's Propaganda Department. Establishment of the society, which
acts as an interlocutor with Western human rights NGOs, reflects
official Chinese acceptance of NGO participation in international
human rights discourse. While Zhu still emphasized the primary significance of the rights of development and subsistence in a speech
given at the Norwegian Nobel Institute in Oslo in June 1997, he also
acknowledged the existence of individual rights: "Some countries in
the West stress democracy is an individual's right to express one's
views and pursue personal interests. We believe individual rights are
certainly not something that can be dispensed with, but they are not
the entire embodiment of democracy."[24] Most important, the society
convened scores of symposia and published scores of books and articles
written by society members and by government officials on the topic
of human rights. In February 2002 it began publishing a bimonthly

international journal on human rights, in Chinese and English, to promote understanding in the rest of the world of China's views on human rights.

By the mid-1990s at least a dozen institutions were doing research on human rights, including major centers at several of China's most prestigious academic institutions, such as Chinese People's University in Beijing and the Chinese Academy of Social Sciences' Institute of Political Science and Institute of Law. They, too, have issued a plethora of publications on the topic of human rights. To counter the U.S. State Department yearly reports on China's human rights conditions, since 1991 China has issued biannual white papers on human rights, with input from GONGOs and academia. China's white papers usually stress the improving conditions in China, which they contrast with the deteriorating human rights conditions in the United States, especially in its inner cities. GONGOs and academics likewise play an active role in spreading and interpreting China's white papers.

Among their tasks, human rights GONGOs and China's human rights experts are to respond to Western criticism of China's human rights record at international conferences. Yet despite their specific responsibilities, within the official parameters of permissible debate, several of them have challenged the government's view on human rights, such as the official view that human rights are granted by the state. For example, Li Buyun, a researcher in the Chinese Academy of Social Sciences and editor of *Studies in Law*, stated in a 1996 article that human rights "exist objectively in the real world prior to being recognized and protected by law." He asserted that human rights are inherent in human nature and one need not wait to achieve socioeconomic or subsistence rights before one has political and civil rights, especially the right of freedom of speech and association.[25] Other scholars joined in this discussion and sought to prove that the concept of human rights was not just a Western or twentieth-century idea; its sources, they asserted, can be traced back to Chinese tradition. One of them, Xia Yong, the associate director of the Institute of Law at the Chinese Academy of Social Sciences (CASS), noted the compatibility between human rights and Chinese tradition. He argued that human rights should not be regarded as only a Western bourgeois slogan. "Even though historically China had no ideology of human rights, within traditional Chinese ideology there were undoubtedly concepts such as the need for moral law and the equality of persons which went beyond the existing laws of that time."[26] Furthermore, "In attempting to redress any injustice, the common people enjoyed the right to beat drums in court and lodge complaints against perceived injustices (that is, petition to the higher authorities)."[27]

One consequence of opening up discussion on human rights in China, therefore, has been the emergence of views in the intellectual establishment that differ from the official government view on human rights. Despite the specific message the Chinese government seeks to convey, the various human rights activities in GONGOs, universities, and institutes have nurtured the blooming of a "hundred flowers" on human rights in various articles, conferences, and publications.[28] Some of the proceedings of these discussions were published, even in the Communist Party's major papers, including its official mouthpiece, the *People's Daily*. Though most of the discussants generally agreed that state sovereignty cannot be undermined and that human rights reflect a particular country's specific history and values, China's human rights experts presented a variety of views that indirectly question the government's view on human rights.

As a result, a substantial domestic constituency for acceptance of the concept of universal human rights has developed, ranging from political activists seeking to set up an opposition party to scholars writing in the mainstream media about the need for civil and political rights. Most of the activists have been suppressed, but establishment scholars, lawyers, and members of the GONGOs continue wide-ranging research, engage in exchanges with one another and with scholars in Western countries, and exert some influence on China's government leaders. Several establishment intellectuals, for example, helped persuade the government that the two UN covenants were compatible with China's laws and values and encouraged China's leadership to sign them.[29] At the same time, a small but important group of intellectuals have raised a new challenge from within the establishment. They emphasize that human rights are natural rights, as opposed to the official view that human rights are given and regulated by the state, and they regard political rights as being as important as economic rights. At a conference on the fiftieth anniversary of the UN Universal

Declaration of Human Rights, political scientist Liu Junning, like a number of other young scholars, asserted that "individual rights belong to the individual and not to one's country and are not to be infringed upon by one's country."[30]

Thus, China's exchanges and contacts with the United States and other Western countries have been important conduits for informing the views of China's scholars and GONGOs on human rights. In 1999, for example, Xin Chunying, the acting director of the Institute of Law and the Institute of Political Science of CASS, spent the fall semester at Yale Law School, where she worked on issues of human rights with members of the Yale faculty. Xin had played an important role in drawing up Jiang Zemin's speech on the fiftieth anniversary of the Universal Declaration of Human Rights in December 1998, in which he repeatedly stressed the connection between economic and political rights. The U.S. and Chinese governments should encourage more engagement between human rights experts in both countries through scholarly exchanges, study abroad, joint projects, and conferences.

RESULTS

The variety of measures that the United States has employed to influence China's conception and practice of human rights has been more successful in modifying China's conception of human rights than in moderating China's human rights practices.

1. The most effective method for achieving these limited results has been through China's participation in international forums, particularly the HRC. It is impossible to evaluate to what degree the threat of public shaming in the international community at the yearly HRC meetings has deterred or prevented even greater Chinese abuse of human rights. Nevertheless, China's active participation in the HRC marks an important shift in the People's Republic because it acknowledges the legitimacy of international monitoring of human rights practices and has helped bring China's view of human rights more into conformity with that of the international community.

2. China's need to respond to public charges of human rights abuses, both in the HRC and from Western nations, specifically the United States, has spawned a corps of human rights experts in China, of whom a small but influential number are leading the way in trying to update China's views and bring China's domestic practices into line with international standards. By including a variety of China's human rights experts in discussions and forums on human rights with Western experts, international norms of human rights practices have penetrated circles beyond official-dom and have evoked interest within China's academic, think tank, intellectual, and dissident communities.

3. U.S. pressure exerted by Congress, bilateral human rights discussions, presidential visits, U.S. NGOs, and the media have resulted in the release of well-known political prisoners, but they have not necessarily changed China's overall human rights behavior. Nevertheless, the U.S. State Department's annual country reports on human rights and the yearly debates in Congress, at least until 2001, when China received Permanent Normal Trading Rights, have forced China to respond to criticisms of its human rights behavior.

4. Because the threats of economic sanctions, such as the U.S. withdrawal of MFN, have not been implemented, it is difficult to know the impact of economic sanctions on limiting human rights abuses. Such threats become increasingly less effective as China becomes increasingly intertwined economically with Western nations.

5. Quiet human rights dialogue between China and the United States and with other Western countries at the governmental, NGO, and academic levels has not yielded significant results by itself, but as one of a number of different forms of pressure, particularly in conjunction with the threat of "public shaming" at the HRC, such dialogue has helped to secure the release of political prisoners, China's signing of the two UN covenants, and visits of the Red Cross to China's prisons. In December 2002 quiet dialogue led to an invitation to UN experts to report on the state of torture and arbitrary arrests and religious freedom in China.

Dialogue works when relations with the United States and China improve, as was the case after September 11, 2001.

6. In addition to presidential visits, bilateral visits by members of Congress and China's National People's Congress and by NGO members, lawyers, and scholars involved in human rights in each other's country are useful in focusing attention on the issue. Exchanges such as those funded by the Ford Foundation, the International Republican Institute on village elections, and the International Democratic Institute on legislative reform at the grassroots level also help engender gradual change. Though the "Rule of Law Initiative" to train judges and lawyers and provide technical aid for public education on legal rights, which Jiang Zemin and Bill Clinton had proposed in 1997, was not funded, private U.S. initiatives have begun, such as that of the Yale Law School on legal reform and the establishment of legal aid centers in China, which U.S. judges, including Justice Anthony Kennedy of the U.S. Supreme Court, have visited and given advice to. The European Union has launched similar joint projects. These efforts should be accelerated, expanded, and regularized

Despite the variety of methods for monitoring China's human rights abuses and promoting legal reforms, none has been particularly effective in changing China's human rights practices, though together they have slowly changed Chinese views of human rights. Moreover, China's participation in multilateral organizations has demonstrated that over time China grudgingly accepts some of the rules and regulations of such institutions, at least conceptually. Even though a resolution critical of China's human rights practices at the annual HRC meetings has passed only once, in the immediate aftermath of June 4, 1989, and then in its subcommission, this does not mean that presenting such a resolution each year has not been totally ineffective, as seen specifically in China's signature on the two covenants. While China's abuses are still egregious, though nothing on the scale of the Mao era, there is no way of knowing how much worse they might have been without the annual meetings of the HRC or without U.S. congressional, NGO, and international media criticism.

Pressure is more effective when the United States and the Western nations cooperate on tactics and goals; it is less effective when the United States acts alone. Even with nations cooperating, however, combined efforts have been halfhearted, not only because of the wavering of the Europeans for fear of impairing trade relations with China, but also because of U.S. concern that protests over human rights abuses may conflict with U.S. efforts to gain China's cooperation on strategic and economic interests. While pressure has not achieved significant results, a combination of multilateral and bilateral monitoring has had some impact. The desire of China's leaders to be seen as cooperative members of the international community has served as a constraint on their behavior. They are well aware that China's international reputation influences their access to foreign investment, modern technology, and trade opportunities as well as China's international stature.

The most successful U.S. methods for dealing with Chinese human rights abuse were exemplified in the Song Yongyi case. Song, a Chinese scholar living in the United States, had returned to China to collect materials on the Cultural Revolution that could be bought on the open market. He was arrested in August 1999 and charged with gathering secret information. As the Chinese demanded, the U.S. government worked for six months through dialogue and quiet diplomacy behind the scenes for Song's release. When the Chinese government in late December announced that Song would soon be brought to trial, it became clear that these behind-the-scenes methods were not working.

Efforts to save Song then went public; quiet engagement was transformed into open confrontation with the Chinese government. Loud and persistent protests came forth from Song's educational institution, Dickinson College, Song's lawyer, the human rights community, the Western media, and the U.S. Congress. One hundred fifty U.S. and Western sinologists signed and sent a petition to the Chinese leadership, warning that if Song were not released immediately, academic exchanges with China would be impaired. Added to this public pressure was the fact that China wanted to join the WTO and feared that the growing protest over Song's imprisonment would hurt its chances of receiving Permanent Normal Trading Rights, a condition for U.S. acceptance of China into the WTO. One month later Song was released.

One can say that the multifaceted public pressure from the U.S. government, the media, interest groups, and educational institutions in Europe and the United States made Song's release possible. But one can also say that Song's case was sui generis—Song was living in the United States, he was about to become a citizen, and the case occurred at a propitious time, when China sought Permanent Normal Trading Rights and entrance into the WTO. Moreover, despite the success of this individual case, as in the past, the release of political prisoners was not a prelude to a broader set of changes in China's human rights practices. In fact, the arrest of Chinese scholars who had worked abroad continued in China.

Comparisons with East Asian Neighbors and the Former Soviet Union

There is no assurance that China will follow the paths of its East Asian and post-Confucian neighbors, Taiwan and South Korea. The movement of these countries toward protection of political and civil rights as well as toward democracy, which took place almost three decades after their economic takeoffs, was facilitated by a leadership trained in the West and by persistent and strong U.S. pressure. The United States has much less leverage, however, with China than it had with Taiwan and South Korea, which are both under U.S. military protection. Moreover, most Chinese, the general population as well as the leadership, fear that political reform will produce the kind of disorder that has characterized the transition to democracy in the former Soviet Union. Fear of chaos, *luan*, has haunted China from time immemorial and has been another factor inhibiting the introduction of human rights and democratic institutions.

China's relative improvement in its human rights record in the post-Mao period has more to do with domestic changes than with external pressure. The reaction to the devastation and chaos of the Cultural Revolution and the softer authoritarian government that followed Mao's totalitarian rule (1949–76) have played a more direct role in moderating China's human rights abuses than outside pressure.

In fact, this moderating trend was interrupted and China's human rights record suddenly worsened in the final years of the twentieth century, just as China became increasingly integrated into the international community. The government arrested virtually all the leaders of the China Democracy Party, an opposition political party established in the fall of 1998, imprisoned scores of organizers of unofficial Christian churches and the leaders of the Falun Gong and other sects, and detained thousands of their followers. It reinforced its repression in Tibet and Xinjiang, particularly after September 11, 2001. And in the spring of 2000, it criticized and purged from CASS four prominent liberal intellectuals, among them Liu Junning, who had spoken on the subject of human rights.

Consequently, the United States introduced a strong resolution at the HRC critical of China's human rights abuses in April 2000 and lobbied several months before to get support for it. At the same time, Beijing's delegation in Geneva lobbied hard to ensure a no-action vote in order to prevent any substantive discussion on the resolution itself. The United States was unable to get any of its Western allies to join in sponsorship. Poland had contemplated cosponsorship but was threatened by China with economic repercussions and begged off at the last moment. Yet Poland cosponsored a resolution with the Czech Republic against Cuba's human rights abuses. Clearly China's economic clout was much greater than Cuba's. Although Washington's allies again joined with the United States in voting against the no-action resolution, no-action won by twenty-two to eighteen with twelve abstentions. Only one more country voted against the no-action resolution in 2000 than in 1999. Immediately after the vote, the Chinese representatives emphatically and repeatedly pointed out that the United States had been defeated nine times on this issue at the HRC.

Nevertheless, as long as China's human rights abuses continue —and they are in fact likely to increase as various social groups in China, such as the millions of discharged workers, unpaid pensioners from bankrupt state-owned industries, and tax-burdened peasants, express their grievances in potentially destabilizing protests—the United States is likely to continue to sponsor resolutions critical of China's human rights abuses at the HRC. And until China's political system changes, the threat of passage of such a resolution may be one of the few tactics preventing even worst abuses.

The fact that the Chinese government seems only slightly responsive to external pressures on human rights issues does not mean that such pressure does not have an effect. Much can be learned from the impact of external pressures on the Soviet Union. When the Soviet Union signed the Helsinki Accords in 1975, it acknowledged a generally accepted set of human rights norms, as China did when it signed the two UN covenants. The Soviets signed the accords in exchange for Western acceptance of post–World War II territorial arrangements in Eastern Europe. Although the Soviet government had no real intention of living up to the human rights provisions of the accords, the fact that the Soviet government had signed the accords and that the Helsinki Commission was established to monitor Soviet human rights abuses encouraged human rights activists in the Soviet Union and Eastern Europe to pressure their governments to live up to the provisions.

Thus, a country's recognition of shared values, even if only in theory, provides a useful tool for those within the country who seek to change its political practices. Also, greater knowledge about international norms provides a basis for comparison and creates internal pressures as such norms become better known. Soviet human rights advocates had memorized Paragraph 2 of Article 19 of the Covenant on Civil and Political Rights: "Everyone has the right to freedom of opinion and expression; this right includes freedom to hold opinions without interference and to seek, receive and impart information and ideas through any media and regardless of frontiers."[31] Similarly, those Chinese seeking political and religious rights in 1999, such as members of the China Democracy Party, organizers of independent labor unions, and the Falun Gong and other meditation and religious groups, similarly began to demand that their government abide by the covenants to which it is a signatory.

While the Soviet Union's signature on the Helsinki Accords helped undermine the Leninist regimes in the Soviet Union and Eastern Europe, progress was erratic and not clearly discernible at the time. It was not until the Gorbachev era in the second half of the 1980s that there was any definite improvement in human rights conditions in the Soviet Union. It may take even longer in China because of deeply embedded practices, but we already see that the international human rights regime is slowly having an impact in activating forces for change, both at the grassroots level and among advisers to the leadership. True civil, political, and religious rights, however, will not come until China introduces democratic political and legal institutions that can protect the freedoms of expression, association, and religion, as stipulated in China's constitution.

External condemnations of China's human rights abuses, therefore, may not have much of an impact on the behavior of the Chinese government, but they help alter international expectations and encourage domestic human rights advocates. Because of China's acceptance of international norms of human rights, violations are no longer treated entirely as a matter of sovereign prerogative. Without such acceptance, it is likely that China's behavior would be even more repressive.

SYMBOL OR SUBSTANCE?

Although China's leaders have incorporated international standards, derived from participation in international organizations, generally their learning has been more symbolic than substantive. Furthermore, China's conscious incorporation has not significantly moderated its human rights abuses. Nevertheless, as shown in the Soviet case, international pressure evokes symbolic concessions, which, even if they are used as bargaining chips or for short-term tactical reasons, can have a profound domestic impact. It is too early to know if the same will hold true in China. So far, China's symbolic gestures have hardly addressed China's systemic violation of human rights and persecution of political dissidents and unofficial religious believers. While China's symbolic acquiescence to international human rights norms has been a long and tedious process, because of China's desire to participate in the international community and achieve international respectability, it has gradually accepted such basic international human rights procedures.

There is still, however, a clear disconnect between China's acceptance of international human rights norms and its domestic human rights practices. The United States, in conjunction with the

European Union, should focus on a handful of specific measures that, if fulfilled, could add substance to China's symbolic gestures. International pressure should be used

- to encourage the National People's Congress to ratify the UN Covenant on Civil and Political Rights;
- to dismantle China's system of "reeducation through labor," which allows officials arbitrarily to sentence political dissidents and noncertified religious believers to labor camps for up to three years without judicial review;
- to expand cooperative efforts to promote legal training, such as training programs for Chinese judges, lawyers, and legal aid workers;
- to open up Tibet and Xinjiang to regular access by UN human rights agencies, the press, and independent monitors and to urge that China negotiate with the Dalai Lama and reduce its repression of the Uighurs in Xinjiang; and
- to encourage the U.S. government and NGOs to put pressure on Americans doing business in China to establish codes of labor conduct and environmental protection, similar to the Sullivan Principles they helped implement in South Africa.

While such reforms will take a long time and may not show results right away, they are already being discussed in China and the United States and between the two countries.

Clearly, it is difficult to monitor a large power in a noncrisis situation, especially a power with considerable international economic and strategic clout. Unlike the internal human rights crisis sparked by June 4, ongoing, systematic abuse of human rights is much more difficult to deal with externally, especially when there are other, equally important, interests in the relationship, as there are between the United States and China. In such a situation, it should be possible to find ways to cooperate with the country on common interests, such as establishing the rule of law, while at the same time confronting it on human rights abuses.

While the United States should not seek to determine the nature of the Chinese regime, it is in the U.S. interest that China adhere to international norms of human rights as much as to other international norms. China has demonstrated normative learning in response to both internal and external pressures and has made a number of symbolic concessions to international human rights norms. External pressure has helped to move China in this direction, but the only way in which China's symbolic human rights actions will acquire substance, and learning become practice, is through domestic political reforms that can be carried out only by the Chinese themselves.

NOTES

1. Minxin Pei, "Creeping Democratization," *China Journal of Democracy* 6, no. 4 (October 1995).

2. Minxin Pei, "Citizens vs. Mandarins: Administrative Litigation in China," *China Quarterly*, no. 152 (December 1997).

3. Minxin Pei, personal communication with the author, March 3, 2003.

4. Lianjiang Li and Kevin O'Brien, "The Struggle over Village Elections," in *The Paradox of China's Post-Mao Reforms*, ed. Merle Goldman and Roderick Macfarquhar (Cambridge, Mass.: Harvard University Press, 1999), 129–144.

5. Murray Scot Tanner, *The Politics of Lawmaking in Post-Mao China* (New York: Oxford University Press, 1998).

6. Andrew Nathan, "Political Rights in Chinese Constitutions," in *Human Rights in Contemporary China*, ed. R. Randle Edwards, Louis Henkin, and Andrew Nathan (New York: Columbia University Press, 1986), 120.

7. Ibid., 117.

8. Ann Kent, *China, the United Nations, and Human Rights: The Limits of Compliance* (Philadelphia: University of Pennsylvania Press, 1999).

9. Marina Swenson, *The Chinese Conception of Human Rights* (Lund, Sweden: Lund University, Department of East Asian Languages, 1996); and *Debating Human Rights in China* (London: Rowman and Littlefield, 2002).

10. Sumner Twiss, "Confucian Contributions to the Universal Declaration of Human Rights: A Historical and Philosophical Perspective" (unpublished paper).

11. Kent, *China, the United Nations, and Human Rights*, 44.

12. Xinhua News Agency, August 9, 1996, as reported in Summary of World Broadcasts, F 2688, G1.

13. Ibid.

14. Ibid., 178.

15. Kent, *China, the United Nations, and Human Rights*, 50.

16. Ibid., 61.

17. Ibid., 235.

18. Kent, *China, the United Nations, and Human Rights*, 237.

19. Jiang Zemin, speech to the National Committee of U.S.-China Relations, Council of Foreign Relations, and the Asia Society, Washington, D.C., October 30, 1997.

20. Steven Teles, "Public Opinion and Interest Groups in Making U.S.-China Policy," in *After the Cold War* (Armonk, N.Y.: M. E. Sharpe, 1998), 40.

21. Ibid., 44–45.

22. Ibid., 55.

23. See Tony Saich, "Negotiating the State: The Development of Social Organizations in China," *China Quarterly*, no. 161 (March 2000): 124–141.

24. Xinhua News Agency, June 11 1997, FBIS-CHI 97-162.

25. *China Rights Forum* (winter 1999–2000): 30.

26. Xia Yong, "Rights and Traditions," in *Streetlife China* (Cambridge: Cambridge University Press), 24.

27. Ibid., 24–25.

28. Kent, *China, the United Nations, and Human Rights*, 151–153.

29. Members of the Institute of Law and the Institute of Politics of CASS, interviews by author, China and United States, 1999.

30. Liu Junning, "Summary Record of the Panel for the Celebration of the Fiftieth Anniversary of the Universal Declaration of Human Rights," ed. Xia Yong, *Gong Fa* (Public Law) 1 (1999): 324–327.

31. Interviews with Soviet human rights activists in the United States.

5

Missing the Point

Human Rights in U.S.-Pakistan Relations

PAULA R. NEWBERG

I N OCTOBER 1999 GENERAL PERVEZ MUSHARRAF led a coup d'état
that returned Pakistan to military rule after just over a decade of
elected governments. The army had never really left politics: for a
half century, Pakistan's political history has repeated a pattern of on-
again, off-again civil-military governance that has compromised the
shape of military engagement, the scope of political participation, and
the nature of South Asia's foreign policies. Musharraf's coup d'état
occurred after Indian and Pakistani nuclear tests in 1998 (which
prompted sanctions from several Western countries), as distaste for
Afghanistan's unending conflict was growing, and amid fears that
Southwest Asia's involvement in narcotics and arms trafficking would
endanger Asia's march toward global prosperity.

This overlay of complex issues colored the international response to the army's appropriation of power and, as has happened so
often in the past, left to the side some of the most important problems
that Pakistani citizens face in their daily duels with a brittle, heavy-
handed state. Misrule, whether civilian or military, has reinforced the
traditional political elite, accentuated class divisions that have left

Pakistan at the distant periphery of a rapidly changing global economy, underlined the army's self-proclaimed role as guardian of the state, and inhibited political change. Authoritarianism, whether dressed in civilian or military garb, has treated civil society as a threat, constrained civil debate, and hardened political discourse. And because its strategic location has placed the country squarely in the ambit of superpower policies, Pakistan's capacity to develop its political resources at its own pace, and to think and act autonomously, has often been weak and misguided.

Pakistan credits its dependencies to insecurity; external powers frequently credit its insecurities to self-defeating domestic intransigence. When U.S. and Pakistani interests converge, they generally do so unequally; when they diverge, Pakistan is rarely able to counter U.S. power; and when Pakistan sets off on its own, it generally annoys almost everyone that it needs without satisfying itself. The overall relationship is without trust: Pakistan and the United States call each other allies but have turned each other into enemies. Nonetheless, Pakistan's governments—whether elected, selected, or imposed—have often sought external validation for their antidemocratic practices, and their favored patron has long been the United States. For this reason, the texture of U.S.-Pakistan relations has been an essential element in the evolution of Pakistan's human rights environment. Equally important, the absence of a serious U.S. human rights policy toward Pakistan has deeply influenced Pakistani politics and public policy since the 1970s.

Although ideologies and actors have changed frequently and dramatically in both the United States and Pakistan since the end of the 1971 Bangladesh war, U.S. policy has consistently allowed—and, more damagingly, at times encouraged—rights to be traded off in its dealings with Pakistan in three related ways. First, Cold War policies favored an autocratic military that limited rights protections in far-reaching ways; the same policies helped to create a diplomatic environment of mistrust on issues related to democracy and rights by defining away the centrality of rights in securing democratic stability. Second, post–Cold War policies have continued patterns of reward and sanction: although they trade off different goods, they still treat other diplomatic discussions as more important than rights. U.S. foreign

policy is often thought to work against rights protections by continuing to empower those least concerned about rights in Pakistan—
but the United States is also quick to blame Pakistan for the weaknesses of its governance institutions. And third, the absence of rights-
respecting regimes in Pakistan has created enormous problems for
Pakistan's closest diplomatic interlocutors and has contributed to an
environment of pervasive regional insecurity.

Human rights protections in Pakistan have always been about
the concurrent, if contradictory, demands of domestic and foreign policies, as seen primarily from the vantage point of power holders and
seekers rather than that of civil society. Like public policy as a whole,
human rights are about what the state and its leaders can afford to do
and afford to ignore. The calculations of leaders have often been at
odds with those of citizens, leaving military rulers unable fully to govern and civilian political leaders rarely able to handle the frustrating
requirements of a postcolonial, praetorian state with an evolving nuclear capacity.

Since the mid-1970s, U.S. global policies have ostensibly
embraced the protection of rights and the promotion of democracy.
But as the U.S.-Pakistan relationship has grown more intricate and
less flexible, rights have become at best one small talking point in
lengthy, often recriminatory diplomatic discussions whose focus is
generally only nearby or next door. The color and texture of the U.S.-
Pakistan relationship—habitually rights-disregarding, paying indirect
homage to ideals removed from political reality—have been far more
important to Pakistan's human rights practices than specific rights-
regarding policies or occasional interventions. In the pursuit of short-
term self-interest on both sides, the results have been dismal: state
power in Pakistan now almost inevitably embraces rights violations,
by design or disregard; and the demands of U.S. foreign policy require
Pakistan to centralize power, minimize dissent, and reinforce imbalances in the economy, polity, and society. The challenge, with yet
another military ruler in Islamabad, is daunting. U.S. policy toward
Pakistan requires a different focus if rights are to be protected and
democracy is to thrive, a different way to do business in and with Pakistan, and the sensitivity to step aside when others can support rights
more credibly and effectively.

Setting the Post-Bangladesh Stage

In 1973 the Pakistan parliament endorsed a new constitution to establish parliamentary rule, maintain civilian control over the armed forces, and provide a foundation for democracy. The 1973 constitution was a retrospective political document as much as an instrument to organize state power. It was intended to remove vestiges of colonial rule; correct the abuses of military rule; repair the political devastation of a civil war that reduced the country's population by half; reinforce the power of central government by reducing habitually contentious interprovincial relations and thus strengthen borders with Iran, China, India, and Afghanistan; and enfranchise populations whose poverty coincided with powerlessness. Prime Minister Zulfikar Ali Bhutto's Pakistan People's Party (PPP) articulated state policy through a triad of ideologies—Islam, socialism, democracy—and its programs through a triad of welfare provisions—*roti, kapra, aur makan* (bread, clothing, housing)—that quickly recentralized power while appearing to broaden political participation.

This short period of constitutional rule, which ended with a coup d'état led by General Mohammed Zia ul Haq in 1977 (and Bhutto's execution in 1979), encapsulated important regional political changes. By the time the Soviet army arrived in Afghanistan in December 1979, South and Southwest Asia had shifted political focus: socialist democracy was waning; so-called Western models of political behavior were overturned or discredited in Pakistan and neighboring Iran; the Afghan monarchy was superseded by a sequence of unstable Soviet-backed communist governments; political corruption was highlighted by the trial of India's prime minister, Indira Gandhi; and OPEC-backed pan-Islamism helped to finance Pakistan's nuclear explorations. In 1980 military rule flowered: General Zia fully abrogated the 1973 constitution and, through the inadvertent good graces of the Politburo's Afghan intervention, received Western and Islamic backing to militarize the state and refocus Pakistan's foreign policy.

In 1973 the U.S. Congress passed laws to anchor human rights in U.S. foreign policy. In 1976 Congress required the U.S. government to report on human rights conditions in aid-receiving countries and modify the provision of bilateral assistance to rights-violating governments; in quick succession, it instructed U.S. policymakers to take parallel actions regarding the use of multilateral development funds and overseas investment insurance. These laws were as much about regaining congressional initiative in foreign policy as they were about protecting rights in foreign countries, and they provoked continuing tussles about accountability in foreign policy. Pakistan was not a major focus of U.S. human rights concern in the early Carter years, even though Bhutto maintained his rule with frequent, often crass, violations of individual rights and democratic process. Pakistan's nuclear program led the United States to invoke sanctions in 1976, leaving human rights problems to the side in U.S.-Pakistan relations. In its last year the Carter administration was beset by problems in Iran that spilled over into U.S. policies toward Pakistan and Afghanistan. The administration's search for an elusive regional stability ignored the importance of rights-protecting governance as an anchor for workable regional policies.

The 1977 coup d'état returned rights to the U.S.-Pakistan agenda, but relatively superficially. U.S. impatience with the Zia regime generally, and with its belligerent pro-nuclear policies more specifically, turned Pakistan into a sideshow in Washington's increasingly complicated foreign policy. By skillfully managing Pakistan's proximity to Afghanistan and coyly playing to the concerns of the Reagan administration, General Zia ul Haq set Pakistan near the center of U.S. interests by making it fundamental to the anti-Soviet war in Afghanistan. Pakistan's early counterpoint to evolving U.S. human rights policy—low priority because bombs are more important—was repoliticized once the Cold War landed in Afghanistan's lap—lower priority because the Afghans were important proxies for the Soviets. During the 1980s the U.S.-Pakistan relationship left human rights problems in Pakistan virtually untouched. The regional paradox—a massive war that Afghans believed was waged to regain them their rights was pursued by ensuring a military regime in Pakistan that held power only by denying rights to Pakistanis—is one that continues today. Indeed, this paradox was renewed after the U.S.-led coalition renewed fighting in Afghanistan in 2001 and strengthened its relationship to Pakistan's military government in order to pursue its new antiterrorism strategies.

Two Decades of Limited Rights and Constrained Policy

Bhutto's PPP government justified political harassment under the aegis of populist ideology and state-led development. Bhutto's opponents were persecuted, minority sects were disenfranchised, and organized dissent among politicians in the northwest Frontier Province and tribal rebels in Baluchistan province was dealt with harshly. The 1973 constitution was gradually amended to remove rights rather than expand them, and Bhutto showed little mercy when he interfered with courts and judges. Supporters of the military justified General Zia's 1977 coup by pointing to the civilian government's unsustainable pattern of rights abuse. But the international community's reaction to the army's unconstitutional appropriation of power was more serious than its tepid response to inequities under PPP rule. General Zia was shunned for his attachment to military rule and stern Islamic injunction until the Soviet army appeared in Afghanistan. After a brief interlude, in which he spurned President Carter's minimalist assistance offer, General Zia was able to step into the growing global engagement in Afghanistan armed with U.S. economic and military aid, and to fashion Pakistan as a linchpin in the long battle for Afghanistan.

Martial Law

The story of the Afghanistan war is often recited in Washington, in Islamabad, and in Rawalpindi's army headquarters as a morality tale justified by its end: the decline and fall of the Soviet empire as a result, in part, of the Afghanistan war. But human rights practices, and policy responses to them, concentrate far more on the means used to achieve that end. From 1980, when General Zia promulgated a Provisional Constitutional Order that ended constitutional government and proscribed judicial challenges to military rule, until 1986, when he was forced to return to very limited, titular representative government, Pakistan lived in a human rights vacuum. Imprisonment and torture were common, political organizing was proscribed, the rule of law was replaced by a regime of ordinances and regulations, and personal privacy was severely circumscribed. Pakistan's politics—with all its divisions and inequalities—moved underground and into exile, leaving only occasional protest against rights violations as a weak form of public engagement. The military used force to maintain quietude, with little regard for individual or community freedoms, and was rewarded with funds to help centralize both the provision of aid to Afghanistan and the imposition of order on civil society. Billions of dollars of official aid went to and through Pakistan as part of the war effort, and billions more were spent unofficially.

Through this period, the requirements of U.S. human rights law were waived. Sections 503(b) and 116(a–e) of the Foreign Assistance Act allowed Congress and the executive branch to ignore or sideline rights abuses in the pursuit of overriding foreign policy objectives. Both did so with relative ease; later, antinuclear sanctions were also waived in order to pursue the Afghan war. Although State Department reporting on rights violations increased in sophistication during the 1980s, Pakistan was not singled out for reconsideration, and the efforts of U.S.- and European-based human rights organizations to draw attention to Pakistan were politely rebuffed. Rarely, an individual case merited attention in Washington or the U.S. embassy in Islamabad. U.S. human rights groups brought Pakistani cases to Washington, but they received real, if strikingly limited, attention only after funds had been committed to provide Stinger missiles to Afghanistan and after General Zia formally lifted martial law in 1986.

The overall effect of this policy environment could be quickly seen in two related ways. First, General Zia was able to tighten control after 1980 precisely because he had external support—not necessarily or directly for repression, but certainly for pursuing goals that made repression a likely form of governance and a concern only for those directly affected by it. Second, political space in the United States was not made seriously available for discussions of Pakistan's problems until they were no longer perceived to compete with U.S. regional and global security policies. And until late 1986, when the Human Rights Commission of Pakistan was inaugurated, no locally based organizations were able to help individuals redress grievances: bar associations had few, if any, powers, and lawyers were as frequently found in jail as in court. General Zia was protected by the silence that surrounded empty courtrooms and full prisons, and by decisions in

Washington, Riyadh, and Beijing to support the Afghan mujahideen at the cost of Pakistani civil liberties.

The formal lifting of martial law allowed some space for political debate—although even the PPP failed to discuss rights issues until they became a useful tool to gain recognition and power—but institutional practices made rights abuse easy to continue. The army was rewarded for its martial law work, financially and politically. Decommissioned soldiers became overzealous policemen, little oversight governed law enforcement bodies, and General Zia's policy of divide and rule—among political parties, religious sects, and interest groups—helped to foment violence among parties and deflect violence away from the state. Lifting martial law came at a high price. Early in 1985 a parliament was elected under restrictive rules that were further tightened before the assembly took office. Consisting primarily of traditional, practiced politicians willing to compromise on matters of political structure, it agreed to far-reaching constitutional amendments at the end of 1985 to facilitate the lifting of martial law. These amendments severely compromised democratic progress long after General Zia was killed in 1988. Zia himself was of mixed mind about Pakistan's political future. Shortly before he died, he dismissed Prime Minister Mohammed Khan Junejo, reconsidered the political value of national elections, and speculated openly about concentrating, rather than devolving, power.

The political cost for Pakistan of the anti-Soviet war was even higher. Almost all the immediate problems of Pakistani political life in the 1990s were exacerbated by the Afghan war. Narcotics and arms trades, sectarian violence, renewed border disputes, and a state organized around control rather than representation—all became the hallmarks of post-Zia political society. Corruption, the structural distortions of army rule, and external debt were combined with macroeconomic incentives (and disincentives) that still contribute to an intermittent fiscal crisis. General Zia's eleven-year rule set the stage for regional instability as well. Afghanistan was then and, in different ways, still remains captive to Pakistan's interests and its self-defeating policies toward Kabul. The accumulation of rights abuses in both Afghanistan and Pakistan and the inability of both states to rise above violence to protect their citizens have joined the two countries in a shared political misery. These trends were predicted by antimilitary observers in the early and mid-1980s but rarely heeded in Pakistan or abroad.

Transition, Round One

The last eighteen months of General Zia's rule witnessed a weak transition—military-led government dressed in civilian clothing— that offered limited but unaccustomed space for free association and expression. Nongovernmental organizations and newspapers tentatively tested the new climate. General Mirza Aslam Beg's decision to allow party-based elections after General Zia's death—a policy sanctioned by President Ghulam Ishaq Khan and later validated by the courts—hinted at an end to some of the political assumptions and practices of the previous decade. The first terms of Prime Ministers Benazir Bhutto and Mian Nawaz Sharif signaled the real transition from military to civilian government. Between 1988 and 1993 each sought to accomplish transition in different ways.

Bhutto, a self-styled representative of the antimilitary establishment, tried to take on the military retrospectively, but she found her government confined at every turn by a political agenda, state apparatus, financial organization, and civil society that was acceptable—if only barely—to the military guardians of the state. The PPP government tried to do everything at once, including reviewing all military sentences, judicial appointments, and rights abuses. Its efforts to repair the depredations of martial law were effective to the degree that it did not fully confront the foundations of praetorianism or challenge the habits of military patronage. Its authority, however, was limited by the bargains it struck to retain power and its intolerance for those who eschewed the icons of PPP history or disagreed with its priorities and practices. Even more, it was constrained by familiar foreign policies that, despite quick PPP embrace, reenfranchised the military-intelligence power elite and reignited regional tensions. Almost inevitably, the PPP government, needing to maintain a public belligerence to the army while pursuing policies that required military acquiescence and approval, faltered in massive contradictions. The fact that it engaged in few overt human rights violations itself—except in the *mohajir* (migrant)-dominated cities of Sind province, where mutual retribution among competing ethnic groups led to officially sponsored bloodshed, massive rights abuses, and ultimately army intervention—did little to persuade many Pakistanis that PPP rule was not synonymous with corruption, compromise, and conflict. The steel frame of the state, it turned out, was built from the tanks and guns that had supported martial law. When the going got tough and General Beg deviated from policies acceptable to the PPP, the governance paradox was wrapped in irony: the army patrolled Sind under rules promulgated by Zulfikar Ali Bhutto but disavowed by his daughter; General Zia's constitutional amendments were invoked to dismiss Benazir Bhutto's government and, after elections, send Sharif's coalition to parliament.

Sharif proclaimed himself a civilian beneficiary of military rule. He sought to combine the interests of the military with those of a more conservative civilian establishment but found this impossible to accomplish without resorting to repression and manipulation. His impatience with judicial oversight was translated into a series of efforts to bypass the courts and, when that failed, to override their decisions. The Islami Jamhoori Ittehad (IJI), an alliance of parties united in their disdain for the PPP, found it difficult to agree on policy and even harder to sanction dissent. When the already dangerous cities of Sind erupted into even greater violence, journalists were threatened (and many killed), freedom of expression was sharply curtailed, and parliamentary predominance was negotiated down to accommodate the wishes of the president and the army. Corruption masqueraded as policy designed to create a vanguard middle class. Seeking redress for grievances was not impossible, as it was under the army, but it was not easy, and many jailed PPP members found it difficult to distinguish General Zia from his political progeny in Sharif's cabinet. By 1993 Sharif's growing list of enemies included some in the military, and a perpetually recrafted military-parliament-presidential triumvirate almost destroyed the foundations of parliamentary precedence. The courts were asked to rule on the validity of his rule, and after a sequence of "he's in, he's out" maneuvers, Sharif and President Ghulam Ishaq Khan both relinquished office to an interim government whose primary task was to organize new elections. The summer of 1993 was a second turning point in Pakistan's lengthy transition; this time, however, previously high expectations were tempered by chastening experience.

Transition brings stress to almost any political society. The first phase of Pakistan's transition, which occurred coincidentally with those in former communist states, was exceedingly difficult. The strains of early electoral governance were added to those of post–martial law transition, and both arose simultaneously. (Antinuclear sanctions, imposed by the United States retrospectively, highlighted the awkwardness of overlapping agendas: the IJI government was forced to live with the results of nuclear policies implemented under General Zia; while it did not disagree with the policies, it resented shouldering the blame.) Social confusion, political division, and economic anxiety were of a piece with the complicated constitutional endowments of the 1980s. The shadows of continuing war in Afghanistan fell not on the military-intelligence complex that guided chaos across the Durand Line, which defined the Afghanistan-Pakistan border, but on the civilians who were left out of decisions about war and weapons. And to maintain policy consistency in Kabul and Kashmir, civilians and military officers spread their wings over a collection of collaborators whose own agendas—whether religious, sectarian territorial, cultural, fiscal, or political—contributed to violence and a wide range of rights abuses in Pakistan, Afghanistan, and Kashmir.

Transition, Round Two

The sequential reelections of Bhutto and Sharif were tainted by the governance environment set by interim prime minister Moeen Qureshi during his short term of office in the summer of 1993. Before elections, he initiated a process of partial public accountability that exposed the fiscal misdeeds of many politicians (who stood for election anyway), exposed the nexus between politics and money, and kept the army away from scrutiny. Although many politicians were incensed, others in Pakistan argue that the benefits of this strategy have yet to be realized; still others suggest that the effects of that strategy are evident in the sequence of political failures that led to, and include, the current military government.

Bhutto's second term paralleled her first. The PPP concentrated on retaining power by concurrently treating the army as an enemy and the guarantor of the party's tenure. This two-pronged approach was reflected in efforts to craft an Afghan policy (patronizing the newly created Taliban proved a dramatic failure), reassert Pakistan's interest in Kashmir through a policy that paralleled Pakistan's interventions in Afghanistan, and patch together an economic policy to save the country from its external and domestic debt. The primary effect on rights was structural rather than specific: the PPP-run state was thought once again to be corrupt, intrusive, incompetent, and, in a vaguely comprehensive manner, malign. Projects such as creating a human rights ministry were dismissed—no power, no authority, too little, too late—and complaints about perversions of justice grew. By late 1996 a precipitous downward spiral—family murders and betrayals, policy failures, and political divisions—led to Bhutto's second dismissal, this time by President Farooq Ahmed Khan Leghari, a longtime PPP member chosen to be president by Bhutto herself. Sharif's return in early 1997, with a small margin of popular votes that yielded the first postmilitary majority in parliament, was greeted less with enthusiasm than with popular resignation at the seemingly inevitable.

Sharif found few new arrows in his quiver. He targeted the press and the courts once again, this time with the threat (never fully realized) of the full implementation of *shariah* (Islamic) law to take the edge off executive manipulations of justice. His government went to war, first against the president—he was able to reduce presidential powers by voting down the one portion of General Zia's constitutional amendments that all parliamentarians found noxious, the power to dismiss parliament—and then against the Supreme Court, by forcing the Chief Justice from office, and finally against the army chief, who also resigned. Critics were persecuted and jailed; public condemnation did little to temper harassment or victimization. His economic policies faltered, not least because a strong commercial sector requires an independent justice system, such as no longer existed. Sharif's tenure was saved, at least for a while, by the decision that ultimately brought him down: popular opinion rallied around nuclear tests in June 1998, even though they provoked new sanctions, constrained the economy, and weakened Pakistan's overseas posture. Unsure of its limited strengths but certain that its praetorian policies required the support of conservative Islamist parties, Pakistan continued to support the Taliban in Afghanistan (or, at the least, continued not to sacrifice the Taliban to the West) and reengaged in fighting in Kashmir. The sum of his policies defeated its parts: Sharif's Pakistan was viewed, at home and abroad, as a dangerous place harboring dangerous people, unable to protect its borders or its citizens, economically bankrupt, and immune to even minute reforms.

Through round two of the transition, U.S. policy diverged only slightly from its earlier models. Both Bhutto and Sharif were greeted with skepticism, cynicism, and distrust, even while the United States tried to use Pakistan as a lever in its regional policies. The U.S.-Pakistan relationship turned on three critical patterns of interaction: a push-me, pull-you contest in which each side demanded what the other would not provide, took affront at rejection, and then repeated earlier demands; a more consistent focus on issues that seemed secondary to the government of Pakistan (Afghanistan rather than Kashmir, nuclear nonproliferation rather than investment) but were of primary importance to the United States; and a distinct aversion to blunt responses to rights abuses. The less Pakistan was able or willing to provide to the United States, the faster U.S. impatience with Bhutto and Sharif accelerated, and the more Pakistanis believed the United States to be contemptuous of struggling democracy. Shrill reports on rights abuses in Pakistan, often edged with understandable panic, were used as a convenient stick with which to hit both Bhutto and Sharif, but few Pakistanis thought that rights were fundamental to the U.S.-Pakistan relationship. The United States often averred, and still does, that its leverage in Pakistan had waned and that its diminished influence had to be conserved to stave off nuclear conflagration and Indo-Pakistan war. Critical links—between rights as prerequisites for democracy and transparency as a fundamental element in democratic governance— were missing as a matter of policy, not accident. Neither country pursued the relationship on the basis of mutually recognized and understood priorities. There is no question that the United States knew full well that the only alternative to weak elected government would be a return to military rule. By confining rights to a small corner of policy, the United States in effect acquiesced in the diagnosis of irretrievability that grounded the army's justification for seizing power.

Back to the Barracks

When General Musharraf led a coup d'état in October 1999, Pakistan had become a place where rights were neither recognized nor protected, and democracy had become irrelevant to the electoral process. But military rule did not change this. Once again, a faulty electoral system was interrupted before it had a chance to fix itself, however painful that process might be. Once again—precisely echoing Zia's strategy—the constitution was abrogated, judges were forced to swear loyalty to the general, the deposed prime minister was imprisoned (for financial wrongdoing, not rights abuses), politicians were arrested without charge or trial, and accountability processes were initiated without due process guarantees. And once again, the military government began a long battle for economic sustainability while maintaining a series of expensive foreign policy engagements that strained the exchequer, foreign relations, domestic harmony, and rights.

The international response was, predictably, strongly stated and weakly executed. The United States and the Commonwealth imposed pallid sanctions. Musharraf avoided declaring martial law in the hope of avoiding instant sanctions and was rewarded with confusion overseas. Foreign powers demanded a timetable for restoring democracy without requiring policies to restore the rights that democracy requires. But the United States also began, almost immediately, to craft a policy that would underscore its distaste for previous leaders without interrupting important business. In so doing, the United States maintained four familiar habits. First, restoring democracy is an oxymoron in Pakistan: if elected governments have yet to become democratic, restoration would mean reempowering familiar elites who have kept democracy at bay. (Public opinion is almost united on this one issue.) To demand restoration is at best to be considered irrelevant and at worst to be seen as complicit in the malign governance of recent years. Fairness and honesty demand that democracy arise from open political engagement, and open politics requires an environment that sustains dissent and change—in short, a rights policy leading to rights-respecting government. In Pakistan, military coups d'état do not bring democracy, bureaucrats are not political vanguards, and voters without protected voices cannot be heard.

Second, sanctions have changed little but the tone of voice and the level of seniority of counterparts and interlocutors. The list of issues that made up the U.S.-Pakistan agenda in mid-2000 was the same as it was in mid-1999: terrorism, narcotics, nuclear nonproliferation, missile proliferation, economic stability, and regional security. This agenda almost benefits from centralized dictate and fits easily into the checklist/sanctions schema of past and present U.S. policy. It seemed possible to pursue most of this agenda with army officers and their civilian subordinates, thereby avoiding the seeming inconveniences of democratic debate. The content of the relationship thus bypasses the messy business of rights, representation, and democracy—even when the cake is iced with televised democracy tutorials from the U.S. president.

Third, bypassing the content of democracy and rights reduces the published goals and objectives of U.S. policy almost to incoherence. The law requires a stern response to military coups d'état, but the executive branch is generally willing to go along with lawmakers who believe that eluding the harshest sanction requirements can help to smooth regional relations. In effect, if not intent, waiving sanctions overtakes a democracy and rights policy by raising other issues above governance concerns. This is a dangerous trend. At the time that General Musharraf took power, he was unlikely to elicit the support that General Zia mustered—not of his own making—to validate his foreign policy. The likelihood that repression might increase as Pakistan's military came under greater pressure to relinquish its tenacious, if desperate, hold on domestic power and foreign policy grew in the months after the coup d'état. By refusing to take seriously the rights and democracy prerequisites for coherent policy, the United States contributed to heightened, rather than diminished, political instability in and among Pakistan, Afghanistan, and India.

Fourth, embedding rights policy in a sanctions-laden policy environment has reduced, rather than increased, the profile of rights and democracy in U.S.-Pakistan initiatives. Too many irritants, too many loopholes, few clear priorities—all lead to a muddled policy arena that protects rights for few Pakistanis but creates an enormous amount of background noise in Washington. By organizing the bilateral relationship around sanctions, the United States structured rights out of the relationship.

These patterns of interaction were highlighted, again and again, during Musharraf's first months in office, when U.S.-Pakistan relations sank publicly to new depths. General Musharraf insisted that he was ending corruption and restructuring Pakistan's nonfunctioning state, and for a few brief months, the Pakistani public seemed to appreciate his efforts. Relatively quickly, however, Musharraf's domestic agenda weakened: corruption was assumed to readjust itself to the new military context, and despite scores of policy papers on government reorganization, the state was still stalled. Even more clearly, his foreign policy agenda seemed to doom whatever domestic progress he may have had in mind. On seizing power, he had vowed to remove militant political groups from the political arena. To do so would have required fundamentally altering Pakistan's policies toward Kashmir and Afghanistan, on whose behalf most of them were flourishing, and this was something that Musharraf seemed incapable of doing.

In the end, it was Afghanistan that called Washington's sanctions bluff, once again. In order to be able to declare war in Afghanistan in October 2001 in response to terrorist attacks on the United States, Washington required Pakistan to change its intelligence command, cease its support for the Taliban, and remove militant parties from active support for both the Taliban and the war in Kashmir. Musharraf agreed to all three demands and acted on the first two. In short order, some sanctions were lifted to make it possible for military relationships to be renewed and Pakistan was back in the good graces of the United States. (Similar sanctions were lifted for India.) Once again, war trumped human rights and, in so doing, condemned, not only the U.S.-Pakistan relationship, but also the substantive goals to which the two countries had mutually agreed, to woeful shortsightedness. The United States presented its renewed cooperation with Pakistan in terms voiced first by Musharraf: because alliance with the United States came at presumed (but not proved) political cost to the military government, the United States would be expected to pay up. This assumption was never seriously tested, and indeed the counterfactual might well have been more accurate: by September 2001 Pakistan had few friends and fewer options, and the United States could well have simply stated a case for the military to resign and civilian government to be restored. Seeking the predictable, the United States opted instead to restore its time-honored relationship with Pakistan.

Habit comes with a price, however. Because Musharraf did not deal with militant parties, no one could: their influence not only in

Kashmir but also along the border with Afghanistan left the tribal belt open to Taliban influence long after a new government was installed in Kabul. Both problems contributed to considerable regional instability and a worsening environment for civil liberties at home. By the end of 2002, relations between Pakistan and India had worsened over Kashmir, and Afghanistan's new government was eyeing Islamabad warily.

Taking yet another page from General Zia's script, Musharraf used an old ploy by calling for elections to local bodies and then national polls—but only after mocking the political process by setting a referendum that ensured his own return to the presidency and embarrassing his U.S. allies, some of whom believed that the military government was a convenient cloak for democratically leaning generals. When national elections brought to office a coalition that included militant Islamist parties (including some from the tribal areas), pundits could not decide whether Musharraf had been hoisted on his own petard, or whether the military had found a way to support Islamist proxies who would maintain Pakistan's traditional agendas in Kashmir and Afghanistan. Either way, the military government was sure to disappoint those in Pakistan who sought broader room for civil and political liberties and was likely to thwart those outside interlocutors who believed that alternating policies of sanctions and engagement could change essential relationships in the subcontinent. Little wonder, then, that when the United States withdrew its democracy sanctions on the eve of the Iraq war in February 2003, civil society in Pakistan greeted the move with little more than a shrug.

THE GOVERNANCE CONUNDRUM

Many Pakistani civilians argue that military rule is the last chance for the Pakistani state. Those who hold this view, and therefore acquiesce in the military's condemnatory picture of politics, are likely to be disappointed. Pakistanis generally distinguish between running a state and running it well or democratically, and U.S. policy generally accedes to this distinction. As a consequence, democracy is often seen as a road to disarray, authoritarianism is seen as a second state of nature, and soldiers are mistakenly seen as acceptable alternatives to civilian government—all because the dominant discourse is about rule rather than governance. But armies and dictators exercise power; they do not govern.

The United States and other foreign interlocutors therefore confront the same choices that Pakistanis do today. To the degree that diplomatic support and financial assistance for administrative reform is provided (or not prevented), external powers deny long Pakistani experience: administrative tinkering, whether tentative or strident, has never brought the cleaner, more clearly defined, equitably oriented politics required to ensure rights. General Musharraf and his advisers have learned some of the vocabulary lessons of the post–Cold War era. Acknowledging that an entire governance environment is required to promote democracy, the military is seeking holistic-sounding assistance to reform the state while at the same time accumulating lists of small things that appear to add up to democratizing tactics even while undercutting them by inaction—adding seats for women in parliament, for example, but not changing laws that repress women. This policy posture builds on another vocabulary problem, and a related problem of concept. Pakistan shares with the United States a reluctance to clarify language in order to clarify the meaning of policy: for most of Pakistan's political life, both sides have been reluctant to call a dictator a dictator, a soldier a soldier, and repression repression. As a result, both act and speak as if rights-disregarding regimes were simply alternative forms of government. Habit discourages change: in truth, rights and democracy have become dispensable in Pakistan because they have been treated as if they were disposable.

Governance, by contrast, requires institutions operating with integrity, and these, in turn, can be built only on a strong political foundation. Politics is meaningless without justice, and justice is a consequence of rights. Moreover, the accountability that the military and outside powers claim to seek is meaningful only when it is integrated into a full program of governance, not a system of punishments. By transforming a language error into political theory, Pakistan indulges in an expensive category mistake: it appears to make administration (modus operandi) into governance (modus vivendi). The United States has taken advantage of this conceptual split because it allows policy to continue without indulging in the uncertain sport of politics. But corruption begins and ends in bad governance and easily undercuts all policy. The crisis of the state is a crisis of bad faith, reflected in complicity with rights-disregarding rule.

LEARNING LESSONS

U.S. policy toward Pakistan too often contradicts four lessons that its democracy policy has already taught elsewhere. Democracy often and almost necessarily creates uncertainty; it is not about specific policy outcomes but is about the process of achieving goals that are legitimated by the polity; it is impossible to achieve without systematic rights guarantees; and it is a reflection of an entire environment, not just a few technical requirements. U.S. policy also ignores the many interlocking lessons—again, learned elsewhere—about the ways that rights and democracy figure in foreign policy. Human rights protection and democracy promotion are two sides of the same policy. Both elements require consistency of purpose and message to cushion the inevitable uncertainties that arise through democratic process and become comprehensible to those affected by policy. Both require clearly articulated priority within foreign policy, whatever that priority is to be, and both must set their sights on long-term trends rather than short-term gains or failures. In so doing, no country should be made to relinquish its rights because another country is considered more important.

Pakistan itself offers two additional, blunt lessons in rights policy. First, when rights are separated from politics, rights cannot be guaranteed. Second, when external powers accede to the diminution of or the disregard for rights in order to achieve other objectives, their complicity in denying rights dramatically limits any capacity to realize those other goals.

Although there is no single point at which U.S. policy might have provided a decisive counterweight to the frequently antidemocratic tendencies of Pakistan's politics, the accumulations of history carry weight. It is clear that the U.S.-Pakistan relationship has provided the political space for successive governments in Pakistan to concentrate power rather than broaden its base and, in so doing, to remove rights protections from their rightful place at the center of politics. Whether or not U.S. policy highlights specific rights issues at every turn, experience demonstrates the fallacy of conducting a wide-ranging relationship—whether military or civilian—that diminishes the importance of rights for Pakistan's citizens. This may sound like theory, but it is based on practice: neither military engagement nor public policy collaborations can encourage or sanction rights-abusing behavior without precipitating a forceful, institutional, seemingly irreversible backlash that, with time and in turn, threatens the viability of future relationships. If there is one lesson to be learned from Pakistan, it is that sound policy rests on sound politics, and fundamental rights make politics possible.

6

U.S. Policy and Human Rights in the Republic of Korea

The Influence of Policy or the Policy of Influence

DAVID I. STEINBERG

T HE EXCEPTIONAL ECONOMIC DEVELOPMENT of the Republic of Korea, its rapid recovery from the Asian financial crisis of 1997, its apparent transformation from authoritarian rule to pluralism and free elections, and the placid retirement of the military from politics are remarkable achievements that have attracted considerable international attention, even acclaim. In less than a decade and a half, the Republic of Korea (hereafter Korea or South Korea) has undergone singular and progressive changes.

Within this very positive context, a state of war still exists between Korea and the Democratic People's Republic of Korea (DPRK, or North Korea). Fears about war were much diminished by the summit of June 2000, but have been reexacerbated by a recalcitrant North Korea and a shift in U.S. policies toward it under the Bush administration. These developments have resulted in a growing divergence of priorities between the United States and South Korea on North Korean relations and have spurred rising anti-American sentiment in the South that could affect U.S. influence there. Policy divergences and differences continue to prompt residual fears about the North's intentions toward the South, which include external aggression and, albeit less important than in previous decades, internal subversion. These palpable concerns have lingered for half a century and have broadly affected internal and external policies on politics, democratic development, and human rights; popular attitudes within South Korea toward politics and human rights; and foreign considerations toward the peninsula. The United States, as the primary supporter of the Republic of Korea, has played a commanding role in the South as the security guarantor for all regimes, first after liberation from Japan in 1945 and then after the republic's inception in 1948. A complex of U.S. national interests as expressed on the peninsula and in the region has resulted in juxtapositions of sometimes divergent, contradictory, or differently prioritized policies emanating not only from the U.S. Department of State but also from diverse executive branch institutions, from sundry wings of the legislative branch, and from the nongovernmental community. Although there has been a fundamental concern in the U.S. policy community for democracy and good governance in Korea, explicit concentration on human rights has been episodic and irregular, and human rights have been accorded a lower priority than other U.S. interests, which has made official influence less effective.

These formal relationships have been supplemented, however, by the important but generalized influence of the United States through a wide network of informal linkages, the training of Koreans in the United States, and the growing Korean-American community with ties back to Korean society.[1] Thus, the multiple roles of the United States in fostering human rights policies in Korea are far more complex than might first be imagined.

INTRODUCTION

Korea has, for over a generation, been a test case of American commitment to human rights. For the critics, it is a poignant case of paradise lost—a land liberated in 1945 from its own decadent past and from forty years of colonial subjugation, only to be divided by its American and Soviet liberators into two antithetic regimes and then dragged into dictatorship and oppression. In this view, the United States, instead of using its tremendous power to bring forth a just society, abetted political retrogression through a mixture of mindless anti-communism, cynicism, national self-interest, and impotent good intentions.[2]

Is this early, preliberalization characterization of U.S. policies in Korea an accurate assessment? There are those who look at the political (and economic) progress in Korea and consider that U.S. policies have been instrumental, even causal, in the country's positive transformation. Others take a more nuanced view. Debate over U.S. human rights policies and their efficacy in South Korea is also often between those who implement policy and those who critique it.

Those with experience in diplomacy tend to minimize U.S. responsibility for human-rights problems in the R.O.K. and also to downplay the value of official pressures in improving South Korean practice. . . . The critics are often convinced that, for historical reasons, the United States bears at least indirect responsibility for South Korean government abuses and could do much more than it does to mitigate human-rights encroachments. . . . They are less concerned with the possible role of Korean historical and political responsibility for existing problems. They are concerned that long-term U.S. political and strategic interests may become fatally undermined by failure to distance the United States sufficiently from abusive practices and regimes.[3]

That there have been remarkable changes in Korea in a generation, and not simply in economics, is not in question. Questions can reasonably be raised, however, as to which changes are profound and/or pervasive and which are more surface manifestations, masking substratum continuities. Further questions can be posed about the purported causes of such changes and whether they may be attributed in part to U.S. policy influences and, if so, to what degree. In other words, can the United States take some credit for pursuing a set of policies related to human rights that can by any standard of attribution and evaluation be considered "successful"? And what, indeed, constitutes success? And when was that success achieved? Or was the United States responsible (and if so, to what degree) for the dismal human rights situation in Korea for almost four decades?

Because there is more data available on Korea's recent history than on that of any other Asian state, because Korea has been a priority focus of U.S. national interests since at least 1950, if not since 1945, and because a considerable number of academic and policy analyses have been conducted, a prevalent perception persists that any study of U.S. policies related to human rights would be a relatively simple matter. This, however, is not the case.

Considerable information has been available on human rights conditions in Korea since the 1980s through the reports of the U.S. Department of State and a variety of nongovernmental organizations, such as Amnesty International and Human Rights Watch. Earlier materials on the human rights milieu from independence in 1948 until the late 1980s are incomplete because of censorship by authoritarian regimes of varying degrees of intensity. The declassified cable traffic of the Department of State does in part deal with these issues, as will be discussed later, but it usually focuses on U.S. priorities. The academic literature on policy issues almost exclusively concentrates on security, political (i.e., issues of democracy and governance), and economic questions, but not on the more fundamental question of rights as distinct from governance, with some exceptions, which are referenced in some of the endnotes that follow. The available materials on this subject are meager indeed compared with the wealth of data on other aspects of the Korean scene.

Korean sources on rights have been markedly circumscribed. Censorship and the fear of criticism of both domestic policies and U.S. policies have been apparent and legally justified under the draconian National Security Law and related legislation and the law's predecessors. Although there has been freer academic inquiry since the political liberalization of 1987, there is more discussion in Korean sources of the actual conditions in Korea than of specific U.S. policy issues, although general criticisms have become more widespread since the Kwangju incident of 1980. A separate subset of materials in Korean has appeared in Japan. Much of this subset is closely related to transparent North Korean interests and thus is virulently anti-American and anti–South Korean. It is not germane to any objective analysis of the issues in South Korea, although it may have affected some South Korean attitudes.

It is tempting to try to assess only the more recent aspects of U.S. policy on human rights in Korea, for the period and the issues seem more relevant to lessons to be learned, yet this would be a mistake, because the patterns of U.S. response and initiative go back to the very founding of the republic. Koreans regard their history holistically, so the roots of the problems, and thus U.S. responses, cannot arbitrarily be truncated. It is, for example, impossible to consider political liberalization in 1987 without understanding the coups of 1961 and 1979 and the Kwangju insurrection of 1980. Thus, we will explore the range of Korean contemporary history in the search for lessons.

As the next section shows, all of these questions are made more difficult by a variety of conceptual problems related to the terminology involved in human rights.

CONCEPTUAL AND PROCEDURAL ISSUES IN HUMAN RIGHTS

Although the Universal Declaration of Human Rights dates from 1948, that document sets forth what evidently became a set of aspirations, often only tangentially related to the conditions in many of the world's states, including some of those regarded as economically most advanced. Although states may have signed that declaration, no enforcement mechanism was set up, and only under the most egregious circumstances were violations of those rights aired at official international fora. The declaration, however important it may be to international prestige and acceptance, is of limited relevance as a policy guide to this study.

However, a series of conceptual and definitional problems relate to analysis of U.S. policy in Korea. The first problem focuses on definitions of human rights, which are treated elsewhere. The second problem relates to the usage of the term "human rights" itself as an element of both analysis and policy, and whether surrogate indicators that convey similar meanings may be used in place of the term. A review of the literature on Korea indicates that in either English or Korean, the term "human rights" (*in-kwon* in Korean) was not in vogue until late in the U.S.-Korean policy relationship. Rather, "democracy" and "freedom" were continuously invoked (sometimes with a certain degree of cynicism) as goals to be attained. The literature also indicates that economic rights were not considered to be of paramount concern, the exploitation and subjugation of labor being one important means by which Korea became economically competitive internationally. Human rights, under the surrogate term "democracy," were limited to the political realm. Since Korea was ethnically homogeneous, the issue of social and ethnic rights was not relevant. Religious rights were also not an issue, for one of the strengths of modern Korea has been its religious diversity and its respect for all faiths.[4] Gender rights have not traditionally been on the U.S. agenda in Korea and have only recently become a matter of internal Korean focus.[5]

A vital question is whether "democracy" is a sufficient surrogate term for "human rights." It seems evident that the terms cannot be used interchangeably, because democracy focuses on only one aspect of human rights, avowedly and public political rights, and does not deal with broader and even more basic issues. Any evaluation of human rights must take into account this limitation as well as a number of other aspects of the problem of attributing to U.S. policies the causes of, or contribution to, change.

Although constitutions are often first examined to evaluate the presence or absence of respect for certain human rights, those documents are often simply aspirations of a populace or regime, unrealistic norms or myths, or cynical attempts by administrations to project internally or externally acceptable images. Eastern European and Soviet constitutions contained many positive provisions on rights that were either ignored or qualified as "subject to law." In the case of Korea, it was not until the Korean 1987 constitution that such provisions were liberalized.[6]

On those occasions when U.S. policy toward Korea has emphasized human rights or democracy, what has motivated Washington? Has this emphasis been prompted by U.S. concern for the interests of the Korean regimes, the Korean people, some other international goal, the U.S. people or political process, or some or all of the above? This question is not irrelevant, as motivation and perceived motivation have helped shape Korean attitudes toward the United States.

A related question is: What have been Korean perceptions of the U.S. role in fostering human rights and democracy? Although this chapter focuses on what that U.S. role was and on the perceptions and lessons from a U.S. vantage point, Korean views of what motivated U.S. policies and what effect they had on Korea are also important. Koreans and Americans may draw markedly different conclusions about the U.S. role. Among Koreans, perceptions will be colored by generational, regional, educational, and occupational differences, and by differences in social and economic status. Both the U.S. and Korean governments encouraged the belief that U.S. policies were fundamentally altruistic (and discouraged or suppressed less flattering interpretations), but the Korean intellectual community has reexamined U.S. motivations, and that review has led to some disillusionment with the United States—and to a greater understanding of realpolitik.

THE KOREAN MILIEU

Just as definitions of human rights have constantly evolved, so too has change been a constant element of the Korean milieu into which U.S. policies have been inserted. The description of the culture of any modern society can capture only a static glimpse of a moving image, one that defies adequate definition over time. This is especially true in the case of Korea, for there are few countries in the world that have undergone such rapid changes. Yet, even as various facets of Korean life have transfigured elements of Korean society, remarkable continuities in terms of traditional values and attitudes are evident—continuities that operate within, and sometimes in conflict with, more dynamic trends. Seven concepts or conditions in Korea help define the Korean milieu within which U.S. policy has operated.[7] They are concepts of individualism, the concept of the appropriate role of the state, the issue of orthodoxy, the role or rule of law, the question of hierarchy, the intensity of Korean nationalism, and conceptions of and reactions to the "other"—North Korea. These policies and attitudes are in a state of flux by time, social group, educational status, and other factors and should not be regarded as static or as internally consistent within Korean society. Yet they are influential and have severely constrained the freedoms associated with human rights. One of the manifestations of these policies and attitudes is found in the National Security Law.

The National Security Law and its antecedents have had the most important influence on human rights and democratic dialogue issues. The law has gone through a variety of incarnations, and its origins predate the Korean War. In the more liberal period since 1987, the Korean courts have somewhat limited the broad scope of the law, which in the past has included criminal procedures for having unauthorized contact with any "antistate" organization (i.e., North Korean–related institutions or individuals); for criticizing the South Korean social or economic system; for reading Soviet, communist, or leftist materials; and for praising the North.[8] Although theoretically designed to be an antisubversion law, in fact it has been an antidissent and antidissident law, as something less than 2 percent of those arrested under it have been charged with spying. The National Security Law was not the product of a single administration, such as the most oppressive legislation under Park Chung Hee's Yushin Constitution (1972–79), but has been a constant factor in all administrations. Even since political liberalization in 1987, and even under the Kim Dae Jung administration, the number of those arrested under the law has not substantially decreased.[9] The "catch-22" aspect of the legislation has been especially frustrating to many: since North Korea vehemently opposes that law and has demanded that the South repeal it, those in the South who advocate replacing it with more focused and appropriate legislation can be arrested under the law for violating its provisions of approving a North Korean demand.

The reaction of the Korean government, and the large and generally conservative middle class, to more radical Korean student adulation of North Korea has been one of extreme concern. Reaction has ranged from the arrest of many students to President Kim Young Sam's pronouncement, after the violent student demonstrations at Yonsei University in August 1995, that Korea needed a "new ideology" to prevent future such outbursts among the students, thus illustrating both the fear of North Korean infiltration and influence and the desire for intellectual orthodoxy.[10]

The atmosphere for human rights and democracy has certainly become more liberal in Korea. The pluralism associated with a vibrant civil society and free elections is enshrined to a degree that anything short of a major national catastrophe, such as a northern invasion, will not cause them to disappear. The fact that members of the Korean elite are increasingly likely to be internationally educated and to have growing foreign family ties, the greater access to more plentiful and more nuanced international information, and the growing realization of the modern, international role that Korea plays (it is, for example, a member of the Organization for Economic Cooperation and Development [OECD] and has the twelfth-largest economy in the world) all encourage more liberal policies toward human rights.

But the atmosphere is not unambiguously favorable for human rights. The distance between the state and civil society (including individuals, private organizations, the business community, and the press) is narrow. The state considers that it has the moral right, even the duty, to restrict actions that in other societies would be sacrosanct under freedoms of expression, and this right is to a considerable degree supported by the acquiescence of the Korean population. As Doh C. Shin, the most respected academic analyst of polling results, notes:

> While about one-half (49%) were in favor [in 1993] of economic development over democratic reform, about one-quarter (26%) chose democratization over economic development. In 1997, however, less than one-tenth (9%) replied that democratization is more important than economic development for their nation. Even among those who believe that democracy is always the best form of government, moreover, economic development outweighs democratic development by an overwhelming margin of 51 to 11 percent. The implication is that the majority of the Korean people would withdraw their support for democratic reforms whenever they saw those reforms interfering with economic development.[11]

The issue, then, may be not only what—if any—effects U.S. policy interests have had on human rights and democracy in Korea but also how lasting the effects are likely to be in alternative scenarios.

U.S. POLICY PRIORITIES IN KOREA

From liberation from Japanese colonial rule and the onset of the Cold War on the Korean peninsula until the present, there has been one singular U.S. policy objective in Korea to which all other considerations have been subservient. This is, quite obviously, security. The United States confronted a Soviet state bent, as it was assumed at the time, on world domination. Korea was one area where the confrontation was palpable. With the rise of the People's Republic of China and the Sino-Soviet bloc, the United States assumed that the North Korean invasion of the South in 1950 was a surrogate for testing U.S. resolve; if the United States did not stand up to this invasion, other communist invasions would follow throughout the world. Although that theory has largely been exploded, security remained a continuing priority in the face of a verbally belligerent and potentially aggressive North Korean regime, and so remains today.[12] Washington's overriding concern with security resulted in conservative stances when it was perceived to be threatened.

Two other policy objectives were articulated over time. These were, in order of priority, economics, which was critical because it was viewed as a corollary to security, and democracy, which was not so closely linked in policy terms. Democracy subsumed the political rights on which it was to rest. Economic motivations themselves were complex and shifted over time as U.S. policies refocused both on the region and on Korea. The earliest economic priority for the United States was to try to make Korea economically self-sufficient. Congress was at first reluctant to allocate the funds that the administration requested for Korean economic assistance, and later there was a continuing congressional impression that the massive foreign aid (that by 1975, when new economic aid ended, totaled some $13 billion in economic and military fields) was not producing the expected results. Such aid was justified to Congress in terms of a security rationale. Washington sought to reduce the amount of U.S. economic aid, to make Korea more self-reliant through import-substitution industries, and then, after 1961, to help develop Korea's exports. The United States pushed for Korean normalization of relations with Japan to help shift the economic assistance burden onto the Japanese; this normalization occurred when U.S. foreign assistance was being redirected toward Vietnam.[13]

As Korea increased its exports and by the late 1980s enjoyed a major trade surplus with the United States, the opening of Korean markets and foreign investment became important political issues in the United States (and were featured in the 1988 Democratic primaries). The cry then became "a level (economic) playing field" as the United States was the largest market for growing Korean exports, but U.S. businesses experienced great difficulty in penetrating the Korean market.

To the outside observer, the U.S. cry for democracy, the third policy objective, was perhaps based more on concern for the international position of the United States, because for much of this early period Korea was internationally considered a "client state." Since the UN and U.S. intervention in the Korean War had been justified on the grounds of preserving democracy and defending the "free world," it behooved the United States to try to ensure that Korea was democratic, or at least was perceived to be democratic by the international community.[14] The public aura of democracy had to be presented, even if the reality diverged. There seems to have been less concern for any internal democratic governance, although if democracy did not threaten security it was certainly desirable. The ambassador to South Korea, Philip Habib, said, "I'm not thinking of it [the serious Korean political situation of 1974] simply from the standpoint of whether or not the Koreans have individual freedom or liberty or not. I'm thinking in terms of if the political situation in Korea deteriorates and continues to move in the direction . . . which is increasingly authoritarian, increasingly oppressive, and generating a greater degree of opposition in Korea." Habib went on to say that the United States should not be associated with repression. Secretary of State Henry Kissinger said, "I do not think it is worth our investment to democratize Korea or Turkey."[15]

Although the U.S. government considered democracy secondary to security, democracy was nonetheless a goal. How the United States intervened to promote, or abstained from promoting, political and other rights will be discussed later. The U.S. government's approach was never, however, monolithic. Not only did the Department of State and the Department of Defense differ in their priorities, as might have been expected, but also individuals and groups of congresspeople contributed their own, often opposing, views on Korea.[16] Meanwhile, Seoul actively sought to influence U.S. policy positions, most egregiously in the "Koreagate" scandal of the 1970s.[17]

The Korean government was aware of the conflicting priorities of the various U.S. actors and was adept at playing one department against another to ensure that Korean state interests as perceived at that time were not compromised. Appropriate attempts to invoke positive responses to Korea's security and economic dilemmas have continued with official and unofficial (albeit officially endorsed or prompted) funding of academic programs and, more important, research and activities associated with various policy think tanks. As Korea liberalized internally, so too the support for Korea among foreign think tanks broadened. It was apparent that the Korean authorities believed that without sponsored activities, Korean issues would disappear from the U.S. policy radar screen, and thus support for Korea would be more vulnerable. Liberalization in Korea also brought with it greater concern for the opinions of the more liberal members of Congress; previously, attention had been focused on conservatives in Congress, who, because of their close association with the regime, were unlikely to criticize the human rights situation and who regarded security as paramount.

Nonetheless, U.S. concern for democracy and human rights had been expressed from the very beginning of the relationship. In 1946 U.S. policy had several objectives: the development of an independent democratic state and a national government that "shall be a democratic government fully representative of the freely expressed will of the Korean people."[18] Secretary of State Dean Acheson in March 1950 told President Syngman Rhee that U.S. assistance was "predicated upon the existence and growth of democratic institutions within the Republic."[19] During the Korean War, U.S. policy statement NSC 118/2 still called for a democratic Korea, and in 1959 the Bureau of the Budget proposed that U.S. support be contingent on the strengthening of democratic institutions in Korea, but the State Department disagreed.[20] The official U.S. emphasis on democracy was repeated even during the 1960s and 1970s, when Korea had its most governments, although U.S. rhetoric had little overall influence.

Syngman Rhee had said as early as 1947 that U.S.-style democracy was not suited for Korea.

The Koreans often responded to criticisms angrily:

> While the United States directly or indirectly attempted to influence Seoul's domestic policies so that human rights would be respected or political prisoners would be freed, the South Korean government resisted such an attempt as an unfair interference in sovereign domestic affairs. Although the Nixon and Ford Administrations were relatively reticent about this issue, the Carter Administration chose South Korea and the Philippines as the major Asian targets of its highly visible human rights diplomacy.[21]

PATTERNS OF U.S. INTERVENTIONS IN HUMAN RIGHTS

The types and patterns of U.S. interventions into the domestic Korean human rights and governance scene have been varied. Although this chapter deals with official U.S. policies and their application, it is impossible to ignore the unofficial aspects of the relationship, for indeed if human rights have improved in Korea (as almost all observers would agree), then the question would be, How much of this change is attributable to external influences, both official and unofficial?

A review of the literature indicates that there were at least five distinct modes by which the United States exerted official pressure on Korean regimes to improve or modify human rights issues on individual, institutional, or national levels (in contrast to generalized influence through training and exposure to the United States and its institutions): public expressions of concern; private expressions of concerns; the threat to cut off military assistance; the threat to cut off economic assistance;[22] and the use of either the U.S. (or international) media or the Korean media for these purposes.

As we will note, a critical factor in the U.S.-Korean relationship was whether protestations about rights were to be publicly or privately expressed. The communications between the State Department and the U.S. embassy clearly indicate that on numerous occasions the Koreans feared that publicly aired criticism would lead to a loss of the regime's credibility and perhaps even to a loss of political legitimacy.[23]

The Koreans went to considerable lengths to persuade the United States to keep such protestations confidential and in some instances compromised on issues to win this point.[24] This approach successfully continued for a considerable period because of Korean government censorship of the press and the limited distribution (and even the suppression) of the international media within Korea.

The declassified documents reveal that the U.S. official community considered leaking stories about problems in Korea to the U.S. press. The community did not wish these stories to be seen as emanating directly from the State Department but felt they would work their way back into the Korean scene and affect Korean policies.[25] The U.S. embassy also dealt directly with the Korean press and even released its own statements in Korean to the press and the people when the Korean government was issuing disinformation about U.S. policies that linked the U.S. official community with repressive Korean actions or was reneging on Korean government–promised public distribution of U.S. position statements.[26]

Unofficial influence on human rights was also important. Considerable impact occurred through the mushrooming Christian community, with its international links. The concept of an egalitarian social system (egalitarian at least before the deity) probably influenced the growth and broad acceptance of human rights among Koreans. Myongdong Catholic Cathedral was a center and sanctuary for dissidents opposing the government's policies on various human rights, including political rights, torture, and labor issues (the arrest of dissidents in the cathedral in the 1970s became, along with Kim Dae Jung's arrest, a cause célèbre). The direct missionary influence was also important. There were mission organizations that specifically dealt with labor rights and organizing workers. It is evident that Park Chung Hee, for example, was careful to avoid unnecessarily agitating the Vatican.[27]

The international NGO community was also active in Korea. The number of such, mostly relief, groups in Korea after the Korean War dwindled from more than one hundred, but many are still active on social concerns and on issues such as the role of law, human rights, democracy and good governance, women's rights, local autonomy, and so forth. The most prominent of these NGOs is the Asia Foundation, which has been in Korea since 1954 and which has focused, not on the abstract concepts of rights, but on law, due process, the media, women's rights, and related issues.[28] Korean NGOs, largely ineffectual before the liberalization of 1987, have become a vital force. Those that managed to survive during the authoritarian period often had links with international counterparts, and this relationship was a form of protection that likely influenced their policies related to rights.

The international intellectual interchange should not be ignored in the process of transformation related to rights. A very large percentage of the Korean elite has been trained in graduate schools, mainly in the United States, and although equating such training with absorption of U.S. mores regarding political and human rights would be a dangerous leap of faith (sometimes one that U.S. sponsors of such training are prone to make), nevertheless the U.S. influence has likely been strong—albeit unquantifiable—in this regard. With such training and exposure has come the influence of international media and academic concepts that reinforce changing views of human rights throughout much of the world. Training in the United States has not always contributed to the advance of human rights in Korea, however. As in Latin America, so in Korea, many have asked whether U.S. training of local intelligence operatives has contributed to the repression of dissident groups and political opponents of the prevailing regime. Similarly, many Koreans question whether U.S. training of tens of thousands of Korean military officers in the United States has contributed to the expansion or the restriction of human rights.

The links to the outside world are further reinforced by the growing Korean American community that continues to have strong familial and social ties in Korea. Officially, more than one million Koreans were resident in the United States in 1990; the current population is likely to be double that number. Korean Americans have not yet become politically prominent in the United States; they are, however, very successful economically and professionally. Their views and those prevalent in the United States filter back into Korea through family and other connections, probably affecting attitudes toward rights to some unquantifiable degree.

The remaining foreign influence is one with a past and a future. This is international sports. The Seoul Olympics of 1988 were an important event affecting human rights in Korea.[29] The spring of 1987 witnessed massive popular outpourings of antigovernment demonstrations against the repressive regime of Chun Doo Hwan. They called for political liberalization, such as direct popular election of the president, freedom of the press, and the release of political prisoners. Those demonstrating were not the usual coterie of radical students and their cohorts, but a broad spectrum of Korean urban society, including the usually conservative middle class. The positive role of the United States at this juncture will be discussed later, but part of the reason for the government's forced political and human rights liberalization was the specter of the possible cancellation of the Seoul Olympics of 1988, toward which the whole nation had been focused. Tear gas floating around the Olympic stadia or the cancellation of the games outright would have been a national disgrace that no administration could have weathered. Thus, international sports had a positive effect on human rights policies. The World Cup soccer tournament, cohosted by Korea and Japan in 2002, was another such event that not only increased Korean pride and nationalism, thanks to the stellar performance of the Korean players, but also encouraged the Korean governments to ensure that their policies on rights remained liberal and were perceived as such in both Korea and the international community.

MAJOR U.S.-KOREAN INTERACTIONS ON HUMAN RIGHTS ISSUES

One approach to assessing the impact of U.S. policies on human rights in South Korea is to regard the constant interaction between the Korean governments and the United States since independence as a seamless dialogue, however effective or ineffective. Such a conception, however, fails to convey a sense of the dynamic and frustration evident (for different reasons) between the players. A more illuminating approach is to pick the cardinal points of dispute in the field of human rights. The following two lists show these points of dispute in cases in which the United States (1) intervened or attempted to intervene and (2) did not intervene or did so in a way so muted as to be completely ineffectual. The cases relate only to episodes in which political or human rights were specifically involved or directly affected.[30] Also included are the nonevents, when the lack of intervention for human rights affected both the policies and the relationships between the two states.

Cases of U.S. Intervention

- *The 1950 elections.* President Syngman Rhee attempted to postpone the 1950 elections for the National Assembly when he realized that he would lose in any fair trial. The United States forced the elections to be held. The constitution specified indirect election of the president through the National Assembly, but Rhee later changed the constitution to allow direct elections, because he believed he was popular and could manipulate the elections, which he successfully did until his ouster in 1960. He also eliminated term limitations without major U.S. public protest.

- *The trial of Cho Bong-am, 1958.* Cho, an opposition politician, was tried and convicted of treason (though he was only opposing Rhee) and sentenced to death. The United States monitored the trial and sought to get the sentence commuted but failed, and Cho was executed.

- *The departure of President Syngman Rhee, 1960.* The rigging of the elections and the death of a student in police custody resulted in the student revolution of April 19, 1960, which forced Rhee from office. The United States convinced Rhee to leave and granted him exile in Honolulu.

- *The elections of 1963.* The United States forced Park Chung Hee to hold elections, which he was reluctant to do, with threats to cut off U.S. economic aid.

- *The kidnapping of Kim Dae Jung and subsequent trial, 1973.* The Korean CIA kidnapped Kim Dae Jung in Japan and was about to assassinate him. His life was saved through the intervention of the U.S. embassy and CIA station chief. Kim and the "Myongdong dissidents" were put on trial. The United States quietly protested that this would undercut U.S. public support for the

Korean regime. The U.S. ambassador reported that "pressures [are] building for public statements" by the U.S. government criticizing the "highly critical human rights situation in Korea." The ambassador also noted the U.S. embassy's "desire to avoid such statements."[31]

- *U.S. pressure on Korea to liberalize, 1979*. After Park Chung Hee's assassination, the United States pressured interim president Choi Kyu-Ha to liberalize the political regime and repair the human rights damage of the later Park years.[32]

- *The trial of Kim Dae Jung, 1980*. Kim Dae Jung was arrested, resulting in the Kwangju uprising and the massacre of at least two hundred and perhaps as many as one thousand people. He was then tried, found guilty, and sentenced to death. On August 27, 1980, President Jimmy Carter wrote to President-elect Chun Doo Hwan:

  > I do not raise this delicate matter [of the Kim Dae Jung trial] with any wish to interfere in your internal judicial process. Nevertheless, I urge you privately to take whatever steps are necessary to avoid having the issue of fair treatment erode your nation's relations with the U.S. and other countries. Mr. Kim's execution, or even sentence of death, could have serious repercussions. . . . I urge you to take the earliest possible action to ensure the stability of the government through the development of popularly supported political institutions and greater personal freedom for your citizens.

  The United States intervened and had Kim's death sentence commuted in return for a visit by Chun to the White House after Ronald Reagan's election.

- *President Reagan's visit, 1983*. After internal debates within the administration in Washington, President Reagan decided not to make any formal protestations on human rights during his visit to Korea, though he did include some in an informal speech at a party at the U.S. embassy residence.

- *The 1987 demonstrations*. The United States intervened in the issue of mass demonstrations against the regime of Chun Doo Hwan, contributing to the liberalization of human and political rights policies and the formation of a more liberal constitution. This was probably the most successful U.S. intervention in support of greater freedom and human rights in the bilateral relationship since 1948. But as William Steuck argues: "Yet it would be inappropriate to end by complimenting the United States for what it did right. Ultimately the credit for democratization in South Korea in 1987 rests with the South Korean middle class, the salary men and women of Seoul and other cities who took to the streets in June to show their support for change."[33] Although this is patently true, the United States effectively limited Korean options, which might otherwise have included such measures as declaring martial law.

Cases of U.S. Nonintervention or Ineffectual Intervention

- *The coup of May 16, 1961*. Both the U.S. embassy chargé, Marshall Green, and the UN commander general, Magruder, privately protested this coup, and Korean troops were ordered back to their barracks but without effect. The United States called for the support of the civilian constitutional government, but "[i]n the absence of a stronger intervention on our part, the junta came into power and was from the outset somewhat hostile toward us."[34] The Korean commander asked the U.S. commander to release Korean forces to put down the coup, but the United States refused.[35]

- *The kidnappings of Korean citizens in Germany, 1967*. The German government formally protested the Korean CIA kidnappings of Korean citizens (some of whom were also tortured) and sent a legal emissary to Seoul, but the United States made no public statements on the issue.

- *The Yushin Constitution, 1972*. The Yushin Constitution came about after the Korean government had monitored the United States for its response to the September 1972 coup against President Ferdinand Marcos of the Philippines, found a negative U.S. response lacking, and decided to usher in the most repressive event in Korea's modern independent history. With the

Yushin Constitution, Park Chung Hee was essentially manipulating the political system to make himself perpetual president.

• *The coup of December 12, 1979.* The coup of Chun Doo Hwan
directly led to the Kwangju massacre and the trial of Kim Dae
Jung. To move troops for the coup, the Koreans had to obtain
permission from the U.S. commander under the Combined
Forces Command headed by the United States. They did so only
after the coup had taken place. There was no public outcry from
the United States about this event, although Ambassador
William Gleysteen personally drafted a strong statement that was
shown to both sides and broadcast over the Voice of America,
the only U.S. channel to the Korean public.[36] As Han Sang-
Jin writes:

> In May 1980, a broad range of Kwangju citizens rose up in
> protest against the arrest of Kim Dae Jung and political
> repression. The Korean special forces (not under U.S. com-
> mand) were sent in and massacred (officially) about 200 civil-
> ians, although informal reports were that the death toll was
> much higher. The U.S. military commander then authorized
> the Korean forces to occupy the town, and the U.S. was thus
> implicated in the event, which has been described as the worst
> event in Korea since the Korean War, and caused the mush-
> rooming of anti-American sentiment. It took until 1989 for
> the U.S. to issue a White Paper on Kwangju, and the silence
> was taken as an indication of complicity. The Kwangju citizens
> had hoped that the U.S. would intervene with the Korean
> government on their behalf, but this did not happen. . . .
> They [Kwangju citizens] had hoped and expected that the
> U.S. would acknowledge the historical significance and value
> of their resistance against the military dictatorship. . . . Some
> citizens regarded the U.S. as the protector of democracy and
> expected U.S. support and alliance. Some, on the other
> hand, feared for the possibility of U.S. support for Chun Doo-
> hwan's military regime. . . . At first, however, most Kwangju
> citizens believed that the U.S. would in the end support their
> democratic movement. . . . "Remembering the U.S. contribu-
> tion to 4.19 [the student revolution of 1960] democratic
> movement, we cannot help feeling betrayed by the U.S.'s

indifference and even duplicity that was demonstrated during the Kwangju uprising. The U.S. changed their initial support for Korean democracy to support the military dictatorship and its massive massacre of innocent citizens. We demand the U.S. correct its mistakes and listen to our people's true desire for democracy."[37]

The United States, however, not only was not in command of the Special Forces but was not aware of their deployment or brutal actions and did not "authorize" Korean troops to occupy the town, although it did authorize them to move troops. "The U.S. did everything it could to make these facts known publicly but was frustrated by censorship and disinformation efforts by the Chun group."[38]

KOREAN PERCEPTIONS OF THE U.S. ROLE IN HUMAN RIGHTS

The U.S. perception of the official U.S. role in improving human rights conditions in Korea is likely to be more sanguine about its effects than that of the Korean elite or students. Most polls of Koreans do not ask questions about rights, although the polls often have asked about democracy. There is a strong generalized heritage of goodwill toward Americans and the United States in general in spite of the rise of anti-American sentiment, but this should not mask the possibility of critical views about the role played by the U.S. government.[39]

Where do Koreans get their impressions of the U.S. relationship to human rights? It is not through academic studies, which in any case tend to be critical of that role. Although there is no quantifiable evidence, it seems likely that opinion about the United States and human rights is shaped in large part by the obvious presence of U.S. troops in Korea and the sometimes bitter, often sensational, stories of criminal or other rights violations by U.S. troops and the manner in which they are handled under the Status of Forces Agreement (SOFA). It seems evident that from a Korean vantage point, the United States has had a lack of trust in the Korean judicial system.[40] A number of published volumes on human rights in the Korean language have concentrated on the overwhelming number of cases in which jurisdiction has been given to the United States under SOFA, even after it has been revised. Negotiations for additional changes have recently taken place.

O Yon-ho, who has written extensively about the violations of law by Americans,[41] notes that, according to the Ministry of Foreign Affairs, between 1967 and 1987, 45,183 U.S. soldiers were involved in 39,452 crimes, and that since 1945 100,000 U.S. soldiers have broken Korean law. (Although the data are unavailable, one suspects that a great number of these crimes were traffic or other violations of limited significance.) He continues that under the 1966 SOFA, only 0.7 percent of all judicial actions against Americans in Korea were taken by the Korean courts, and that when U.S. property, security, or families are involved, or when Americans are on U.S. official business, the United States has jurisdiction. If the United States thinks the case is of high priority, then the United States will have jurisdiction. Korean police have no authority within U.S. compounds. O Yon-ho notes that even if the United States is held responsible for a crime, the Korean side must pay 25 percent of the costs of the settlement. This is more restrictive than U.S. agreements with Japan, the Philippines, or Germany, according to the author.

Kim Chin-ung undertook an interesting major survey of younger people (aged between twenty and thirty), most of them students.[42] In 1989, 54.9 percent believed that the United States was in Korea to occupy the country, not to liberate it, and one-third thought that Korea was unable to unify because of U.S. influence. Ninety-one percent wanted Korea to control military operations conducted in Korea, while 67 percent believed that the United States indirectly supported the Korean government and 28.5 percent thought the United States was in full control of the government. About 75 percent thought the United States was involved in the Kwangju massacre. A significant shift in attitudes occurred in the late 1980s: in 1987, 70 percent of these younger Koreans were pro-American, but by 1990 that number has dropped to 40 percent. In a survey that encompassed a much broader age cohort, 66 percent of Koreans believed that the United States was in Korea for profit, not to foster democracy, and 64.5 percent wanted U.S. forces to be gradually withdrawn from the peninsula.

Another writer, Cho Nam-gi, notes that the Kwangju massacre marked a turning point in anti-American sentiment, leading many Koreans to believe that the United States supported dictatorial governments.[43] A 2002 survey indicated that Koreans believed that the United States could no longer be relied on as the foremost friend of Korea—in ten years' time that position would fall to China.

Whether these authors have accurately portrayed generalized Korean attitudes may be questioned, but their findings likely represent an important element in the equation and should not be dismissed as simply serving the special interests of certain groups in Korea. The heritage of Kwangju is still real, but that of the Korean War is too old to be remembered by the bulk of the population. Thus, U.S. efforts to save Korea (for whatever purposes) in the 1950s were virtually forgotten until the revelations in the fall of 1999 about the massacre of civilians by U.S. troops at No-Gun-Ri in the early days of the Korean War. Now other stories of various killings or atrocities have surfaced, which will further inflame the erroneous but popular perception that the U.S. official role in human rights not only was not positive but may have been negative.

Once confined to a small minority of ideologically committed youth, anti-American sentiment has become widespread and markedly pronounced in South Korea. It is based in part on the ideology of a small number of young people; a generalized and growing distrust of U.S. policies on the Korean peninsula; a feeling that the United States is responsible for not only the initial division of Korea in 1945 but also its continuing division; specific incidents such as crimes committed by U.S. soldiers; trade frictions; and a sense that the United States is arrogant in dealing with the republic. Although the Korean government tends to downplay this sentiment, it is serious and growing, exacerbated by the Bush administration's policies toward President Kim Dae Jung and his administration, Bush's public diminishing of President Kim at their summit in Washington in March 2001, and U.S. policies toward North Korea. President Roh Moo Hyun was elected in December 2002 in part because of his previous questioning of the presence of U.S. troops in Korea and his appeal to Korean youth, who share his concern about U.S. dominance. Roh's election is likely to mean that U.S. influence on Korea, including on human rights issues, will diminish. President Roh is said to have indicated to a highly placed American that he could not be seen publicly to be subservient to the United States.

THE FUTURE OF HUMAN RIGHTS IN KOREA AND THE ROLE OF THE UNITED STATES

Although there is little doubt that the status of human rights in Korea today is the best in Korean history, questions necessarily arise about whether the present limitations on those rights, outlined earlier, will dissipate in the foreseeable future. What are the pressures for continuity of some of the traditional constraints of Korean society on rights? What forces exist for convergence of Korean practices in this area with worldwide trends toward democratization and the expansion of rights? And what role, if any, might the United States have in either process? Although Dante Alighieri assigns soothsayers to a very low circle of hell, to assay an estimate of the future seems essential within the context of this study.

The forces for a continuing progressive transformation of rights in Korea are manifold. That Korea needs to trade internationally to survive is self-evident. That this globalization will give Korea access to more and varied international information is obvious. Korea is already one of the world's most extensive users of the Internet on a per-capita basis. So too will Korea be more subject to international scrutiny concerning not only its economic policies and adherence to the international norms of the World Trade Organization and the OECD but also its social and political forces. The extreme sensitivity of Korea to international opinion (witness the 1988 Seoul Olympics), the World Cup in 2002, and a myriad of international fora that continuously take place in Korea all mean that the political restrictions on rights will likely be limited. As Korea in the past has regarded the hosting of such meetings as a tangible demonstration of its political and international legitimacy, these forces are likely to continue.

The civil forces within Korea that have been major elements in the growth of political pluralism in that society will contribute to sustaining human rights. Korea is irretrievably pluralistic, and as civil society has mushroomed in all fields, so concerns about the protection of political, economic, and social rights, and organizations devoted to those ends, have also grown. Any government that attempted to restrict fundamental political or economic rights without the most obvious of dire crises—for instance, a North Korean attack—could not long exist.

Korea has materially expanded the rights of labor, previously the most exploited and suppressed element of the society. Labor is now able to form political parties and back candidates for office. This change came about through Korea's entry into the OECD, which mandated improved rights for labor.[44] The status of women has improved; however, although equality is legislated in the constitution and in other laws, the reality is still far from the goal.[45] Violence against women in Korean society is profoundly disturbing. Koreans have greater access to international culture (Japanese "mass culture" was allowed to be imported only in 1999), there is less censorship of the cinema, and Koreans are freer to travel abroad. As Koreans travel and study overseas and have relatives who live overseas, these generally positive factors will continue to influence liberalization in Korea. That is the good news.

The constraints to fuller realization of human rights goals lie in the traditional attitudes toward power and authority, as mentioned earlier and discussed in the appendix, which continue to influence, if not govern, approaches to the exercise of power and its domination by the state. We may expect to see the gradual reduction of these constraints, but the process will likely be slow and even tedious, with glitches that may set back progress as crises prompt more strenuous government intervention. The social science attitudinal surveys that have been conducted indicate that a simple generational change will not prompt dismissal of some of these more traditional attitudes, although their attrition is likely. The tendency to use the National Security Law, in spite of President Kim Dae Jung's interest in its reformation, the charges regarding surveillance by the intelligence agencies that figured prominently in the press in 1999 (the very fact that they appeared was in itself progress), and attempted improper influence on the media all point to the continuity and tendency of coercive control, although these practices have been mitigated by the June 2000 summit meeting. If the term "procedural democracy" has meaning in the present, it is likely to be applicable in the future for some time.[46]

The role for the United States in these future developments is likely to be circumscribed. Even before anti-American sentiment became vociferous and widespread, the growth of Korean nationalism and pride and the absence of any appreciable degree of U.S. leverage on Korean political or social processes (in spite of continuing U.S. security concerns on the Korean peninsula even after the end of the Cold War) indicate to this observer that attempts at direct intervention are likely to be counterproductive. All Korean governments have been well aware that because of Korea's importance to the U.S. interest in protecting Japan, the United States will not take any precipitous action against the Korean state in relation to its abuses of rights. Even with the end of the Cold War, and even if North Korea should disappear or become a sleeping paper tiger, the nature of the balance of power in East Asia between Japan and China will mean that the U.S. relationship with Korea will be important to the stability of the region, although immediate security needs will likely be replaced by longer-term strategic interests. One of the dangers in Northeast Asia is an arms race, and a democratic Korea respectful of rights will mitigate some of the fears in Japan and China over a united Korea. More productive and likely to curb excesses would be the encouragement of close relationships between the international NGO community and Korean NGOs involved in the field of human rights. The international media also have a major role to play in ensuring that the prestige that Korea values so highly is not tarnished by negative reporting on conditions within Korea.

At one point the United States considered forming a regional human rights group for Northeast or East Asia. This would have been seen in the region as inappropriate (although it may have satisfied an internal U.S. constituency). Rather, the United States should continue to monitor progress in Korea but not take a leadership role. The United States could also try to employ regional organizations with which Korea is affiliated to remonstrate, should that seem appropriate. Such organizations include the OECD, the Association of Southeast Asian Nations (ASEAN), the ASEAN Regional Forum, and perhaps in the future the Asia-Pacific Economic Cooperation Group (APEC) and a Northeast Asia regional grouping devoted to security—which has been under discussion for some time. The United States should seek a delicate balance between remaining committed to the region and its security and the well-being of the Korean people and attempting to ensure through indirect means the broadening of their rights, for the preservation and expansion of those rights are in the U.S. security, as well as moral, interest.

Yet human rights are likely to be circumscribed in the future because of the cultural norms that are in tension with globalized norms, as represented to a significant degree by the United States. The Korean milieu is likely to evolve, but slowly.

THE EFFICACY OF U.S. POLICY

That official and unofficial U.S. institutions and relationships have had a positive impact on Korean governance and human rights is evident. The questions of attribution, however, are complex and involve both public and private institutions; their relative weights cannot be demonstrated. Under the worst of authoritarian regimes, the growth of U.S. influences on human rights attitudes among the population has been apparent. It seems clear, however, that in spite of the cumulative positive impact on rights, no administration (with the possible exception of the Carter administration, though his was complicated by the issue of potential U.S. troop withdrawals) had a policy that effectively incorporated human rights as a primary priority. Moreover, the evidence available does not show that a plausible and comprehensive strategy for improving rights existed, however much the development of such a milieu was deemed desirable and however much the responsible bureau in the State Department attempted to foster such rights. Democracy and human rights may have been goals of all U.S. administrations, but their pursuit was ad hoc, responsive to dire situations but not proactive, and subordinate to other, more palpable, U.S. government objectives.

William Stueck has argued that the U.S. response differed over time. The United States was more effective in the 1980s because influences outside the peninsula were significant and the U.S. role in democratization was "at best secondary" to internal conditions.[47]

In all probability, the private and cumulative effects of a variety of U.S. relationships were more important over the longer term than single policy decisions, but with one major exception. The U.S. role in the spring of 1987 was the most critical official act of the U.S. government that affected positively the rights situation in Korea. It may be argued that the changes were inevitable and that the United States simply was swept along by the tide of popular disaffection with the Chun regime. It was, however, Assistant Secretary of State Gaston Sigur's February 1987 declaration that signaled the change before the demonstrations reached crisis proportions. This was followed by later statements and visits. The motivation for that change probably occurred not because of any inherent belief in the sanctity of such rights in Korea, nor because of the inherent interest in human rights in the Reagan administration, but because the security stance of the United States and Korea on the peninsula seemed threatened, and the administration may have feared a congressional backlash if no action were taken. Thus, even when human rights were vigorously pursued, it was because of the preoccupation with security.

A second occasion when the United States acted for human rights was, in effect, damage control: the United States convincing President Syngman Rhee to leave the country in the wake of the student revolution of April 1960. There the revolution had already succeeded, and Rhee's departure avoided further violence rather than effecting change.

A seemingly positive step by the United States, the virtual forcing of General Park Chung Hee to hold elections in 1963 or face the cut-off of foreign assistance, was in fact less of a liberalizing event than it might appear. It was, rather, a legitimizing act, for it must have been evident that the military regime under no circumstances would allow Park to lose that election. The United States, thus, in effect acted as an unindicted coconspirator to ensure that tranquility on the peninsula was enforced and that Korea in international eyes was regarded as governed by an appropriate regime in power through an appropriate process. Korea is not unique in this regard; elections in other states were also intended to be internationally legitimating.

The United States did engage in positive acts on an individual level as well in response to ill-conceived Korean repressive initiatives.

The United States saved Kim Dae Jung's life twice, in 1973 and in 1980, the latter case as the quid pro quo for President Chun's invitation to the White House as President Reagan's first foreign visitor in 1981. Other, lesser-known, individuals were enabled to leave the country under U.S. ambassadorial initiatives.

Korean perceptions of these U.S. roles differ from those expressed here. Koreans have accused the United States of supporting dictatorial regimes that systematically violated human rights, and even Korean academicians have downplayed the positive U.S. role in 1987. On a number of occasions the United States either acted against liberalization or took no strong action, thus enabling repression. The continuous U.S. focus and priority on security on the peninsula has resulted in Korean perceptions that the United States condoned dictatorships. These attitudes were reinforced during periods of press censorship when there was no objective reporting on events and when the United States chose to try to influence change through quiet dialogue. Such critical points include the military coup of May 16, 1961,[48] the declaration of the Yushin Constitution of 1972, the coup of Chun Doo Hwan on December 12, 1979, and the Kwangju incident of 1980.

The emphasis on human rights issues had general effects on the U.S.-Korean relationship. President Carter's policy on human rights exacerbated the already difficult relationship between the two states, which had been dampened by his demand for total U.S. troop withdrawal (later rescinded).[49] Immediately thereafter, President Reagan's decision to avoid emphasizing human rights after Kim Dae Jung's life had been spared downplayed U.S. interest in that whole area (the U.S. ambassador did not call on any opposition figure during that period, although some of his staff did).

If, then, the record of official U.S. policies has been mixed, the overall relationship with the United States, including religious groups, the NGO community, international academic and nonprofit contacts, and Koreans living overseas, has contributed to furthering human rights in Korea. Korea's gradual transformation on human rights has been slow, with egregious regressions that have hurt both nations and their relationship. There is, thus, no cause for rejoicing over the efficacy of U.S. policies. Although it is difficult to ascertain what might have happened if the United States had intervened strongly at a number of different stages in Korean development, to this writer it seems evident that the United States could have more effectively intervened without threatening the security relationship between the two states. In the period following independence, U.S. competence on Korea was so limited that we were not prepared to deal effectively with these issues. The Cold War was still too hot, and the Korean War made a simplistic emphasis on security more palatable to both Korean and U.S. leaders. So opportunities were lost, but the Koreans have been the leading force in positively affecting change in human rights in Korea, and it has not been the government that has led this charge. Instead, reform has come in response to pressure from below.

OBSERVATIONS AND POLICY RECOMMENDATIONS BASED ON THE KOREAN EXPERIENCE

Because of the particularity of the U.S.-Korean relationship, including that evolving from the Korean War, there are issues that do not relate to U.S. policies toward other nations. Yet some generalized lessons from the Korean experience could be useful in considering actions in other countries. These lessons include the following:

- The United States has less leverage in the area of human rights (and other matters) in "client states" dependent on the United States in some way because the very fact of such a state as a client means that U.S. interests are intensive and extensive and will not be sacrificed for human rights issues alone.
- The corollary is that the fewer U.S. security or economic interests present, the more intense will be human rights concerns (e.g., Burma/Myanmar).
- The cultural milieu of each state in which human rights are a concern must be studied to see what the most effective means might be to improve such rights, and what the internal sociocultural constraints to achieving U.S. human rights policy goals are.
- The United States must avoid the arrogance and ethnocentrism that has accompanied many of the policy priorities related to

rights and other matters while at the same time continuing to advocate rights in appropriate fora. The United States should recognize that individual and group rights are real, but that the "Asian values" argument (namely, that human rights as presently formulated is a Western concept, inapplicable to Asia, which has its own set of equally valid and more germane values) is erroneous.

- The United States should appropriately distance itself from repressive regimes because otherwise, when regimes change, the United States will be accused of supporting dictatorships and repressing rights.

- A policy of transparency related to rights and regime support will prove more effective over the long term.

- Security concerns, even during the Cold War, were probably overstated, and short-term priorities given too great an emphasis over longer-term goals. Care should be taken to avoid overstressing these concerns in the future.

- The United States should question regimes that use security considerations (internal or external) as excuses for repressing rights.

- The lack of public statements on rights will be interpreted and used by repressive regimes as indicating U.S. acquiescence in or even support for their policies.

- Lack of initiative on human rights problems in a state may negatively affect the long-term U.S. relationships with that state and subsequent governments.

- U.S. embassies should be in touch with intellectual and opposition figures to be able more accurately to appraise the intellectual climate, rights issues, and relations with the United States.

- U.S. human rights policy in any state should not solely be directed toward the rights of any eminent person but should be more broadly focused (while assuring the safety of such important figures at the same time). One does not substitute for the other.

- Democratic or human rights reforms in Korea did not emanate from the elite but were forced on the elite by the society below (sometimes with U.S. support). Liberalization in Asia (except

Taiwan) has generally come from below, not from the elite power structure, and thus the United States should seek to be in contact with such elements. This raises questions of how much progress can be made on rights in difficult countries by working only with the authorities and by quiet diplomacy.

- As the single superpower, the United States can exercise overwhelming influence, but is also vulnerable to charges of domination. It should seek to work through international, regional, and private organizations without issuing strident statements that produce backlashes that can defeat the very policies being pursued. At the same time, clear indications of U.S. policy interests in human rights are important. This is a fine line requiring deft diplomacy.

- The U.S. Congress will continue to have strong interests in human rights, and any administration should attempt to seek consensus, when possible, in pursuing policies related to rights.

- The international NGO community has become important in pursuing rights and in protecting local human rights organizations, and the United States should seek to work with this community whenever possible. The explicit encouragement of the NGO community might have contributed to improvement in rights on the margin.

• • •

Appendix

STATE, SOCIETY, AND HUMAN RIGHTS IN KOREA: THE CULTURAL CONTEXT

Fundamental to any consideration of human rights are at least seven general concepts or conditions that define the discourse on rights and create sets of expectations of what those rights have been and what they might be, how far they might be pursued, and what role foreign interventions may have played. These are the concept of individualism, the concept of the appropriate role of the state, the issue of orthodoxy, the role or rule of law, the question of hierarchy, the intensity of Korean nationalism, and conceptions of and reactions to the "other"—namely, North Korea.

It is tempting for the foreign observer to view the issues of and debate about human rights, broadly defined, in Korea in a dualistic construct: the "struggle" between residual but strong Confucian values and more modern concepts, some of which evolved out of the Christian experience. The predilection to assume the validity of such an approach should be avoided because the dichotomy is intellectually unnecessary and inaccurate in the Korean context; both sets of values may exist simultaneously in different contexts, and one may reinforce the other. We understand too little about these issues to make such a generalization, however tempting it might sound.[50]

Human rights, as the term is employed in Western societies and especially in the United States, are based on an explicit concept of individualism. We tend to think of rights globally but in the singular rather than in some form of plurality or group rights. It is evident, however, that in a variety of societies, of which Korea is one, certain patterns of group cohesion and loyalty are, or may be, more important than individual interests. In Korea, the concentric circles of loyalty start with the family, both nuclear and extended, and proceed outward, invoking the clan, the associations formed from school ties and by extension the geographic region, and then broader interests.[51] It is said, for example, that in Korea marriages are a union more of families than of individuals. This concern with the group has been fundamental to Korean society, although it is undergoing change, especially among the younger generation and those who have been at least partly educated abroad. It is this very concept of what many Koreans would consider extreme individualism that in many Western societies, but especially in the United States, has been the object of criticism because of the implications that such individualism leads to the repression of group interests in the incessant pursuit of selfishness—individual economic or social gain.

The second factor is the role of the state. The template for the functions of the state and its ruling elite is that of the Confucian family. This pattern has been evident in Korean literature and governance for almost a millennium and a half, and it remains an unstated but vital element even though it is evolving in response to exposure to international cultural practices and the impact of economic globalization.

The unarticulated role of the state and its ruler is that of the father in the Confucian family. As the leader, the father has almost unlimited authority to impose his (supposedly benign) will on the members of the family. In spite of the fact that Korea now holds free and fair elections, the role of the Korean president is an "imperial" one—he is strong and expected to be strong and is able to garner the power associated with that of the father.[52] The distance between the state and the individual is very narrow, with the government having the right, indeed the moral justification as well as the authority, to intrude. The analog of the father allows the state to intervene in the lives of its children, the citizenry, for their own good and that of the collective family. Thus, as a father would tell his children what they should do, read, eat, see, study, with whom they might associate, all for their own good and that of the family, so too the state has the implicit right to regulate the lives of its citizens in manners more intrusive than might be tolerated in many other societies. Traditional and modern sumptuary laws are simply one rather benign aspect of such intervention. State intrusion on freedoms of speech, assembly, publication, advocacy, and the press has been endemic, and even the close association of the state and the business community, supposedly a cause of the Asian financial crisis of 1997, may be in part attributed to this tendency and thus is far more fundamental than economists are likely to assume. This predilection for intrusion has profound implications for perceptions of what are human rights and their place in Korean society. The literature is full of references to these aspects of Korean life, but the outside observer should not necessarily assume that the populace necessarily views such interventions with disfavor. Their tolerance of the intrusive role of the state is far greater than, for example, that of Americans. But a marked difference between today and even a decade earlier is that individuals and groups now bring their complaints on violations of rights to the courts.

Human rights and issues of law, because they are based on issues of governance and traditionally did not flow from theistic origins, tend to be more situational. That is, rights are considered in a set of hierarchical relationships, with obligations relatively more important depending on who is doing what to whom. Although these considerations are obviously important in Western societies ("mitigating circumstances" often affect trials), the tendency is more pronounced in Korean society, and the question may be asked whether the increasing enrollment in Christian churches will affect this concept.

The Confucian concept of personal patriarchal authority is supplemented and strengthened by a more theoretical concept common to many traditional societies: that is, the finite nature of power, as opposed to the modern administrative theories on the infinite nature of power. If power is infinitely expandable, then sharing, delegating, or devolving it personally or institutionally (from father to son or from central government to provincial governments, etc.) may result in more power to all at all levels (a "win-win" situation). But if power is considered finite, such delegation becomes more difficult because sharing automatically involves loss. The Korean presidency under all administrations has been called "imperial." Power then becomes personal in nature, and this results in factionalism. Loyalty relates to individuals and less to institutions or concepts, such as freedom or human rights. A cardinal example is that of political parties in Korea, all of which have been simply vehicles for personal power—its retention or gain. Since loyalty is intensely personal, a "loyal opposition" is an oxymoron with important implications for rights.[53]

Orthodox responses to the views of the leader and the state are expected. Fathers, and leaders, speak and are seen to speak ex cathedra, which means there is little diversity of viewpoint and disagreement expressed. A sense of orthodoxy is expected, and other divergent political, social, or economic views are effectively discouraged (those on the left were simply illegal). The terms used in Korean are instructive—opposing views are "impure" or "polluted," thus implying that only the authorized versions are "pure" and can be correct. Even in the present era of relative press freedom in Korea, the tendency to manipulate and control all information, which is considered a form of power, is prevalent.

Francis Fukuyama has summed up the argument this way:

> If we take Confucianism as the dominant value system in Asia, we see that it describes an ethical world in which people are born not with rights but with duties to a series of hierarchically arranged authorities, beginning with the family and extending all the way up to the state and the emperor. In this world, there is no concept of the individual and individual rights; duties are not derived from rights as they are in Western liberal thought, and although there is a concept of reciprocal obligation between ruler and ruled, there is no absolute grounding of government responsibility either in the popular will or in the need to respect an individual's sphere of autonomy.[54]

But the influence of Confucianism is not static; the pluralism now so evident in Korean society is shifting these concepts. There is a contrast between the Western reiteration of law as fundamental to the protection of rights and that in Confucian societies. The role of law in Western and Confucian societies has been profoundly different, although the pattern is now changing with pluralism and a more open judiciary since 1987. Rather than law, as in the West, being considered as a series of normative rights (involving deistic origins in many instances) as well as obligations, law in traditional Confucian societies, and in Korea as well, was invoked as punishment.

According to Dai-kwan Choi, the gradual transformation of law from traditional Korea through the Japanese occupation and liberation was not efficacious for rights:

> The law thus understood was equated with the command of the sovereign and, particularly, with criminal punishment. The arts of politics consisted in the practice of virtue and moral propriety. Therefore law in its close associations with shame and moral impropriety was conceived as to wither away when morality was fully realized with ideal politics. Law comes into play only when morality fails.[55]

But the transition from traditional attitudes toward law that occurred during the Japanese colonial era produced disastrous precedents for human rights and good governance:

> With no constitutional law, no separation of powers, and no constitutional guarantees of human rights, there was no judicial review of the exercise of political power. There was no bill of rights for Koreans. There was no notion of torts committed by the government against which a private person could claim damages. There was no way for a detained criminal defendant to request compensation from the government if he was acquitted as innocent (as provided in the present constitutional law of Korea). Koreans had nothing, as a right, to claim redress for abuse of the government-general's power, no right to be vindicated against the government at the court. The legal system of Korea under Japanese rule was a system composed essentially of rules of duties and obligations alone.[56]

Gregory Henderson has commented on the lack of change upon liberation:

> In this way it came about that, unlike in the north, no clear break occurred in the systems of security, arrest, imprisonment, torture, and legal processes in South Korea despite the complete departure of the Japanese. . . . The post-1945 police and judiciary were thus tempted toward an even more brutal repressiveness than the more secure colonialist era had usually found necessary. . . . Hence it was the character of the Japanese colonial system and the attitude toward human rights that dominated the situation, not the old, indigenous Korean system, not the aims of the independence movement or the ideas or reforms of the incoming Americans.[57]

Law also was irrelevant except as a state-sponsored tool of control under all the republics until the 1987 liberalization. The taut military command system after 1961 supplemented the heritage of the Japanese so that legal recourse was not possible until a decade ago.[58] It was not until December 1999 that the United States and Korea put into effect an extradition treaty, although discussion of such a treaty had proceeded for decades. The reason for the delay was U.S. mistrust of Korean law.[59] Even after the treaty was signed, persons charged in Korea under the National Security Law did not become subject to extradition because the United States has no such legal provisions and could not be seen to be associated with the National Security Law's repressive characteristics.

This tendency for orthodoxy was manifest in the traditional period of the Yi (or Chosun) dynasty (1392–1910), through the Japanese colonial period, under the three-year U.S. military occupation following World War II, and under the republic since 1948. This is why civil society, those organizations that are independent of the state, did not effectively develop until the political liberalization after 1987.[60] Civil society is now, however, a vital element in political and social life and a force for pluralism.[61]

Another aspect of Korean social structure relevant to human rights is that of hierarchy, which is an important element of Korean society. This is reflected in the structure of the Korean language and has been evident throughout Korean history. When Chinese institutions, such as the examination system for civil service appointments, were introduced into Korea, more hierarchical class elements were included than existed in China. Although modern Korea has evolved out of a class system, and war, destruction, economic progress, and physical mobility, as well as education, have all resulted in the elimination of the worst effects of a class society, the sense of hierarchy has not disappeared. It is less reflected in class origins but is apparent in terms of age, gender, region, occupation, and other desiderata and is retained in language. This should in no way imply that human rights or democracy may not flourish in societies that were traditionally strongly hierarchical (e.g., England), but it is the case that the concepts of human rights and democracy are based on at least a theoretical concept of equality, at least for certain purposes.[62]

Nationalism has a significant influence on the atmosphere within which foreign suggestions to reform Korean human rights policy are considered. The growth of Korean nationalism has been apparent in both states on the peninsula and cannot be ignored in any discussion of foreign policy issues.[63] Nationalism has grown in the South as a natural aspect of economic development, but also because the South Korean state depends for its survival on two external factors: the U.S. security umbrella and international trade. This dependency creates an acute sensitivity to U.S. pressure—a sensitivity exceeded only in the case of Korean-Japanese relations—and makes it likely that such pressure will generate a nationalistic backlash. Thus, U.S. pressures on any Korean administration to take any action (known as "humiliating diplomacy"), including action to improve human rights and to revise the provisions of the Status of Forces Agreement that involve human rights, have always elicited strong dissent in some Korean quarters. In fact, the more the United States propounded democracy and rights, the more the nationalistic reaction among some prompted Koreans to equate democracy with not following U.S. guidance.[64]

The final aspect of the human rights milieu relates to the contest for legitimacy and even survival with North Korea. The competition with North Korea means in part that both North and South have defined themselves in contrast with the "other." The threat of invasion and subversion from North Korea, at least in earlier years, should not be underestimated. Nevertheless, it is also evident that this threat has been used to perpetuate the intrusive role of the state in South Korea and has been a means, through various legislation and social pressures, to ensure ideological conformity and behavior and media compliance, and to perpetuate the power of the various governments in the South.[65] Thus human rights have been severely and continuously circumscribed on this basis.

NOTES

The author is indebted to Kim Sang-in of Korea University for his assistance in researching Korean source material, and to the members of the United States Institute of Peace's review committee, who offered many valuable suggestions.

1. One senior U.S. embassy official of the 1970s said that an "'inordinate" amount of time was spent trying to respond to congressional inquiries about individual human rights violations brought to the embassy's attention by Korean Americans. U.S. embassy official, interview by author, Washington, D.C. In 2002 more than 49,000 Korean students were studying in the United States.

2. Donald S. Macdonald, "U.S. Human Rights Objectives and Korean Realities," in *Human Rights in Korea: Historical and Policy Perspectives,* ed. William Shaw (Cambridge, Mass.: East Asian Legal Studies Program, Harvard Law School, 1991), 253–254.

3. William Shaw, introduction to *Human Rights in Korea,* 11–12.

4. Korea has elected Buddhist, Protestant, and Catholic leaders. Although only 2 percent of Koreans count themselves as religiously Confucian, the population as a whole retains Confucian social values. There has been a remarkable transition from the persecution of Western religions (Catholicism particularly) and large numbers of martyrs in the eighteenth and nineteenth centuries to the essential indigenization and expansion of Christianity, which now conservatively accounts for some 25 percent of the Korean population.

5. In 1945 the U.S. military government in Korea had three education objectives: democratization, decentralization, and coeducation after primary school. The United States expended considerable funds in education to achieve these objectives, none of which have been realized.

6. A constitutional review commission existed for fifteen years before 1987. It was designed to review legislation for adherence to the constitution, but it never reviewed a case. This situation has now changed, and the court does occasionally find against the government.

7. These are set forth in some detail in the appendix to this essay.

8. In the Kim Dae Jung administration, there were efforts to change the National Security Law by limiting its enforcement. After the June 2000 summit in Pyongyang between Chairman Kim Jong Il and President Kim Dae Jung, much of the law seemed to be irrelevant, as censorship was restricted and speaking ill of the North was discouraged. The future of the law in its present form is questionable; it is likely to be significantly altered. President Roh Moo Hyun, who took office in February 2002, is interested in continuing President Kim Dae Jung's "Sunshine Policy" (engagement policy) with the North.

9. See David I. Steinberg, "The Republic of Korea: Human Rights, Residual Wrongs, New Initiatives," *Asian Perspective* 20, no. 2 (fall-winter 1996): 185–209. See also Park Won Soon, *The National Security Law: Instrument of Political Repression in South Korea* (Los Angeles: Korea Human Rights Network, 1993). In 1958 the U.S. embassy said that the National Security Law was a threat to civil liberties—this view endured until April 2000, when the summit plans were announced. See Donald S. Macdonald, *U.S.-Korean Relations from*

Liberation to Self-Reliance: The Twenty-Year Record (Boulder, Colo.: Westview, 1992), 195–199. (This study, based on State Department archives, was originally classified and then declassified for publication.)

10. See David I. Steinberg, "On Ideological Orthodoxy," in *Stone Mirror: Reflections on Contemporary Korea* (Norwalk, Conn.: EastBridge, 2002), 197–199.

11. Doh C. Shin, *Mass Politics and Culture in Democratizing Korea* (Cambridge: Cambridge University Press, 1999), 252. Shin did not directly poll on human rights. It would be interesting, but probably impossible, to know what rights and freedoms South Koreans would be prepared to give up if unification were to take place.

12. The question of whether the end of the Cold War has altered this policy will be discussed later. The nuclear crisis with North Korea of 2002–03 has reinvigorated security concerns because nuclear proliferation and weapons of mass destruction are global U.S. priorities (not so for South Korea, whose security interests are, first, peninsular, and then regional). Since September 11, 2001, U.S. security has focused on terrorism as well.

13. Beginning in 1965, when normalization of relations with Japan occurred, Korea received $800 million in loans, grants, and credits from Japan over a ten-year period.

14. The Korean government was to be "responsive to popular needs, with objectives, institutions, and methods compatible with Free World ideals," and Korea was to be a "showcase for democracy in Asia." Macdonald, *U.S.-Korean Relations from Liberation to Self-Reliance*, 31, 33, 141.

15. Secretary of State Henry Kissinger's staff meeting, Washington, D.C., January 25, 1974, secret (declassified). It may be that Habib, knowing Kissinger's predilection for realpolitik, stressed those aspects.

16. Many congressional supporters of Korea did voice concern about human rights issues. In April 1976, 119 senators and representatives signed a letter to President Gerald Ford that complained about "continuing suppression" of rights after Christians were arrested, and warned that continuing U.S. military support to Korea could make the United States "an accomplice to repression." Six months later, 154 congresspeople wrote to the president on Korean "disrespect for human rights," undermining U.S.-Korean relations. Donald Oberdorfer, *The Two Koreas: A Contemporary History* (New York: Basic Books, 1997), 91–92. Such broad congressional concern occurred during the infamous, repressive Yushin period of Park Chung Hee's presidency. Although individual congresspeople may have been upset over Syngman Rhee's repression or Chun Doo Hwan's authoritarianism, those periods did not evoke the same level of response.

17. According to Lee Chae-Jin and Hideo Sato, "Beyond furthering the Korean interest in ensuring consistent and favorable policies from the United States, the scheme that produced the Koreagate scandals was launched to blunt

the growing U.S. criticisms of President Park's repressive policies and human rights violations." Lee Chae-Jin and Hideo Sato, *U.S. Policy toward Japan and Korea: A Changing Influence Relationship* (New York: Praeger, 1982), 75.

18. Macdonald, *U.S.-Korean Relations from Liberation to Self-Reliance*, 3.

19. Jerome Alan Cohen and Edward J. Baker, "U.S. Foreign Policy and Human Rights in South Korea," in *Human Rights in Korea*, 173.

20. Macdonald, *U.S.-Korean Relations from Liberation to Self-Reliance*, 25. The importance of human rights to the Carter administration was apparent in Korean policy. The U.S. embassy in Seoul believed that public criticism of Park Chung Hee would encourage other Koreans to try to replace him. According to William Gleysteen, "When Park was assassinated, quite a few Koreans on the left and right of political center were convinced that my very public recall to Washington in early October to protest Kim Young Sam's ouster from that National Assembly was a deliberate action to withdraw legitimacy from Park and invite others to take charge." Ambassador William Gleysteen, letter to author.

21. Lee and Sato, *U.S. Policy toward Japan and Korea*, 90–94.

22. This type of threat, however, had limited usefulness. A classified study noted that the U.S. Agency for International Development (USAID) threatened to cut off program loans unless certain economic stabilization measures were taken, but USAID recognized that the cutoff could only be temporary because of security considerations. Of course, the Koreans also realized this, so the initiatives had limited effectiveness. Elizabeth Carter, "Korea," in *The Use of Program Loans to Influence Policy*, AID Evaluation Paper 1A, March 1970, confidential (later declassified).

23. The fear of the loss of legitimacy indicates both the fragility of that factor and the continuing influence of the United States, suggesting that the United States could have exerted more pressure for human rights on the government than it did. How much this might have affected security concerns is questionable.

24. There are many examples of this behavior. In Department of State cable Seoul #3365 (April 25, 1977, secret [declassified]), the Korean ambassador urged the United States to avoid any public attacks on President Park, because this would give Park a chance to modify his policies without U.S. pressure. The U.S. ambassador (Seoul #2723, April 5, 1977, secret [declassified]) wrote, "I stressed [to the Koreans] pressures so far resisted to publicly criticize ROKG on this [human rights] issue."

25. For example, Ambassador Dowling recommended that Washington "stimulate" U.S. press coverage to convince Koreans to eliminate repressive press provisions. The State Department response was not helpful at first; it claimed that these provisions were an internal Korean affair and would not comment on Dowling's proposal. The United States did say later in a personal letter to Rhee (dated December 14, 1958) that "it hoped it [the National Security Law] would not be used to hinder democratic development." Macdonald, *U.S.-Korean Relations from Liberation to Self-Reliance*, 196. That the Korean press is still reluctant to do investigative reporting is illustrated by the fall 1999 revelations in the *New York Times* about the No-Gun-Ri massacre during the Korean War. Only then did the Korean press publicize the massacre. It seems likely that the Korean press had either been earlier warned off the story by the regime or indulged in the often-employed self-censorship. See David Steinberg, "Stone Mirror" column: "On Atrocities and the Press," *Korea Times*, October 6, 1999.

26. This was especially true during the Kwangju uprising in 1980.

27. Habib, in the Kissinger staff meeting of January 25, 1974, noted, "I think [Korean] Christian ministers have not been persecuted because of the reaction of the United States." The use of churches is still important in the protection of human rights. In January 2000, 450 civic organizations organized a blacklist of corrupt and otherwise inappropriate legislators who, the organization hoped, would abstain from or be defeated in the National Assembly elections of April 13, 2000. These organizations remained anonymous under the protection of the Anglican church in Seoul.

28. The German foundations after World War II associated with political parties were also active in fields such as labor rights, women's affairs, and local autonomy and rights.

29. The Koreans openly asserted before the Seoul event that as the Tokyo Olympics of 1964 put Japan back on the international map, so the Seoul Olympics of 1988 would do the same for Korea.

30. For example, the dispute over the armistice of the Korean War in 1953 was serious, as Syngman Rhee did not want it and refused to sign; the United States had to give certain guarantees (a defense treaty and an increase in Korean forces). But since human rights were not specifically included, this dispute is not listed here.

31. Seoul #2878, April 9, 1977, secret (declassified).

32. According to William Gleysteen, "In my experience with Korea this was the most systematic and sustained effort to achieve progress in governance as well as human rights. It continued quite seriously after the 12/12 power play [Chun Doo Hwan's coup of December 12, 1979] by Chun and was only snuffed out in April 1980 by Chun's progressive encroachment into the civil area." Gleysteen, letter to author.

33. William Steuck, "Democratization in Korea: The United States Role, 1980 and 1987," *International Journal of Korean Studies* 2, no. 1 (fall-winter 1998): 1–26.

34. "U.S. Relations with the Korean Military Junta," memorandum, March 27, 1963, secret (declassified). No author given.

35. May 16, 1961, cable (no number, retyped), secret (declassified). There were sufficient U.S. forces to accomplish that. When the coup succeeded, the United States asked the embassy to "confer on successor government to maximum attainable [to] extend an *aura* of legality, continuity, and legitimate constitutional succession" (emphasis added). State-to-Seoul #1321, May 17, 1961, secret (declassified). The United States considered cutting off military and economic aid but did not do so.

36. Gleysteen, letter to author.

37. Han Sang-Jin, "Popular Sovereignty and a Struggle for Recognition from a Perspective of Human Rights," *Korea Journal* 39, no. 2 (summer 1999): 184–204. The last part of the quotation is from the "Announcement of May 1981 in the name of the Chonnam people. For the views of one of the critical participants in both the coup of December 12, 1979, and Kwangju, see William H. Gleysteen, Jr., *Massive Entanglement, Marginal Influence: Carter and Korea in Crisis* (Washington, D.C.: Brookings Institution Press, 1999). He also has extensive material on the Carter human rights concerns in Korea. A volume on Kwangju is Donald N. Clark, ed., *The Kwangju Uprising: Shadows over the Regime in South Korea* (Boulder, Colo.: Westview, 1988). For a strong conflicting view critical of the lack of a positive U.S. response, see Chalmers Johnson, *Blowback: The Costs and Consequences of American Empire* (New York: Henry Holt, 2000), 95–118.

38. Gleysteen, letter to author.

39. See the summary report on the conference "Korean Attitudes toward the United States: The Enduring and Endured Relationship" (Georgetown University, Washington, D.C., January 30–February 1, 2003); a copy is available on the Asian Studies website, www.georgetown.edu/sfs/programs/asia/publications/ conferences/Korean.Anti-American.Conference.3.5.pdf. A volume of papers presented at the conference is forthcoming: David I. Steinberg, ed., *The Enduring and Endured Relationship: Korean Attitudes toward the United States* (New York: M. E. Sharpe, 2004).

40. The most serious incident involving the U.S. military was the deaths of two middle-school girls caused by a U.S. armored vehicle in 2002. Two soldiers were tried by U.S. court martial and found innocent, prompting massive anti-American demonstrations in front of the U.S. embassy. The trial, which was ineptly timed, illustrated the differences between the Korean and U.S. judicial systems. In Korea, someone must be found guilty and responsible, while in the United States this need not be the case. Koreans made strong statements on the need to revise the SOFA to give Koreans jurisdiction in cases involving U.S. forces and Korean civilians.

41. O Yon-ho, *Singminji ui adul ege: pal ro ch'ajun panmi kwogwaso* (The son of a colony) (Seoul: Paeksan Sodang, 1989). Another volume similarly critical of the SOFA is *In-kwon Paekso* (White paper on human rights) (Seoul: P'yonghwa Minjudang In-kwon Wiwonhoe, 1990).

42. Kim Chin-ung, *Han'gugin ui panmi kamjong* (Korean anti-American sentiment) (Seoul: Ilchogok, 1992).

43. Cho Nam-gi, *Yoksa wa inkwon* (History and human rights) (Seoul: Taehan Kidokkyo Sohoe, 1989).

44. Changes in labor legislation and labor's entry into politics are directly attributable to Korean entry into the OECD, which was pushed for political, not economic, reasons.

45. It may be worth noting that regulations that gave (male) veterans a certain point advantage on civil service examinations and placements were overturned by the Korean courts in 1999 on the grounds that women were not subject to the draft and thus were discriminated against in violation of the constitution. Women occupied about 6 percent of the National Assembly seats after the April 13, 2000, elections, about triple their previous representation (though some seats were gained by appointment, not election).

46. Procedural democracy refers to the existence of all the modern institutional elements of a democratic system, but with the concepts of power remaining traditional, thus affecting how those institutions operate. See the appendix.

47. Stueck, "Democratization in Korea." Progress no doubt was due to the Koreans themselves, but the United States in 1987 played an important role by limiting the parameters of official Korean response.

48. The United States did protest the 1961 coup but then decided to live with the event and the resulting military regime.

49. Had troops been withdrawn, however, perhaps potential U.S. influence on rights would have been lessened. Gleysteen, letter to author.

50. For example, see C. Fred Alford, *Think No Evil: Korean Values in the Age of Globalization* (Ithaca, N.Y.: Cornell University Press, 1999). This volume discusses the role of the concept in Korea and the Korean perceptions of Western dualism.

51. The ties that are closest are those forged at high school (which by their nature are also regional ties), college, military academy, and so on.

52. The most flagrant example of the leader as father is that of North Korea's Kim Il Sung, who was constantly referred to as the father of the people and the state. The use of the phrase "father of his country" to refer to George Washington in no way conveys the intensity of the use of the term in North Korea, nor to the role of fathers in general. One of the major criticisms of Roh Tae Woo as president was that he was *mul* (literally, water; wishy-washy) and did not fulfill the role of a strong leader.

53. See David I. Steinberg, "'Continuing Democratic Reform in the Republic of Korea: The Unfinished Symphony," in *Deepening Democracy in Korea*, ed. Larry Diamond (Boulder, Colo.: Westview, 1998). A recent example was the January 2000 transformation of President Kim Dae Jung's party into the new "Millennium Democratic Party."

54. Francis Fukuyama, "Asian Values, Korean Values, and Democratic Consolidation," in *Institutional Reform and Democratic Consolidation in Korea*, ed. Larry Diamond and Doh Chull Shin (Stanford, Calif.: Hoover Institution Press, 2000), 307–308. Fukuyama disagrees with the concept of "Asian values," as does this author, yet the description does accurately portray a traditional viewpoint relevant to Korea. The issue is not its past relevance, but its contemporary impact.

55. Dai-kwan Choi, "Development of Law and Legal Institutions in Korea," in *Traditional Korean Legal Attitudes*. Korean Research Monograph no. 3, ed. Chun Bong Duck, William Shaw, and Dai-Kwon Choi (Berkeley: University of California, Center for Korean Studies, 1980), 59–60.

56. Ibid., 77.

57. Gregory Henderson, "Human Rights in South Korea, 1945–1953," in *Human Rights in Korea*, ed. Shaw, 133.

58. President Park Chung Hee was in the Japanese military, and many of his attitudes stem from that experience.

59. David Steinberg, "Stone Mirror" column: "On Law and Extradition," *Korea Times*, January 2000.

60. The issue of civil society has evoked considerable debate in Korean academic circles. For a view of the lack of such institutions, see David I. Steinberg, "Human Rights and Civil Society in Korea: The Influence of Orthodoxy and Ideology," *Korea Journal* 37, no. 4 (winter 1997); and "The Republic of Korea: Human Rights, Residual Wrongs, New Initiatives," *Asian Perspective* 20, no. 2 (fall-winter 1996): 185–209.

61. This is evident from the "blacklisting" of corrupt and inappropriate potential candidates for the National Assembly elections by more than four hundred NGOs in January–February 2000.

62. The causes for the extremely rapid expansion of Christianity in Korea over a generation (from perhaps 10 percent of the population to more than 25 percent, mostly Protestants) are under debate, but one reason may have been the stress on egalitarianism and democracy, which may have struck a responsive chord among many Koreans. The hierarchy of traditional Korean society was apparent not only in the gentry system (the *yangban*) but also in the large slave population in the Yi dynasty (1392–1910), a population significantly larger than that in China. Peasant rebellions in Korea often focused on the destruction of the slave registers.

63. One of the appeals of North Korea to South Korean youth is the apparent stress on nationalism, which is manifest in the Kim Il Sung theoretical doctrine of *juche*, or autonomy or self-reliance. This has been built into a religious-like orthodoxy to which titular adherence is required, but whose accuracy is dubious.

64. Kim Sunhyuk, *The Politics of Democratization in Korea: The Role of Civil Society* (Pittsburgh: University of Pittsburgh Press, 2000), 75.

65. According to Youm Kyu-ho, "No matter how the status of press freedom under American military government rule in 1945–1948 is characterized, Koreans in general for the first time experienced a taste of press freedom as part of their daily life. . . . The unprecedented exposure of Koreans to the Western concept of a free press during the era of the American military rule has contributed enormously to the future sociopolitical development of South Korea. The American military government strove in principle to cultivate a free press in Korea modeled after the American press. When it came to the actual implementation of its policy, however, the government employed a number of authoritarian mechanisms that often contradicted its own political and ideological commitment to a liberal democracy." Koreans learned from the United States to cherish a free press, but they also adopted some U.S. military restrictive provisions on it. Youm Kyu-ho, *Press Law in South Korea* (Ames: Iowa State University Press, 1996), 74.

Part III
Europe

7

U.S. Policy and Human Rights in Bosnia

The Transformation of Strategic Interests

JON WESTERN

FROM 1992 TO 1995 BOSNIA was a human rights and humanitarian nightmare. More than two hundred thousand people—mostly civilians—were killed; between two and three million civilians were physically and psychologically terrorized and forcibly evicted from their homes; tens of thousands were incarcerated in concentration-style camps and thousands of prisoners were summarily executed; and thousands of women were victims of systematic rape campaigns. The country's major cities were held under siege for most of the war as combatants deliberately tried to freeze and starve the civilian inhabitants; whole villages were razed to prevent the return of refugees; civilians were routinely used by combatants as human shields; and delivery of humanitarian relief supplies was obstructed and supplies were frequently looted.

Despite these egregious human rights violations, for three and a half years U.S. policy on the Bosnian war remained largely unresponsive and ineffective. Driven principally by domestic politics and entrenched

Cold War–era conceptions of geostrategic interests, the United States only occasionally deterred abuses and in fact awkwardly, albeit unintentionally, contributed to them.

The cornerstone of U.S. policy from the earliest stages of Yugoslavia's disintegration and later during the war in Bosnia was that this region was not vital to Washington's interests. Consequently, senior U.S. policymakers—in both the Bush and Clinton administrations—did not significantly commit U.S. diplomatic or military resources to prevent or stop the human rights abuses until 1995, when the ongoing systematic violations of international humanitarian and human rights law transformed U.S. interests.[1] In mid-1995, following Serb massacres of civilians in the UN-designated safe areas of Srebrenica and Zepa, senior U.S. officials concluded that the human rights and humanitarian crisis in Bosnia threatened the fundamental credibility of the United Nations and NATO and, consequently, threatened core U.S. interests in those institutions. With the perception of NATO credibility at stake, the persistent human rights and humanitarian violations in Bosnia evolved from subordinate foreign policy concerns into a central geostrategic interest for U.S. foreign policy. In August 1995 President Clinton committed extensive U.S. diplomatic and military leadership to end the war.

The U.S.-brokered Dayton Peace Accords signed in November 1995 effectively ended the war. At Dayton the parties agreed to demobilize their military forces, to share power in a unified Bosnian state, and, at the behest of U.S. negotiators, to respect and implement several European Convention human rights protocols and provisions —including pledges to ensure the security and liberty of all citizens, to cooperate with the International Criminal Tribunal on Yugoslavia, to allow the freedom of movement, to support the right of refugees to return to their prewar homes, and to hold free and fair democratic elections. The United States led an international Implementation Force (IFOR) to provide security for the postwar transition.

In the years following the war, the human rights record has substantially improved. IFOR, which became the Stabilization Force (SFOR) in December 1996, has largely stabilized the security environment throughout the country. In each successive year since the war, political killings, ethnic violence, and police torture have declined dramatically. Still, despite their rhetoric to the contrary, the United States and SFOR have consistently refrained from participating in full implementation of the Dayton human rights provisions, and critical human rights issues remain unresolved. Only a small number of refugees have been allowed to return. And many of those who have returned continue to face obstruction and endure hostility from local officials. Fewer than a hundred of the thousands of war criminals have been indicted and far fewer have been arrested or prosecuted. And the nationalist parties still dominate most of the political and economic resources.

This chapter examines U.S. human rights policy toward Bosnia —from the dissolution of the Yugoslav federation and the formal recognition of Bosnia to the war, the peace process, and finally the initial phases of the postwar peace implementation. In particular, this chapter demonstrates the influences of human rights and humanitarian issues on the formulation of that policy and how events on the ground in Bosnia and subsequent pressure by the media, nongovernmental organizations, and the bureaucracy changed senior policymakers' conceptions of U.S. interests.

DISINTEGRATION OF THE FEDERATION, U.S. INTERESTS, AND THE ABSENCE OF PREVENTIVE DIPLOMACY

During the Cold War, U.S. policy toward communist-controlled Yugoslavia was motivated principally by geostrategic interests.[2] Yugoslavia, under the control of Josip Broz Tito, broke from the Soviet Union in 1948 and maintained an independent socialist foreign policy throughout the Cold War. The country's geographic proximity to NATO and Warsaw Pact countries and its long and deep coastline on the Adriatic convinced U.S. policymakers that Yugoslavia's independence from Moscow was vital to U.S. and European interests. Warren Zimmerman, the last U.S. ambassador to the Yugoslav Federation summed up the relationship: "As long as the cold war continued, Yugoslavia was a protected and sometimes pampered child of American and Western diplomacy."[3]

Tito's death in 1980, coupled with the global recession, precipitated economic and political turmoil in Yugoslavia. Tito had left a
cumbersome power-sharing political structure enshrined in the 1974
constitution, in which power was dispersed among the country's six
republics. To prevent Serb domination of a post-Tito federation, the
1974 constitution also granted autonomy and federal representation to
Kosovo and Vojvodina, two provinces within Serbia. The result, however, was a system unable to deal with political rivalries and economic
disparities among the republics. By 1988, under the pressure of extensive foreign debt and paralyzed by increasing ethnically based political
cleavages, Yugoslavia's economy collapsed. Unemployment reached
nearly 40 percent in the southern republics and the inflation rate
topped at nearly 25,000 percent—the fourteenth-highest inflation
rate in world history. Soup lines emerged on the streets of Belgrade for
the first time since World War II.

At the same time, Slobodan Milosevic surfaced in the Serb
leadership by tapping into a growing sense of unease among Serbs and
reigniting Serb nationalism. Beginning in 1988 Milosevic launched a
crackdown against Kosovar Albanians, and in 1989 Milosevic and the
Serb parliament usurped the 1974 Yugoslav constitution and revoked
Kosovo's autonomous status. Milosevic also began an effort to recen-
tralize and take control of Yugoslav federal political and economic
authority at the expense of the republics. While Milosevic's repressive
Kosovo policy and recentralization schemes were extraordinarily popular among Serbs, they fueled nationalist secessionist movements in
Slovenia and Croatia and further fragmented the federation.[4] By late
1989, as repressive centralized communist structures fell throughout
the rest of Eastern and Central Europe, all the warning signs suggested that Yugoslavia was headed for a violent breakup.

The disintegration process in Yugoslavia coincided with the easing of U.S.-Soviet tensions in the late 1980s and ultimately the end
of the Cold War. Without the superpower rivalry, Yugoslavia was no
longer significant to Washington's security interests in Europe, and as
a result, its overall importance among U.S. foreign policy priorities
significantly declined. The focus of the Bush administration's Yugoslavia policy shifted from one of geostrategic importance, in which the
United States courted Yugoslavia and accommodated its socialist

system, to one of only marginal importance, in which the United States modestly pursued a more ambivalent task of encouraging and promoting unity, democracy, human rights, and economic reforms.

In 1989 President George Bush appointed the U.S. ambassador to the Conference on Security and Cooperation in Europe (CSCE), Warren Zimmerman, an experienced diplomat on human rights and democracy issues, as ambassador to Yugoslavia. Despite the elevation of human rights and encouragement for democratic transition that Zimmerman's appointment signaled, overall the United States pursued a rather passive, minimalist policy that was limited almost exclusively to diplomatic démarches and other rhetorical pronouncements supporting Yugoslav unity, although Zimmerman also repeatedly condemned Serb actions in Kosovo.[5]

In the absence of stronger and more persuasive policy instruments to shore up Yugoslavia's economy and assist in the development of democratic institutions, however, U.S. efforts to slow or control the disintegration process were ineffective. In 1989 and 1990, for example, the United States gave rhetorical support to Yugoslav premier Ante Markovic and his market-based economic reform program. The United States encouraged Markovic and the Yugoslav government to implement IMF-prescribed austerity measures that included tightening credit, reducing government spending, and raising taxes to constrict the money supply.[6] Despite repeated requests for financial assistance from the Yugoslav federal government and warnings from Markovic that without such assistance the economic reforms would fail and further unleash ethnic nationalism, the Bush administration and Congress refused to provide any significant financial resources.[7] In fact, Yugoslavia was shut out of virtually all U.S. assistance earmarked for Eastern Europe (all of the 1989 Support for East European Democracy Act was targeted at Poland and Hungary).[8] Furthermore, not only did the U.S. policy fail to stem the economic collapse; it also failed to deter Slobodan Milosevic's policy of repression and the subsequent dramatic rise in human rights abuses by Serb secret police in Kosovo.

By the fall of 1990, the U.S. intelligence community concluded that Yugoslavia was on the verge of civil war and predicted a catastrophic human rights and humanitarian crisis.[9] Nonetheless, the Bush administration ignored pleas from within the State Department bureaucracy for more aggressive preventive diplomatic initiatives and continued to limit its policy focus.[10] Throughout much of 1990 and early 1991, Bush and his chief advisers were focused on German reunification and the massive diplomatic effort to forge the international coalition to support Operation Desert Shield (and ultimately Operation Desert Storm). With their plate full, they were unable to (and unwilling to) delegate additional diplomatic resources at the critical juncture before the disintegration of Yugoslavia was complete and showed little interest in or concern about the situation. As Susan Woodward concludes:

> The summer of 1990 was clearly a time when foreign warnings against the violation of human rights wherever it occurred—in Serbia, Croatia, or Macedonia—could have made a difference in establishing legitimacy for the CSCE norms and for individual rights, preventing the escalation of conflict in the Krajina, and giving support—through even-handed behavior—to moderate forces in Serbia and Croatia that were pressing for dialogue with minorities against their nationalist governments.[11]

It was not until June 1991, however, that Secretary of State James Baker finally focused on the region and attempted a last-ditch effort at preventive diplomacy. Baker made his only trip to Yugoslavia just four days before Slovenia and Croatia declared their independence. During his eleven-hour visit, Baker impressed most of the Serb, Croat, and Slovene leaders with his rhetorical skills. However, he offered no tangible diplomatic initiatives or committed leadership to avert the impending conflict.[12] He paid lip service to the Helsinki principles on border changes and minority rights, but the purpose of his visit was to discourage the two republics from taking unilateral action and declaring independence. He also issued an ambiguous call for the Serb leadership in Belgrade not to use force to keep the country together.[13] Robert Hutchings, then director of European affairs at the National Security Council (NSC), later concluded that since it was apparent to those in Yugoslavia that the United States was only minimally interested in the crisis, Baker's statements may even have been somewhat counterproductive:

> [B]y warning equally against unilateral declarations of independence and [against] the use of force to hold the federation together . . .

[the United States] seemed to be sanctioning the latter [by the Serbs] if the Slovenes and the Croats resorted to the former.[14]

In sum, by 1991 Yugoslavia was no longer a significant interest or priority for U.S. foreign policy. Baker and other U.S. officials were well aware of the potential for violence and the potential for violence to lead to widespread violations of international human rights and humanitarian law. And in response to the impending violence, Baker and others in the Bush administration expressed support for human rights and hope for peaceful resolution of the political crisis. But without broader strategic concerns in Yugoslavia, they were not interested in committing significant diplomatic or economic energy to resolving the crisis nor were they willing to do so. Within days of Baker's only trip to Yugoslavia, war erupted in Slovenia and in Croatia.

Many of those most intimate with U.S. policy formation during this period have since concluded that a more robust preventive diplomatic effort could have forestalled the surge of violence and massive human rights violations. Ambassador Zimmerman has concluded that Milosevic might have been deterred had Baker issued threats of a U.S. or NATO military response to Serb attacks in Slovenia or Croatia.[15] NSC staffer David Gompert also has concluded that

> [s]ince the Bush administration was not prepared to take military action, it chose not to issue any explicit warnings, even though nothing less would have changed Serb policy. Milosevic could see by 1990 that he was safe to ignore American pressure, since no concrete threats, much less actions, accompanied Washington's stern demarches.[16]

WAR IN CROATIA AND BELATED PREVENTIVE DIPLOMACY IN BOSNIA

The Yugoslav wars began with a short, six-week conflict in Slovenia in the summer of 1991. In response to Slovenia's efforts to take control over its borders, the Serb-dominated federal leadership in Belgrade deployed the Yugoslav National Army (JNA). After six weeks of sporadic battles, the JNA withdrew and Belgrade largely conceded Slovenia. Croatia, however, was much more problematic. Whereas

Slovenia was largely ethnically homogenous and distant from Belgrade, more than a half million Serbs lived in Croatia. The fighting in Croatia erupted with much more intensity and violence. Warring factions deliberately targeted civilians: hundreds were murdered and thousands were forcibly displaced from their communities. Throughout the fall, the Serb-led Yugoslav army and navy encircled cities and towns and indiscriminately launched artillery attacks against civilian targets—most notably Vukovar in eastern Slavonia and the historic Adriatic seaport of Dubrovnik. For eighty days the Serbs shelled Vukovar, one of the most peaceful and ethnically mixed communities before the war. When the city finally fell in November 1991, all non-Serbs were forcibly expelled and, in a particularly egregious violation of international humanitarian law, Serb paramilitaries and JNA units attacked and executed more than 150 wounded Croat soldiers and civilians at the Vukovar hospital.

After these human rights violations occurred, the Bush administration came under increased pressure from the media, Congress, several nongovernmental organizations, and staff members within the State Department to issue explicit military warnings to the Serbs to stop their attacks on civilians.[17] At the Pentagon, as part of their standard regional planning process, U.S. military planners prepared contingency plans for the demonstration and use of U.S. naval and air power in the Adriatic to stop Serb attacks. Nonetheless, despite reports of massive human rights violations and gross breaches of international humanitarian law, President Bush and his advisers maintained that, while the events in Yugoslavia were unfortunate, the crisis in Yugoslavia was "simply a humanitarian issue" that did not threaten U.S. strategic interests in the region.[18] No one in the Bush administration, working under this basic assessment of U.S. interests, considered using U.S. force. Furthermore, no one considered using the threat of U.S. force to support Washington's diplomatic efforts. Instead, Bush and his advisers concluded that Yugoslavia was a "European problem" and subsequently deferred international leadership and mediation efforts to the Europeans and to the United Nations. The United States' response during this phase of the Yugoslav wars was limited to modest efforts to condemn the fighting and to secure the passage of United Nations Security Council Resolution 713, calling for an international arms embargo on Yugoslavia.

In January 1992, after Serb and Croat forces reached a stalemate on the battlefield, UN negotiator Cyrus Vance successfully mediated a cease-fire in Croatia that included the deployment of UN peace-keepers. With Croatia stabilized (at least for the time being), the future of Bosnia took center stage in the region. Throughout 1991 the U.S. intelligence community warned that war in Bosnia would invariably be a much greater human rights and humanitarian crisis than the war in Croatia. Demographically, Bosnia was the most ethnically mixed and integrated republic in Yugoslavia. Muslims constituted 44 percent of the Bosnian population; Serbs, 31 percent; and Croats, 17 percent. Throughout 1991 leaders in Belgrade and Zagreb routinely intimated their desire to establish control over Bosnia as part of the drive for Greater Serbia and Greater Croatia.[19] In the fall of 1991 the Bosnian Muslims, under the leadership of President Alija Izetbegovic, concerned about the future of Muslims in a Serb-dominated rump Yugoslavia and seduced by their own increasingly nationalistic agenda, introduced a resolution on Bosnian independence in the Bosnian parliament. For their part, the Bosnian Serbs—already preparing for a military showdown in Bosnia—used the event as a pretext to walk out of the Bosnian parliament and establish their own autonomous Republika Srpska within Bosnia.

Despite these warning signs throughout 1991, the Bush administration ignored the Bosnia question until early 1992. By then the administration was on the defensive for its passive response to the Serb attacks at Dubrovnik and Vukovar. Aware of predictions that an even greater humanitarian crisis was looming in Bosnia, the Bush administration, despite its limited interests in the region, examined U.S. options in Bosnia. It concluded that diplomatic démarches, public condemnations, and economic sanctions would not prevent the outbreak of war. But, as they did in Croatia, Bush and his advisers immediately ruled out any form of U.S. military action in Bosnia—including any type of support for preventive peacekeeping. That left only one policy instrument: international recognition of Bosnia. According to Brent Scowcroft, the Bush administration wanted to prevent violence that inevitably would target civilians, create a massive humanitarian problem and could eventually undermine regional stability. We believed at the time that, given our lack of strategic interests, recognition was the only available option. We hoped that recognizing Bosnia would "internationalize" the conflict (i.e., transform Bosnia from civil war to an international conflict) and thus deter Milosevic. Obviously, it did not work.[20]

In early April the United States pressed the Europeans and the international community to recognize Bosnia as an independent state. Rather than deterring the war, however, the recognition of Bosnia strengthened the hand of Serb nationalists, who saw it as a clear affront to Serb national rights. Within days of recognition, Bosnia was at war.

The disintegration of Yugoslavia, the war in Bosnia, and ultimately the massive human rights violations and gross breaches of international humanitarian law were widely predicted. But in the wake of the Cold War's end, the Bush administration concluded that the region did not affect the traditional conceptions of U.S. strategic interests. As a result, the United States deferred international leadership to the Europeans and the United Nations and limited its preventive diplomatic efforts to diplomatic démarches. Only occasionally, as in the case of recognizing Bosnia, did Washington exert international leadership. Ultimately, though, the United States, the Europeans, and the United Nations pursued differing and conflicting strategies, and without strong focused leadership, the international community failed to prevent the spread of war to Bosnia.[21]

THE WAR: AVOIDANCE IN THE ABSENCE OF STRATEGIC INTERESTS

Almost immediately at the outset of the war, Bosnia deteriorated into a human rights and humanitarian catastrophe. The first few months of the war in Bosnia were particularly brutal. Serb forces—a coalition of Yugoslav National Army, Bosnian Serb Army, and Serb paramilitary units—led an onslaught that captured nearly two-thirds of Bosnian territory. By early June more than 100,000 were killed in deliberate and systematic attacks and more than 750,000 were expelled from their homes and villages.

As reports of the horrors of ethnic purification surfaced and video footage of concentration camps and massacres in the streets of Sarajevo outraged international public opinion, critics of U.S. and international policy demanded U.S. military intervention to break the siege of Sarajevo and to free the concentration camps. Nonetheless, the administration remained emphatic on the limits of U.S. interests and involvement in Bosnia. The overriding objective of the Bush administration—especially in the run-up to the 1992 presidential elections, with the campaign emphasis on the U.S. economic recession—was to keep U.S. troops out of Bosnia. As Warren Strobel concluded in his study of the policy, the focal point of the Bush administration on Bosnia was not to control the human rights abuses themselves but the "political problem created by the images." In sum, "U.S. government officials believed they had to be seen to be reacting, even as they kept policy [of nonintervention] virtually intact."[22] In this regard the administration deliberately framed the conflict as an inevitable Vietnam-style quagmire—a conflict fueled by age-old ethnic hatreds about which nothing could be done—while military planners inflated estimates of the number of troops necessary to undertake even the most limited military actions.[23]

While the administration exerted considerable political resources to keep military intervention off the table, congressional and media pressure as well as pressure from within the State Department bureaucracy did compel the administration to alter its policy of rigid avoidance of Bosnia.[24] In the UN Security Council, the United States condemned the violence. It also called for cease-fires and demanded the demilitarization of paramilitary forces and the withdrawal of Yugoslav and Croatian forces (UN Security Council Resolution 749). In response to Serb attacks on humanitarian relief convoys and mortar attacks on Muslim civilians in the streets of Sarajevo, the United States led diplomatic efforts in the passage of UN Security Council Resolution 757 in May 1992, invoking a complete economic embargo against the Serb-dominated rump Yugoslavia.

The paradox of the administration's policy is that while Bush and his senior advisers routinely argued that the United States could do nothing to stem the violence—"that until those people decide they want to stop killing each other, there is nothing that can be done"—there is evidence that the United States did influence events in Bosnia.[25] For example, for six weeks before the public disclosure of the existence of Serb-controlled concentration camps, the U.S. intelligence community collected and presented information about these camps to senior officials. Apparently fearful that the disclosure would generate a public backlash against the administration's avoidance policy, Bush and his team silenced the information.[26] Yet when the existence of the camps was publicly disclosed in early August, after "waffling" for a few days, President Bush and his advisers emphatically demanded the closure of the camps.[27] Within a month almost all of the camps were shut down. Strong and unambiguous U.S. diplomatic condemnations coupled with intense international media scrutiny altered the Serb behavior. This suggests that concerted U.S. leadership and more focused U.S. attention on the crisis might have been effective in altering the course of the war and deterring the systematic campaign of human rights violations.

More often, however, U.S. policy had unintended effects that awkwardly, albeit unintentionally, contributed to human rights violations. For example, in May 1992 the Bush administration argued successfully in the UN Security Council that the international arms embargo imposed on Yugoslavia in 1991 should also apply to Bosnia. The logic behind the administration's argument was that it was unwise to increase the number of weapons in an already destabilized situation. However, the unintended consequence of the arms embargo was that it fixed huge force asymmetries in favor of the Bosnian Serbs and rendered the Bosnian Muslim areas largely defenseless. The Bosnian Serbs used these military advantages with impunity to prosecute their ethnic cleansing campaign throughout northern and eastern Bosnia.

Another unintended effect of the Bush policy on Bosnia was that all of the political and rhetorical effort aimed at mitigating political pressure for the use of force undercut the potential effectiveness of the administration's other policy instruments. For example, in the fall of 1992 State Department officials in the Legal Advisors office, the Bureau of Human Rights and Humanitarian Affairs, and the Bureau of European and Canadian Affairs began developing strategies for the formation of an international criminal tribunal. In response to bureaucratic initiative and requests from Congress, Secretary of State

Lawrence Eagleburger tasked the intelligence community to collect evidence that might constitute gross violations of international humanitarian law and genocide.[28] Between October 1992 and July 1993, the intelligence community worked with the Bureau of Human Rights and Humanitarian Affairs to compile and declassify reports containing extensive evidence of atrocities and war crimes. It then submitted these reports to the United Nations and released them to the press. The intelligence community's intention with this exposure was to put the perpetrators—most notably the Serb and Bosnian Serb leaderships in Belgrade and Pale—on notice that the international community was moving toward the development of an ad hoc tribunal that would hold them accountable for gross violations of international humanitarian law. In addition, in December 1992 at the International Conference on the Former Yugoslavia Steering Committee in Geneva, Eagleburger announced that Milosevic, Ratko Mladic, and Radovan Karadzic were war criminals.[29]

While these events ostensibly threatened the Serb leadership with diplomatic, political, and legal reprisals, the administration simultaneously (and quite emphatically) continued to argue that Bosnia was not in Washington's vital interests and that it would not accelerate its policy to stem the violence.[30] The signal to the Bosnian Serb leadership was essentially that the United States cared only rhetorically about the crimes and that it was not really interested in the conflict.

By early 1993 the war showed no signs of abating and U.S. policy seemed to be on the verge of a new direction. The Clinton administration came into office highly critical of the Bush administration's passive response to the human rights situation in Bosnia. Bill Clinton ridiculed the Bush administration during the 1992 presidential campaign for "turning its back on violations of basic human rights."[31] Secretary of State Warren Christopher suggested during his Senate confirmation hearings that the Serb ethnic cleansing campaign constituted "near genocidal or perhaps really genocidal conditions."[32] Clinton and Christopher suggested that their policy would be much more aggressive in stemming the systematic human rights abuses in Bosnia.

During the first several months in office, however, Clinton and his advisers found themselves caught between the set of idealistic human rights principles they had espoused during the campaign and a desire to avoid getting the United States into Bosnia—regardless of the human rights conditions on the ground. On the one hand, some of Clinton's advisers, such as Anthony Lake, National Security Council adviser, and Madeleine Albright, U.S. ambassador to the United Nations, abhorred the massive human rights violations and believed that the United States and the international community had a responsibility to stop the war and punish the guilty—primarily Serbs—for their crimes. They led the campaign within the administration to oppose a plan developed by UN special envoy Cyrus Vance and European Union special envoy Lord David Owen (the Vance-Owen Peace Plan) because they believed that it was a veiled attempt to partition the internationally recognized Bosnia and that it rewarded Serb aggression.

On the other hand, for Clinton, who had campaigned on ending the domestic recession and whose relationship with the military had soured during his first days in office over the question of gays in the military, the policy of avoiding any military involvement in Bosnia quickly dominated his administration's policy.[33] While the administration showed general disdain for Vance-Owen and other international diplomatic initiatives that it believed would be unfair to the Muslim victims of the violence, it was unwilling to assert its own leadership on Bosnia. Within the Clinton administration, Bosnia quickly became seen as a political issue that had to be controlled rather than as a foreign policy priority. Christopher and other senior officials reverted to the Bush strategy of rhetorically framing the conflict as outside U.S. strategic interests and as one of intractable ancient ethnic hatreds about which the United States could do little. Christopher also backtracked from using the term "genocide" to describe the atrocities in Bosnia.[34] For example, during testimony before the House Foreign Affairs Committee on May 18, 1993, Christopher stressed that the situation in Bosnia foreclosed most U.S. policy options because all sides were equally guilty of committing atrocities.[35] And in June Christopher announced that while "Bosnia is a human tragedy, just a grotesque humanitarian situation . . . the United States has no vital interests in Bosnia."[36]

Like the Bush administration, however, the Clinton administration ultimately found the strategy of avoidance difficult to sustain. The persistence of gross human rights abuses, massacres of civilians, indiscriminate Serb shellings of UN-designated safe areas, and overall international impotence in the face of systematic violations of international humanitarian law kept putting Bosnia back on the president's agenda.[37] It had become clear to many in the Clinton administration by the summer of 1993 that the policy instruments of wishful thinking, international condemnations, expressions of outrage, and economic and diplomatic sanctions were not effectively altering the situation. Between the late summer of 1993 and early 1995, the Clinton administration frequently, albeit briefly, considered more robust diplomatic and military responses. On several occasions, the United States contemplated the use of NATO air strikes to break the siege of Sarajevo and to block Serb artillery attacks against the UN safe areas.

In each instance, however, generating a domestic and international consensus authorizing NATO air strikes required more political capital than the domestically oriented Clinton was willing to spend on a foreign policy crisis. The Joint Chiefs of Staff remained heavily opposed to any gradual escalation of U.S. military involvement, and public opinion polls repeatedly suggested that while most Americans might be persuaded otherwise, they did not believe the United States had a responsibility to lead international efforts to stop the violence.[38] And, for their part, the European allies who had troops on the ground as part of the United Nations Protection Force (UNPROFOR) argued that NATO air strikes would only complicate matters for their forces on the ground. Caught between the criticism over inaction and an unwillingness to try to overcome the constraints, Clinton's policy on Bosnia festered amid fits and starts while the atrocities mounted.

SREBRENICA AND ZEPA

In the spring of 1995, the Bosnian Serb army launched a major offensive in an effort to end the war on the battlefield. The offensive included direct attacks against the UN-designated safe areas of Srebrenica and Goradze. In early July, while lightly armed Dutch peacekeepers stood by, the Bosnian Serb army rounded up roughly eight thousand Muslim men from the safe area, marched them into the woods, and summarily executed them.[39]

Within the Clinton administration, the initial reaction was limited to assessing the constraints facing U.S. policy: the United States
would not deploy troops to Bosnia, and air strikes were limited by the
"dual key" arrangement, in which the United Nations and NATO
would have to concur. With European forces on the ground, the
Clinton administration proclaimed that the United States was "not a
decisive actor" in Bosnia.[40]

This position, however, generated intense scrutiny within elements of the U.S. diplomatic corps. In the immediate aftermath of the
Srebrenica massacre, Bosnian Serb forces turned their attention to
Zepa, a second UN safe area. Peter Galbraith, U.S. ambassador to
Croatia, and John Shattuck, assistant secretary of state for human
rights, began warning of the dangers of allowing Zepa to fall. Shattuck,
aware of constraints, especially the resistance within the U.S. military
to any policy that might lead to U.S. military involvement, warned
that if Zepa fell, the United States would be forced to follow through
on its commitment to its European allies to assist their withdrawal. In
doing so, Shattuck argued, "U.S. troops will be on the ground helping
the UN force pull out while Bosnian Serbs . . . fire upon them, and
fearful Muslim civilians try to block their exit."[41] Shattuck's warning
was that the situation in Bosnia was already messy and was certain to
get worse if the United States continued to ignore it.

For his part, Ambassador Galbraith sent an urgent cable to Secretary of State Christopher on July 25 titled "Possible Mass Execution
of Srebrenica Males Is Reason to Save Zepa." The cable warned of a
massive humanitarian catastrophe if the United States failed to take
immediate action. The message struck a resonate chord throughout
the State Department. Christopher's aides pressed the secretary of
state to dispatch a senior-level team to investigate.

In response, Christopher sent John Shattuck and Phyllis Oakley,
assistant secretary of state for refugees, to Bosnia to assess the situation. Shattuck conducted two days of interviews and reported back to
Washington that there was "substantial new evidence of genocide."[42]
While Shattuck's recommendations were limited to calling for renewed
pressure to prosecute those responsible for war crimes, his report sent
shock waves throughout the State Department and the National Security Council. Individuals within the bureaucracy—notably Madeleine

Albright, U.S. ambassador to the United Nations, and Richard Holbrooke, assistant secretary of state for European and Canadian affairs —renewed their pressure to reformulate U.S. policy.

Elsewhere in Washington as well, Srebrenica and Zepa were stark illustrations of international impotence in the face of systematic violations of human rights and international humanitarian law. Horrified by images of UN peacekeepers standing by observing the slaughter of civilians, the media, a growing number of senators and representatives, and the human rights and humanitarian NGO community dramatically escalated their calls for the administration to take more forceful action.

For nearly six months before the events in Srebrenica and Zepa, Senators Robert Dole and Joseph Lieberman had been leading the charge in the U.S. Senate to lift unilaterally the UN arms embargo on Bosnia. Their efforts had been assisted by Marshall Harris and Steven Walker, two former State Department officials who had resigned in 1993 and who had founded a nongovernmental organization to lobby Congress for a more robust U.S. military response to Bosnia. Throughout the first part of 1995 their efforts steadily generated additional support on Capitol Hill. The events of Srebrenica and Zepa, however, fundamentally tipped the balance. In late July the House and the Senate voted overwhelmingly to end U.S. participation in the UN arms embargo, and two senior senators—Jesse Helms and Robert Dole—introduced legislation authorizing $100 million in immediate military assistance to the Bosnian Muslims.[43]

After years of trying to avoid asserting U.S. leadership in Bosnia, President Clinton was now feeling pressure from the horrific events on the ground and from Congress, the media, and the NGO community and within his own bureaucracy. A policy of avoidance was no longer sustainable.

THE ENDGAME, DAYTON, AND BEYOND

Even as he was briefed on the fall of Srebrenica in mid-July, Clinton angrily lamented: "This can't continue. We have to seize control of this. . . . I'm getting creamed!"[44] More worrisome for President Clinton and his advisers was their perception that the human rights and humanitarian crisis in Bosnia ultimately threatened the fundamental credibility of the United Nations and NATO and, hence, core U.S. interests in these institutions.[45] President Clinton, for the first time in his presidency, demanded that the United States take the lead in the international effort to end the war in Bosnia and the humanitarian catastrophe.[46] Anthony Lake developed an "endgame strategy" that laid out an explicit blueprint for a comprehensive U.S. diplomatic and military initiative to end the violence in Bosnia. By early August, Lake had sold the plan to the president, the Joint Chiefs of Staff, and—after extensive high-level negotiations—the European allies. The plan included, for the first time, a formal commitment by the United States and the European allies to launch massive and sustained NATO air strikes against Bosnian Serb targets throughout the country in response to any future attacks on safe areas.[47]

Meanwhile, the Bosnian Serbs continued their offensive in an attempt to win a decisive military victory. In late August the Serbs stepped up their attacks on Sarajevo, and on August 28 they launched an artillery attack against the Sarajevo marketplace, killing thirty-eight civilians and wounding eighty-five others. Within hours of this egregious violation of international humanitarian law, the United States and its NATO allies began the most extensive air campaign in NATO history, striking Bosnian Serb targets throughout Bosnia. The NATO aerial bombing, along with military gains by Croats and Muslims in the summer of 1995, finally compelled the Serbs to sign a cease-fire agreement on September 14. On September 20 the siege of Sarajevo ended as the Bosnian Serbs removed their heavy artillery from the hills surrounding the Bosnian capital. And they, along with the Muslims and Croats, signed a countrywide cease-fire on October 5.

To reach a comprehensive settlement, however, the Clinton administration continued to fully commit U.S. diplomatic efforts. In November the United States hosted the Dayton proximity talks in Dayton, Ohio, and pressed the parties to reach a comprehensive peace. After nearly three weeks of intense negotiations, the parties agreed to end the war, demobilize their military forces, and share power in a unified Bosnian state. At the behest of U.S. negotiators, the warring factions also formally agreed to respect and implement several European

Convention human rights protocols and provisions. In Annex 6 of the Dayton Peace Accords, the warring factions pledged to ensure the security and liberty of all citizens, to cooperate with the International Criminal Tribunal on Yugoslavia, to establish a Commission on Human Rights, to lift restrictions on the freedom of movement, to support the right of refugees to return to their pre-war homes, and to hold free and fair democratic elections for the country's postwar leadership. In support of these provisions, the United States led an international Implementation Force (IFOR) to carry out and administer the Dayton Peace Accords.

Ultimately, however, the accords were first and foremost a territorial and political compromise among the radicalized, nationalist warring factions and the international community to end the war. As a result, the principal element of the Dayton framework was the establishment of a dual entity structure premised on the 1994 Contact Group's position on territorial and political arrangements. The accords separated Bosnia into two entities, with Muslims and Croats in control of 51 percent of Bosnian territory and the Serbs in control of 49 percent. And although the framework established Bosnia as a single state committed to European conventions on human rights, it did not require the dismantling of the nationalists' wartime regimes. Instead, it specifically codified constitutional provisions establishing constituent peoples with national vetoes and political institutions that reinforced ethnic divisions in the country. Thus, in the immediate wake of the agreement, the warring nationalist regimes—which had little strategic interest in integrated and democratic institutions and some of which had no commitment to human rights—were able to consolidate their control of most of the country's political and economic resources.

These compromises have had mixed results on the human rights situation. On the one hand, the human rights record in Bosnia has improved dramatically since the wartime atrocities. IFOR, later SFOR, stabilized the security environment throughout the country. The war is over, the sieges of cities and safe areas have been lifted, and SFOR has effectively deterred most instances of organized violence. In each successive year since the end of the war, political killings, ethnic violence, and police torture have declined dramatically. Internationally monitored open elections have been held and freedom of movement and of association (but not of residence) has become a reality. The Human Rights Commission and the Human Rights Ombudsman established at Dayton have increased their caseload each year since the end of the war and regularly adjudicate individual cases of property, employment, and education discrimination.

Nonetheless, many of the human rights promises embedded in the Dayton framework remain unfulfilled. Many of the obligations within the Dayton agreement that relate to international covenants and European human rights protocols have not been implemented.[48] The country's political institutions and economy are divided ethnically, and minorities often confront discrimination in housing, employment, education, and voting. As of mid-2003, more than half a million people displaced from the war had not returned to their homes.[49] Many of those who have returned continue to face obstacles related to security, property, housing, employment, and education. Fewer than a hundred of the thousands of suspected war criminals have been indicted and far fewer have been arrested or prosecuted.[50] The most notable war criminals in the Bosnian Serb leadership have not been arrested and still exert political and economic influence throughout the country. Many victims of violence during the war continue to face fear and intimidation from the perpetrators of violence, many of whom continue to hold positions of economic or political power and influence. There is also still no formal multiethnic investigation into the wartime activities nor is there an official forum in which victims can express their anguish.

Following Dayton, Washington has pursued an overall strategy in postwar Bosnia that has once again subordinated human rights to more traditional conceptions of security: force protection is the primary objective of U.S. troops in Bosnia. Unlike the efforts of British and Canadian military units, U.S. troops have not actively supported or provided security for the return of refugees displaced from their homes, nor have they actively pursued war criminals still exerting influence throughout the country. Furthermore, while U.S. diplomats routinely endorse and encourage moderate multiethnic political parties, overall Washington has been remarkably timid in its efforts to break the nationalist parties' control over the country's political and economic resources. In particular, in its first two years in office, the administration of George W. Bush frequently overlooked and ignored or only minimally discouraged noncompliance with international human rights provisions. As a result, several years after the Dayton Peace Accords, Bosnia has only rudimentary working administrative infrastructures on criminal law, property rights, and minority rights, and many of these are frequently obstructed with impunity.

In sum, while ambitious human rights and humanitarian protocols were incorporated into the texts of the Dayton Peace Accords and substantial progress has been made, neither the warring factions nor the U.S. government has been committed to aggressively supporting or implementing them.

CONCLUSION

Until 1995, U.S. policy was not effective in stopping mass human rights abuses. In fact, throughout the war U.S. policy tended to be counterproductive. For example, while Bush and Clinton hoped that the war and the human rights abuses would end, both presidents were principally concerned with avoiding U.S. military intervention in Bosnia. Consequently, both administrations exerted considerable political effort to contain the pressure for military intervention. Indeed, one of the focal points of each administration's public policy on Bosnia was to represent the conflict as outside U.S. interests and as being fueled by age-old ethnic hatreds about which the United States—and military intervention—could do little.

The irony is that concerted and sustained diplomatic and political devices such as formal and public protests, condemnations, and expressions of outrage did occasionally alter the Bosnian Serb behavior and stem human rights abuses—as in the case of the concentration camp closures. However, more often Bush and Clinton coupled verbal protests with explicit—and counterproductive—statements that expressed explicit limits on what the United States was ultimately prepared to do in Bosnia. These limits were seen in Bosnia and in Serbia as a sign that, despite the rhetoric, the United States did not fundamentally oppose the Serb actions in Bosnia. As a result, both administrations ultimately undermined their modest ability to curtail human rights abuses by simultaneously engaging in a domestic political campaign to limit U.S. involvement in Bosnia.

Another counterproductive component of U.S. policy was the application of the international arms embargo on Bosnia. While the motives for the policy were seemingly sound—the United States did not want to see the introduction of arms into an already destabilized conflict region—the result was that the embargo ensured huge disparities in military capabilities. The Serbs possessed superior arms, equipment, and training and used these capabilities to prosecute the systematic and egregious campaign of human rights violations. In neither case—the contradictory signals nor the arms embargo—did the Bush and Clinton administrations systematically review the effects of their strategy or seek to alter it.

More broadly, the case of Bosnia demonstrates how unchecked human rights and humanitarian abuses can evolve from insignificant U.S. foreign policy concerns into significant geostrategic imperatives. Despite adequate early warning signs on the likelihood of violence in the Balkans, the Bush administration dismissed the potential problems as being outside U.S. interests. The United States only belatedly attempted to forestall the disintegration of the federation. Throughout three and a half years of war, the Bush and Clinton administrations continued to premise their policy toward Bosnia on traditional Cold War conceptions of U.S. interests: Bosnia, a "simple humanitarian crisis," was of no geostrategic or economic importance to Washington. What neither administration had expected was that U.S. and international indifference in responding to widespread, systematic, and egregious violations of international human rights and humanitarian law could transform the fate of Bosnia into a core interest for the United States.

Even though public opinion never supported direct U.S. engagement in Bosnia, the persistence of gross violations of human rights coupled with protracted critical media attention and congressional and NGO criticism compelled President Clinton to fundamentally shift course on Bosnia. The final catalyst for U.S. action came in the wake of the massacres at Srebrenica, when U.S. policymakers concluded that Bosnia was in Washington's interests. As Mark Danner described it:

> In the post cold war world, highly visible and widespread violations of human rights could threaten the prestige and thus the power of both the United States and international institutions. When soldiers of a small European power methodically murder great numbers of unarmed people virtually in front of the world's television cameras, and American leaders appear to do little more than look on and wring their hands, this will inevitably come to make the United States "look weak." And when American officials and their counterparts in Paris and London and Bonn spend their time exchanging nasty public criticisms, this will eventually make the Western alliance look impotent and irrelevant.[51]

In sum, the persistent failure of the United Nations and of NATO to prevent systematic slaughter of civilians led senior officials to conclude that the credibility and the reputation of NATO, the United Nations, and ultimately the Clinton administration were on the line.[52]

BROADER LESSONS

Human rights historically have been subordinated to traditional material-based conceptions of national interests in the formulation of U.S. foreign policy. Since the end of World War II, realist scholars and policymakers in the United States routinely have expressed the position that U.S. foreign policy should not be guided by "idealistic" and lofty humanitarian notions. However, in light of global trends, this view seems to be increasingly anachronistic. The cascade of international human rights norms and protocols in the past few decades and the increasing global transparency associated with dramatic improvements in information technology—both remarkably young processes—make it increasingly difficult for the United States to ignore systematic violations of international human rights and humanitarian laws.

Indeed, the events in Bosnia served as the impetus for institutional reform within the U.S. bureaucracy. The intelligence community was called upon for the first time in its history to dedicate intelligence assets for the purpose of systematically collecting evidence of war crimes and crimes against humanity. Within the State Department, a new position of U.S. ambassador-at-large for war crimes was established with explicit responsibilities for coordinating the collection and analysis of war crimes. And the United States led international efforts for the creation of ad hoc tribunals on Yugoslavia, which ultimately also led to the creation of a tribunal for Rwanda and provided much of the initial political momentum for the creation of the International Criminal Court.

From these historical, political, and institutional legacies, future administrations that categorically reject policy responses to massive human rights violations almost certainly will find themselves faced with persistent and intensifying criticism, especially if the crises persist over time. This is even more likely as Congress, the media, the State Department's own human rights bureaucracy, and the NGO community gain greater technological resources to collect, analyze, and report information on human rights abuses in previously remote areas of the world. In short, policies of avoidance and indifference will become only more difficult to sustain.

Given this likelihood, the United States can better serve this broader (and transformed) conception of national interests by developing more sophisticated early-warning methods to detect instances in which massive violations of international human rights and humanitarian law are likely and by bolstering its capacity for preventive diplomacy to meet these challenges before the onset of systematic violence against civilians.

NOTES

1. The United States consistently condemned the violence and supported multilateral sanctions in hopes of stemming it. At times this minimal effort was effective. On several occasions the threat of NATO air strikes and other international punitive measures arrested the atrocities. But overall, U.S. policy consisted largely of isolated and ad hoc reactions to highly publicized massacres and abuses.

2. Susan Woodward, *Balkan Tragedy: Chaos and Dissolution after the Cold War* (Washington, D.C.: Brookings Institution, 1995), 24–29.

3. Warren Zimmerman, *Origins of a Catastrophe* (New York: Times Books, 1999), 7.

4. For a comprehensive examination of the disintegration process, see Woodward, *Balkan Tragedy;* and Laura Silber and Allan Little, *The Death of Yugoslavia* (London: Penguin Books/BBC Books, 1995).

5. Zimmerman, *Origins of a Catastrophe*. See also David C. Gompert, "The United States and Yugoslavia's Wars," in *The World and Yugoslavia's Wars*, ed. Richard Ullman (New York: Council on Foreign Relations, 1996), 124. Zimmerman also participated in an international boycott of the Milosevic ceremony at Kosovo Polje in June 1989. Milosevic subsequently refused to receive him until early 1990.

6. Zimmerman, *Origins of a Catastrophe*, 43–51.

7. Markovic's appeals for greater U.S. financial assistance to support the austerity measures were rejected by Washington in both 1989 and 1990. Zimmerman, *Origins of a Catastrophe*, 46–52; and Woodward, *Balkan Tragedy*, 154.

8. See Francis T. Miko and Jon Western, "Eastern Europe: U.S. and International Assistance," CRS Issue Brief, Congressional Research Service, May 24, 1990.

9. David Binder, "Yugoslavia Seen Breaking Up Soon," *New York Times*, November 28, 1990, A7.

10. In a highly unusual event, unnamed State Department officials deliberately leaked a draft of the highly sensitive National Intelligence Estimate on Yugoslavia to David Binder of the *New York Times* to generate public and political pressure on the administration to pay more attention to the Yugoslav crisis. James Hooper, interview by author, Washington, D.C., March 24, 1999. At the time of the leak, Hooper was the deputy director of the Office of Eastern Europe and Yugoslavia in the Bureau of European and Canadian Affairs, U.S. Department of State.

11. Woodward, *Balkan Tragedy*, 152.

12. See Mark Danner, "The U.S. and the Yugoslav Catastrophe," *New York Review of Books*, November 20, 1997, section 4.

13. Gompert, "The United States and Yugoslavia's Wars," 125.

14. Robert Hutchings, quoted in Danner, "The U.S. and the Yugoslav Catastrophe."

15. Zimmerman, *Origins of a Catastrophe*, 138–140.

16. David Gompert, quoted in ibid.

17. Brent Scowcroft, interview by author, April 29, 1999.

18. Ibid.

19. In March 1991, Milosevic and Croatian president Franjo Tudjman met at Karadjordjevo and discussed the partition of Bosnia. See Steven L. Berg and Paul S. Shoup, *The War in Bosnia-Herzegovina: Ethnic Conflict and International Intervention* (New York: M. E. Sharpe, 2000), 82.

20. Scowcroft, interview by author.

21. While the United States, Europe, and the United Nations squabbled among themselves over the best strategy to stop the wars and on the question of recognizing the independence of the breakaway republics, they all agreed on the imposition of an international arms embargo on the territory of the former Yugoslavia.

22. Warren Strobel, *Late Breaking Foreign Policy* (Washington, D.C.: United States Institute of Peace Press, 1997), 147.

23. Jon Western, "Sources of Humanitarian Intervention," *International Security* 23, no. 4 (spring 2002).

24. Warren Zimmerman, telephone interview by author, March 24, 1999.

25. One of the most emphatic statements was the oft-repeated line from Secretary of State Lawrence Eagleburger: "I have said this 38,000 times and I have to say this to the people of this country as well. This tragedy is not something that can be settled from the outside and it's about damn well time that everybody understood that. Until the Bosnians, Serbs and Croats decide to stop killing each other, there is nothing the outside world can do about it." Lawrence Eagleburger, quoted in Mark Danner, "Clinton, the UN, and the Bosnian Disaster," *New York Review of Books*, December 18, 1997. For military estimates on Bosnia, see Michael Gordon, "Conflict in the Balkans: 60,000 Needed for Bosnia, a U.S. General Estimates," *New York Times*, August 12, 1992, 8.

26. Zimmerman, interview by author.

27. As Lawrence Eagleburger told Warren Strobel in an interview, "We took too much time to deal with it. . . . We kind of waffled around a little bit. All of us were being a little bit careful . . . because of this issue of whether or not it was going to push us into something that we thought was dangerous." Strobel, *Late Breaking Foreign Policy*, 150.

28. William Hill, interview by author, March 24, 1999. William Hill was the division chief of the Office of East European Analysis, Bureau of Intelligence and Research, U.S. Department of State, from 1992 to 1994.

29. Elaine Sciolino, "U.S. Names Figures It Wants Charged with War Crimes," *New York Times*, December 17, 1992, A1.

30. See, for example, Colin Powell, "Why Generals Get Nervous," *New York Times*, October 8, 1992, 35.

31. Zimmerman, *Origins of a Catastrophe*, 221.

32. Richard Johnson, "The Pin-Stripe Approach to Genocide" (unpublished manuscript, January 1, 1994), 6.

33. During the first year of Clinton's presidency, the administration's policy and political priorities focused almost exclusively on containing the economic recession and reforming the U.S. health care system.

34. Neither the 1993 nor the 1994 human rights report used the term "genocide." In June 1993, as Washington celebrated the opening of the Holocaust Museum, the United States endorsed a recommendation by the UN

World Conference on Human Rights presented to the Security Council to take "necessary measures to end the genocide in Bosnia and Herzegovina." Almost immediately, however, the administration backed away from the recommendation. According to Richard Johnson, there was no record of the conference's appeal in the official files of the Bureau of Human Rights and Humanitarian Affairs. A Clinton administration official described it as "not really an official act of the Conference." See Johnson, "The Pin-Stripe Approach to Genocide," 5.

35. Christopher's testimony angered his top human rights adviser. Richard Shifter, then acting assistant secretary of state for human rights and humanitarian affairs, wrote an unprecedented response to the secretary, declaring that, contrary to Christopher's public statements, U.S. intelligence and official investigations revealed that the vast majority of war crimes committed in Bosnia had been perpetrated by Serb and Bosnian Serb forces. He suggested that Christopher's attempt to morally equalize the conduct of the warring combatants was a deliberate effort to mitigate growing public and political pressure.

36. AFP, "U.S. Has No Vital Interests in Bosnia: Christopher," June 2, 1993.

37. For a discussion of the internal political dynamics and discussions, see Ivo Daalder, *Getting to Dayton: The Making of America's Bosnia Policy* (Washington, D.C.: Brookings Institution, 2000), 19–23.

38. For a summary and analysis of public opinion polling data on Bosnia and other crises, see Andrew Kohut and Robert C. Toth, "The People, the Press, and the Use of Force," in *The United States and the Use of Force in the Post–Cold War Era: An Aspen Strategy Group Report* (Queenstown, Md.: Aspen Institute, 1995), 133–169.

39. For an excellent account of the events surrounding Srebrenica, see David Rohde, *Endgame: The Betrayal and Fall of Srebrenica—Europe's Worst Massacre since World War II* (Boulder, Colo.: Westview Press, 1997).

40. Samantha Power, *A Problem from Hell: America and the Age of Genocide* (New York: Basic Books, 2002), 406.

41. Ibid., 415.

42. Ibid., 418.

43. Elaine Sciolino, "Defiant Senators Vote to Override Bosnian Arms Ban," *New York Times*, July 27, 1995, A8; Elaine Sciolino, "House, Like Senate, Votes to Halt Bosnia Embargo," *New York Times*, August 2, 1995, A6; and Adam Clymer, "Dole-Helms Bill Asks $100 Million in Arms Aid for Bosnia," *New York Times*, August 11, 1995, A3.

44. Bob Woodward, *The Choice* (New York: Simon and Schuster, 1996). See also Mark Danner, "The U.S. and the Yugoslav Catastrophe."

45. Several factors ultimately propelled the Clinton administration to take a stronger role. First, events changed on the ground. Croatia defeated the

Serbs in Krajina. The joint Muslim and Croat offensives were wearing down the Bosnian Serb army. Milosevic was increasingly weary of economic sanctions. Second, escalated Bosnian Serb massacres in the safe areas at Srebrenica, Zepa, and ultimately Goražde generated even greater media and NGO criticism of the administration. Third, the Republican-controlled House and Senate both passed legislation to unilaterally lift the international arms embargo on Bosnia. Fourth, the British and the French were threatening to withdraw by November and the United States had committed itself to deploying U.S. forces as part of a NATO operation to provide safety for a withdrawal of UNPROFOR.

46. The details of this political maneuvering are detailed in Daalder, *Getting to Dayton*.

47. Ibid., 79.

48. For a critical assessment, see Zoran Pajic, "A Critical Appraisal of Human Rights Provisions of the Dayton Constitution of Bosnia and Herzegovina," *Human Rights Quarterly* 20, no. 1 (1998): 125–138.

49. According to the UN High Commissioner for Refugees, as of June 2000 the total number still displaced was 1,115,000.

50. "Who's in the Custody of the ICTY," a list produced by the Coalition for International Justice, updated June 26, 2000, in the author's files.

51. Danner, "The U.S. and the Yugoslav Catastrophe."

52. According to Douglas C. Foyle's analysis, "As the war dragged on, [Clinton] began to worry that Western ineffectiveness in dealing with the issue was beginning to reflect poorly on his administration, and he watched the events in the spring and early summer [of 1995] with an increasing sense of foreboding." See Douglas C. Foyle, *Counting the Public In: Presidents, Public Opinion, and Foreign Policy* (New York: Columbia University Press, 1999), 248.

8

U.S. Policy on Human Rights in Relations with the USSR, 1961–91

JACK F. MATLOCK, JR.

The observations that follow derive from my experience in dealing with the Soviet Union during my Foreign Service career. From 1956 to 1958, I was an analyst of Soviet internal developments in the Bureau of Intelligence Research. From 1961 to 1963, I was assigned to the U.S. embassy in Moscow as consular officer (first year) and political officer (second year) reporting on internal politics. From 1971 to 1974, I was director of Soviet affairs in the Department of State, and from 1974 to 1978, deputy chief of mission at the embassy in Moscow. I returned to Moscow for most of 1981 as chargé d'affaires and then served on the National Security Council staff as senior director for Europe and the USSR (1983–86). From that position I was sent to Moscow as ambassador, where I served until shortly before the collapse of the USSR in 1991. Thus, I was able to observe the development and implementation of U.S. human rights policy over a thirty-five-year period. I will attempt to describe that development and then draw some conclusions from the experience.

• • •

UNTIL THE 1970S, it was difficult to speak of a U.S. human
rights policy in regard to the Soviet Union. Before then there
was, of course, interest in the Soviet regime's treatment of its
own citizens and, to the degree events could be followed in the tightly
closed society Stalin created, some effort to document abuses. But this
effort was made more to expose the nature of the Soviet regime than in
a hope that the United States could directly influence these practices.

The United States did attempt to resolve "cases," as they were
called, when there was direct U.S. citizen interest, particularly after
Nikita Khrushchev's "thaw" of the late 1950s. Some U.S. citizens had
been imprisoned or forced to accept Soviet citizenship. Some of the
more determined began—with great difficulty on their part—to contact the U.S. embassy in Moscow and appeal for help in leaving the
Soviet Union. If they were still U.S. citizens, or close relatives of U.S.
citizens, the State Department authorized the embassy to make representations on their behalf, normally by formal note to the Soviet
Ministry of Foreign Affairs.

With the partial opening up of Soviet society by Khrushchev,
there also occurred a few marriages of Soviet citizens with Americans.
If a Soviet woman married an American, she was usually allowed to
leave the country to join her husband, though she was subjected to an
involved and uncertain bureaucratic procedure. Not all were, however; if the Soviet wife or her close relatives had been employed in
work considered secret, they were usually denied exit visas. Also, if the
husband was the Soviet citizen, he was usually denied permission to
emigrate on the grounds that the wife should join the husband at his
place of residence. If the husband pressed his request for exit permission, the Soviet authorities sometimes proceeded to annul the marriage
over the objection of both parties.

The State Department and the U.S. embassy in Moscow normally did what they could to persuade the Soviet authorities to resolve
these cases as the U.S. citizens wished. This, however, was not done
as part of an overall human rights policy, but as consular representation of U.S. citizens. The Soviet authorities never challenged the
right of the U.S. government to defend the interests of its citizens.
(After all, they took a proprietary attitude toward their citizens abroad.)
When they rejected U.S. approaches they would dispute the facts,

not the right of the U.S. government to make a representation. For example, they might claim that John Doe was not an American but a Soviet citizen, or that some violation of Soviet law had occurred that justified whatever action they had taken. When there was a warming of U.S.-Soviet relations, some long-standing cases would be resolved, as if to suggest that the rights of U.S. citizens would be respected only if political relations were cordial.

Following Khrushchev's denunciation of Joseph Stalin and the release of many political prisoners from gulags in the late 1950s, more reliable information began to seep out about past abuses, and by the early 1960s critics of the system within the USSR began to speak more openly. In 1962 Khrushchev authorized publication of Aleksandr Solzhenitsyn's *One Day in the Life of Ivan Denisovich,* which encouraged many others to speak out. The relaxation did not last long, however. As exposure of Stalin's atrocities threatened to create public pressure to reform the communist system, the door to public discussion of Soviet shortcomings was slammed shut; it was locked after the Warsaw Pact invasion of Czechoslovakia in 1968 to end Alexander Dubček's attempt to create "socialism with a human face." Soviet official media were thereafter (until the late 1980s) closed to criticism of the system, except on those limited topics favored by the regime. For example, if there was a campaign to change methods of agricultural management, some discussion of defects (usually called "distortions") in management practice was encouraged.

When the media were muzzled on most critical topics, however, critics simply resorted to self-publication, the literal meaning of samizdat—that is, circulation of articles in manuscript or typescript. Manuscripts would be typed in as many carbon copies as could be stuffed in a typewriter, and the copies distributed to circles of trusted friends, in chain-letter fashion. (Copiers and printing presses were tightly controlled and usually not available to authors of samizdat.) Very quickly, these samizdat productions found their way out of the country, and many were published abroad and then smuggled back into the Soviet Union. They also, increasingly, served as material for Western radio stations broadcasting to Soviet audiences. Radio Liberty, in particular, would broadcast even book-length productions at dictation speed, so that they could be transcribed by listeners in the Soviet Union.

As more and more concrete information accumulated about the violation of human rights in the Soviet Union, public sentiment grew in both the United States and Western Europe to do something about it. Initially, much attention was focused on the plight of Soviet Jews, who were subject to periodic waves of officially sponsored anti-Semitism, including, by the late 1960s and early 1970s, severe limitations on higher education and employment in positions considered sensitive as well as prohibitions on religious education, the closure of synagogues, and even a ban on teaching Hebrew. Beginning in the early 1970s, a small number of Soviet Jews, for the first time since World War II, were allowed to emigrate to Israel. Once emigration became possible (though uncertain and exceedingly difficult), thousands began to apply to leave. Some genuinely wished to settle in Israel, but most used emigration to Israel, the only destination for which Soviet authorities would grant Jewish citizens an exit visa, as a pretext to leave the country and settle in the United States. Many had relatives in the United States who had a natural interest in their right to emigrate, the more so that the future well-being of Jews in the Soviet Union seemed under serious threat.

During the period leading up to the 1972 Nixon-Brezhnev summit meeting, when the Antiballistic Missile (ABM) Treaty was signed, the amount of Jewish emigration increased rapidly, and the numbers continued to rise in 1973 and 1974. President Richard Nixon attempted to deal with the issue by quiet diplomacy, pointing out that the right of Soviet Jews to emigrate was an important issue in the United States and that denial of that right could affect Senate ratification of arms control and trade agreements. (One of the Soviet objectives during this period was to increase trade and particularly access to U.S. technology.) The Soviet authorities gave private assurances that restrictions on emigration would be eased, but only if the administration did not make a public issue of the matter. Leonid Brezhnev was unwilling to be seen bowing to foreign, particularly U.S., pressure on a matter most Soviet leaders considered under their domestic jurisdiction.

Although Brezhnev allowed a growing number of Jews, along with some Armenians and ethnic Germans, to emigrate (the latter to West Germany), Soviet authorities suddenly imposed an "education tax" on emigrants. The official rationale was that an emigrant had been educated at state expense, and if he or she left the country for permanent residence elsewhere, the state should be reimbursed for the cost of the education received. The tax was in fact within the means of most intending emigrants, who could pay with assets not otherwise legally transferable out of the Soviet Union, but it raised serious questions of principle since it appeared to be, in effect, a demand for ransom. The "education tax" became a major political issue in the United States. Although it eventually was dropped under U.S. pressure, Soviet restrictions on Jewish emigration continued to be an issue in the U.S. Congress, and the Nixon administration was charged with giving it insufficient attention.

Congressional frustration with Soviet restrictions on the right to emigrate eventually led to the Jackson-Vanik and Stevenson Amendments to the Trade Act of 1974. The Jackson-Vanik Amendment prohibited extension of Most Favored Nation tariff treatment (MFN) to "non-market-economy countries" that did not already enjoy MFN status (e.g., Poland and Romania) unless the president could certify that there were no restrictions on the right to emigrate. The Stevenson Amendment severely restricted the size of loans by the Export-Import Bank for U.S.-Soviet trade. These amendments were opposed both by President Nixon and by his successor, President Gerald Ford, on grounds that more could be achieved by quiet diplomacy than by formal legal strictures. They had, however, overwhelming support in the legislative branch, and all subsequent administrations were careful to enforce them. In fact, they had no choice, since waivers had to be approved by Congress and could be of only one year's duration.

Initially, in early 1975, it appeared that the Jackson-Vanik Amendment would produce higher levels of Jewish emigration. The number of exit permits continued to rise and reached a rate exceeding fifty thousand a year. The administration, in effect, encouraged the Soviet authorities to come to terms with Senator Henry Jackson, and they made some attempt to do so. In principle they were willing to guarantee a level of sixty thousand emigrants annually, but only if the agreement was tacit and unofficial. It was important to them to be able to deny at home that they were reacting to U.S. pressure. Senator Jackson, however, went public with his demands, and the Soviets ended their effort to meet his terms. From 1976 the number of Jewish and other emigrants fell rapidly, and from then on, until the late 1980s, the number of exit visas issued by Soviet authorities seemed rigidly linked to the overall state of U.S.-Soviet relations. As détente frayed, the numbers declined; when there was hope of a major agreement, such as Strategic Arms Limitation Treaty (SALT) II, signed in 1978, the numbers would rise. When it became clear that the U.S. Senate would not ratify SALT II and the United States reacted vigorously to the Soviet invasion of Afghanistan, the number of exit visas issued plunged toward zero.

Soviet emigration policy thus became a hostage to the general state of U.S.-Soviet relations. In addition, external pressure to allow Jewish emigration had reverberations on the treatment of Jewish citizens by Soviet authorities. Jews were considered a separate "nationality" and were so identified by their internal passports. As the numbers of those applying to emigrate rose, the feeling that Jews were more likely than Russians to be disloyal encouraged a wide array of restrictive practices, few of which were officially acknowledged. Admission to the most prestigious higher educational institutions became practically impossible for most Jewish young people, and there was a general reluctance to place Jews in supervisory positions, thus limiting professional advancement in many fields. Informal restrictions on the practice of religion grew. These tendencies inevitably encouraged many persons who previously had given little thought to leaving the country to take an interest in emigration. Thus the pressure to be allowed to emigrate began to grow within the Soviet Union. Some Soviet Jews, largely for religious reasons, considered Israel their desired destination. Many, however, wished to settle in the United States or, to a lesser degree, in another Western country.

Support in the Soviet Union for reform and greater regard for human rights began to develop independently of the pressure to allow free emigration. The "dissident movement" (actually not a single movement) had its roots in the brief thaw Khrushchev introduced. Those who produced samizdat were generally intellectuals who were seeking fundamental reform of the system and who had no desire to emigrate. When they faced repression, as they did in the 1960s and 1970s, some were forced to emigrate to avoid martyrdom and others, like Aleksandr Solzhenitsyn, were simply deported against their will. Most of the dissidents intellectually supported the right to emigrate in principle, even if they had no desire to avail themselves of it. The right to travel abroad and return to their country was more important to them personally.

Even though they were not united, were pitifully organized, if at all, and were brutally repressed, the dissidents of the 1960s and 1970s began to revive a Russian tradition of liberal thought that had been virtually eradicated by the communists following the Bolshevik revolution. Except for a brief period in 1917, this tradition had never been the dominant political force in Russia, but it was a powerful intellectual strain in Russian society from the end of the nineteenth century up to the Bolshevik revolution itself. The "February" revolution of 1917, which attempted to establish a parliamentary regime in Russia, was led by persons of a liberal persuasion (in the nineteenth-century sense of the term). The dissidents of the 1960s and 1970s had the dual task of catching up with modern political and philosophical thought in the West and recovering a lost Russian tradition that had been compatible with it. They were always weak numerically, but their thought, particularly that of prominent figures like Andrei Sakharov, was eventually of critical importance for the reforms of the late 1980s and early 1990s.

In addition to the intense political pressure it brought to bear on emigration issues, the United States increased attention in the 1970s on solving the plight of a growing number of divided families and on the defense of persons arrested for political reasons. Traditionally, the Soviet authorities adamantly refused to discuss human rights concerns other than those with a direct U.S.-citizen interest. Often, officials in the Ministry of Foreign Affairs would refuse even to take a list of problem cases for official consideration. A démarche, for example, regarding a political prisoner or a dissident incarcerated in a mental asylum would be summarily rejected. This attitude, however, changed, at least superficially, with the signing of the Helsinki Final Act in 1975.

The Conference on Security and Cooperation in Europe (CSCE), which produced the Helsinki Final Act, was in part the culmination of a Soviet campaign for an All-European Conference. The Soviet goal initially was to exclude the United States and thus drive a wedge in the NATO alliance. When it became clear that such a conference would be impossible without U.S. participation, the Soviets agreed to include the United States and Canada, along with the European countries. (Only Albania refused to participate.) The second Soviet objective, which became the primary one once the United States and Canada were admitted to the conference, was to secure international endorsement of the "territorial results of World War II"—that is, of the division of Europe and the division of Germany. The United States finally agreed to participate in the conference as a part of the Nixon administration's détente policy, but (like most of its NATO allies) it was determined not to accord legitimacy to the Soviet position in Eastern Europe or to the Soviet annexation of the three Baltic states. Western negotiators therefore faced a formidable task: to establish principles that could contribute to stability without freezing the political division of Europe, and at the same time to secure a Soviet commitment to protect specific human rights.

The most difficult negotiations involved so-called Basket I (security) issues and those in Basket III (human rights and freedoms). Regarding Basket I, Western negotiators finally secured agreement to a set of principles regarding security and borders (e.g., that borders could not be changed by force, but only by the mutual agreement of the states involved), which avoided endorsement of any particular border. (President Ford made the point explicit when he announced before he signed the document that his signature did not imply U.S. recognition of the inclusion of the Baltic states in the Soviet Union.) As far as Basket III was concerned, the Soviet Union was compelled to agree to a set of principles that it had systematically violated and continued to do so. Soviet agreement was doubtless hypocritical, but Brezhnev needed to claim a successful result of the "All-European Conference" the Soviet Union had long sought. The imagery of success was more important to him than the actual results. Soviet propagandists would claim that Moscow had secured an endorsement of "the results of World War II," and some critics of the accord in the West accepted the claim, but anyone who read the document with care could see that it did not, in fact, legitimize the division of Europe.

The Soviet Union did little initially to bring its practices in line with the Basket III principles. The Helsinki Final Act, however, had two positive effects, one of limited but the other of profound importance. The effect with limited importance was the willingness of Soviet officials in the Ministry of Foreign Affairs to discuss specific human rights problems, even when there was no U.S. citizen interest. As long as the representation was related to a principle in the Final Act, Soviet officials could not deny that it was a legitimate subject for international discourse. They might, and did, continue to deny the facts as presented by the United States (or other countries), but they no longer refused to discuss the issues.

Far more profound, however, was the impact of the Final Act on opinion within the Soviet Union. The Final Act gave dissidents a legitimate reason to organize, since they could say that they were merely monitoring the observance by Soviet authorities of an international document the Soviet leader had signed. This did not prevent brutal attempts to suppress the movement. Many organizers and activists were jailed or exiled, but these actions were so flagrantly in violation of the obligations the Soviet regime had assumed in Helsinki that they further discredited the Soviet authorities abroad (preventing, for example, closer relations with the countries of Western Europe, despite the strong desire there for a relaxation of tension). In time, the repression also acted to discredit and gravely weaken the Soviet regime at home.

The United States immediately took advantage of the opening provided by the Final Act by proposing concrete negotiations on Basket III issues. It proposed that each country specify practices in the other country that it considered in violation of Helsinki principles, that these be discussed regularly at a responsible diplomatic level, and that unresolved issues be placed on the agenda for higher-level meetings, such as by foreign ministers or heads of government. The Soviets, somewhat to our surprise, accepted the proposal, and a channel was established for meetings, twice a year at a minimum, between the deputy chief of mission at the U.S. embassy in Moscow and the deputy chief of the USA Department in the Soviet Ministry of Foreign Affairs. I was at that time deputy chief of mission in Moscow and thus the designated U.S. interlocutor. My Soviet counterpart was Viktor Komplektov, who much later—in 1991—was Soviet ambassador to the United States for a few months.

The U.S. practice was for the embassy in Moscow to compile a suggested list of problems and cases, send it to the State Department for correction, amendment, and approval, and then present it to the Soviet ministry. The Soviets, by then, had prepared their own list of alleged human rights violations in the United States. Each side, in theory at least, consulted the relevant authorities in its own country to obtain an explanation or, if a violation had actually occurred, corrective action. There were several such exchanges. The U.S. list, if memory serves, grew to eighty-odd specific complaints. The Soviet list was somewhat shorter, and most complaints misrepresented the facts, though there were some instances of questionable arrests and jury verdicts. We treated the Soviet list with respect and had every allegation investigated. In a few cases local authorities took corrective action in order to avoid a questionable police action becoming the subject of international attention. Similarly, but for quite different reasons, a few of the cases the United States cited were resolved.

Unfortunately, this exchange did not continue after the inauguration of President Jimmy Carter. The assumption at the U.S. embassy in Moscow was that, given President Carter's vocal espousal of human rights, including copious criticism of Soviet practices, his administration would vigorously utilize the mechanism that had been established to clarify, discuss, and if possible resolve specific abuses of human rights. The embassy rapidly prepared a draft of a démarche to follow up on the earlier talks and sent it to the State Department for approval. It never came back. When, weeks later, we questioned our colleagues on the Soviet desk, they replied that they had cleared the draft and sent it to the National Security Council for approval, where it still languished. Weeks stretched into months, and to the best of my knowledge, the "Helsinki human rights channel" established during the Ford administration was simply allowed to die. I do not know whether this was the calculated result of a decision or the inadvertent result of inattention.

The failure to continue a dialogue on specific human rights issues was ironic given the public emphasis President Carter personally (and no doubt sincerely) gave to human rights. Soviet diplomats could not avoid the cynical conclusion, which their political authorities would have encouraged in any event, that the professed U.S. interest in human rights was merely a propaganda ploy, designed to gain some advantage over the Soviet Union. When relations soured following the abortive effort in March 1977 to alter the terms of the Vladivostok understanding for strategic arms control, the Soviets were in no mood to grant the United States any favors. U.S. policy had resulted in the conviction on the Soviet part that permitting emigration and releasing political prisoners were simply a sop to the United States and should be reserved for those periods when the Soviet Union was obtaining a quid pro quo. Jewish emigration went into a steep decline and dissidents continued to be arrested and expelled. There was no reversal of these negative trends until, for a brief period in 1979 when SALT II was under active consideration in the Senate, some easing of barriers to emigration occurred. By 1980–81, however, the human rights situation in the Soviet Union was as bad as it had been at any time since Khrushchev's thaw of the early 1960s. After the Soviet invasion of Afghanistan in December 1979, virtually all genuine communication between the U.S. and Soviet governments ceased. Diplomacy was replaced by mutual public denunciations.

This was the situation when President Ronald Reagan took the oath of office in 1981. The U.S. public and the Soviet leaders focused on what they considered his "hard-line rhetoric," largely ignoring what he had to say about reducing nuclear weapons and developing cooperation with the Soviet Union. Reagan personally put great emphasis on human rights in his policy deliberations, but he was reluctant to make public issues of specific cases. He sought solutions through private diplomacy (as Nixon had done, but in Reagan's case more from a conviction that human rights were important than as a response to public pressure). When there were results, Reagan was more forthcoming in negotiations on other subjects. In 1983 he made a personal, unpublicized request to General Secretary Yuri Andropov for exit permission for the Pentecostalists who had taken refuge years earlier in the U.S. embassy. When they were allowed to leave the Soviet Union, he took no public credit but instructed the State Department to initiate serious negotiations on other issues. The summit meetings he sought with Andropov and Konstantin Chernenko, who became general secretary in March 1984, never took place, in part because of the infirmity of the Soviet leaders, and in part because of the Soviet reaction to the deployment of U.S. intermediate-range missiles in Europe beginning in November 1983. Reagan, therefore, was not able to engage the Soviet leaders as he desired until Mikhail Gorbachev came to power in 1985.

Even before Gorbachev came to power, however, Reagan articulated a policy that melded support for human rights with other issues important to the United States. In January 1984 he set forth an agenda for U.S.-Soviet interaction that aimed to end superpower military involvement in regional conflicts, reduce nuclear weapons, and "improve the working relationship," a euphemism for raising the Iron Curtain and respecting human rights. In extensive correspondence with the Soviet leaders and subsequent public statements, he made it clear that while he established no rigid linkages among the various areas for negotiation, none could get very far unless there was improvement in all. By 1985 what had been listed as three points on the agenda became four, when human rights and improved communications were designated as separate categories. The four-part agenda linked Soviet external behavior with the nature of Soviet rule at home.

By the early 1980s the Soviet leaders understood that they needed to end the arms race, which was ruining their economy and putting the unity of the country under increasing stress. Gorbachev's predecessors, however, wanted to end the arms race without changing anything else. Reagan in effect said, "If you want to end the arms race, you must start changing some things at home." Gorbachev, too, tried to end the arms race without making other adjustments, but by early 1987 he concluded that this would be impossible. From that time on, progress on all points of the U.S. agenda took place with accelerating speed that surprised everyone. The jamming of foreign broadcasts ended in early 1987; editors of several mass publications were replaced with people determined to challenge Communist Party control of the press. In September of that year Secretary of State George Shultz met Foreign Minister Eduard Shevardnadze in New York during the session of the United Nations General Assembly. He began the meeting, as he always did, by presenting Shevardnadze with a list of human rights cases that needed resolution.

Instead of complaining, as his predecessor would have done (if he deigned to accept the document at all), Shevardnadze reached out across the table for it and said something like, "Thank you, George. We'll look into these cases and if the facts are as you say, we'll do our best to correct them. But I want you to know one thing. I'm not doing this because you ask me to. I'm doing it because it is something my country needs to do."

Shultz immediately stretched out his hand and replied, "Eduard, that's the only reason you should ever do anything. Rest assured that I'll never ask you to do something unless I think it is in your country's interest."

This was one of the most dramatic moments I witnessed as we negotiated the end of the Cold War. It did not come out of the blue, and it was not simply a matter of yielding to U.S. pressure. It was the result of many separate developments that began to coalesce in 1987: the dissident movement that had spread ideas among the Soviet elite far beyond the dissident circles themselves, the cultural and educational exchange programs begun by the Eisenhower administration, the long frustration of many party officials who began their careers in the 1960s and sympathized with Dubček's reforms in Czechoslovakia (several of whom became key members of Gorbachev's staff), the growing Soviet economic malaise caused in part by the enormous burden of military expenditures and in part by the irrationalities of the command economy. Those tendencies affected mainly the Soviet elite, but they developed as the broader public grew more aware of how much better people lived in the West—and, what was more galling to them, in rapidly developing East Asia, not only in Japan, but also in the smaller "Asian tigers."

Shevardnadze was as good as his word. He not only acted to resolve the cases brought to his attention but also created a division in the Ministry of Foreign Affairs to deal with other Soviet agencies in defense of human rights. He requested and obtained support for a CSCE conference on human rights to be held in Moscow, obviously with the intent to demonstrate that respect for human rights was important for

Soviet prestige and authority in world affairs. (The conference occurred after he left office.)

By 1988 emigration had become so free that the U.S. embassy
was suddenly flooded with applicants for immigration or political asylum. Waiting lists for immigration skyrocketed to half a million, while
more than a hundred thousand Soviet citizens applied for and received
visas for temporary visits. The United States had campaigned so long
for freedom to emigrate that its inability to accommodate all applicants
quickly was considered by many in the Soviet Union as evidence of
hypocrisy. "You have insisted that we open our doors. Now that we
have, you refuse to open yours!" was a common complaint when only
one out of ten Soviet applicants for immigration received permission to
settle in the United States. There is, of course, a difference between a
country's forbidding its citizens to leave the country and a country's
placing limitations on immigration. The distinction was, however,
blurred in the perception of most Soviet citizens. More serious from
the point of view of the Soviet government was the U.S. refusal to
eliminate the restrictions imposed by the Jackson-Vanik Amendment
(as opposed to merely waiving them for a time) even when Soviet
restrictions on emigration were removed. To many, this seemed proof
that the United States was intent on using human rights issues to
achieve advantages in other areas.

In the last years of the Soviet Union protection of human rights
went hand in hand with democratization of the political system.
From 1989 there were, for the first time in Soviet history, relatively
free elections. The democratic movement that formed out of liberal
elements of the Communist Party, along with intellectuals and profes-
sionals who entered the political arena for the first time, placed issues
such as freedom of speech and assembly, freedom of the press, and freedom to travel at the top of their agenda. Increasingly they sought not
so much foreign support as foreign advice. In 1990 and 1991 we could
pack the ballroom at Spaso House, the U.S. ambassador's residence,
with members of the Soviet parliament for discussion with U.S. experts of topics such as First Amendment rights or federal-state relations.
Days later, these discussions would be echoed on the floor of the Soviet
parliament. Frequently, key provisions in U.S. law would turn up in
draft legislation (without, of course, reference to their provenance).

There was, of course, opposition, and a lot of it, from many elements in the Communist Party, reluctant to see power slip from their grasp, and also from the military and the KGB. Until August 1991 Gorbachev managed to keep them at bay, in part by deceit and in part by using the traditional authority of the Communist Party general secretary. The challenge of secessionist movements in the three Baltic states, in Georgia, and eventually in Ukraine posed the most serious threats to Gorbachev's reforms in 1990 and 1991.

This was, to a degree, a paradoxical situation, since the principle of self-determination is one of the recognized human rights, and the Soviet constitution gave the union republics a formal right to secede. However, the Soviet political establishment was overwhelmingly opposed to the breakup of the Soviet Union and was prepared to use force to prevent it. If the Communist Party apparat, the KGB, and the army had had their way, civil rights, still a new and fragile growth, would have been suppressed throughout the country in order to curb the secessionist movements. Though he toyed with these forces, Gorbachev ultimately blocked the extensive use of force, and this was the issue that precipitated the attempt to remove him from power in August 1991. Although the attempted coup d'état failed to achieve its purpose, it so undermined Gorbachev's authority and public confidence in the voluntary federation he sought that the Soviet Union collapsed within months.

The events that brought on the Soviet collapse occurred so rapidly that a salient fact has rarely been noted. It is that by the summer of 1991 most fundamental freedoms were being observed in practice in the capital of the Soviet Union and in most of the areas it controlled. There was freedom of speech, of press, and of assembly. People could travel freely and leave the country if they could afford a ticket and another country would admit them. Of the most important rights, only that to own land was still being denied. The country, however, had not yet developed a political structure to ensure these freedoms, and they were, to varying degrees, challenged in many corners of the vast empire over which Moscow still held formal sway. Much of the opposition to Gorbachev's reforms was in fact opposition to the introduction of property rights and the protection of other basic human rights. In many of the union republics this opposition eventually cloaked itself in nationalist garb. For communist officials in Central Asia and some of the other republics (but not the Baltic states), national independence was used as camouflage to conceal an effort to retain political power and the control of property.

It is for this reason that regard for human rights has retrogressed since 1991 in several of the successor states of the Soviet Union. Only the Baltic states, and to a more limited degree Russia and the Republic of Georgia (which experienced a destructive civil war before taking steps to protect human rights), have been able to develop more reliable protection for civil and human rights than existed in the Soviet Union in its final months. President George Bush was correct when he told the Ukrainians in Kiev on August 1, 1991, that freedom and independence were not synonymous, and that freedom should take precedence.

CONCLUSIONS AND LESSONS

The Cold War ended, communist rule collapsed in the Soviet Union, and the Soviet Union disintegrated in such quick succession that many conflate these three seismic events, perceiving, for example, that the Cold War ended with the collapse of the Soviet Union, or that the Soviet Union was freed from communist rule by pressure from abroad. These perceptions are, however, not supported by a close look at the facts. The Cold War ended before communist rule collapsed in the Soviet Union. It ended because the Soviet leader at the time came to understand that the terms the United States offered were in fact in the interest of his own country. Communist rule ended in the Soviet Union because the Communist Party was incapable of adapting to the reforms Gorbachev demanded and because Gorbachev ultimately chose to undermine the party he headed in order to save the state it controlled. The Soviet Union then collapsed because of its inherent structural contradictions and Gorbachev's inability to control the process and pace of reform.

Foreign pressure, particularly that from the United States and its allies, played a key role in creating conditions that gave Soviet leaders a strong incentive to end the arms race. President Reagan's implicit linkage of arms reduction and internal reform gave Gorbachev little choice but to proceed with internal reforms if he was to reduce the external tension that perpetuated the arms race. It was also important that this linkage was implicit rather than formal and explicit. It was important for Gorbachev to present the reform effort as a response to internal needs rather than to pressure from the outside. The manner in which U.S. policy was implemented was as important as the policy itself.

In sum, the United States set the conditions for ending the Cold War and, as these conditions were met, cooperated to do so. It did not, however, bring down communist rule in the Soviet Union or cause its breakup. These things happened because of internal forces, some, but not all, of which benefited from U.S. and Western support.

Bearing these general observations in mind, I would draw the following conclusions regarding the effect of U.S. human rights policy on the Soviet Union:

1. Soviet leaders began to respect human rights when they understood that it was in their interest to do so. Once Gorbachev, Shevardnadze, and the small group of officials who supported them grasped that the Soviet Union could benefit from democratization, more openness, and stimulation of individual creativity, they began an effort to eliminate the abuses of the past and to develop protections for the future. This required fundamental political reform in the Soviet Union from a totalitarian to a law-based democratic state. It inevitably evoked the opposition of those who had benefited from the Soviet system (the Communist Party apparat and the nomenklatura). Increasingly, Gorbachev's personal political future was linked to his reform program. Therefore, he had an objective interest (though for tactical reasons he did not always show it) in supporting creation of an open society with a government that protected human rights. He was a practical politician who knew very well that this could not happen overnight, but who understood that the country needed to set a course that would eventually bring this result.

2. The principles set forth in the Helsinki Final Act were of crucial importance in improving the protection of human rights in the Soviet Union. Since the Soviet Union had formally endorsed

the principles it set forth, it could not be plausibly argued that these were alien concepts promoted by an outside power for its own benefit. (In fact, it was so argued, but not convincingly.) *The Helsinki Final Act turned out to be a critical prerequisite for the political acceptance in the Soviet Union of protection of human rights as a legitimate goal.*

3. A confrontational policy limited largely to direct pressure (e.g., the Jackson-Vanik Amendment to the Trade Act of 1974) could produce specific concessions regarding individuals and groups when the United States could offer a political quid pro quo (e.g., increased Jewish emigration when an arms control treaty was up for ratification), but direct pressure did little, if anything, to promote protection of human rights across the board. The reason is obvious: policies involving carrots and sticks lead to the impression that respect for human rights is a concession to a foreign power rather than something a healthy, successful society requires.

4. The fact that the Soviet Union was a nuclear power precluded any temptation to threaten the use of force to solve human rights or other political issues (such as the right of the Baltic states to be independent). This, ultimately, turned out to be an asset, since it directed our attention to support for groups in the Soviet Union that were campaigning for human rights, to establishing international norms, and to persuasion. Once Gorbachev set a course of democratization, the United States kept most of its criticism private, so as not to make his position weaker at home or to tempt him to play to his grandstands by "standing up" to the United States.

5. During periods of reform, the governing institutions of a state come under intense stress. If central authority collapses, the result is likely to be quasi anarchy at best or civil war at worst. Inevitably, human beings suffer the consequences. While the state may no longer be capable of exercising authoritarian rule, it is also incapable of protecting the individual from criminals, corrupt bureaucrats, or those who have seized the state's wealth. This means that there will always be a certain tension between

the need to reform a dictatorial system and the need to preserve enough authority to enforce just laws. Outsiders are rarely able to judge the delicate balance of principle and expediency reformist political leaders must achieve.

• • •

These conclusions, derived from our experience in promoting regard for human rights in the Soviet Union, may not have universal applicability. Every country is unique and there is no magic policy potion that inevitably induces political leaders not only to respect human rights but also to develop the institutions that will compel their successors to do so. However, they do suggest that establishing regard for human rights in a society that traditionally has neither understood nor protected them is inevitably a slow and gradual process. The most important contribution the United States can make to human rights throughout the world is to set an example, by demonstrating that U.S. society is successful because it protects the individual. Cultural and educational contacts are vitally important in spreading this message —assuming that we do, in fact, protect human rights and are seen to do so.

It is also important to distinguish between what private nongovernmental organizations can do and what governments can and should do. It is important to know about and to publicize human rights abuses, but this is best done by nongovernmental organizations, preferably international ones. Egregious violations may require some public comment by political leaders, but it should be minimized. On these issues, governments are almost always more effective using private diplomacy than public pressure. Private organizations, however, are most effective when they stimulate public opposition to reprehensible practices and affect a regime's prestige and standing in the world. Least effective of all are rigid legislative linkages that tend to create in the target country a zero-sum attitude on human rights issues and the presumption that the United States is using human rights as a pretext for demanding some selfish advantage.

Part IV
Latin America

9

First Do No Harm

U.S. Foreign Policy and Respect for Human Rights in El Salvador and Guatemala, 1980–96

SUSAN BURGERMAN

THE UNITED STATES IMPLEMENTED its human rights foreign policy more in the breach than in the observance during the 1980s in El Salvador and Guatemala. This was primarily because of competing interests in foreign policy decision making, with regional security typically being accorded higher priority than the promotion of human rights. El Salvador and Guatemala are states located within the United States' historical sphere of influence, and as with several other such countries caught in the web of Cold War geopolitics, the U.S. government actively supported one side of their internal armed conflicts. In both El Salvador and Guatemala, the United States sided with the existing government against leftist insurgent forces. Especially with respect to El Salvador, the obstacles to implementing a human rights policy were found as much in the U.S. government as in the target government. Finally, the fact that these polities were torn by civil war created a different configuration of constraints and opportunities for implementing human rights measures

267

than exist in cases of "ordinary" repression found in other countries whose human rights practices have come under scrutiny.

While a bilateral human rights policy can often be effective in promoting respect for international human rights principles, in both of these cases *conditions improved when the U.S. government lost interest in supporting the violators* and permitted the United Nations to step in. What most clearly contributed to the marked change in the Salvadoran and Guatemalan governments' human rights compliance were the irreversible momentum of their respective mediated peace processes and the intrusive presence of UN human rights observers, who were deployed throughout both countries. Ultimately, foreign policy decision making is largely about competing values, and moral concerns such as human rights promotion will usually sink on the policy agenda where they compete with security or powerful economic interests.

Aside from the problem of competing values, we run into trouble evaluating the effectiveness of human rights sanctions because the outcome is often overdetermined. Evaluating foreign policy initiatives implies finding a causal relationship between pressure over time and outcomes over time, but changes in state behavior usually have many causes or influences. Even when an action (for example, sharp diplomatic protest or the threat of sanctions) appears to result in an immediate behavior change (for instance, prisoner release or the arrest of a perpetrator), the change is usually limited to a single act, which can also be reversed. The violator's behavior may change for a number of reasons, which include U.S. pressure but also factors that have nothing to do with U.S. pressure—for example, changing domestic interests, a realignment of international coalitions, or because repression has achieved its goal of eliminating the opposition. Therefore, an evaluation of the outcome of human rights pressure must include an analysis of the domestic political context.

Further, the measure of the result itself may be ambiguous. What constitutes reform? How profound need it be to justify the measures taken? Does compliance with a list of specific but narrow demands constitute reform? In order to approach an evaluation, this chapter defines "human rights reform" as change in either state action or state structures that the relevant elites acknowledge was initiated in response to pressure and in order to conform to international human rights standards. Reforms can be indicated by an actual change of practice, such as restructuring the judicial system to guarantee legal rights or demilitarizing the internal security forces, or by a change in the way state leaders communicate their priorities to society and to other governments and international actors, such as frequent allusion to human rights in public statements. Admittedly, change in government rhetoric is often empty of substance and used to cloak or justify inaction, but it also provides opportunities for advocates or other states to hold that government accountable for complying with human rights standards that it has publicly endorsed.

This chapter first gives an overview of U.S. interests in these two war-torn countries. Next, it explains how the outcome of U.S. human rights pressure varied with changes in their domestic political contexts. Third, the chapter examines the results of the major policy instruments the U.S. government used to promote human rights.

U.S. GOALS AND COMPETING INTERESTS: HUMAN RIGHTS VERSUS REGIONAL SECURITY

El Salvador

During El Salvador's civil war (1980–92), the executive branch of the U.S. government publicly exhorted the Salvadorans to comply with human rights and humanitarian law. But however stern the protests were in words, in deeds the U.S. government clearly subordinated human rights principles to its interest in containing leftist insurgent movements in Central America. This produced two near-term adverse consequences: it provided decision makers with a justification for turning a blind eye to human rights violations, and it prevented the government of El Salvador from pursuing a negotiated settlement with the guerrilla opposition (the Farabundo Martí National Liberation Front [FMLN]) when President José Napoleón Duarte (1984–89) sought to open a peace process. That said, the U.S. government under Ronald Reagan did pay limited and rhetorical attention to human rights principles in its dealings with the Salvadoran government, which I argue elsewhere is a testament to the effectiveness of the human rights lobby in the United States.[1] The Reagan human rights policy focused on promoting elections that resulted in civilian governments, broadly conflating human rights compliance with electoral democracy. Elliott Abrams, assistant secretary of state for human rights and humanitarian affairs (assistant secretary of state for inter-American affairs in the second Reagan administration), spearheaded this policy.

The association of the Salvadoran conflict with Cold War geo-strategic interests was initially established during the administration of Jimmy Carter, and it was under Carter that the military counterin-surgency strategy was first promoted. The Carter State Department's fledgling human rights policy came up against overriding security concerns in Central America after the July 1979 Sandinista victory in Nicaragua. Human rights concerns were thereafter subordinated to a policy of maintaining government stability in the region and prevent-ing further socialist gains, a policy that persisted throughout the Reagan administration and well into that of George H. W. Bush.

The government of El Salvador had preemptively rejected U.S. military assistance in 1977, in protest over congressional criticism of its human rights record.[2] A relatively low level of military assistance was reinstated in March 1980, when the House Foreign Operations Subcommittee approved the reprogramming of $5.7 million toward nonlethal aid for the Salvadoran military (ironically, one week after Archbishop Oscar Romero's assassination by government-supported paramilitaries). The Carter administration decided to ease restrictions that June, in an effort to bolster the shaky ruling junta, which was perceived as the sole means of preventing another marxist revolution in Central America.[3]

For at least the first half of the decade, members of Congress sympathetic to human rights concerns struggled with the executive branch over U.S. policy in El Salvador. They utilized the human rights provisions of State Department foreign assistance legislation as lever-age to gain a measure of control over President Reagan's military appro-priations requests. The Reagan administration's hard-line ideological stance polarized the issue of human rights protection, as it did all policy discussion concerning Central America. During the 1980s, debate on Central America policy, especially with regard to human rights viola-tions, became a source of acute conflict between the executive branch and human rights advocates, with sympathetic members of Congress mediating on the side of the advocates.

Several highly publicized incidents of abuse by Salvadoran state or paramilitary agents early in the civil war provoked international nongovernmental protest and heightened congressional opposition to military aid. The fact that two of these incidents involved U.S. nationals provided the congressional opposition with greater leverage in their efforts to overrule White House appropriations requests. First, on December 2, 1980, three U.S. nuns and a Catholic layworker were arbitrarily detained by national guardsmen, raped, and murdered. This case generated a tremendous outrage among the U.S. public and by far the greatest degree of interest in Congress. State Department officials were pressured to investigate the situation personally and to maintain supervision of the Salvadoran military's investigation.[4] One month later, on January 3, 1981, two labor advisers from the American Institute for Free Labor Development (AIFLD) were shot at the Sheraton Hotel in San Salvador while dining with the director of the Salvadoran Institute for Agrarian Reform. These two cases were specified in legislation that conditioned military aid on a presidential certification of progress toward reform (certification is discussed later in this chapter). These became rare instances in which the material, albeit not the intellectual, perpetrators of egregious violations in El Salvador were eventually prosecuted.

Ultimately, congressional efforts wavered before a determined White House. After the election of Christian Democrat José Napoleón Duarte in 1984, the majority chose to abide by the fiction of democratic government in El Salvador and forged a bipartisan policy consensus. Duarte's election paved the way for the U.S. Congress to release withheld military funds, much of which went into augmenting the air force. This led to an intensification of the air war. Indiscriminate aerial bombing, intended to disrupt the FMLN's supply lines of provisions and information from rural supporters, caused massive dislocation among the rural population.

The U.S. embassy initially supported aerial attacks on the grounds that they were necessary to deprive the guerrilla force of its base of support. However, in response to the ensuing international media and NGO outcry, the embassy in San Salvador retracted its claim that civilians living in combat zones were legitimate targets. As another result of international human rights pressure at this time, President Duarte issued a new rules-of-engagement order in September 1984. The new orders limited air strikes to combat situations or to attacks on guerrilla columns. They also required that strike orders be accompanied by statements disclosing the location of civilian populations and International Committee of the Red Cross operations that were to be avoided. The rules-of-engagement order was unfortunately disregarded by the air force, and aerial attacks on civilians continued.[5] For all of his express desire to protect the rights and lives of noncombatants, Duarte lacked the ability to impose civilian authority on the armed forces as long as they enjoyed an independent and seemingly unconditional supply of funds from the United States.

Following the transition from Ronald Reagan's administration to that of George Bush, the government of the United States continued to support military assistance and a military settlement of the civil war in El Salvador. The White House maintained its position that the Salvadoran government was a democracy under threat, and that the Salvadoran armed forces were capable of winning the war with continued assistance, until the end of 1989.[6]

However, the military capabilities demonstrated by the FMLN in a November 1989 urban offensive (and, despite this, their inability to establish an urban base in the capital), combined with the armed forces' poor performance, convinced U.S. military decision makers that the war had reached a stalemate. The congressional bipartisan consensus on cooperating with the administration's El Salvador policy was definitively shattered in the months following the November 1989 offensive. An act committed by the armed forces during the offensive—the November 16 assassinations of six Jesuit scholars, their cook, and her daughter—set off a visceral and bipartisan wave of moral condemnation that finally motivated Congress to draw the line on military assistance. In May 1990 an investigative commission headed by Representative Joe Moakley (D-Mass.) released a report implicating the Salvadoran military in the Jesuit murders, causing an unprecedented degree of moral outrage in Congress. Within a year, U.S. military assistance was cut by 50 percent, with conditions placed on the remainder.

U.S. strategic interests in Central America shifted to a more pragmatic posture after 1989, in any event. Foreign military support for both the Salvadoran government and the FMLN eroded. The collapse of the Soviet bloc and the loss of Nicaraguan assistance after the Sandinistas were defeated in the 1990 elections deprived the FMLN of much of its international political support. The U.S. Congress, now joined by an administration that was less ideologically polarizing than Reagan's, exerted unilateral pressure on the Salvadoran government and military to negotiate a peaceful resolution of the civil war. In the end, the U.S. and Soviet foreign ministries joined in bilateral efforts at diplomatic persuasion to keep the Salvadoran negotiated peace process on track.

Guatemala

Relations between the Guatemalan and U.S. governments in the 1980s were very different from U.S.-Salvadoran relations of the same period. The Salvadoran armed forces' dependence on U.S. financing and training was so great that the threat of losing that aid was a principal factor leading to their eventual subordination to civilian authority. In contrast, U.S. military assistance had helped build the Guatemalan armed forces into a modern, well-equipped, and well-organized institution during the 1960s and 1970s, but official military assistance was then cut off under the Carter administration. By the time it was reinstated in 1986, the military had established other arms sources, notably in Taiwan and Israel.

At least as relevant was that the Guatemalan high command had developed independent financial sources in banking, real estate, and other enterprises. The military maintained a nationalist foreign policy attitude at the core of which lay the determination not to become (like the Salvadorans) dependent on U.S. assistance. Because of this relative independence, the change in U.S. regional strategy with the end of the Cold War did not have the same effect on prospects for human rights in Guatemala that it had in El Salvador. Less military assistance to the violator government meant less leverage over the armed forces, and therefore less positive change in behavior with the withdrawal, or threatened withdrawal, of U.S. assistance. Throughout the 1980s congressional debate focused on the other security issues in the region. Given the much smaller U.S. investment in Guatemala's low-intensity conflict, supporters in Congress could not muster the political will to exert consistent and strong pressure on the Reagan administration to sanction human rights violations in Guatemala or on the Guatemalan government to change its practices.

Nonetheless, the shift in geopolitical interests under the George H. W. Bush government did bring about increasing levels of State Department scrutiny of Guatemalan government and military behavior, which contributed to the growing international pressure to enact human rights reforms. Several attempts were made to bring the material authors of major crimes to trial in the early 1990s, but the pressure did not result in any consistent change in policy or increase in civilian control over the military—until a significant realignment of domestic political alliances took place in the mid-1990s.

COMPETING INTERESTS WITHIN THE TARGET COUNTRIES: PRAGMATIC VERSUS HARD-LINE ELITES

El Salvador

National and local elections were held in El Salvador on a regular basis (albeit with notable interruptions) throughout most of the twentieth century. The political system was, however, highly restrictive. In October 1979 a cadre of young reformist officers staged a coup, overthrowing the repressive and corrupt government of General Carlos Humberto Romero (1977–79). The ensuing five-member junta was reshuffled four times. Two interim presidents were appointed by the junta: José Napoleón Duarte (December 1980–March 1982) and Álvaro Magaña (March 1982–June 1984). Two presidents, Duarte (1984–89) and Alfredo Cristiani (1989–94), were elected in what were declared by international observers to be fair and free contests. All three presidents, whether elected or appointed, were civilians, and all three expressed concern for their country's human rights record. Neither Duarte nor Magaña was capable of exerting civilian authority to modify the military's behavior, because of the autonomy that continuing U.S. assistance afforded the military, and because of their reluctance to confront the armed forces during a civil war, not a palatable task for a civilian leader with a weak political base.

The Salvadoran government did make some show of responding to U.S. and international human rights pressure in certain cases. These cases (albeit minor ones) of positive change suggested that the Salvadoran government would respond to human rights pressure when the message was delivered unambiguously and if the threatened sanctions directly affected military interests.

In the early to mid-1980s, the massive increase in U.S. financial, matériel, and training support caused the military to shift from its traditional dependence on agrarian elites and to affiliate itself more closely with its U.S. backers. Whereas officers had formerly sought to advance their careers through ties to the oligarchy, in the 1980s overtly supporting U.S. policies—propping up a weak centrist presidency, promoting a compromised agrarian reform—became the key to personal and institutional enhancement. This inevitably led to a weakening of the long-standing alliance between the institutional armed forces and the traditional economic-political elite. Just how weak the alliance had become was evident after the 1985 assembly elections, in which the Christian Democratic Party (PDC) received an absolute majority. The National Republican Alliance (ARENA), the party representing the agrarian and industrial elites, challenged the results. Rather than support its former oligarchic patrons, on this occasion the military aligned itself with the PDC and that party's patron, the Reagan administration.[7]

The military-oligarchy alliance remained tenuous and often unstable through the civil war years. Wealthy landowners required the military to conduct the war and to keep popular organizations under control, but they consistently thwarted the land reform efforts that the more moderate military faction considered necessary in order to stabilize the country and, especially, to retain U.S. support. A split formed between hard-line officers, who supported ARENA and participated in paramilitary operations, and more pragmatic members of the high command, who were concerned that refusal to cooperate on land reform and electoral issues would mean the loss of U.S. military assistance. The armed forces were able to retain a great deal of autonomy from political elites of both the political center and the right wing throughout the civil war, thanks to independent funding from the United States.

Operating between the institutional armed forces and traditional economic elites were several paramilitary organizations, or death squads. Some of these groups worked directly out of state security offices; others were civilian based and associated with ARENA party leadership. At the height of death squad operations in 1983, an average of eight hundred murders per month were attributed to these shadow organizations. Despite the evidence of official complicity, both the Salvadoran government and the Reagan administration insistently maintained a sharp distinction between military and paramilitary violations. State Department and CIA reports characterized the death squads as "right-wing terrorists" in order to deflect responsibility from the Salvadoran military and security apparatus. Evidence indicates that the White House was aware of official complicity. For example, an October 1983 classified CIA briefing paper documented the paramilitary activities of, among other Salvadoran government officials, Lt. Col. Rene Emilio Ponce, director of the National Guard Police Department.[8]

The Reagan administration officials who were guiding Salvador policy must have been aware of the involvement of Salvadoran security forces in death squad operations. Nonetheless, in order to justify continued military assistance, the U.S. administration publicly insisted that the problem was not a lack of political will to reform the security forces, but rather that the death squads were part of an autonomous civilian right wing that neither the government of El Salvador nor the armed forces high command was capable of controlling. The Salvadoran government was depicted as fighting for its very survival, under fire from the guerrilla forces on the left and civilian terrorists on the right.

The 1984 presidential election in El Salvador has been referred to as a "demonstration" election, intended for domestic audiences in the United States as evidence that El Salvador was a representative democracy under threat from a communist insurgency and deserving of military support.[9] The reality in El Salvador was that of a corrupt and inefficient government, incapable of promoting its social and economic policies, and facing implacable opposition from the private sector and agrarian elites over its attempts at agrarian reform, nationalization of banks, and electoral recoding. Duarte's capacity to promote more than rhetorical compliance with human rights standards was very weak.[10] He lacked the political base to control the military during a civil war, and the U.S. embassy failed to lend him the support he would have needed to reform the military.

By the end of the 1980s, the preferences of Salvadoran domestic leaders had changed. A schism formed in the right wing, from which arose a pragmatic contingent seriously concerned with the opportunity costs stemming from the country's international image as a human rights violator. Alfredo Cristiani, who represented this faction, was elected president in 1989 by promising to bring the civil war to a peaceful settlement. The center-right pragmatists' capacity to subordinate the military reflected the change in U.S. interests as much as it did Cristiani's internal influence. His predecessor, Duarte, expounded human rights discourse and attempted to initiate peace talks, but, given the Reagan administration's support for the armed forces, Duarte did not exercise sufficient authority to enact reforms. It was not until the U.S. Congress credibly threatened to withdraw military support after November 1989 that Cristiani was able to enter negotiations with military endorsement (and even then cooperation among the high command was not absolutely assured). As the evidence piled up of high-command involvement in the Jesuit murders, junior officers began to express their dissent, particularly with their commanding officers' efforts to block the investigations.

In sum, the alignment of the Salvadoran armed forces with patrons in the U.S. government changed radically in 1990, when the reevaluation of U.S. geostrategic priorities, combined with the Defense Department's perception that the civil war had reached a stalemate and the discovery of armed forces' complicity in the Jesuit assassinations, caused the United States to withdraw its unconditional support. In the end, this allowed a pragmatic and politically moderate faction of the oligarchy, led by Alfredo Cristiani, to gain the upper hand in its power struggle with the military—and to negotiate a peace agreement that established an international human rights mission and that restructured the armed forces, removing internal security from its control and reducing the size of its forces nearly by half.

Guatemala

As in El Salvador, Guatemalan governments under both military and civilian administration failed to comply with human rights pressure. The UN Human Rights Commission passed annual resolutions expressing concern for egregious violations in Guatemala throughout the presidencies of General Romeo Lucas García (1978–82), General Efraín Ríos Montt (1982–83), and General Oscar Humberto Mejía Víctores (1983–86). International condemnation continued through the civilian governments of Marco Vinicio Cerezo Arévalo (1986–91), Jorge Serrano Elías (1991–93), and Ramiro de León Carpio (1993–96).

Guatemalan politics between 1966 and 1985 were conducted under a regime of regularly held elections with an extremely limited, nonpluralist military-dominated party system. Because of the way it controlled the political system, the Guatemalan military was able to impose a top-down structural control over the countryside and to circumvent civilian attempts to limit its authority. General Lucas García launched a crackdown on nonviolent political dissent and opposition politicians of the incipient center and moderate left in 1978. The crackdown coincided with the onset of the most brutal stages of combat against guerrilla organizations that had been operating in different parts of the country since 1961 (organized in 1982 as a coalition, the Guatemalan National Revolutionary Unity [URNG]).

The Lucas García administration was also remarkable for the degree of corruption at the highest levels of the military. With an economic crisis brought on by the international recession of the early 1980s, capital flight, and a drop in tourism caused by extreme violence in the countryside, the corruption among high-command officers exacerbated military factionalism. The army was riven by political contests among officers over fast-diminishing state resources, and between young officers in combat zones and their commanding officers, whom the officers in the field considered incompetent to defeat the guerrilla forces. Meanwhile, many of the military's civilian allies in the business sector were alienated by the fact that a small group of ranking officers was increasingly monopolizing government positions and economic benefits.[11]

General Efraín Ríos Montt overthrew the Lucas García government in March 1982, suspended the constitution, established himself as the head of a military junta, and proceeded to reorganize the government around a national counterinsurgency plan. The intensity of scorched-earth warfare and the number of rural massacres increased sharply during this period. Meanwhile, the junta developed a system of conscripting the indigenous rural male population into local security units called civil defense patrols (patrullas de autodefensa civil [PACs]). PACs were deployed in sweeps to round up villagers displaced by rural warfare and bring them under military control in "development poles," a resettlement system along the lines of the strategic hamlets used in Vietnam. Development poles were located on land depopulated during scorched-earth attacks and then resettled under military command.

However, Guatemala's economic crisis worsened considerably under Ríos Montt, even further alienating the middle class and agrarian and industrial elites. In August 1983 Defense Minister Mejía Víctores removed Ríos Montt (who reemerged in the mid-1990s as a party leader in Congress) and declared himself chief of state. Mejía Víctores engineered a transitional election to civilian government in 1985, in an effort to increase Guatemala's international legitimacy. Given the Reagan administration's emphasis on regularly held elections as the best indicator of respect for human rights, this was considered necessary to attract U.S. development assistance (which leapt from $20 million in 1984 to $107 million in 1985),[12] to regain private-sector confidence and reduce capital flight, and to limit social protest. The process was tightly controlled through the exclusion of organizations or parties that sought substantive change or that threatened military power and prerogatives.[13] Human rights protection under the first two civilian governments improved insofar as the orders for political violence evidently no longer came from the executive office. What did not change were the use of summary execution, torture, disappearance, and other violations of the rights of the person by the military apparatus, particularly the intelligence units, and the climate of impunity within which they were able to operate.

Any efforts by the first civilian president, Vinicio Cerezo, to identify and prosecute those responsible for violations were aborted early in his administration, because he never had the political capacity to assert his authority over the military. Cerezo did not enjoy the support of economic elites, who remained unified in their obdurate refusal to cooperate with his modest efforts to restructure the economy. Further, by the time Cerezo left office, his government was thoroughly discredited by successive scandals and widespread corruption. Finally, the critical factor that weakened Cerezo was that a powerful faction of the military remained opposed to civilian rule and retained its capacity to overthrow any civilian government that threatened the military's prerogatives.

The second civilian president, Jorge Serrano, became increasingly isolated in office and intolerant of criticism during 1992 and 1993, as the rampant corruption in both the executive branch and legislature became public and his administration's economic adjustment policies caused extremes of social dislocation and mass protest. On May 25, 1993, Serrano launched an executive coup and suspended the constitutional order, probably with the backing of members of the military who found the conditions of social unrest and ungovernability intolerable.[14]

A variety of civil sectors reacted immediately to oppose the executive coup, including the association of popular organizations and trade unions, attorneys and judicial workers, and the association of industrial and agricultural producers. Within a few days the United States, the European Union, and the Organization of American States had responded to the breakdown of constitutional order with threats to suspend aid and block loans. Given the private sector's opposition and the threat of economic isolation, the majority of the military high command (which had been bitterly divided over Serrano's coup) joined the civilian opposition in demanding Serrano's resignation. On June 5 Congress elected Ramiro de León Carpio, then the national human rights ombudsman, to serve the remainder of Serrano's term.

As ombudsman, de León Carpio had been an outspoken critic of the military's human rights record, but during his two and a half years as president he lacked the political strength to exert civilian authority over the military. Violations targeting civilians and perpetrated by state security forces continued, although at a generally lower level than under previous administrations, and he failed to follow through with several policy changes he had strongly advocated as human rights ombudsman.

The November 1995 elections brought in a president, Álvaro Arzú, who, like Alfredo Cristiani in El Salvador, represented modernizing elements among the industrial and agrarian elites. Although he ultimately failed to comply with many of the commitments his government undertook in the peace accords, Arzú did have the political capacity and will to conduct two major purges of corrupt and abusive ranking officers during his first year in office. He was able to do so owing to the support of a faction of the high command that clearly understood it to be in the interests of the military, as an institution, to improve Guatemala's international human rights reputation.

TOOLS OF U.S. POLICY: CARROTS AND STICKS, CONGRESSIONAL APPROPRIATIONS, AND THE CERTIFICATION PROCESS

El Salvador

When governments apply pressure on a military or a military-dominated government to change its behavior during time of war, the most relevant point of leverage is military assistance. Congress began to apply pressure on the government of El Salvador through appropriations decisions in 1977. When demonstrations called by the opposition to protest fraudulent elections in March of that year were brutally repressed, Representatives Robert Drinan (D-Mass.) and Tom Harkin (D-Iowa) and Senator Edward Kennedy (D-Mass.) held hearings on the subject. A few months later, in July, the House Committee on International Relations Subcommittee on International Organizations conducted an inquiry into the persecution of Jesuit priests. Had these congressional findings determined that the Salvadoran government was a gross and consistent human rights violator, Foreign Assistance Act Sections 116 and 502(b) would have prohibited the State Department from dispensing military and security-related aid.[15] However, the military government in San Salvador, offended by the inquiries, preemptively rejected U.S. military assistance and thus deprived Congress of what leverage it had at the time. When aid was reinstated

in 1980 in the wake of the Sandinista government's increasing movement toward socialism, Congress justified overriding the human rights
conditions on strategic grounds.

By the end of 1981, with the civil war reaching uncontrollable
heights in rural El Salvador and death squad–style assassinations
becoming commonplace occurrences, Congress responded to the public outcry mobilized by human rights NGOs by voting to impose conditions on further military aid appropriations. In December 1981 the
House and the Senate approved legislation requiring the president to
biannually certify that the government of El Salvador was making a
genuine effort to comply with international human rights standards
and to bring its armed forces under control (HR 4042).

Presidential certification was based on vague requirements of
"progress toward" general goals of political and military reform. These
goals were given some definition, however, by including the requirement that progress be made in the prosecution of specific cases of violations against U.S. citizens. One of the conditions of certification
was good-faith effort to investigate and bring to justice the perpetrators
in the rape and murder of the four U.S. churchwomen killed in December 1980 and the death squad shooting of the two U.S. labor advisers
in January 1981. This measure held the administration responsible for
substantiating its claims of progress on human rights reforms and accountable for what the Salvadoran government and armed forces did
with U.S. funding, in return for requested military assistance.

The certification process became part of the human rights advocates' mobilization calendar. Every six months from January 1982 to
January 1984, the State Department and intelligence services would
prepare reports based on which the White House would make its decision to certify. To ensure accurate reporting, human rights organizations would provide the State Department with information linking
the Salvadoran government and the military to human rights violations. The reports, unrealistically mild at first, finally growing more
critical at the end of the period, invariably found that the government
was doing its best under the circumstances. Although this process did
not directly produce improvements in El Salvador, the certification
requirement provided at least a minimal check on the Reagan administration's support for the Salvadoran government. It also caused the

State Department to exert itself more seriously in pressing its Salvadoran allies to conform to human rights standards. After two years of this, President Reagan terminated the certification bill by pocket veto in November 1983. This did not entirely silence congressional opposition. For example, Senator Arlen Specter (R-Pa.), previously reluctant to limit military spending in El Salvador, amended the 1984 appropriations bill in November 1983 to make 30 percent of aid conditional on achieving a verdict in the churchwomen case.[16]

Congressional appropriations pressure had a greater effect in keeping the military hard line in check during the peace negotiations (1990–92). Again, this reflects the extent to which the military was financially dependent on the United States. A bill coauthored by Senators Christopher Dodd (D-Conn.) and Patrick Leahy (D-Vt.) was passed in November 1990, which cut military assistance by 50 percent and made the remainder conditional on good faith in negotiations, acceptance of UN mediation, progress on the Jesuit case, and control of military violence against civilians.[17] The Dodd-Leahy Amendment was intended to provide both sides with incentives to negotiate in good faith. The proviso for the FMLN was that the 50 percent of military aid that was cut would be reinstated if the FMLN were to leave the negotiating table, instigate military action that would threaten the government's survival, or receive foreign military aid. In fact, the FMLN managed to meet the last condition in January 1991 by using surface-to-air missiles acquired from the Nicaraguan government to shoot down a military helicopter and summarily execute two U.S. advisers. U.S. financing was therefore partially restored to the Salvadoran armed forces in March 1991. Despite the reinstatement of funds, Congress had made its point. Continued U.S. military support, which the armed forces had been able to take for granted for over a decade, was now insecure. This had an impact in ensuring military cooperation with the peace process that cannot be overemphasized.

Guatemala

Neither members of Congress concerned for human rights nor the State Department's Bureau of Human Rights and Humanitarian Affairs was able to exercise the kind of leverage over Guatemala that they could in El Salvador, because Guatemala never enjoyed the attention and financial assistance lavished on El Salvador and Nicaragua during the 1980s. Military assistance to Guatemala did not provoke the kind of debate in Congress that there had been over El Salvador or Nicaragua. This was partly due to the low intensity of the conflict itself after a surge of massacres in 1981–83; the Guatemalan guerrilla forces never posed a significant threat to the government. Another factor was that Guatemala solidarity groups in the United States were less well organized and less active than their Salvadoran counterparts.[18] The amount of assistance the administration was requesting for Guatemala was comparatively negligible, while U.S. commercial investment and interest in Guatemala were conversely much greater than in El Salvador, so appropriations requests did not excite as much controversy.[19] Finally, unlike El Salvador, Guatemala did not share a porous border with socialist Nicaragua. Despite the low level of attention, international human rights organizations working on Guatemala devoted a great deal of their advocacy work to lobbying the U.S. government, because the United States was the major economic and military force in the region and was therefore expected to wield considerable influence over military behavior.

Guatemalan president Kjell Laugerud rejected U.S. military assistance in 1977 to protest the interventionary human rights conditions placed on appropriations. Congress responded by terminating military aid in 1978. In reality, the cutoff was only partial, as support still in the pipeline continued and many military supplies could be reclassified as nonmilitary. Sales of military equipment actually increased from $2.8 million in 1977 to $3.6 million in 1979. Private commercial sales also continued, with licenses issued by the Departments of State and Commerce. No conditions were placed on nonmilitary economic assistance. Conditionality in lending was inconsistent: the United States voted against international development bank loans to Guatemala in October 1979 and May 1980, but approved five other loans during the period. Nonetheless, military aid was technically cut off and no congressional hearings were held on Guatemala from 1976 through 1981.[20]

The Reagan administration increased pressure on Congress to reinstate military assistance to Guatemala in 1983, and human rights lobbyists responded by calling on the United States and other governments to prohibit military aid and arms sales and to curtail all financial assistance, including multilateral loans, except for carefully overseen distribution of basic humanitarian aid. Reagan's requests to renew military appropriations to Guatemala were rejected until elections were held in 1985, because of the publicity over evidence of ongoing government use of arbitrary detention, disappearance, extrajudicial killing, and torture. When the request was approved, Congress attached conditions to future military aid, stipulating that the aid must be requested in writing by the civilian president of Guatemala, rather than directly by the military, and that the State Department must certify that human rights conditions had in fact improved. Overall economic assistance to Guatemala increased sharply with the election of a civilian government, and U.S. military personnel became directly involved in combat operations, training, joint exercises, and logistical support.[21]

By the time lethal aid was finally reinstated in 1986, the Guatemalan guerrilla war had been confined to occasional skirmishes in a few isolated combat zones and could not be construed as a threat to an elected government. From the U.S. strategic perspective, the most likely purpose for the increase in military support was to overcome the Guatemalan high command's defiantly independent policy of support for the regional (Contadora) peace process and refusal to officially participate in the U.S.-financed contra war in Nicaragua. The policy had been established under General Ríos Montt, in part to assert Guatemala's independence from U.S. aid and in part because the high command was convinced that Reagan's war in Nicaragua would destabilize the entire region. In fact, Cerezo was able to attract nearly $300 million in loans and credit and $58.4 million in outright grants from the European Community and various member-states in 1986, in support of his refusal to cooperate with the Reagan administration against the Contadora process.[22] The U.S. State Department countered in mid-1988 with threats of economic sanctions and promises of additional aid in return for cooperating in an effort to isolate the Sandinista government. Cerezo backed down in August 1988 and adopted the U.S. regional policy.[23] In this case, the carrots and sticks produced the intended effect of weakening the regional peace process, with the side effect of prolonging Guatemala's internal conflict.

Lethal aid to Guatemala was again cut back under the administration of George H. W. Bush, and deliveries were temporarily suspended in December 1990, owing to evidence that senior military officers were obstructing the investigation into the June 1990 murder of U.S. citizen Michael DeVine. Congressional appropriations legislation for fiscal 1993 prohibited all military aid but permitted commercial arms transfers.[24] Following the May 1993 executive coup and the successful threat of economic sanctions from the United States, the European Union, and the international financial institutions, the Clinton administration sought to bolster the newly appointed civilian government by temporarily resuming security assistance, military and police training, and joint military exercises, although direct military assistance remained suspended.[25] However, revelations that the CIA had retained a Guatemalan army officer on its payroll who was implicated in the Michael DeVine murder caused the Clinton administration to announce on March 13, 1995, that all remaining military assistance, including officer training programs, had been terminated.[26]

In any event, as a 1996 investigation revealed, covert funding and CIA operations continued throughout the period. Following the suspension of direct military assistance in 1990, overall CIA funding levels decreased from approximately $3.5 million in fiscal year 1989 (a sizable amount, considering how low the level of direct military assistance was) to approximately $1 million in 1995. "The funds the CIA provided to the Guatemalan liaison services were vital to the D-2 and Archivos [the security agencies most closely associated with human rights violations]. . . . The CIA, with the knowledge of ambassadors and other State Department and National Security Council officials, as well as the Congress, continued this aid after the termination of overt military assistance in 1990."[27]

Overall, insofar as foreign assistance can be used as an incentive for compliance with human rights standards or to sanction noncompliance, the amounts of lethal assistance to Guatemala were too small to impress the military, and the signals from U.S. administrations were too mixed and inconsistent to bolster the weak civilian leaders.

TOOLS OF U.S. POLICY: DIPLOMATIC REPRESENTATIONS, PUBLIC STATEMENTS, AND STATE DEPARTMENT COUNTRY REPORTS

El Salvador

The U.S. ambassador to El Salvador, Deane Hinton, warned Salvadorans in October 1982 that the United States might withhold assistance if the Salvadoran government failed to seriously investigate and prosecute the murders of U.S. citizens, despite the U.S. commitment to fight communism in the region.[28] One year later Hinton's successor, Thomas Pickering, speaking at an American Chamber of Commerce event in November 1983, issued a barely disguised threat, warning that the United States could no longer ignore "terrorism of the right" in determining financial assistance. He noted that Congress had already proposed to reduce military spending by $22 million and place conditions on what remained, owing to the protest raised in the United States against death squad activities.[29] Pickering's remarks were targeted at right-wing civilians associated with ARENA and at the military. They carried a direct threat of economic sanctions that most directly affected the armed forces and drew an immediate, albeit purely rhetorical, response. That same month, Defense Minister Vides Casanova declared that the high command was determined to combat terrorist organizations "regardless of their political persuasion."[30]

Vice President George H. W. Bush visited San Salvador a month later, to underscore the Reagan administration's concern that the human rights situation was seriously undermining El Salvador's prospects for continued military aid. The fact that the vice president was sent to deliver this message indicates that the White House was not impervious to pressure from human rights activists and found it necessary to demonstrate its concern. This was probably the clearest single instance in which human rights pressure—initially generated by NGO lobbying, and then exerted by Congress on the administration, which then turned it on the Salvadoran government—resulted in some measurable action in El Salvador. The visit occurred less than a month after Pickering's unsubtle warning in his Chamber of Commerce speech. Bush clearly stated that his mission was critical to administration

policy and that he spoke for the president. He provided a nonnego-
tiable deadline for reforms: January 10, the date when Congress would
reconvene. The visit was precipitated by the Salvadoran government's incapacity to stem increasing paramilitary activity, CIA findings
linking military and security forces to the death squads, and growing
evidence that Salvadorans living in Miami were funding death squad
operations.[31]

Bush met first with Álvaro Magaña and then in a restricted session with the top three military commanders. After forty minutes, the
military session was expanded to include the full high command. Bush
was characteristically straightforward in stating the problem to the
high command:

> I must tell you frankly that it has not been easy for us either. Pro-
> viding assistance to you is not a popular cause in the United States.
> Publicity about death squads, great inequalities of income, the kill-
> ing of American citizens and military setbacks make it a very un-
> popular proposition in my country. President Reagan has supported
> you at considerable political cost, because we know it is the right
> thing. . . .
>
>   Without actions in these areas there is no point in trying to
> obtain additional funds for El Salvador, and to be honest, we will
> not even make the effort, because it would be fruitless.[32]

The "actions" required of the military in order to ensure continued U.S. assistance were clearly specified. Eduardo Avila, an officer
indicted in the murder of the U.S. labor advisers, should be arrested.
Other officers involved in death squad activities should be arrested
and prosecuted. Salvadoran government investigations should be
conducted for a series of rural massacres. The military should support
land reform efforts and transparency in the upcoming elections, and a
number of specific military practices should be reformed. Most sensa-
tionally, Bush handed the military commanders a "short list" of officers and civilians (rumored at around thirty) linked to death squad
activities, who would have to be assigned abroad by January 10, 1984.
Civilians who chose not to leave the country for an extended period
of time would face intensive investigation and prosecution in El Salvador.[33] General Vides Casanova protested, correctly, that the military
had no constitutional authority to order civilians into exile. Pickering

noted in response that "Vides is a stickler in finding legal problems in things he finds difficult to do or does not want to do, but not quite so scrupulous when it comes to legal requirements to carry out actions such as dealing with the death squads."[34]

The outcome of Vice President Bush's visit was a heavily qualified success. Avila, the officer implicated in the AIFLD case, was detained on lesser charges; however, with the help of an uncle on the Supreme Court, he managed to avoid prosecution.[35] Although the names on the list of officers to be sacrificed remained confidential (General Vides made this a condition for compliance), shortly following the visit an officer of the National Police Intelligence Department was reassigned to Spain. An officer from the Treasury Police was sent to Paraguay (but brought back and promoted in January 1986).[36] And Hector Regalado, ARENA death squad director and chief of security for the National Assembly, was told to leave the country.[37] According to the CIA, the two police officers were immediately replaced with "ultra-rightist officers, one of whom is a [excised] leader of a police death squad."[38] Worse yet, several officers closely associated with death squads (most of whom were rumored to be on the Bush list) were reassigned to prestigious posts, including Lieutenant Colonel Denis Morán, considered to be one of those responsible for ordering the assassination of the AIFLD labor advisers. The CIA's conclusion regarding the reforms that followed the visit was that

> efforts by the civilian government and military high command to crack down on right-wing violence have made little progress and have been aimed almost exclusively at placating Washington. . . . Defense Minister Vides—whose room to maneuver is limited— appears both personally disinclined and professionally unable to effect a major cleanup within the armed forces any time soon.[39]

The period from late 1983 through 1984 also witnessed an intense effort on the part of the U.S. Military Group to professionalize the Salvadoran army by promoting a National Plan (along the lines of winning hearts and minds) and holding human rights seminars for Salvadoran troops.[40] But despite the emphasis on reforming military combat and public security practices, combat-related violations continued, as did abuse by security forces.[41] Statistical analysis suggests that, although the number of death squad killings decreased appreciably during 1984, in the aftermath of Bush's visit, the decrease was compensated for by a significant increase in military attacks on civilians.[42] Assassinations attributed to death squads rose again in 1987–88, indicating that the incentives to conduct politics in this manner had not disappeared.[43] Essentially, in this case episodic, inconsistent diplomatic pressure produced brief and easily reversed responses. Diplomatic pressure has to be continual and to consistently maintain a credible threat of sanctions in order to produce significant policy change.

Guatemala

The State Department's willingness to criticize the Guatemalan government for human rights violations increased radically with the end of the Cold War. State Department *Country Reports* began using much stronger language from 1989 on, criticizing first Cerezo for lacking the political will to stem military and paramilitary violence, then Serrano for not following through with his stated intention to control the military. For the first time, reports openly acknowledged that the majority of human rights abuses were committed by security forces and civil patrols and questioned the government's rationale that victims were guerrilla sympathizers.

The U.S. government raised the volume of pressure in the early 1990s, through several diplomatic actions. First, in March 1990 U.S. ambassador Thomas Strook was temporarily recalled to Washington to protest a lack of progress in key human rights investigations.[44] Secretary of Defense Richard Cheney visited Guatemala in February 1992 and delivered a strong statement emphasizing the importance of human rights in relations with the United States. In October 1992 Assistant Secretary of State Bernard Aronson pressed the Guatemalan government to investigate the 1990 murder of Guatemalan anthropologist and human rights activist Myrna Mack. The following month Aronson telephoned President Serrano to express his deep concern over judicial harassment of indigenous rights organizers. Probably in response to U.S. pressure, the Cerezo and Serrano governments made several arrests of lower-ranking military and intelligence officials in the major cases specifically indicated in State Department communications.

The Clinton administration acted quickly and forcefully to oppose the May 1993 executive coup. In fact, a major factor in the private sector's critical decision to ally with popular organizations was the Clinton administration's announcement on May 27 that it would suspend special trade status and vote against World Bank and International Monetary Fund loans unless democratic rule was reestablished. The U.S. Congress immediately suspended most economic aid programs that were channeled through the Guatemalan government and all security assistance, military and police training, and joint military exercises. Similar threats emerged from the European Union. The Organization of American States acted quickly to support the constitutional system on the basis of the 1991 Santiago Resolution, which requires the organization to adopt procedures to restore democratic government in the event of a disruption of constitutional rule. The U.S. government's willingness to take a firm stand against the 1993 executive coup and the rhetorical support that the U.S. embassy gave pro-democracy activists emboldened and helped to generate confidence among Guatemalan civil sectors.

Parenthetically, in addition to the human rights leveraging tools available to the executive branch and Congress, in rare instances U.S. courts have been used to prosecute violators. Federal courts have jurisdiction over tort cases between foreign nationals in which the offense has been committed on foreign soil, provided that the violator is staying in the United States. By this means, in April 1995 a U.S. federal court judge in Boston awarded Sister Dianna Ortiz, a U.S. citizen, and eight Guatemalan plaintiffs $47.5 million in their civil suit against former defense minister Héctor Gramajo. Prosecutors were able to bring this case before a U.S. district court because Gramajo was at the time attending Harvard University's Kennedy School of Government.[45]

ASSESSMENT

It is especially difficult to attempt a neutral evaluation of how effectively U.S. human rights policy was implemented in Central America during the 1980s, because it was so extremely politicized. More than any other factor, competing interests within the U.S. government, among its agencies and branches, undermined human rights promotion. That said, U.S. human rights pressure did effect limited behavior change and occasionally measurable improvements in those instances in which action—whether economic sanctions or public statements—was forceful, directly targeted at the offending agency, and/or specific in its objectives.

El Salvador and Guatemala fall into the sizable category of cases in which human rights policy is overridden by national security concerns or commercial relations or because the country is perceived as having strategic importance solely because of its size or geopolitical location. In these cases the difficulty of implementing a bilateral human rights policy is a good argument for strengthening multilateral institutions. This is, indeed, one of the stated objectives of the State Department's policy. In the end, U.S. human rights values were most effectively achieved in Central America when they were expressed through support for multilateral efforts: UN mediation of peace talks and deployment of human rights observer missions.

Another conclusion can be drawn from this comparison. By itself, however consistently applied, U.S. human rights pressure will not directly result in reforms if the target government has the resources to refuse to comply irrespective of the consequences and is not concerned about the opportunity costs of a damaged international reputation. Improved human rights conditions are often the result of a change of government in the target state. While U.S. pressure can assist or accelerate this process, the more immediate causes for such change will be domestic. One need only consider Slobodan Milosevic's ability to hold on to the Yugoslav presidency for years, despite defeat in war, NATO bombing, indictment for war crimes, and continued economic sanctions aimed at forcing his resignation. Human rights diplomacy in this respect can be one of many factors leading to a change in leadership and thus to improved conditions.

The existence of domestic leadership willing to and capable of promoting reforms was necessary but not sufficient in these cases. Alfredo Cristiani was able to exert civilian authority over the Salvadoran army only when the U.S. government ceased its unconditional support for a military victory. Had the pipeline of U.S. assistance not become threatened, the Salvadoran military would have retained its independence from civilian authority, business confidence in El Salvador would have remained low, and Cristiani would have been in a weaker position to advance a political settlement, much less to request the UN secretary-general's mediation. By the same token, diplomatic pressure for human rights reform will be successful only insofar as important domestic elites—in these cases, both the military and the civilian leadership—are willing and able to cooperate.

It is important for U.S. policymakers, especially elected officials with narrow time horizons, to bear in mind that a foreign policy can be sound even if it appears unlikely in the near term to achieve tangible rewards. Success may be measured in intangible terms, and the policy can be considered effective in less obvious ways. Several such beneficial side effects are mentioned in the introductory chapter to this volume: increased public perceptions of U.S. moral authority, gradual delegitimization of abusive governments, increased coherence in the State Department's human rights policy, and strengthened civil sectors in repressive states.

In conclusion, it is important that this effort to understand "what works" not result in a template of policy instruments to be applied according to a fixed schematic. When no opportunity exists for issue linkage, when a government prefers autarky to cooperation, or when strategic considerations automatically override human rights implementation, it would be naive to seek measures that will "work," if what works is defined as a measurable change in violator behavior. Maintaining a policy of promoting human rights norms and protecting vulnerable populations is a good in and of itself, and we should avoid placing unrealistic expectations on a *bilateral* policy promoted by a state with diverse, often competing, interests. Human rights diplomacy must be context sensitive and flexible, and evaluation criteria should include such intangible values as exercising moral leadership, empowering victims of abuse, and reinforcing nascent democratic civil sectors.

NOTES

Research for this chapter was assisted by an International Predissertation Fellowship from the Social Science Research Council and the American Council for Learned Societies, with funds provided by the Ford Foundation. The author thanks the participants of the United States Institute of Peace Human Rights Implementation Project for their insightful comments and useful advice. An earlier version of much of this chapter is in Susan Burgerman, "The Evolution of Compliance: The Human Rights Regime, Transnational Networks, and United Nations Peacebuilding" (Ph.D. diss., Department of Political Science, Columbia University, 1997).

1. Susan Burgerman, "Mobilizing Principles: The Role of Transnational Activists in Promoting Human Rights Principles," *Human Rights Quarterly* 20, no. 4 (November 1998).

2. Cynthia J. Arnson, *Crossroads: Congress, the President, and Central America, 1976–1993* (University Park, Pa.: Pennsylvania State University Press, 1993), 27.

3. My thanks to Ambassador Robert White for pointing out that the Carter administration renewed military assistance only very cautiously, and at funding levels considered minimal to maintain the Salvadoran government's stability.

4. U.S. Embassy in El Salvador, "Assassinations of Four U.S. Religious Persons, December 2, 1980," internal memorandum dated January 16, 1981 (microfilm of declassified document, viewed at National Security Archive, Washington, D.C.).

5. Americas Watch, *El Salvador's Decade of Terror: Human Rights since the Assassination of Archbishop Romero* (New Haven, Conn.: Yale University Press, 1991), 53–54.

6. See William LeoGrande, "From Reagan to Bush: The Transition in US Policy towards Central America," *Journal of Latin American Studies* 22, no. 3 (October 1990).

7. Cristina Eguizabal, "Parties, Programs, and Politics in El Salvador," in *Political Parties and Democracy in Central America,* ed. Louis W. Goodman, William LeoGrande, and Johanna Mendelson Forman (Boulder, Colo.: Westview, 1992), 141–142.

8. Central Intelligence Agency/U.S. Department of State, "Briefing Paper on Right-Wing Terrorism," October 27, 1983, as cited in National Security Archive, "Escuadrones de la muerte: Declassified Documentation on Death Squad Activities in El Salvador" (mimeograph, 1996), 9.

9. Terry Karl, "Imposing Consent? Electoralism vs. Democratization in El Salvador," in *Elections and Democratization in Latin America, 1980–1985,* ed. Paul Drake and Eduardo Silva (San Diego: University of California, San Diego, 1986).

10. Rodolfo Cardenal, vice rector of the University of Central America, September 12, 1994; Héctor Dada, Facultad Latinoamericana de Ciencias Sociales (FLACSO), January 3, 1995; and Francisco Díaz, director of the Centro de Estudios para la Aplicación del Derecho (CESPAD), September 9, 1994, interviews conducted by author in San Salvador.

11. Jim Handy, "Resurgent Democracy and the Guatemalan Military," *Journal of Latin American Studies* 18, no. 2 (November 1986): 400–401.

12. U.S. Agency for International Development, *U.S. Overseas Loans and Grants, Obligations, and Loan Authorizations July 1, 1945–September 30, 2000 [Greenbook]*, online at http://qesdb.cdie.org/gbk/index.html.

13. See Héctor Rosada Granados, "Parties, Transitions, and the Political System in Guatemala," in *Political Parties and Democracy in Central America*.

14. Rachel M. McCleary, *Dictating Democracy: Guatemala and the End of Violent Revolution* (Gainesville: University Press of Florida, 1999), 129–130.

15. Section 502b contains an exception clause that enables the executive to override the prohibition on military aid in cases of "extraordinary circumstances." The legislation does not specify what circumstances qualify as extraordinary, but humanitarian need and strategic importance are most commonly referred to in justifying continued assistance to human rights violators.

16. Arnson, *Crossroads*, 140.

17. For details of the debates over this bill, see Teresa Whitfield, *Paying the Price: Ignacio Ellacuría and the Murdered Jesuits of El Salvador* (Philadelphia: Temple University Press, 1995), 174–189.

18. Juan Méndez, interview by author, New York City, August 14, 1996.

19. Susanne Jonas, *The Battle for Guatemala: Rebels, Death Squads, and U.S. Power* (Boulder, Colo.: Westview, 1991), 197.

20. Lisa L. Martin and Kathryn Sikkink, "U.S. Policy and Human Rights in Argentina and Guatemala, 1973–1980," in *Double-Edged Diplomacy: International Bargaining and Domestic Politics*, ed. Peter Evans et al. (Berkeley: University of California Press, 1993), 336.

21. By way of comparison, U.S. military assistance (not including fungible Economic Support Funds) to Guatemala was $5.5 million in 1987, as compared with $117 million to El Salvador. According to the Latin America Working Group, total direct military assistance to Guatemala had reached $9 million before the 1990 cutoff, still miniscule by comparison.

22. Americas Watch/British Parliamentary Human Rights Group, *Human Rights in Guatemala during President Cerezo's First Year* (New York: Americas Watch/BPHRG, February 1987), 96. None of these funds came from the British government. Great Britain had broken off diplomatic relations with Guatemala over the question of Belize in 1963, which were restored only at the end of 1986, and it is highly unlikely that Prime Minister Margaret Thatcher would have joined a European campaign against the Reagan policy in Central America.

23. Jonas, *The Battle for Guatemala,* 206.

24. Human Rights Watch, *Human Rights Watch World Report 1993: Events of 1992* (New York: Human Rights Watch, 1993), 117–118.

25. Human Rights Watch, *Human Rights in Guatemala during President de León Carpio's First Year* (New York: Human Rights Watch, June 1994), 114.

26. "U.S. Cuts Off Remaining Military Aid to Guatemala," *International Herald Tribune,* March 13, 1995. Harbury is a U.S. attorney who is an extremely active member of the Guatemala solidarity community. Her protest was aimed at forcing the administration to release information concerning the fate of her husband, URNG commander Efraín Bámaca, who was reported to have been captured in battle, tortured, and killed by ranking Guatemalan officers, at least one of whom was at one time on the CIA payroll. The Bámaca case has become a cause célèbre for the human rights network.

27. Intelligence Oversight Board, *Report on the Guatemala Review, June 28, 1996* (Washington, D.C.: Government Printing Office, 1996), 20.

28. Deane Hinton, quoted in Arnson, *Crossroads,* 103–104.

29. Thomas R. Pickering, "Address before the American Chamber of Commerce in San Salvador" (mimeograph of text of speech, delivered November 25, 1983).

30. "Statement by the Minister of Defense of El Salvador, General Carlos Eugenio Vides Casanova, San Salvador," November 2, 1983 (mimeograph).

31. In fact, an FBI investigation was under way of the "Millionaire Murderers," a group of six Salvadoran émigrés living in Miami, suspected of financing and directing death squad operations, including the Sheraton Hotel murders. U.S. Embassy San Salvador/Secretary of State cable, "Millionaires' Murder Inc.?" January 6, 1981 (microfilm of declassified document, viewed at National Security Archive, Washington, D.C.); U.S. Department of State internal memorandum, "Investigation of Domestic Support for Violence in El Salvador," December 8, 1983 (microfilm of declassified document, viewed at National Security Archive, Washington, D.C.).

32. U.S. Embassy San Salvador/Secretary of State cable, "Vice President Bush's Meetings with Salvadoran Officials," December 14, 1983 (microfilm of declassified document, viewed at National Security Archive, Washington, D.C.).

33. Ibid.

34. U.S. Embassy San Salvador/Secretary of State cable, "Early Assessment, Vice President Bush's Visit," December 13, 1983 (microfilm of declassified document, viewed at National Security Archive, Washington, D.C.).

35. Directorate of Intelligence, Central Intelligence Agency, "El Salvador: Dealing with Death Squads," January 20, 1984 (microfilm of declassified document, viewed at National Security Archive, Washington, D.C.).

36. The Watch Committees and Lawyers Committee for Human Rights, *Critique: A Review of the Department of State's Country Reports on Human Rights Practices in 1986* (New York: Lawyers Committee for Human Rights, 1987), 30.

37. U.S. Embassy San Salvador/Secretary of State cable, "Talk with President Magaña, Bush Visit Reaction," December 15, 1983 (microfilm of declassified document, viewed at National Security Archive, Washington, D.C.).

38. Central Intelligence Agency, "El Salvador: Dealing with Death Squads."

39. Ibid.

40. See interviews with General Wallace Nutting, U.S. Southern Command, and Colonel John Waghelstein, U.S. Military Group, in *El Salvador at War: An Oral History*, ed. Max Manwaring and Court Prisk (Washington, D.C.: National Defense University Press, 1988), 222–223.

41. Americas Watch, *El Salvador's Decade of Terror*, 51–63; and U.S. Department of State, "Security Force Human Rights Abuses, Part One: Murders," May 2, 1989.

42. U.S. Embassy San Salvador/Department of State cable, "Human Rights in El Salvador," June 29, 1988 (microfilm of declassified document, viewed at National Security Archive, Washington, D.C.); see also UN General Assembly, *Situation of Human Rights in El Salvador* (A/43/736, October 21, 1988), para. 32.

43. See especially William Bollinger and Deirdre A. Hill, "The *Index to Accountability*: Identifying Perpetrators of Human Rights Violations in El Salvador, 1980–1990" (paper presented at the International Congress of the Latin American Studies Association, Washington, D.C., September 1992), 25–30. Bollinger and Hill suggest that this represents an alteration in government policy, which shifted the emphasis from one category of violation (paramilitary killing) to another (armed forces attack).

44. U.S. Department of State, *Country Reports on Human Rights Practices for 1990*, 631.

45. See "Welcome Mat Gone for Guatemalan Linked to Atrocities," *Miami Herald*, April 20, 1995, A18.

10

U.S. Human Rights Policies and Chile

HARRY G. BARNES, JR.

C HILE'S TRADITIONAL, RARELY INTERRUPTED DEMOCRACY long made it a special case in the Western Hemisphere. For the United States, Chile in the 1960s represented an attractive, alternative model of development and democracy in the face of the Cuban revolution, which was seen as threatening the Americas with communism. Chile's democracy was shattered, however, on September 11, 1973, by a military coup that removed the controversial Popular Unity government of President Salvador Allende. The return to democracy took nearly seventeen years. This chapter attempts to understand how four successive U.S. administrations may have influenced human rights in Chile from 1973 to 1988 during the military government of General Augusto Pinochet. U.S. policy toward the Chilean regime oscillated from complicity to condemnation. Human rights, however, gradually became entrenched in U.S. policy toward Chile—and in U.S. foreign policy in general. Tools to press Pinochet to improve human rights were manifold, ranging from behind-the-scenes as well as public diplomacy to economic sanctions. Two features of U.S. policy remained constant during the period: pressure by Congress to address the human rights situation in Chile, and difficulties faced by each administration to communicate a coherent and consistent policy line to Pinochet—regardless of how important human rights were as a policy priority. The chapter also seeks to analyze the key dynamics at play in Washington and in Santiago during the Pinochet era.

THE NIXON AND FORD ADMINISTRATIONS

There was no official U.S. human rights policy during the Nixon and Ford administrations. Given the anticommunist priorities in U.S. foreign policy, Washington generally supported the Chilean junta despite its deplorable human rights record, though Congress began to serve as a strong counterweight, gradually inserting human rights considerations in the U.S. foreign policy equation.

The Nixon Administration Faces Congress

In the first few days following the 1973 coup, the Nixon administration expressed relief that Allende was gone and support for the new Pinochet regime. The September 20, 1973, meeting of the Washington Special Action Group (WASAG) led to an agreement to authorize the U.S. ambassador to Chile, Nathaniel Davis, to talk to the junta on the following day to inform them "of our goodwill, our intention to recognize them in the next few days." The administration made an early commitment to the new Chilean government to meet its urgent economic needs through credits for the purchase of wheat and feed corn. Davis was also authorized to discuss Chile's longer-term economic needs.

Concerned members of Congress, however, quickly started questioning the administration's approach. Along with representatives of church groups, Congress called on the State Department and the embassy in Santiago to discover what had happened to two Americans, Charles Horman and Frank Teruggi, who had gone missing in the wake of the coup, and to press the Chilean junta to respect human rights. The strongest congressional critic was Senator Edward Kennedy of Massachusetts. Within weeks of the coup, Kennedy offered an amendment to the Foreign Assistance Act, which called on the administration to make a definitive finding that the government of Chile was protecting the human rights of all individuals in the country.[1]

In April 1974 a member of Kennedy's staff, Mark Schneider, and former U.S. ambassador to Chile Ralph Duncan pushed the congressional agenda further by going to Chile. They were given access to detention centers and allowed to interview prisoners. They also attended military trials, held discussions with a number of people opposed to the government, and met junta head General Pinochet himself.[2] Duncan gave his assessment to the embassy, arguing that while human rights violations had decreased recently, the situation was still "abhorrent." He urged the U.S. government to be more forceful in urging the junta to moderate its policies, for instance, by using Chile's debt to the international creditors group known as the Paris Club and U.S. government PL 480 credits for agricultural products as levers.[3]

The embassy and the State Department did convey to Chilean officials the concern about the persistent human rights problems, particularly relating to political prisoners, detentions, and torture.[4] The administration's attitude was likely fueled by its caution in the politically volatile atmosphere of Vietnam, the continuation of the Watergate affair, and public attention on the disappearance of Horman and Teruggi—which had led to questions about U.S. government complicity. But in the end, the weight of the Nixon administration's behavior toward Chile came down on the side of understanding and supporting the junta.[5] In his memoirs Henry Kissinger writes, "How was the United States to reconcile its geopolitical interests and its concern for human rights? The new Chilean government, whatever its faults, would not assault our interests in every international forum as its predecessor had."[6] The persistence of serious human rights abuses was not, in short, considered sufficiently important to alter the basic decision to give the regime a chance.

The dispute between Congress and the administration over Chile policy did not cease with the advent of President Gerald Ford. When Congress reconvened in November 1974, there were amendments to fiscal year 1975 bills to limit, condition, or completely cut off military assistance to the Pinochet government.[7] In December the Kennedy Amendment finally became law. It prohibited Chile from receiving military grant aid, foreign military sales (FMS) and credits, and training. But the administration was torn between domestic constraints

and what it viewed as pressing geopolitical imperatives. Without con-
sulting Congress, Kissinger approved the sale and delivery to Chile of
add-ons to existing military sales contracts and naval spare parts that
had been contracted before the enactment of the congressional ban.[8]
Ambassador David H. Popper articulated the administration's dilemma: abandoning congressional restrictions on aid to Chile would
give the Chileans the wrong message, but ending all economic aid and
continuing an absolute ban on arms aid would reduce the Chileans to
hopelessness about their relationship with the United States—which
might result in a "much harsher cycle of repressiveness" and search by
Chile for aid "from any quarter whatsoever."

Congress, however, was growing adamant about human rights.
By 1975 congressional efforts had filled the void of human rights in
the U.S. foreign policy repertoire with a fairly coherent policy framework. The crafting of the framework was gradual, however, because of
the slowness of the legislative process and because the executive
failed to carry out fully the congressional intent—and, at times, deliberately evaded the specific provisions emanating from Capitol Hill.
The interbranch strife notwithstanding, the new policy forbade military or economic assistance as well as lending from the international
financial institutions, such as the Inter-American Development Bank,
with the exception of assistance for basic human needs. Similar, albeit
vaguer, criteria applied to assistance from the World Bank and the
International Monetary Fund (IMF). Moreover, as a result of congressional pressure, the State Department established the position of coordinator for human rights and humanitarian affairs in April 1975.[9]
At the end of the year, the United States voted for the first time in
favor of UN resolutions condemning Chile's human rights abuses and
also subsequently opposed an industrial credit to Santiago by the
Inter-American Development Bank.

Kissinger in Chile: Mixed Messages, Lost Opportunity

Against the backdrop of these developments, many hoped that Secretary of State Kissinger's trip to the Organization of American States
(OAS) General Assembly in Santiago in June 1976 would eliminate
the remaining ambiguities about the importance of human rights to
Washington.[10] Kissinger's signals were mixed at best. He did use the

occasion of the OAS meeting to deliver what he called "a major speech on human rights" and supported the separate resolution criticizing Chile. But in a prior meeting with Pinochet, Kissinger had explained that the speech was a response to congressional pressures at home and that the U.S. policy was to help the government of Chile.[11] Commenting in his memoirs on the Kissinger visit, then Christian Democratic party leader and later president of Chile Patricio Aylwin says that "Kissinger gave the image of very friendly treatment toward the regime and on his return openly made very favorable declarations."[12]

The administration's complacency was apparent also in deed. First, despite additional restrictions on arms sales by a congressional conference on security assistance, the administration rushed to conclude new contracts for spare parts in order to include them in the pipeline, which was exempt from the new restrictions. Second, the U.S. government abstained on the annual UN resolution condemning human rights abuses in Chile. And third, the U.S. government continued to support loans to Chile from the international financial institutions on grounds of their meeting the "basic needs" criteria set up by the Harkin Amendment—or maintained that the amendment did not apply. The administration also argued that Chile was moving in the right direction on human rights.

In sum, the last few months of the Nixon administration and the Ford term in its entirety were marked by a growing awareness of the human rights issues. But some potentially encouraging measures to promote human rights unfailingly came second in U.S. policy priorities to the need to support the antimarxist government that inherited "the revolutionary situation." This behavior was particularly pronounced during the Ford administration. Importantly, however, Congress worked diligently to incorporate human rights into the government's activities by devising new policies and prompting the construction of institutions geared to addressing human rights.

What was the impact of these U.S. policies in Chile? Not only was the impact relatively limited, but also Chileans on both sides of the ideological divide were unhappy with Washington. Chilean military officers, expecting reciprocal friendship and support from the United States, were dismayed by the continuing efforts by Congress to limit their access to weapons—including those already paid for. Opponents of the regime, meanwhile, saw nothing that indicated the emergence of a forceful official human rights policy in Washington, nor did they detect any strong or visible support or concern from the U.S. embassy on human rights issues. Indeed, many saw continuity between the anti-Allende efforts of the Nixon administration and the support for the junta by the Ford administration.[13] The opponents of Pinochet took some solace from the support by the Chilean Catholic Church's Vicariate of Solidarity and by U.S. universities and scientific laboratories that absorbed those dismissed from their teaching and research jobs in Chile. In short, those who had expected significant U.S. support because of the overthrow of the Allende regime got much less than they felt they deserved, particularly in terms of much-hoped-for backing against the apparently hostile intentions of Chile's neighbors, Peru and Argentina. Meanwhile, those who counted on the efforts of the congressional human rights champions found that the latter could not deliver very much.[14]

The policy equation was about to be shaken, however. The most significant single event in U.S.-Chilean relations since the coup took place on September 21, 1976, when Orlando Letelier and his American coworker Ronni Moffitt were killed in a car bomb explosion in Washington, D.C. Letelier had been Chilean ambassador to the United States from 1971 to May 1973 and then defense minister for Allende. Following the coup, he had settled again in Washington in the new role of organizing support for opposition to the military regime. The Letelier-Moffitt case and the earlier discovery that Horman and Teruggi had been killed shortly after the coup would serve to keep the Chilean situation alive in Congress and continue to harm Pinochet's image.

THE CARTER ADMINISTRATION

One well-informed Chilean has commented that Chileans do not usually pay much attention to U.S. presidential campaigns, but that 1976 and 1980 were different because of Jimmy Carter. With the advent of the Carter administration in early 1977, human rights advocates in both Chile and the United States expected much more headway to be made. It appears as though the mere anticipation of Carter's assuming office was enough to prompt Pinochet to release a number of political prisoners. It is difficult to prove that U.S. pressure and attitudes caused the junta to ease up on some of its restrictions and cut back on the abuses in the latter part of the 1970s; however, for those seeking a change, there was the sense that because Washington now cared, things would at least not get worse.

The First, Difficult Steps

The first indication of a policy shift in Washington came at the annual meeting of the United Nations Commission on Human Rights, which took place six weeks after Carter's inauguration. Unlike in the past, the U.S. delegation decided to cosponsor the resolutions critical of Chile.[15] Other contrasts with the past emerged. Vice President Walter Mondale met with former president Eduardo Frei in Washington in May 1977, while Kissinger had declined to meet Frei in Santiago the previous June. According to a report prepared by National Security Council (NSC) staff member Robert Pastor, Mondale indicated that the administration was for human rights "not because we are against Communism, but because we believe in human rights."[16] National Security Advisor Zbigniew Brzezinski took pains, though, to clarify to Frei that the goal of U.S. human rights policy was to create a moral framework, not to interfere in the internal affairs of any country. The change in policy did not make policy choices any simpler. The administration struggled to decide whether to isolate Chile or to seek to bargain with Pinochet.[17] Nor was the policy implementation any easier. Pastor complained to Brzezinski that there were at least two widely divergent Chile policies in the State Department.[18] At the other end of Pennsylvania Avenue, members of Congress kept changing sides on human rights votes. At one point that summer, the House voted to deny funds for military training for Argentina by a fair-sized margin. The next day it approved, by almost the same vote, restoration of aid for Anastasio Somoza's Nicaragua. Human rights advocates in Congress were also split on responses to the administration's plea for greater flexibility of policy action[19]—even though the administration sought to review carefully the human rights aspects of U.S. foreign assistance and multilateral bank loans through the

Christopher Committee, named after Deputy Secretary of State Warren Christopher.[20]

Pinochet in Washington

President Carter had a chance to take the measure of Pinochet himself on September 6, 1977, at the signing of the Panama Canal treaties, which brought all heads of state of the hemisphere to Washington. Carter had overruled staff advice and decided to invite Pinochet, possibly to seek to persuade the general to allow a visit by the UN Human Rights Commission's Ad Hoc Working Group.

In the meeting with Pinochet, Carter stated that the issue of human rights was the only major bilateral problem between the two countries and that he wished to ventilate the matter in a frank and positive way.[21] He noted the progress with prisoner releases, trial procedures, and the proclamation of future elections. Carter also commended to Pinochet the new U.S. ambassador, George Landau. In response, Pinochet called attention to the August 1977 replacement of the much-criticized Directorate of National Intelligence (DINA) with the National Information Center (CNI) and argued that Chileans enjoyed press freedoms, freedom of thought, and freedom of travel. He also stressed that he greatly admired democracy and very much wished to leave office having built one—albeit "not one liable to attack from underneath as had happened before."

Carter insisted, however, that confirmation of progress in human rights could not be made without a visit by an independent body. The issue of UN human rights observers became the point of contention in the ensuing correspondence of five months between the two presidents.[22]

Nonetheless, the meeting was followed by discernible improvements on human rights in Chile. The number of disappearances went from one hundred fifty in 1977 to twelve in 1978. The state of siege was lifted in March 1978, and in April an amnesty law was proclaimed covering crimes committed since the 1973 coup. It excluded the Letelier-Moffitt case.[23] The UN Ad Hoc Working Group was finally allowed to visit in July 1978. The following month, Michael Townley, an American who had been working for the DINA and was suspected of having played a key role in the Letelier-Moffitt case, was expelled to the United States.[24] And Pinochet was drafting a new constitution in order to deliver on his earlier promise to move Chile from the "recovery" to the "transition" phase.

These developments allowed the U.S. embassy to conclude that "systematic institutionalized, widespread, gross violations of the rights of the person no longer exist. . . . Prolonged detention without charge is a thing of the past; technically illegal detentions still occur on occasion but at least the arrests are acknowledged; some mistreatment and torture may still exist, but rarely. Lack of institutional safeguards and ample residual emergency authority keep the lid on dramatic improvement in the area of political freedoms."

The Impact of U.S. Policies

But to what extent were the positive changes in Chile due to the Carter administration? Inconsistencies in policy implementation make it harder to reach conclusions on its impact. What is more, the relatively good economic times strengthened the regime and probably accounted for some of the decline in repression. Besides, the Carter administration was not the only U.S. actor that played a role in Santiago. For example, in light of the continuing repression of any trade union activity, the AFL-CIO began planning for a boycott of Chilean fruit entering the United States. Rapport between AFL-CIO head George Meany and shipping magnate Peter Grace provided for a unique "united front" and led to the formulation of the Labor Plan of 1979, which was based to a considerable extent on the U.S. model.[25]

The Carter administration's impact was significant, however. Carter undoubtedly brought to the relationship with Chile a new and very visible, if not always consistent, set of criteria. Without U.S. pressure, the DINA would probably have continued its previous murderous practices. But perhaps the greatest—albeit one of the least tangible—benefits of the Carter human rights emphasis was the encouragement it gave to the democratic opposition and to the work of groups like the Catholic Church's Vicariate of Solidarity. It was what Chileans called *solidaridad* (solidarity)—the feeling that they were not alone, that the powerful United States was sympathetic and would try somehow to be helpful. Indeed, Ambassador Landau is still remembered for his persistence in promoting human rights. This encouraged

Chileans to build organizational capabilities in order to gear up to fight for the restoration of democracy.

Could Washington's new policy line have had a greater impact had it been pushed harder? Pinochet certainly felt he could handle the challenge posed by the Carter administration. The final draft of the new Chilean constitution was approved in a plebiscite held under opaque conditions with 67 percent in favor on the anniversary of the coup, September 11, 1980.[26] After all, for Pinochet, investment was available from the U.S. private sector, and arms could be obtained from U.S. friends and allies.[27] The U.S. embargo also stimulated the growth of a domestic (and later export-oriented) arms industry. One astute journalist argues that a more forceful approach would have allowed for progress in the Letelier-Moffitt case; and the administration could have sought to constrain Pinochet's leeway by seeking to influence the flow of private credit to Chile.[28]

In its last two years in office, the Carter administration faced such problems as the hostages in Iran and the Sandinistas in Nicaragua. Then came the Soviet invasion of Afghanistan, which shifted the focus primarily to security issues. Interest in Chile, by comparison, faded. It is clear nonetheless that one of the principal legacies of the Carter administration was to incorporate human rights into U.S. foreign policy, and that Chile was an important factor in that shift.

THE FIRST REAGAN ADMINISTRATION

Human rights issues did not play a significant role in the 1980 U.S. presidential campaign. In his autobiography Carter noted that Ronald Reagan made only "some evasive statements concerning civil rights and human rights."

The new administration, however, did come in with very unevasive thoughts. Indeed, it was convinced that one of the major changes required in the Carter legacy was correcting the overemphasis on human rights. The most prominent voice was that of Jeane Kirkpatrick, whom Reagan appointed as ambassador to the United Nations. In her much-publicized 1979 article in *Commentary*, she had drawn a sharp distinction between totalitarian and authoritarian regimes. The former were communist; the latter were military and/or rightist. The former by definition controlled all aspects of a society; the latter were less intrusive, particularly in people's personal lives, and could be influenced through "quiet diplomacy."

The new approach had two effects. First, there was an effort to "understand" leaders, like Pinochet, who were fighting communism. Second, even though these leaders paid little attention to their citizens' rights, there was a reluctance to complicate things for them with open criticism. Rather, quiet diplomacy was thought to modify behavior in ways that hectoring never would.

Policy Overhaul

George Shultz became President Reagan's secretary of state in mid-1982. A former professor at the University of Chicago, Shultz had reason to be impressed with the economic accomplishments of his erstwhile students and colleagues in Chile. He was also critical of what he called Carter's "light switch diplomacy, an effort to turn trade and investment on and off in order to influence a country's human rights practices."[29]

In concrete policy terms, Washington's change of heart involved moving from abstentions or no votes in the international financial institutions to yes votes. It also meant opposing UN resolutions critical of Chile's human rights practices, often on the grounds that they were no worse than those of other countries. Visible military ties were revived by including the Chilean navy in inter-American exercises. Prominent persons such as General Vernon Walters and Ambassador Kirkpatrick were sent to visit Chile. Kirkpatrick's August 1981 visit attracted particular attention because she did not have time to meet with leading human rights advocates—one of whom, Jaime Castillo, was exiled a few days after her visit. A new ambassador, James Theberge, was assigned to Santiago. He commented that the Castillo exile was "absolutely legal and does not have anything to do with the policy of human rights in Chile." Theberge was not new to Latin American caudillos: he had been ambassador in the 1970s to Somoza's Nicaragua.

The relatively amicable ties between the executive and Congress on the human rights front during the Carter administration were replaced by antagonism. Congress resumed its role as a critical check on the executive. While there was no spurt of congressionally initiated legislation as in the mid-1970s, the strengthening of the Kennedy Amendment showed how much ground those concerned with human rights had gained in Congress. The administration sought on several occasions to get rid of the amendment's prohibitions on military assistance; however, the efforts only resulted in its being replaced by still more stringent conditions. Military aid required not only a certification by the president as being in the national interest but also a certification that Chile had made "significant progress" in complying with international standards. The most onerous condition was the requirement for a certification that Chile had "taken appropriate steps to cooperate in bringing to justice" those implicated in the Letelier-Moffitt assassinations. The conditions on that score clearly could not be met and the administration did not persist. Moreover, the Senate Foreign Relations Committee, faced with lobbying by Americas Watch and Helsinki Watch, defeated the administration's nomination of Ernest Lefever to be assistant secretary of state for human rights and humanitarian affairs on the grounds that Lefever saw human rights in only the anticommunist dimension. The post went later to Elliott Abrams.

Promoting Democracy: Connection with Human Rights?

The U.S. approach to human rights clearly changed with the Reagan administration. The administration's global crusade for democracy, set out in President Reagan's June 1982 speech to the British Parliament, however, did provide a mechanism for addressing human rights— even though the relationship between democracy and human rights remained somewhat unclear. Noting that the UN Universal Declaration of Human Rights provides guarantees for free elections, Reagan stated that "we must be staunch in our conviction that freedom is not the sole prerogative of a lucky few but the inalienable and universal right of all human beings."

For Chile, the speech came to mean that U.S. "understanding" of Pinochet had its limits. This was particularly the case as quiet diplomacy was not producing any visible results from the Chilean government. In the course of 1983, Chileans began to notice the frequency of critical State Department comments about progress toward restoring democracy. By the end of the year, the Chilean foreign minister complained that fourteen such statements had already been issued; this, he said, amounted to interference in Chile's internal affairs.

The United States became increasingly focused on Chile following the rise of political unrest in the context of severe economic problems in the country and the subsequent failure of the talks between the government and the Democratic Alliance (a grouping of center-left parties). The impasse, it was feared, might lead to a new confrontation reminiscent of the Allende period. Concern in Washington was deepened by the fact that the overall human rights situation had been deteriorating for some time.[30] Detentions, sometimes accompanied by torture, censorship, and internal or external exile were still features of the system. In March 1984 James Michel, deputy assistant secretary for inter-American affairs, linked political stability in Chile with the need for a centrist coalition. This became an increasingly prominent goal.

As Reagan was elected for a second term in the fall, a state of siege was reimposed in Chile, the first in six years. The proximate causes were the continuing strikes and demonstrations, as well as violent incidents attributed to the Communist Party's Manuel Rodriguez Patriotic Front and the Movement of the Revolutionary Left (MIR). The state of siege undercut any illusions about the Pinochet government's smooth and stately progress toward the future. Whereas earlier these phenomena might have reinforced Pinochet's standing in the U.S. administration, now they worried Washington[31]—and seemed to contradict Pinochet's argument that in Chile it was a choice "between Pinochet and chaos." Now, Pinochet meant chaos. The way out began to appear to be a democratic Chile, one without Pinochet. And that presaged U.S. pressure, even if at the cost of abandoning the reliance on quiet diplomacy. On December 10, International Human Rights Day, President Reagan termed the lack of progress toward democracy in Chile and Paraguay "an affront to human consciences." Pinochet was disillusioned, viewing the United States as an undependable ally.[32] Meanwhile, in the United States, NGOs branded the administration's efforts political.[33]

THE SECOND REAGAN ADMINISTRATION

By the start of the second Reagan term, the administration had come to understand Pinochet: he was not changing. But Pinochet did not understand Washington. In Chile, what the U.S. government wanted was a more open government, the rule of law, and a government headed by elected officials.

In Washington, George Shultz moved Elliott Abrams to assistant secretary for inter-American affairs and selected Harry Barnes, then ambassador to India, to head the U.S. embassy in Santiago. Barnes went to Chile with a clear mission, based on extensive discussions within the administration, as well as with members of Congress and NGOs. The three principal U.S. objectives were to push for an early return to democracy, promote full respect for basic human rights, and support free markets.[34]

A few months earlier, the democratic opposition, encouraged by the new cardinal, Juan Francisco Fresno, had adopted a "National Accord for Transition to Full Democracy." The document called for respect for basic human rights, protection for private property, and free elections for congress and the president. The hope was that it would serve as a basis for discussion with the government. The United States was supportive of the effort. Pinochet, however, held off until Christmas Eve, when he invited the cardinal to meet him. Pinochet bluntly told Fresno that the accord was no longer relevant and that it was "time to turn the page."

Pinochet's intransigence, the U.S. administration's impatience, and a number of dramatic events in Chile widened the gulf between Washington and Santiago in 1986. In the UN Human Rights Commission the United States joined the ranks of the cosponsors of a resolution highly critical of the human rights situation in Chile. Washington's concerns grew in July over the case of Rodrigo Rojas, a teenaged U.S. resident, and his companion, Carmen Gloria Quintana. They had been taking part in a protest demonstration in Santiago when they were seized by soldiers, doused with gasoline, and set on fire. He died a few days later; she survived and recovered after extensive surgery. The Rojas killing and the lack of progress toward a political transition were the background for intense discussions within the U.S. government over how the United States should vote on a World Bank structural adjustment loan (SAL), which was due for consideration in the fall. In September a nearly successful attempt to assassinate Pinochet brought reimposition of the state of siege in Chile. President Reagan sent a message to Pinochet expressing his concern over the assassination attempt, but also about the reimposition of the state of siege.[35]

At the end of 1987, the U.S. government took five concrete steps to make the point that it knew what it wanted from Pinochet. First, the United States abstained rather than voted no on the annual UN General Assembly resolution on Chile in order to underscore the U.S. commitment to a return to democracy and to promote enhanced respect for human rights. Second, the United States deprived Chile of the benefits of the generalized system of preferences for developing countries (GSP) and of access to the U.S. government's Overseas Private Investment Corporation (OPIC) loans because of abuses of workers' rights. Third, Washington voted not to support a $240 million structural adjustment loan from the World Bank, citing human rights violations as the reason. Fourth, on December 17 President Reagan and Secretary Shultz issued a statement of support for democracy in Chile, a step the Chilean opposition had been hoping for. The thrust of the declaration was that the fuller the observance of basic and civil rights up to and during the expected plebiscite, the greater the legitimacy of the outcome. Fifth, in December Congress adopted a proposal by Senator Tom Harkin to provide $1 million to the National Endowment for Democracy to support voter registration and civic education in Chile.[36]

Perhaps for the first time in the Reagan years, the administration and Congress were not working at cross-purposes in human rights in Chile. Members of Congress at this time formed a group to support free elections in Chile and a number of House members in midsummer had written to Pinochet urging the creation of an open atmosphere before and during the plebiscite. In August the House passed a resolution calling for the restoration of a full and genuine democracy in Chile and for lifting the still prevailing status of "states of exception."[37]

Impact in Chile

Was the shift to stress democracy and human rights in U.S. policy having an effect on the ground? Events ostensibly unrelated to the U.S. policies inspired hopes for a democratic transition in Chile. First, there was an emergence of a broader coalition of democratic parties. In February 1988 the coalition decided to contest the plebiscite by campaigning for a no vote against the expected official candidate, Pinochet. Earlier attempts to persuade the government to accept free elections had failed.[38] Second, there began to appear some difference between members of the junta and Pinochet. In July air force commander Fernando Matthei told visiting Robert Gelbard, deputy assistant secretary of state for inter-American affairs, that differences existed between Pinochet and the junta over such matters as the number of signatures required to legalize a party. Matthei also indicated that he had pushed for competitive elections instead of a plebiscite. Non-army junta members began to meet with opposition leaders.[39]

Although the key developments propelling the transition were undoubtedly indigenous to Chile, U.S. policies and actions were invigorating the pro-democracy movement. In January 1988 Carl Gershman, president of the National Endowment for Democracy, visited Chile to discuss assistance to the transition in light of the legislation adopted in the U.S. Congress. The U.S. Agency for International Development (USAID) channeled aid for voter registration through the OAS. Meanwhile, the embassy promoted the sharing of ideas among opposition leaders and with NGOs working in the areas of voter registration and civic education—and with members of the junta, human rights NGOs, the church, and the media. The message stressed was the importance of fairness and transparency, not only of the plebiscite itself, but also of the atmosphere in the months leading up to it. The embassy also sought to provide opportunities for Chilean entrepreneurs to think more about the links between democracy and the free market. It was harder to find ways of reaching the armed forces with the message that democracy was not incompatible with honorable military careers. A beginning was made through orientation programs, organized by the U.S. Information Agency (USIA) and the Department of Defense, for Chilean officers to come to the United

States. Opportunities were also provided for Chilean appeals court judges to become familiar with the work of their counterparts in the United States. In short, even though it was the opposition movement and the intrajunta divisions that drove the transition in Chile, various U.S. actors—Congress, USAID, NGOs, and also the White House—can be said to have furthered the course of events in Chile.

The weekend before the plebiscite, the embassy had learned that the government might attempt to use expected demonstrations to invalidate the plebiscite. The Chilean ambassador was called into the State Department and told of U.S. concerns over these reports, and the next day the press spokesman made those concerns public. It now seems clear that on the night of the plebiscite, as the negative results came in, Pinochet was prepared to decree his own continuation in office. The other members of the junta refused to go along.

The plebiscite took place on October 5, 1988. The government initially suppressed the news of the victory of the no. Sergio Molina's free elections committee then provided the results of their quick count, a 53 percent to 44 percent victory for the no. Former interior minister Sergio Onofre Jarpa, appearing on a Catholic University TV program, acknowledged the opposition victory, but it took the government spokesman another several hours to do so.

The Two Terms of the Reagan Administration and Chile

Chilean recollections of the first Reagan term are vague. Jeane Kirkpatrick remains as a short-lived but still clear symbol of the administration then. There was an obvious contrast with the Carter years, as well as a difference between George Landau's openness to many sectors of Chilean life and James Theberge's identification with the government. But after two or three years, the picture became more complex. This was true especially because of the high priority accorded to the promotion of democracy, as well as the fact that some of the feeling from the late 1970s that the United States was indeed on the side of human rights began to resurface.

Indeed, the emergence of Reagan as a visible champion of democracy eventually led to a reduced reliance on quiet diplomacy. While there was little effort to articulate the links between human rights and democracy, it was implicitly understood that a country could not become truly democratic if it did not at least try to respect human rights. Despite an occasional UN General Assembly negative vote on Chile human rights resolutions, the shift in the administration's policy from understanding authoritarian leaders to overt support for an early return to democracy effectively put the United States on the side of change.

In the end the Reagan administration conveyed a coherent message. Everyone knew where the U.S. government stood. Particularly central were effective coordination between the State Department and the embassy in Santiago, the maintenance of close links with a number of key members of Congress, and the assistance provided by NGOs. To be sure, other countries cooperated to make significant contributions, but history, geography, and sentiment all still endowed the United States with a special influence. The abandonment of ambiguity meant that the government of Chile had to calculate on U.S. criticism rather than U.S. silence or approval as the norm. That was a message that got through clearly as well to the democratic opposition.

● ● ●

It seems fitting that not much more than a year after Pinochet's departure from presidential office, the Organization of American States should adopt in Santiago a Commitment with Democracy and the Renewal of the Interamerican System. The commitment is to convene special meetings "in the event of any occurrences giving rise to the sudden or irregular interruption of the democratic political institutional process or of the legitimate exercise of power by the democratically elected government in any of the Organization's member states."

A decade after the plebiscite, ex-president Pinochet was detained in the United Kingdom on the basis of a Spanish judge's charges of gross human rights violations. He was allowed to return to Chile two years later for health reasons, and in July 2002 the Chilean supreme court concluded he was too ill to stand trial. In March 1999, with the Letelier-Moffitt murders in mind, U.S. attorney general Janet Reno told a news conference that in light of the British decision, "what we want to do is look at the determination by the House of Lords, make a determination as to how that might impact on our issue.

But what we're faced with is a situation that occurred here in the United States. And if there is a basis for holding someone accountable, whoever it may be, we would like to proceed in every possible way to do that." In April 2000 a Chilean court was taking testimony from a number of individuals based on letters rogatory from the United States about their possible knowledge of the 1976 assassinations in Washington.

CONCLUSION: LESSONS FROM THE THREE ADMINISTRATIONS

What can be learned from the U.S. experience with its human rights policies toward Chile between September 1973 and October 1988?

There are three lessons: (1) overall U.S. impact on Chilean behavior was marginal, but marginal does not necessarily mean insignificant, (2) democracy and human rights reinforce each other, but they are not identical, and (3) formal governmental structures tasked with the promotion of human rights do matter.

First, internal factors are most often of greater importance than external influences. In the case of Chile, however, and Latin America and the Caribbean more broadly, U.S. influence is a major given. That influence is often disproportionate to actual U.S. interests in a country. But those interests are perceived in the region as significant precisely because they are *U.S.* interests.

In the Nixon and Ford years, U.S. attitudes were of some limited help to the military regime. It is also true that the persistent efforts of Congress to restrict the administration's flexibility complicated Chilean government calculations. During the Carter years, the balance was reversed. The clear insistence on the importance of human rights and of the Letelier-Moffitt assassinations constituted permanent pressure. It was one factor behind the 1978 amnesty law and also behind some lessening of abuses. But the continued availability of foreign investment and military assistance gave Pinochet substantial leeway. For Chileans concerned with human rights and with aspirations for a return to democracy, the pressure had the marginal benefit of providing important psychological support. The Reagan administration's pro-democracy approach forged a firm identification of the United

States with democracy and also with human rights (although the relationship between the two concepts remained somewhat confused).

Second, democracy and human rights are not the same, however much they relate to each other. One of the problems the post–Cold War period has brought to the fore is that elected democratic governments do not necessarily provide adequate protection for basic rights. U.S. policymakers need to develop policy guidelines on the interrelationships between democracy and human rights promotion. Such policy development should begin with some analysis of how the two differ as well as how they reinforce each other. The State Department's own experience in trying to combine democracy, human rights, and labor matters in one entity would be a useful subject to study as well.

Third, although the administration and Congress were working at cross-purposes in the early 1970s, the mechanisms created by legislation have turned out to be quite useful in promoting human rights and in mitigating abuses. In all probability, the fact that every February the annual report on human rights observance will appear has an impact both on those who would like to ignore human rights and on those who want to promote them still further. Similarly, the existence of a State Department office that has an ongoing responsibility for monitoring and furthering human rights is a built-in reminder of the importance of the topic. These structures serve a sort of watchdog effect in keeping at least some attention focused on human rights. More broadly, one of the dilemmas facing both human rights NGOs and government officials dealing with human rights is determining the right mix of criticism of and collaboration with other countries on common aims. In contrast to some earlier periods, there is overall a greater disposition more recently to cooperate more and criticize less. But there is also some uneasiness over possible confusion of roles when security considerations enter in. Kosovo illustrated this question— even if it did not necessarily clarify it. To what extent, for instance, did human rights reporting and advocacy increase the likelihood of (if not directly cause) military intervention in Kosovo or in East Timor? Since September 11, 2001, the question has been posed in the context of searching for the optimum approach to cooperation with and criticism of human rights abuses by undemocratic or partially democratic countries that are allied in the war on terrorism.

Are there some useful ideas that could be drawn from the U.S. experience with Chile in the Pinochet years? There is room for government and NGO representatives to develop joint agendas. They could undertake a critique of the existing structures from the standpoint of effectiveness, for example, of the annual reports. Similarly, they could look together at the advantages and problems raised by their partly adversarial and partly collaborative relationship.

There are some further lessons, but these may be difficult to replicate across cases. For one, coalitions increase impact. The compatibility of views in the late 1980s among influential members of Congress, key elements of the administration, major human rights groups, and the embassy in Santiago gave an important coherence to policy and increased the effectiveness of each particular actor. Coordinated support from other influential countries, such as Spain, Brazil, Argentina, and France, emphasized that human rights concerns were not just an American fad. Last, just as all politics is said to be local, so it is clear that local activities count. While capitals are important for setting policy, day-to-day policy articulation and implementation by U.S. ambassadors and embassy staffs are often key.

NOTES

1. The Senate approved the amendment in December 1973; however, it was later deleted in conference.

2. The regime's patience was said to have worn thin, however, as the delegation insisted on visiting Dawson Island, where the best-known political prisoners were being held.

3. The group felt the embassy was not being aggressive enough, though Ambassador David Popper told them he had been making U.S. interest in human rights questions known at all levels of the Chilean government.

4. Cables sent by Ambassador Davis to the State Department reflect the mood. In an October 12 message reporting on a conversation with Pinochet, Davis said, "I took the occasion to point out . . . the political problems we are encountering. A discussion of the Kennedy Amendment, the Teruggi and Horman cases, and the human rights environment ensued. Pinochet intimated that the Chilean government shares fully our concern for human rights and is doing its best to prevent violations and loss of life." Embassy Santiago cable to State Department 4992. (An October 29 meeting of the WASAG, which focused on economic and military aid to Chile, was similarly torn

between efforts to maintain the credibility of U.S. commitments to the government of Chile, particularly to meet its urgent economic needs, and criticism from the public, media, and Congress over the human rights issue.) Davis continued, "He [Pinochet] added that this is not easy as the left extremists continue to attack officers and soldiers, engage in sniping and attempt acts of sabotage. . . . I reiterated assurances of the good will of the USG [U.S. government] and our desire to be helpful. I noted that we had our problems, which would oblige us to defer consideration of Chilean requests in some areas. So far as economic and military aid were concerned, I said we would want to wait before addressing this question until the Kennedy Amendment had been clarified through a Senate-House conference." Assistant (and later Under) Secretary William Rogers has said that he made it clear that human rights were a legitimate U.S. concern and should be treated as such.

5. Using his position as the chairman of the judiciary subcommittee on refugees, Senator Kennedy held a hearing on July 23, 1974, focusing on refugees, detention camps, military triennials, and the cases of the two disappeared Americans. There, Deputy Assistant Secretary for InterAmerican affairs (ARA) Harry Schlaudeman summarized the administration's view that, while important in U.S. relations with other countries, the observance of human rights "is not the only factor." Schlaudeman also noted that the military sales program with Chile was a nonpartisan contribution to regional stability and helped avoid paternalism in U.S. relationships with the countries of the hemisphere in general. For his part, Ambassador Popper submitted a detailed statement in response to criticism of the role he and the embassy were playing as being indifferent regarding rights issues in Chile, highlighting his contacts with religious leaders, defense attorneys for detainees, and political leaders in Chile.

6. Henry Kissinger, *Years of Upheaval* (Boston: Little Brown, 1982), 410. Kissinger answers his own question by saying, "The Nixon administration was not as insensitive to the Chilean junta's clumsy and occasionally brutal practices as our critics alleged. But we considered that the change of government in Chile was on balance favorable—even from the point of view of human rights. . . . We were therefore prepared to give the military leaders a chance; we made repeated private approaches to ease their methods. There is no doubt that our insistence on quiet diplomacy weakened our case at home, even as it succeeded with Chile in many individual cases" (p. 411).

7. The administration, for its part, was trying to push what it called a defensive arms package for Chile, which included 110 tanks and an antitank system. In a December 17 memorandum to Under Secretary for Political Affairs Joseph Sisco, then ARA assistant secretary William D. Rogers noted the importance of taking the opportunity to promote a dialogue with the Chilean government on human rights: "This problem and the reaction to it in the Congress jeopardize our ability to conduct normal, productive relations with Chile."

8. A useful description of the overall approach taken toward Chile in the first year of the Ford administration comes in the form of a briefing memorandum written by the officer in charge of Chilean affairs in the State Department and dated April 4: "[W]e have sought with other members of the United Nations . . . to assure concerned and objective attention to human rights problems in Chile. Depending on their nature, we have supported or abstained on resolutions. Our objective has been to encourage a useful dialogue between the US and Chile rather than politically motivated invective. We have also supported the efforts of the Inter-American Human Rights Commission and have taken the position that its recent report and the Chilean observations . . . merit the consideration of the OAS General Assembly. We believe, however, that the IAHRC [Inter-American Human Rights Commission] report based on findings 18 months old, is now of less relevance than the findings of the UNHRDC working group expected to visit Chile presently."

9. The first incumbent, however, spent much of his time urging that "quiet and friendly persuasion" was the way to combat human rights abuses.

10. In a cable of April 26, 1976, the chargé of the U.S. embassy, Thomas Boyatt, argued to Assistant Secretary Rogers that "the Secretary's visit provides us with a unique opportunity to impress upon senior Chileans—and particularly on Pres. Pinochet—how deeply and how negatively GOC [government of Chile] human rights practices affect our traditionally good bilateral relations." Boyatt went on to say, however, that Pinochet was not an easy person with whom to deal. "Pinochet is shrewd and hardheaded, but finds it difficult to deal with contrasting viewpoints. He is so narrow-minded and convinced of his righteousness that it takes sledgehammer blows to call his attention to some unpleasant facts of life." Boyatt, however, recommended against Kissinger's seeing ex-president Frei. Boyatt noted, "On balance I come down against the Secretary meeting Frei because such an obviously political gesture (and it would be only a gesture with no immediate practical results) would operate against improvement of human rights, our primary policy goal toward which we could make measurable progress."

Just before the visit, Ambassador Popper provided a checklist of what he called "matters to provide encouragement and/or incentives to the GOC." They included assurances with respect to the pending Security Assistance Bill, specifically the Kennedy Amendment—which, he argued, would "stop all military deliveries cold"—and the Fraser Amendment, introduced by Representative Don Fraser of Minnesota, which would cut economic assistance from $90 million to as low as $24 million, well below the administration's aim of at least $60 million to $70 million. Other items were the delivery of 18 F-5 aircraft, purchased and paid for already and scheduled for delivery in July, the timing of delivery of PL-480 wheat, and the resumption of Overseas Private Investment Corporation (OPIC) activities, along with raising the limits of Exim bank guarantees. Citing political rationales, the ambassador also suggested that the admission of Chilean political detainees be increased from three thousand to four thousand. Undated memorandum from Ambassador Popper to the secretary of state in preparation for the meeting with Pinochet.

   11. Referring to his forthcoming speech, Kissinger told Pinochet, "I will treat human rights in general terms and human rights in a world context. I will refer in two paragraphs to the report on Chile of the OAS Human Rights Commission. I will say that the human rights issue has impaired relations between the U.S and Chile. This is partly the result of congressional actions. I will say that I hope you will shortly remove these obstacles. . . . The speech is not aimed at Chile. I wanted to tell you about this. My evaluation is that you are the victim of all left-wing groups around the world, and that your greatest sin was that you overthrew a government that was going communist. But we have a practical problem we have to take into account. Without bringing about pressures incompatible with your dignity, and at the same time does not lead to U.S. laws which will undermine our relationship." Kissinger also highlighted the importance of constitutional guarantees. Pinochet's response touched on several matters, such as the institutionalization of Chilean society, the efforts to provide constitutional guarantees, the threat from Peru, and the verbal attacks from many quarters, including the United States. He argued that "we are constantly being attacked by the Christian Democrats. They have a strong voice in Washington. Not in the Pentagon, but they do get through to the Congress. Gabriel Valdes has access. Also Letelier . . . on the human rights front, we are slowly making progress. We are now down to 400. We have freed more. And we are also changing some sentences so that the prisoners can be eligible for leaving." Memorandum of conversation, June 8, 1976, between Secretary of State Henry Kissinger and President Augusto Pinochet.

   12. Patricio Aylwin, *El reencuentro de los Democratas* (Santiago, 1998), 120.

   13. As one politician put it, people felt that at first the United States stood aside but was favorably disposed to the new government. Whether this disposition came in the form of military assistance or food, it was seen as confirming the belief held by many that somehow the United States had been part of the coup plotting. In addition, the work of the congressional Church Committee on CIA activities (the committee discovered a lot of questionable and some illegal actions) was familiar to many. The fact that the administration also did little to take in Chilean political refugees reinforced this appearance of support for the regime and indifference to the regime's behavior. In contrast, the efforts of members of Congress (of whom Senator Kennedy was the best known) were warmly welcomed as signs of hope for the future.

   14. In his memoirs, Ambassador Davis also mentions that despite Chilean government assurances that Chile would uphold all its obligations in the field of human rights, "neither my representations nor those of other ambassadors and international representatives were welcome . . . Washington was clearly not prepared to institute Draconian reprisals and I doubt that anything less would have produced a turnaround." Nathaniel Davis, *The Last Two Years of Salvador Allende* (Ithaca, N.Y.: Cornell University Press, 1985), 377.

15. The head of the U.S. delegation, Brady Tyson, went as far as to say that the delegation "profoundly regretted the role that some United States agencies, officials and private groups had played in the overthrow of the previous Chilean government in the coup d'etat of 11 September 1973." Telegram 1964 from the U.S. Mission in Geneva to State Department, March 22, 1977. Tyson was, however, called back to Washington and the next day President Carter asserted congressional investigations had shown no link between the United States and the coup.

16. Mondale continued that "in the past . . . we had gotten these two objectives—anti-communism and human rights—confused, and we often intervened in a clumsy way; a good example was Chile . . . what we did in Chile in the last decade imposes on us a special responsibility to deal with the situation in Chile with good sense and respect for our own values as well as Chile's." Memorandum of conversation between Vice President Walter Mondale and former Chilean president Eduardo Frei, May 25, 1977.

17. Indicative of these dilemmas is Pastor's memorandum to Brzezinski a few days before the Frei meeting. Pastor notes that the "policy which we set towards Chile in the months ahead will also have very serious and lasting implications for our policy on human rights. We could draw the line of 'gross violators' around Chile, declare it a pariah and seek support for such a policy among other democratic countries. If we followed this direction, we would vote against loans to Chile in the IFIs [international financial institutions], meet with opposition leaders and essentially keep a distant posture. The expectation would be that an alternative to Pinochet would emerge. An alternative policy would be to try to bargain with Pinochet, seeking specific and concrete signs of moderation and minimal respect for human rights." Pastor added, "Both alternatives have important consequences, and I really have not yet thought through these issues sufficiently to give you recommendations. I have, however, asked State for a recommendation and have called an informal inter-agency meeting for Monday to discuss these issues." Memorandum to National Security Adviser Zbigniew Brzezinski from Robert Pastor, "Proposed Visit of President Frei," May 23, 1977.

18. For example, "on August 3, the State Department spokesman said that the human rights situation in Chile had improved this year, but that the US had made a number of recommendations on human rights areas of continuing American concern. On August 3 President Pinochet is reported to have said that he had just received a message that Assistant Secretary Terrence Todman said there was no truth to the reports that the State Department had issued new recommendations to the Chilean Government on human rights." Memorandum to National Security Adviser Zbigniew Brzezinski from Robert Pastor, "State Department Press Guidance and Policy Inconsistency," August 5, 1977.

19. This was the case, for example, with the appropriations bill for the IFIs. President Carter wrote to the chair of the House banking committee that "we want to implement this country's commitment to promoting human rights without adopting an overly rigid approach which would subvert the integrity and effectiveness of the institutions in providing economic and social development to poorer countries." Quoted in ADA legislative newsletter, May 15, 1977, 1. Staunch human rights advocates such as Harkin and Fraser would occasionally find themselves voting differently on such bills, with Fraser more inclined to respond to the plea for executive flexibility.

20. The committee decided, for example, that the United States should vote no on an agricultural loan for Chile and also decided to postpone a decision on a loan for Argentina and one for El Salvador.

21. Carter had begun the conversation by talking about Chile's relations with Peru and Bolivia. Pinochet noted that despite problems with the neighboring countries (which included some "uncomfortable problems" with Argentina over some islands in the south), Chile had decided to apply its limited resources to economic difficulties rather than arms purchases. Carter also raised Chilean support for nonproliferation in the hemisphere. Memorandum of conversation between President Carter and President Pinochet, September 6, 1977.

22. In his last letter of the series, on January 30, 1978, Pinochet made much of the popular support he had obtained in the January 4 "consultation" he had called to "defend the dignity of Chile." The proximate cause of the consultation was the final vote on the UN resolution critical of Chile, and its sponsorship by the United States. Chileans were simply asked to respond yes or no to the statement, "In the face of the international aggression unleashed against the government of our fatherland, I support President Pinochet in his defense of the dignity of Chile and I reaffirm the legitimacy of the government of the Republic of Chile to lead in a sovereign manner the institutionalization of the country." The official tabulation showed that 75 percent voted yes. A few excerpts from the letters will illustrate the gulfs of perception between the two:

> CARTER: I am concerned . . . that there will be little change without increased evidence that your government is taking steps to safeguard and promote human rights and to establish in Chile open and democratic institutions in keeping with the democratic tradition of which all Chileans have justly been proud.

> PINOCHET: [M]y government's concern [is] for the safeguarding and protection of human rights. This is a broad field of action and one which is always subject to improvement. . . . This is so, not because of external pressure which, contrary to what is assumed, and above all in the case of my country, is paradoxically counterproductive, but because of the imperative of deeply rooted humanitarian and moral convictions.

CARTER: Let me mention the very important role played by the non-governmental human rights organizations, and my hope they will continue to contribute to the advancement of human rights and my firm belief that they should retain their consultative status at the United Nations.

PINOCHET: I share your ideas about the non-governmental organizations concerned with human rights and the hopes which you have placed in their work in this field. Chile has at all times demonstrated its willingness to cooperate with them. This does not obviate the fact, however, that many of the non-governmental organizations are politically manipulated and have thereby lost the objectivity which should always prevail in human rights concerns.

CARTER: The United States co-sponsored the resolution [in the UNGA] because of our concern over the welfare and freedom of the people of Chile in the light of persistent reports of gross violations of human rights. We hope that such expressions of concern will ultimately cease to be necessary as violations of human rights and fundamental freedoms of persons in Chile are further reduced and finally eliminated.

PINOCHET: Both my government and the people of Chile were profoundly affected by the United States attitude toward the case of Chile in the United Nations. Your government sponsored the resolution and did so, moreover, in close union with countries such as Cuba.

CARTER: I continue to hope that differences over the terms of reference can be resolved which will allow a visit to Chile by the ad hoc Working Group or members of it on a basis which would be fully consistent with both the national dignity of Chile and the urgent need for full protection of human rights.

PINOCHET: [W]e proved that the entire investigation [of the Ad Hoc Working Group] was conducted without any respect for the essential requirements of due process, [therefore] my government has demanded that in the future the international jurisdiction that is being exercised over Chile conforms strictly to the law.

23. The lack of Chilean cooperation in the Letelier-Moffitt investigation resulted in Ambassador Landau being called back to Washington in June 1978. Landau told Pastor that he thought the Letelier-Moffitt case had the potential to induce other Chilean generals to replace Pinochet. According to the ambassador, Chileans were feeling great pressure not only because of the Letelier-Moffitt investigation but also because of the visit of the UN Ad Hoc Working

Group on July 12 and the political pressures that would likely follow from the visit. The junta was also disturbed by the Beagle Channel dispute with Argentina, which made the Chileans genuinely worried that the Argentines were considering war.

24. In principle, Townley had the right to appeal his expulsion within twenty-four hours. To make sure nothing went wrong at that point, the legalistically minded Chileans cut the phone lines to the competent court so there could be no appeal.

25. It provided for union elections at the plant level and for the right to strike (but also for dismissal of strikers after two months). It was enough of an advance for the boycott to be called off and enough to lay the foundation for renewed labor-organizing activity, which was important for the protest movements of the 1980s. To this day, Chilean trade unionists speak with great respect and affection of U.S. union official William Doherty, who for many years embodied the strong support of the U.S. labor movement. At the end of the 1970s, thanks to a number of economic reform measures, including innovative work in the pension field, people began to talk about the Chilean "economic miracle."

26. The constitution provided for two terms of eight years each for the president. It made the armed forces the guarantors of the constitution and contained a special article for the use of various extraordinary measures for suspending constitutional rights and for denying certain persons their civic rights if they were associated with violence.

27. What made matters worse in the late 1970s was the real threat of an invasion by Argentina, which had denounced the arbitration award made by Britain over the islands in the Beagle Channel. To the Chilean military, U.S. indifference was tantamount to betrayal. Hence the military turned to European arms suppliers and to Israel. At the end of 1978 the United States tried to get the OAS involved in mediating the dispute at about the same time others were seeking papal mediation. The two sides accepted the pope's subsequent decision.

28. In mid-1978 Kennedy and Harkin were working on legislation to require private banks to report loans they make to Chile and "other continual human rights violators." The legislation got no support from the Carter administration. In fact, some Chileans in the late 1970s were critical of the U.S. government for not trying to influence the private banking sector to be more aware (and even critical) of Chilean shortcomings. Such people juxtaposed the steady pursuit of the Letelier-Moffitt case with the tolerance of private U.S. "money pouring in." Others saw this as a sign of U.S. appreciation of the private-sector emphasis being put into practice in Chile.

29. According to Shultz, "In the first years of the Reagan presidency, an effort was made to understand Pinochet's problems in the hope of moderating the repressive practices of his authoritarian regime. Certainly important was the fact that Pinochet's economic policies were working well at the start of the 1980s. So as the United States tried to work with the Chilean government, various US-Chilean relationships that had been suspended during the Carter years were revived." George P. Shultz, *Turmoil and Triumph* (New York: Scribner's, 1993).

30. In February 1982 one of the country's most prominent labor leaders, Tucapel Jiménez, was murdered.

31. Still, in the view of Ambassador Theberge as late as December 1984, putting too much pressure on Chile would be "counter-productive." A staff member in the embassy in that period recalls the struggles within the staff over the contents of the annual human rights report, given the close relations with the government at the time. In individual human rights situations, though, the ambassador appears to have been helpful. A labor leader recalls how the ambassador's phone call got him released rapidly from detention.

32. In December 1984 Pinochet received three members of Congress. In response to their critical questions he told them not to stick their noses in matters that didn't concern them. Citing what he considered all of the U.S. losses in the past forty years, he asked them, "What kind of allies are you? You are not dependable."

33. Writing in 1985, Cynthia Brown, consultant for Americas Watch, says that the "Reagan administration's position is not so different from Pinochet's. The perception of Chilean history and traditional democracy is the same. The view of military guiltlessness—even of military mission—is the same. And for both, human rights are a matter of expediency."

34. Barnes's and Pinochet's remarks at the presentation of credentials ceremony in November symbolized the differences between the two countries. Barnes noted that "in our country . . . we have concluded that the ills of democracy can best be cured by more democracy." Pinochet responded by citing the uniqueness of the Chilean experience, which "demonstrated how, and to what extremes, democratic mechanisms themselves can be utilized to destroy democracy's own free institutions."

35. According to a September 16 memorandum from the Latin American Bureau to Secretary Shultz, "Both the President's message and our statements have stressed our hope that the state of siege can be removed quickly and progress made toward a democratic transition.

"These events in Chile have reinforced congressional opposition to U.S. support for MDB [multilateral development bank] loans to Chile, and produced calls for economic conditions.

"We are trying to convince sympathetic Senate staff to move forward the stalled Senate resolution supporting the National Accord, which you raised with Dole and Lugar before the summer recess. The Congressional environment is increasingly conducive to new anti-Chile legislation, as demonstrated by the

Deconcini sense of the Congress amendment to the FY87 appropriations bill, calling for U.S. opposition to MDB loans to Chile."

36. One prominent Chilean business executive called U.S. policy in the mid- and late 1980s a "declaratory" one. A politician said the declarations made it clear that the United States was moving from a policy of "indifference" to one of clear support for an effective return to democracy. It was like saying, he commented, "here we are. This is what we believe." A case in point involved the head of the Vicariate of Solidarity, Bishop Sergio Valech. A government prosecutor had begun to express interest in obtaining the records of the vicariate's human rights activities. From time to time, he made it appear that he might actually try to seize them. On one such occasion, the bishop asked Barnes to come to see him. He said that he would invite the press as well to make sure there were photographs of their meeting. The pictures appeared the next morning and served the purpose of reminding the prosecutor of U.S. interest in the work of the vicariate.

37. That human rights were still part of the U.S. concerns had been demonstrated once again in April. In a conversation with U.S. Treasury officials, Chilean finance minister Hernan Buchi indicated that Chile needed still more World Bank loans. He was told that the United States would have to consider human rights guidelines in existing legislation. It was suggested to him that he provide Treasury a document outlining Chile's economic adjustment/debt reduction plan plus another one providing a definitive description of "the steps taken by the GOC on human rights."

38. Sergio Molina, the head of the committee for free elections, sought to use the goal of free elections as a new way of uniting the democratic opposition and as an idea that might be acceptable even to the army. Free elections might also serve to encourage people to register to vote. But here again, in part because of financial constraints, such an appeal had only limited success. In addition, it was turning out to be hard to create much enthusiasm for either registering or supporting free elections while the opposition couldn't find a way to speak with more unity. The Catholic bishops, for example, were reported to be reluctant to endorse free elections until the parties could sort out their own plans. Compared with 1986, nothing that dramatic happened in U.S.-Chilean relations in 1987, but the context began to be modified as it became apparent that there would be a plebiscite, though no one, except perhaps Pinochet himself, knew for sure just when.

There continued to be periodic contacts between junta members and opposition leaders, with the former complaining about the opposition's inability to organize itself. Ironically, the promulgation of a political parties law complicated the oppositions' task even more. The parties had now to decide whether to register as legal parties and whether to encourage their adherents to register as voters, since only registered voters could count toward the quota set by the law for parties to be recognized.

Even before the political parties law came out in March, Humberto Gordon, a new army junta member, told Ambassador Barnes that the very existence of the new law would rescind any bans on parties holding meetings. This had been a major opposition complaint. Gordon agreed that there would have to be new laws to permit adequate access to the media, particularly TV. When the ambassador asked when such changes might come, Gordon responded by citing a favorite Pinochet expression, "all in good time." He added that only Pinochet would define what was the right moment.

39. However, old difficulties had not completely disappeared. There remained major limitations on television access for the opposition as well as on news coverage in both radio and television. There were occasional detentions and incidents such as an attack on church offices in a provincial capital. The government used "public service" ads on TV showing successful programs in education and health services. Pro-government newspapers ran pictures of opposition leaders Aylwin and Lagos alongside those of Allende to try to link them with the "bad times" of Allende. Cable no. 4994 from Embassy Santiago to Department of State.

11

U.S. Human Rights Policy toward Colombia

MICHAEL SHIFTER AND JENNIFER STILLERMAN

COLOMBIA FACES A GRAVE HUMAN RIGHTS SITUATION, the most dire in the hemisphere. The country's internal conflict claimed the lives of more than thirty-five thousand Colombians during the 1990s and displaced a staggering two million. According to the United Nations, Colombia has the third-largest displaced population in the world, following Sudan and Angola. Some twenty-five thousand Colombians die each year from diverse acts of violence, including common criminal acts unrelated to the conflict, and at least half of the world's kidnappings occur in the Andean nation. Whatever the source—nongovernmental or governmental—the human rights data are profoundly troubling.

Colombia's deep human rights crisis stems primarily from a complex internal conflict involving the state and three main violent groups—two on the left and one on the right. The FARC (Revolutionary Armed Forces of Colombia) and the ELN (National Liberation Army) are two of Latin America's longest-standing insurgencies; both trace their roots to the 1960s. The FARC is the stronger and larger of the two, with some seventeen thousand combatants, whereas the ELN is estimated to number roughly four thousand. Both groups derive a significant share of their income from criminal activity, including kidnapping, extortion, and (the FARC particularly) the drug trade. In this regard, one of the FARC's most common methods includes "taxing" coca farmers and drug traffickers in exchange for protection. Though these groups enjoy very little popular support, they have become increasingly powerful both financially and militarily in recent years.

Exacerbating Colombia's already explosive conditions are formidable paramilitary forces—the third group—that emerged several decades ago in response to the government's lack of authority and the incapacity of security forces to combat the leftist insurgencies. These paramilitary groups or militias—until July 2002 centrally organized under the umbrella AUC (United Self-Defense Forces of Colombia) and numbering around twelve thousand combatants—are responsible for the bulk of political killings in Colombia. According to credible governmental and nongovernmental reports, these paramilitary forces have some links, at some levels, with the Colombian military. Using "taxing" methods similar to those of the FARC, the paramilitary forces also derive most of their funding from the drug industry. In fact, in a TV interview conducted in 2001, Carlos Castaño, the leader of the AUC, acknowledged that his organization obtained some 70 percent of its income from the drug trade. Adding to the mix of violence are drug traffickers, no longer organized in large cartels of Medellín or Cali, but rather increasingly fractured and spread out, making them even more difficult to control.

How has the United States responded to this alarming situation? Without question, human rights concerns have in part motivated U.S. policy toward Colombia over the past several decades. The U.S. government has applied pressure, imposed conditions on U.S. aid, and provided some assistance to Colombian institutions responsible for promoting human rights guarantees.[1]

But U.S. policy responses to the deteriorating human rights and humanitarian conditions in Colombia have also been substantially shaped and constrained by the U.S. interest in combating illegal narcotics. The drug issue—of such enormous domestic political salience in the United States—has long overridden other interests, including human rights. To the extent that the United States has succeeded in positively influencing the human rights conditions in Colombia, it has done so within a framework focused on fighting drugs. Indeed, while the drug connection in Colombia may be the principal hook commanding the attention of key policymakers, this emphasis has also resulted in significant policy distortions and contradictions, as well as the subordination of human rights as a second-tier issue in the bilateral relationship.

In recent years U.S. policy toward Colombia has more often been the product of default than of conscious, deliberate decisions made at the highest level of the U.S. government. A formula for fighting drugs, made up of three essential elements—eradication, interdiction, and extradition—has largely framed U.S. policy over the past several decades. But the policy toward Colombia can most fruitfully be understood as the reflection of competing domestic interests and agendas. While many actors have found counternarcotics policy to be the most compelling, and most politically rewarding, issue, other interests and agendas—human rights included—are promoted by domestic political leaders and play an important role in the formulation and implementation of U.S. policy. The result has been an unusually personalized policy, in which the role of individual actors in supporting a particular interest or agenda matters a great deal. U.S. Colombia policy has also been marked by a high degree of "parallel diplomacy," in which key actors and institutions take up different issues tied to a set of common goals and perform critical functions to advance them. In the case of Colombia, this can be seen within the executive branch itself, the U.S. Congress, and nongovernmental groups. The role of such actors and institutions is hardly new and in fact characterizes most important policy questions, but it has arguably become more pronounced in the absence of an overarching foreign policy framework and strategy.

BACKGROUND

Throughout the Cold War—indeed, throughout much of the twentieth century—the United States and Colombia enjoyed close and friendly relations. This was due in some measure to Colombia's exemplary economic management and its adherence to civilian, constitutional government since the early 1960s. For many years Washington held up Latin America's third-largest country as a model of good governance and a reliable partner in President John F. Kennedy's Alliance for Progress aid program.

In the early 1970s, however, the drug issue (Richard Nixon had coined the phrase "war on drugs" in 1968) began to influence U.S. policy toward Colombia. Since human rights abuses during that period were not as extensive as they would subsequently become, such concerns did not then significantly influence U.S. policy decisions. In 1973 the U.S. government began to provide Colombia with counternarcotics assistance, approving a four-year, $6 million aid package that would train six hundred Colombian law enforcement officers.[2] Despite this new counternarcotics assistance, the drug issue remained a relatively minor piece of the overall bilateral relationship throughout the 1970s. As former U.S. ambassador to Colombia Viron Vaky has noted, "We had DEA [Drug Enforcement Agency] guys in the embassy but it was not a central element of our policy."[3]

With the election of Colombian president Julio César Turbay in 1978, the drug issue acquired greater prominence. In his inaugural speech, Turbay announced that counternarcotics efforts (at that time directed principally at traffickers and marijuana production) would be a top priority of his administration. He stressed that Colombia's success in this area would depend largely on the United States' willingness to provide financial assistance to the Andean nation as well as to address its own problem on the demand side.[4]

The Carter administration welcomed Turbay's commitment to the fight against drugs and worked to foster greater cooperation between the two countries.[5] The two presidents negotiated a bilateral extradition treaty in 1979, which greatly pleased U.S. officials.[6] Further, at the United States' suggestion, Turbay directed the Colombian armed forces to play a greater role in counternarcotics efforts.[7] He instructed the army to focus on drug cultivation in the Guajira Peninsula, where some ten thousand troops seized more than six thousand tons of marijuana over a two-year period.[8]

However, Turbay's determination to restore law and order to Colombia led him to carry out a variety of authoritarian measures that ran counter to the Carter administration's fundamental concern with human rights. In 1978, for example, Turbay issued a "Security Statute" (or Decree 1923), which gave greater authority and autonomy to the military,[9] identified new, vaguely defined crimes such as "disturbing public order," and restricted press freedom.[10] The statute was directed at drug traffickers as well as the country's growing insurgent groups. An investigation conducted by Amnesty International uncovered multiple cases of human rights violations—including disappearances and torture—committed by military officers acting under Decree 1923.[11]

Such reports troubled Jimmy Carter, who had stated in his inaugural address that "our commitment to human rights must be absolute."[12] Nevertheless, his administration was pleased with Turbay's counternarcotics efforts. At the urging of Diego Asencio, the U.S. ambassador to Colombia, the United States rewarded the Colombian president with $16 million in additional antidrug assistance[13]—despite his military's poor human rights record. As Bruce Bagley pointed out, however, Congress later prohibited the use of those funds for aircraft, radar, and communications technology, concerned that U.S. assistance might finance counterinsurgency activities.[14]

The next several years would witness the deterioration of Colombia's human rights situation, as drug traffickers and private citizens armed themselves against the guerrilla groups waging war in the country. December 1981 was a turning point, as more than two hundred drug traffickers created a new organization, Muerte a Secuestradores, or Death to Kidnappers (known by its Spanish initials as MAS), to combat the insurgents.[15]

The creation of MAS had considerable impact. Many outside the drug trade viewed the group as a model of effective organization against the guerrillas. In fact, following MAS's example, the Colombian army's Bárbula Battalion in Puerto Boyacá, Santander, and the military mayor of the town, Oscar de Jesús Echandía, provided civilians with arms, uniforms, and money to fight the insurgents. The Colombian military offered tactical support and advice. This new, legally constituted paramilitary group chose the same name as that used by the drug traffickers: MAS. The organization's initial objective —to free the region of insurgents—soon expanded to include attacks on any person or organization that resisted it. Within two years MAS was participating directly in extrajudicial killings carried out by members of the Colombian armed forces.[16]

It was against this backdrop that Colombian president Belisario Betancur took office in 1982. Vice President George Bush represented the Reagan administration at Betancur's inauguration in Bogotá. Within the context of the ideological conflict that dominated the Cold War (and especially the Central American conflicts), Bush concentrated on the guerrilla rather than the paramilitary phenomenon, suggesting that the United States build a military base in Colombia to monitor the country's insurgents. Betancur, unwilling to accept such a strong U.S. presence, declined the offer. He did, however, allow the Reagan administration to install radar surveillance stations in Colombia to hinder the drug traffickers' efforts to transport raw coca leaf from Bolivia and Peru to Colombia.[17]

Yet Betancur remained deeply concerned about the rise of paramilitary activity, in light of reports that MAS had committed nearly 250 assassinations since its creation. He directed Attorney General Carlos Jiménez Gómez to conduct an investigation—which concluded that 59 of 163 individuals linked to MAS were police and military officers in active service. Though Jiménez sought to broaden his investigation, Colombia's Disciplinary Tribunal determined that the case fell under military jurisdiction. Key officers spoke on behalf of the paramilitary group, arguing that its members sought only to defend themselves against the guerrillas. Not surprisingly, the officers identified by Jiménez were never reprimanded or prosecuted for their participation in the extrajudicial killings carried out by MAS. The Reagan administration had little to say in response to the findings.[18]

At the same time, Betancur pursued peace talks with the Colombian guerrillas. Seeking a way to end the conflict, the Colombian president took the controversial step of offering the insurgents amnesty without requiring disarmament as a precondition. This strategy was at sharp odds with the Reagan administration's approach to guerrilla movements in the region and created some tension between the two governments.[19] Moreover, the U.S. government found the Betancur administration insufficiently attentive to the drug issue and particularly uncooperative when it came to the question of extradition.[20] The Colombian president refused to implement the bilateral treaty negotiated between Carter and Turbay in 1979.[21] This frustrated Ronald

Reagan, who viewed extradition as an essential element of his administration's antidrug strategy.

Betancur's stance on extradition took a sharp turn following the 1984 assassination of Minister of Justice Rodrigo Lara Bonilla, who had pursued Colombia's *narcotraficantes* in collaboration with U.S. drug enforcement agents. Betancur declared "war without quarter" on the drug traffickers and abandoned his previous position on extradition.[22] Over the next two years, he extradited ten Colombian citizens and three foreigners to the United States, expanded illicit crop eradication programs, and seized record-breaking quantities of illegal drugs.[23] In response to Betancur's actions, by 1985 U.S. counternarcotics aid for Colombia had tripled from its 1983 level.[24]

The United States' unwavering insistence on extradition—and the Colombian government's cooperation on that question—would take a heavy toll on Colombian society. Between 1981 and 1986 drug lords opposed to extradition assassinated more than fifty judges (including twelve Supreme Court justices).[25] Meanwhile, Betancur's efforts on the peace front seemed to pay off, as the principal guerrilla group, the FARC, agreed to a cease-fire in 1984 and created a new political party, Unión Patriótica (UP), or Patriotic Union.[26] But over the next few years, paramilitary forces assassinated more than one thousand UP party members.[27] The systematic killings, and the government's inability to stop them, deepened the FARC's distrust toward the Colombian government and have severely impacted subsequent peace negotiation efforts.

Another important dimension was introduced into U.S. policy on Colombia when, for the first time, in 1984 the State Department publicly acknowledged the existence of Colombian paramilitary forces in its human rights report. The report attributed a series of assassinations, disappearances, and cases of torture to these self-defense units. Nongovernmental human rights organizations had criticized the State Department's previous reports, arguing that they presented violations committed by armed actors in Colombia in a way that downplayed their relationship with state forces.

In April 1989 Colombian president Virgilio Barco responded to the growing human rights crisis in Colombia, calling the paramilitaries "terrorist organizations" and noting that their victims included primarily unarmed civilians, not guerrilla combatants. His government took steps to locate and bring to justice the paramilitaries' leaders and declared their organizations illegal. Barco removed two military officials associated with MAS from their posts, dismantled several training centers, and organized a special police unit to pursue the paramilitaries.[28]

He also issued Decree 815—which stated that only the president had the authority to establish "self-defense" groups, subject to the approval of his ministers of defense and government—as well as Decree 1194—which created criminal consequences for civilians and military officers who helped train, finance, or organize paramilitary organizations.[29] Despite these actions, Colombia's self-defense groups continued to grow, with sustained support from parts of the military.[30]

While Barco devoted most of his energies to Colombia's internal conflict, the U.S. government had turned its attention even more sharply to drugs. In the spring of 1986, Reagan issued National Security Directive (NSD) 221, which identified illegal narcotics as a "lethal" threat to the United States.[31] The State Department mentioned the drug trade for the first time since the late 1970s in its 1987 Human Rights Report, which identified traffickers as the principal threat to human rights in Colombia.[32]

From 1989 on, drugs would remain the central—and, at times, virtually the only—component of U.S. policy toward Colombia. That year, President Bush, free to take on a new battle with the Cold War finally over, announced his Andean Initiative, a five-year, $2.2 billion plan designed to heighten the United States' war on drugs. The program—intended to attack drugs at their source—aimed to wipe out coca cultivation, eliminate processing labs, and halt the delivery of precursor chemicals by offering greater military and economic assistance to Colombia, Bolivia, and Peru.[33]

President Bush's increased emphasis on the drug issue was accompanied by an even greater militarization of counternarcotics efforts pushed by both Congress and the White House. In 1989 Congress passed the National Defense Authorization Act, which identified the Pentagon as the "single lead agency" for the detection of illicit narcotics shipments to the United States.[34] In August of that year, the U.S. president authorized $65 million in emergency counternarcotics assistance for the Colombian armed forces and police.[35] The aid package, developed at President Barco's request, included equipment, aircraft, and helicopters, as well as some military training. "We intend to work closely with the Colombian government to bring justice to those responsible for the scourge of drug trafficking," Bush said.[36] While Barco supported this aid package, his request for technical assistance for the judicial system went unanswered.[37]

Also in 1989 Colombia became Latin America's top beneficiary of the United States' International Military Education and Training (IMET) program.[38] More than two thousand military and police received training in U.S. schools over the next several years. This policy was not, however, without its critics. In fact, Human Rights Watch warned, "U.S. officials insist that the United States tracks these students through military-to-military contacts, but it is doubtful that the involvement of U.S.-trained personnel in human rights abuses comes to light in any but the most egregious cases."[39] As Peter Zirnite noted, "Militarization of counternarcotics efforts in Latin America undermines recent trends toward democratization and greater respect for human rights while threatening regional security."[40]

Despite serious concerns about the impact of U.S. assistance on human rights conditions in Colombia, the United States provided $504 million in aid to Colombia between 1990 and 1992 under the Andean Initiative. Of the total amount, $397 million went to military and law enforcement assistance. The remaining $107 million included economic aid intended to address Colombia's balance of payments problems, strengthen its judicial system, and support the Colombian National Police's poppy eradication programs.[41]

During this period the United States took a number of controversial steps as part of its efforts to fight the drug war and implement the Andean Initiative. For example, seeking to enhance the effectiveness of the Colombian military's counternarcotics operations, the U.S. government focused on the armed forces' intelligence capabilities and formed an advisory commission of Pentagon and CIA officials to develop a set of recommendations for Colombia's Ministry of Defense.[42]

In 1991 the Colombian government adopted the commission's recommendations in the form of Order 200-05/91, which laid out a plan for reorganization of Colombia's military intelligence networks.

Despite the Bush administration's stated objective—better equipping the Colombian military to fight the drug trade—Order 200-05/91 had minimal, if any, relation to counternarcotics. According to Human Rights Watch, the document did not so much as mention drugs in its sixteen pages and appendices. The central focus was on fighting the insurgents.[43]

Operating under Order 200-05/91, the Colombian armed forces incorporated paramilitary organizations—which President Barco declared illegal in 1989—into their intelligence apparatus, directing these armed civilians to carry out surveillance of opposition leaders and attack individuals selected by the army's high command.[44] In Barrancabermeja, for example, a paramilitary-military network organized by the Colombian navy committed dozens of killings.[45]

At the same time, there was heightened concern regarding the impact of U.S. assistance on human rights conditions in Colombia. In September 1991 the U.S. General Accounting Office issued a report warning that U.S. officials did not "have sufficient oversight to provide assurances that [U.S.] aid is being used as intended for counternarcotics purposes and is not being used primarily against insurgents or being used to abuse human rights."[46] Indeed, as Human Rights Watch noted, the sheer number of U.S. programs that channeled funds to Colombia made effective oversight a serious problem.[47]

But even when Colombian military officials explained to congressional staff members their intentions to use the bulk of U.S. aid provided under the Andean Initiative to launch a new offensive ("Operation Tri-Color 90") against the guerrillas, the U.S. government did not react negatively.[48] Thomas McNamara, U.S. ambassador to Colombia at the time, stated, "I don't see the utilization of the arms against the guerrillas as a deviation. The arms are given to the government in order that they may use them in the anti-narcotics struggle . . . but this is not a requirement of the United States."[49]

Such a policy was being carried out despite the fact that the State Department's own 1991 human rights report implicated some members of the Colombian armed forces in human rights violations and took note of the high levels of impunity that protected them from prosecution. Moreover, despite growing evidence of human rights violations by the armed forces, between 1989 and 1993 the State

Department granted thirty-nine licenses to U.S. companies for the export of arms to Colombia.[50]

In 1993 the General Accounting Office (GAO) issued another critical report, noting that the State Department had not yet established end-use monitoring procedures to ensure that U.S. aid did not go to Colombian military units implicated in human rights violations. The GAO found "two instances where personnel who had allegedly committed human rights abuses came from units that received U.S. aid."[51]

Political affairs officer Thomas P. Hamilton defended the U.S. government's commitment to human rights, explaining that "throughout the year the Ambassador and other representatives of the Embassy pursue our human rights policy through private diplomatic channels."[52] But, as Human Rights Watch argued, "Elsewhere in Latin America . . . experience has shown that quiet diplomacy means no diplomacy as long as the armed forces feel assured of an uninterrupted stream of military aid."[53]

It was during the administration of César Gaviria that the United States began funding substantial judicial reform efforts in Colombia, with the aim of complementing and reinforcing antidrug policies. In 1991 the U.S. government agreed to provide Colombia with $36 million over a six-year period in support of Colombia's Public Order Courts. Many human rights organizations viewed the courts, with their anonymous judges, prosecutors, and witnesses and secret proceedings, as part of a wider system that routinely violated the rights of Colombian citizens. According to the Lawyers Committee on Human Rights, for example, "the special procedures which [the Public Order Courts] employ impinge on basic due process rights guaranteed under the Colombian constitution and international law. Most notably, the right to a public trial, to confront one's accusers, and to petition for judicial review of detention have all been compromised by Colombia's unorthodox approach to certain criminal prosecutions."[54]

The U.S. government's moments of greatest irritation with the Gaviria administration can best be understood through the primacy of the illegal narcotics question. To cite the two most problematic instances: in 1992 drug kingpin Pablo Escobar escaped from prison (though he was subsequently killed by security forces trying to apprehend him); and two years earlier, extradition had been banned in the country's 1991 constitution (although legislation in December 1997 overturned the ban).

Yet, even with its predominant emphasis on the drug issue, the U.S. government took a number of important steps in the early 1990s in response to Colombia's worsening human rights conditions. Recognizing that the Colombian army remained focused on counterinsurgent rather than counternarcotics operations, the U.S. government redirected most aid in 1992 from the army to the police, navy, and air force.[55] The kidnapping and presumed deaths of three U.S. missionaries by the FARC in 1993 prompted action on the U.S. policy side as well. That year Congress asserted a stronger role in the policymaking process. It included language in the foreign assistance appropriations bill that prohibited the administration from providing security or economic support to Colombia without notifying two congressional committees with authority to block the aid.[56] Although this shift was encouraging and generally welcomed by human rights organizations, it added yet another twist and complication to the Colombia policy puzzle, further highlighting the contradictions and complexities that have long made it difficult for the U.S. government to devise a coherent and constructive strategy.

At the same time, however, despite increased concern for human rights abuses, in 1994 the United States provided more training and equipment for a string of Colombian military brigades involved primarily in combating insurgents, not narcotics.[57] Most of these brigades have since been implicated in human rights abuses. As the executive director of Amnesty International stated that year, "There is now good reason to believe that the United States has been a collaborator in the charade, that much of the U.S. aid intended for counternarcotics operations has in fact been diverted to the killing fields."[58]

TURN FOR THE WORSE

With the inauguration of Ernesto Samper in 1994, U.S.-Colombian relations reached unprecedented levels of tension and mutual distrust. In 1995 the Colombian president was accused of accepting

$6 million from the Cali drug cartel during his presidential campaign. As a result, the State Department revoked Samper's visa and "decertified" Colombia in 1996 and 1997 for lack of cooperation in the war on drugs. The decertification policy, which subjected Colombia to aid sanctions, did little to bolster the government's credibility and legitimacy. An enfeebled government only enabled the violent, nonlegitimate forces—the guerrillas, paramilitary groups, and drug traffickers —to advance and gain the upper hand in multiple conflicts, with severe consequences for human rights throughout the country.

Despite the strained relations between the United States and Samper, it was precisely during this period when the question of human rights in Colombia acquired greater importance in the bilateral relationship. President Samper himself took some positive, noteworthy steps in the area. For example, he established the General Administrative Special Directorate for Human Rights within the Ministry of the Interior; accepted the Office of the UN High Commissioner for Human Rights (at the time, the only such office in all of Latin America); adopted Protocol II to the Geneva Conventions; and approved legislation that compensated victims of human rights violations in cases brought before international tribunals.[59] Perhaps most significant, in 1995 Samper acknowledged the findings of a commission established under the Organization of American States' Inter-American Commission on Human Rights and accepted Colombia's responsibility for the murders of more than one hundred people in Trujillo between 1989 and 1991.[60]

But Samper also resorted to some hard-line measures to deal with Colombia's human rights problems. He twice declared a state of "internal commotion"[61] and his Decree 0717 passed over the civilian authorities, allowing the military's high command to request that the president declare "special public order zones" where fundamental rights would be suspended.[62] Moreover, Samper authorized civilians to form the controversial rural security cooperatives. Through these organizations, referred to as CONVIVIR, private citizens would monitor guerrilla activity and provide intelligence to military personnel in their regions. Members' identities would remain secret and CONVIVIR would keep close ties with both police and military commanders.[63] Human rights groups protested that these government-sponsored self-defense groups involved civilians directly in the country's internal conflict, making them increasingly vulnerable to guerrilla attack.[64]

Also, responding to mounting concerns from nongovernmental organizations and constituents about the human rights situation in Colombia, the United States suspended all aid to the country's military in 1996, directing assistance instead to the Colombian police.[65] This marked a redirecting of its more than twenty-year policy of military aid for counternarcotics. Further, in September of that year, Senator Patrick Leahy (D-Vt.) proposed a ban on U.S. assistance for any foreign military units implicated in gross human rights abuses, unless effective measures had been taken to bring those responsible to justice. The so-called Leahy Amendment applied to counternarcotics aid controlled by the State Department's Bureau for International Narcotics and Law Enforcement and was passed by the U.S. Congress as part of the Fiscal Year 1997 Foreign Aid Spending Bill. To the extent that it has been applied, this U.S. instrument had a positive effect on human rights conditions in Colombia. In 1998, for example, it helped bring about the dismantling of the Twentieth Intelligence Brigade, a group credibly charged with committing grave abuses. In addition, the State Department delivered a sharp message to the Samper administration by issuing highly critical human rights reports on Colombia in 1996 and 1997. Such reports, together with those issued by the UN High Commissioner for Human Rights and Human Rights Watch, pointed to and condemned the ties between Colombian security forces and paramilitary organizations.

Whatever the merits, making U.S. policy toward Colombia contingent on improved human rights and curbing the drug problem has been the result of a complex web of different U.S. domestic agendas and interests seeking to shape policy. It would be difficult to argue that the U.S. stance toward Colombia derived from a clear and coherent policy that reflected sustained and serious high-level political attention. Rather, U.S. Colombia policy can most usefully be interpreted as an attempt to fill the vacuum formed precisely by the absence of such attention. As a White House official acknowledged to the *Washington Post* on December 27, 1998, "Colombia poses a greater immediate threat to us than Bosnia did, yet it receives almost no attention. So policy is set by default."[66]

A NEW BEGINNING?

When Andrés Pastrana became Colombia's president in August 1998, many saw an opportunity to build a more constructive and balanced bilateral relationship. Many U.S. officials, who hoped to get the relationship back on track, viewed Pastrana, unlike his predecessor, favorably. The new president appeared committed to working with the United States, pursuing a negotiated settlement to Colombia's internal conflict, and addressing the grave human rights situation facing his country.

From the outset, however, it was clear that wiping the slate clean after several years of mutual antagonism would not be easy. The cumulative effect of Colombia's pariah status was to encourage various expressions of "parallel diplomacy," particularly between key Republicans in the U.S. Congress (who had assumed control of that body in 1995) and the head of Colombia's antinarcotics police, General José Serrano. The irony, in fact, was that during a low point in the bilateral relationship—when President Samper was denied a U.S. visa—Colombia nonetheless received an increased level of counternarcotics assistance.

In 1999 the United States provided $289 million in such aid to Colombia, which was three times the 1998 amount.[67] As a result, Colombia ranked third in the world, after Israel and Egypt, as a recipient of U.S. security assistance.[68] (The amount of security assistance to Colombia would reach even higher levels the following year after the approval of Plan Colombia legislation.) Although the bulk of the money appropriated in 1999 went to Colombia's national police, the country's military received about $40 million, chiefly for equipment and the training of an elite counternarcotics force.[69] In contrast, U.S. Agency for International Development (USAID) programs directed toward reforming the judicial system, strengthening the enforcement of human rights, promoting civil society activity, and supporting alternative development activities received only $3.3 million in 1998.[70] Although the amount increased to $6.3 million in 1999,[71] the disparity between USAID funding and the financial support received by Colombia's security forces reveals the overwhelming thrust of U.S. policy toward Colombia. Additionally, roughly two hundred U.S. military advisers and trainers continued to rotate in and out of the country.[72] And, according to a report issued by the General Accounting Office in June 1999, the U.S. government had been sharing intelligence on antinarcotics and guerrilla activity with the Colombian military since March 1999.[73]

Indeed, in 1999 it appeared that U.S. policy toward Colombia might begin to take more definite shape and firm direction. High-level attention unquestionably intensified. The focus stemmed in large measure from a pervasive apprehension about the deteriorating conditions in Colombia and President Pastrana's disappointing attempts—chiefly through a peace process with the FARC—to reverse them. As tempting as it may have been to do so, Colombia became nearly impossible to ignore.

Few events are as powerful in mobilizing political and bureaucratic resources in the United States as the deaths of its citizens. The kidnapping and presumed deaths of three U.S. missionaries in 1993, reportedly at the hands of the FARC, already weighed heavily on U.S. policy toward Colombia. The brutal killing of three U.S. human rights workers in March 1999, which the FARC acknowledged had been carried out by its forces, proved to be a turning point. The murders effectively constrained a U.S. role in any peace effort, since the incident made further meetings between State Department officials and FARC representatives (which had taken place in December 1998) politically impossible. The assassinations aroused substantial concern among key members of Congress, as did the deaths of five Americans in July, when their plane crashed during a United States Air Force antidrug reconnaissance mission (the full details of which remain unclear).

Just a month after the March 1999 assassinations, Harold Koh, assistant secretary of state for democracy, human rights, and labor, delivered the Clinton administration's most forceful message on human rights in Colombia at a Medellín conference.[74] He especially urged the Colombian government to sever "any and all remaining ties between the military and paramilitaries."[75] Although it is unclear whether Koh's speech, lauded by human rights groups, had any effect, the State Department's 1999 human rights report on Colombia recognized that the Pastrana government had dismissed four army generals under investigation for alleged links to paramilitary groups. Still, the State Department continued to point to high levels of impunity and continuing collaboration between some members of government security forces and members of paramilitary groups.[76]

The sheer brazenness and growing brutality of the conflict also helped bring Colombia into high-level focus. While President Pastrana's peace initiative struggled to gain traction, Colombians were appalled at the savagery occurring in their country. A record number of FARC and paramilitary atrocities were carried out, and some of the most spectacular kidnappings were the work of the ELN and the FARC. Colombians were left wondering if any place in their country could still be considered secure. In addition, the media, especially CNN, increasingly publicized the humanitarian and human rights crises, particularly the plight of the country's displaced people. A number of community groups in the United States—many with ties to various churches—also began to organize in response to the humanitarian crisis.

Responding to such a critical situation, the U.S. government, chiefly through USAID programs, expanded support for judicial reform efforts, as well as initiatives related to human rights. Training programs have sought to improve the capacity of Colombian investigators and prosecutors of rights violations committed by all armed actors in the country's conflict. USAID also joined with the United Nations and the International Committee of the Red Cross to develop a program of some $23 million for Colombia's internally displaced.[77]

The growing regional and international dimensions of Colombia's crisis also helped account for Washington's more intense focus on Colombia. Emigration had been on the rise, to a considerable degree related to the country's worst economic problems in nearly seven decades. After many years as the region's steadiest economic performer, Colombia had been reeling, with unemployment reaching 20 percent and a sharp decline in real gross domestic product (GDP). According to an August 20, 2002, BBC News report, more than 1.2 million Colombians have left their country since 1997, most of them going to the United States. There were also increasing concerns about regional instability as violence from Colombian paramilitary and guerrilla groups began spilling into bordering countries.

Finally, in addition to the human and geopolitical consequences of Colombia's crisis, the matter of drugs continued to concentrate Washington's attention. Despite increased assistance to Colombia for counternarcotics efforts, the drug problem only worsened. In 1998 production of coca, which supplies the raw material for cocaine, was up by 28 percent[78]—three times the 1994 level.[79] Pressure mounted for government officials at the highest levels to make Colombia a priority and fashion a more productive policy.

THE U.S. RESPONSE AND THE INTERNATIONAL CONTEXT

One of the main impulses in the United States has been to react to deteriorating conditions by getting tough and calling for increased security assistance. Such an impulse was plainly on display during the debate that took place within the U.S. government at the beginning of the Pastrana administration. Leading congressional Republicans, most notably Benjamin Gilman of New York, the chairman of the House International Relations Committee, pressed for more support for the national police. At the same time, General Barry McCaffrey, who headed the United States' antidrug efforts under President Bill Clinton, and General Charles Wilhelm of the United States Southern Command, urged higher levels of assistance to Colombia's military for counternarcotics programs (including the formation of additional elite battalions).

Others, worried that the United States might get sucked into a Vietnam-like quagmire, were far more reluctant to advocate greater involvement. Those holding this view included the human rights community, some members of the Defense and State Departments, and select Republican congressional figures who had previously questioned the U.S. role in Bosnia. Many congressional Democrats shared the concern about a potential "slippery slope" in Colombia and argued that greater resources should be directed toward domestic efforts to reduce demand and consumption of illegal narcotics. Thus, increased attention to the Colombia policy issue tended mainly to muddy the political picture.

Against this backdrop, President Clinton and Secretary of State Madeleine Albright had little choice but to deal more directly with

the Colombia question. In September 1999 the Colombian government unveiled "Plan Colombia," a document created at the urging of
high-level U.S. government officials. Ambassador Thomas Pickering,
under secretary of state for political affairs, played an especially prominent role in shaping the policy framework. Plan Colombia addressed
the full gamut of Colombia's major problems—from illegal narcotics
and political violence to social development, economic stability, and
broad, institutional reform—and outlined possible solutions. President
Pastrana announced that implementing the plan would cost $7.5 bil-
lion over a three-year period, and that Colombia would contribute
$4 billion. The remaining $3.5 billion would come from the international community: the multilateral financial institutions, the European Union, other supportive governments, and, of course, the United
States. The Pastrana administration hoped that the United States
would provide between $1.5 billion and $2 billion of that amount.

In July 2000, after a year of intense debate and political bicker-
ing, Congress finally passed legislation supporting Plan Colombia.
Reduced from Clinton's original $1.6 billion proposal to $1.3 billion,
the aid package received strong bipartisan support. Approximately two-
thirds of its funds were designated for military and police counternarcotics activities. However, owing in large part to the growing, and
increasingly publicized, concerns of critics of the policy's excessive
security emphasis, the package included $81 million for alternative
crop development and $122 million for both human rights support
and the judicial system.[80]

The legislation contained human rights conditions—chiefly
concerning the reported links between the Columbian armed forces
and paramilitary groups—that needed to be met before funding could,
in principle, be released. Yet at the first opportunity President Clinton
waived those requirements by declaring the situation in Colombia a
national security interest. That decision, and the waiver issue more
generally, has become one of the strongest areas of concern among
many in the U.S. human rights community who maintain that permitting the signing of a waiver essentially undermines the strength of
human rights conditionality as an effective policy tool. The subsequent
removal of the waiver provision did little to solve the problem, however. Cutting off U.S. security aid would be likely to make Colombia's

human rights situation even more critical. At the same time, Plan Colombia introduced more regular consultations between nongovernmental human rights organizations and relevant U.S. government officials about the country's progress in addressing human rights problems.

Still, even with the provisions for economic development and the strengthening of the rule of law, one of the main reservations about Plan Colombia remained that it was heavily skewed toward the military. It was also overwhelmingly an antidrug program, with a marked emphasis on the "push into southern Colombia," especially the Putumayo region, where coca production is highest. Not only did human rights organizations such as Amnesty International criticize the U.S.-backed plan, but so did the European Union, Colombia's neighbors, and some of the country's own citizens. A common complaint among Latin American governments and an array of Colombian nongovernmental organizations was that the Pastrana government failed to consult adequately with them beforehand and get their input in the process of policy formulation.

Even as Plan Colombia started to be implemented and bilateral relations grew significantly closer, President Pastrana's peace process with the FARC faltered. Pastrana's decision in November 1998 to cede a demilitarized zone (or *zona de distensión*) to the FARC as a way to advance peace negotiations ultimately proved unsuccessful. The FARC was accused of using the zone as a resupply-and-training area for combatants, and—amid rising violence—growing numbers of Colombians began wondering whether the country's strongest insurgency was really prepared and willing to negotiate in good faith. In February 2002, at the beginning of his last year in office, Pastrana, facing growing pressure, decided to take back the demilitarized zone and officially end the peace process.

The collapse of the Colombian peace talks with the FARC took place within a changed international context. The election of George W. Bush in November 2000 raised questions among many observers about how U.S. policy toward Colombia might change. In essence, though, there was more continuity than change. In an effort to counter some of the strong controversy that had been generated by Plan Colombia, especially among European and Latin American governments, the Bush administration in 2001 proposed the Andean

Regional Initiative, a $731 million proposal, of which $625 million was approved by Congress. This initiative, already contemplated under the Clinton administration, was more geographically balanced than Plan Colombia and directed a higher share of resources to Colombia's neighbors to help them deal with the "spillover effects" of the spreading conflict.

That the funds designated were more evenly distributed for both military and nonmilitary purposes also alleviated some of the sharp criticism that had been leveled against Plan Colombia. The final details of the package revealed considerable sensitivity and concern with human rights questions, as conditionalities of U.S. aid remained at the forefront of the public debate. Nonetheless, for most of 2001 U.S. policy toward Colombia remained squarely focused on the drug issue, as U.S. officials proposed various combinations of instruments and levels of resources to address the serious problem.

9/11 AND COLOMBIA

The terrorist attacks in New York and Washington on September 11, 2001, brought about a significant shift in the way that the United States viewed the Colombian conflict. Security concerns became paramount, and politically it became easier to make the case that U.S. resources should not be limited strictly to fighting drugs but instead could be used more broadly to assist the Colombian government contain the violence. In fact, just over a month after the attacks, U.S. ambassador Anne Patterson, invoking the discourse that especially resonated in Washington, characterized Plan Colombia as an "antiterrorist" policy. Indeed, even though before September 11 the FARC, ELN, and AUC appeared on the State Department's list of terrorist organizations (the AUC was included on September 10), the "antiterrorist" rationale had not dominated the U.S. policy justification until the attacks.

The antiterrorist justification for U.S. Colombia policy acquired even greater importance and momentum in light of the deteriorating security conditions within Colombia itself. Immediately after the collapse of talks between the Pastrana administration and the FARC on February 20, 2002, the Colombian president for the first time began to invoke the term "terrorist" to describe the insurgents. Before then, while peace talks were still alive, such a designation was deemed to be inappropriate. With Pastrana's changed rhetoric, and heightened frustration among most Colombians with the FARC's intransigence, many—even including some European governments—began to slowly accept the new discourse to describe Colombia's violent actors.

The striking coincidence of these developments both in the international context and within Colombia itself opened up an opportunity to shift the terms of U.S. aid to Colombia. As a result, the distinction between counternarcotics and counterinsurgency aid—a distinction that had long been drawn for political purposes but that had, in practice, become increasingly blurred—was essentially jettisoned. In a noteworthy departure in U.S. Colombia policy, in August 2002 Congress passed an emergency supplemental appropriations bill that lifted restrictions on U.S. security assistance and allowed the Colombian government to use funds directly in the armed conflict, to combat the FARC, ELN, and AUC. Even though human rights conditionality on the aid has been strictly maintained—and the Leahy Amendment still applies—many human rights groups have expressed serious concerns about such a policy shift, in light of the Colombian military's problematic human rights record and documented links with some paramilitary organizations.

Nonetheless, despite such reservations, the environment both in the United States and Colombia has, in the wake of the disappointments and frustrations with President Pastrana's fruitless peace effort, become increasingly hospitable to a stronger focus on the question of security. On August 7, 2002, Álvaro Uribe assumed the presidency in Colombia, buttressed by an overwhelming mandate to combat the country's violent actors. President Uribe has promised to deal with Colombia's insurgents and paramilitaries with a firm hand but in keeping with democratic principles and practice. His discourse has been favorably received by most Colombians, as well as by the U.S. government. Uribe's public support for the U.S. position in the Iraq war in March 2003—the only major South American leader to offer such support—further enhanced his stature in Washington.

To be sure, there are a number of important human rights concerns surrounding Uribe's proposals. His idea to set up a civilian force of one million Colombians, possibly armed, to cooperate with the military and police has generated the greatest controversy and will no doubt be subjected to considerable scrutiny. There is substantial nervousness that Uribe's state-of-emergency measures may disguise antidemocratic practices. The concern is that security issues will increasingly join drugs to further trump Colombia's compelling human rights agenda. In some sectors there is now a growing appetite for greater U.S. military support for Colombia on more flexible terms than prevailed in previous years. At the same time, however, among some other nongovernmental rights groups and members of the U.S. Congress, there is deepening concern about the direction of U.S. Colombia policy.

Despite his tough stand on Colombia's security challenges, Uribe has also called for the United Nations to play a role in mediating an end to the country's conflict. His objective is to create the conditions on the battlefield to make serious negotiations more likely. Though the United States continues to assist Colombia through considerable levels of aid, it is unclear to what extent there is an overall strategy aimed at supporting President Uribe's efforts to move toward greater security and peace. Such a strategy, together with applying the necessary pressure to keep human rights concerns high on the bilateral agenda, is essential. Despite a change of administration in Colombia and a new international climate shaped by September 11, mounting pressures and political activity mean that human rights issues will, of course, continue to influence U.S. policy on Colombia. The task is likely to be chiefly defensive, concentrating on questions of conditionality and monitoring the use of U.S. assistance.

POLICY CONTRADICTIONS

The rapid succession of developments in Colombia since the beginning of the Pastrana administration has resulted to a large extent in more lucid diagnoses, deeper concern, and greater attention among key United States government officials. Yet such concern and attention, however laudable, have not led to greater coherence in U.S. policy toward Colombia, and a political consensus for that policy does not seem any closer to being forged. In fact, developments in Colom-

bia since 1999 appear to have led to sharply conflicting policy proposals and prescriptions.

Despite congressional approval of Plan Colombia and the Andean
Regional Initiative, there still appears to be little agreement on a set of
fundamental questions: Where does Colombia fit among the diverse
foreign policy challenges facing the United States? What can the
United States realistically do to help Colombia? How far is the United
States prepared to go in backing the Uribe administration's approach
to ending the country's decades-long conflict? How long will it take
and how much will it cost? These are the basic questions about the
role the United States should play in the new world that is being significantly shaped by the tragic events of September 11, 2001. To date,
however, there have been few convincing answers to such questions.

At a more immediate, practical level, United States officials and
lawmakers must soon deal with a host of issues related to military aid
and drug policy. Where do human rights fit into support for Colombia's military? Will the underlying purpose of security support be posed
in terms of strictly "winning the war" or in terms of professionalizing
the country's armed forces with the longer-term aim of reaching a
political settlement? And should the United States continue to insist
on three key instruments—eradication, interdiction, and extradition—
in dealing with the drug challenge, or should more serious attention be
given to broader security, or development, aims, within a multilateral
framework? What are the human rights implications of such choices?

The U.S. government also must confront the manner in which it
deals with an international community increasingly concerned about
Colombia but unsure how best to act, if at all. It is noteworthy, but
hardly surprising (in light of the marked legacy of U.S. intervention
and the recent involvement in the Balkans), that many Latin Americans appear to be as worried about what the United States is planning
to do as they are about the deteriorating conditions in Colombia
itself. The 2003 Iraq war has only further heightened such concerns.

UN secretary-general Kofi Annan's appointment in December
1999 of a special envoy for Colombia and President Uribe's call for
UN mediation in 2002 add another interesting element to the mix,
posing an important challenge for the United States. If the United
States becomes even more involved in Colombia, will it be inclined

to act unilaterally or in conjunction with the relevant international organizations and its hemispheric neighbors? Experience and logic suggest that the efficacy of U.S. policy generally—and particularly on human rights questions—would be greatly enhanced through more coordinated, multilateral efforts with Colombia's neighbors.

For U.S. support to make a difference will require a much broader, longer-term strategy toward Colombia, one that goes substantially beyond the current emphasis on counternarcotics and, most recently, counterterrorism. A strong case can and should be made to the American people about why the United States needs to assign the Colombia issue highest priority. The risk is that whatever legislation is adopted in the short term will be viewed as having in some way "taken care of" the Colombia policy challenge—without facing the longer-term, higher-level responsibilities associated with such engagement. Stronger leadership, and a clearer articulation of what the United States hopes to achieve in Colombia, are crucial.

Further, for U.S. support to be effective will also require a clear demonstration of Colombians' will and commitment to do their part in carrying out policies aimed at improving the country's conditions related to security, human rights, narcotics, and the economy. Moreover, institutional corruption needs to be squarely and vigorously addressed. The election of Álvaro Uribe and his repeated commitment to addressing these issues open a window of opportunity in this regard. At the beginning of his term, Uribe commanded widespread support, and the levying of a "war tax" on wealthy Colombians appears to be a good sign in this direction. There is an opportunity for the U.S. government, together with Colombia's neighbors and international organizations, to play a more constructive role in attempting to shape the will and build the national commitment necessary to make progress on questions related to peace.

There is no question that in Washington, and throughout the United States, there is growing understanding of Colombia's multiple and immensely complicated problems. There is also ample goodwill and a disposition to help. It would, however, be a serious mistake to interpret the mere lifting of restrictions on U.S. aid or the passage of future assistance packages as reflecting a sufficiently clear consensus about how the United States can most productively engage

Colombia. More will be involved in successfully advancing national interests and goals such as the protection and promotion of human rights. There is, after all, a critical difference, too rarely recognized, between *instruments* of policies and the policies themselves.

The fundamental truth is that a lot more will unquestionably be required, not only from Washington and Bogotá, but also from European and other Latin American capitals. It is hard to see how progress can be made in dealing with Colombia's human rights and humanitarian crises without such collective and constructive engagement by external actors.

Notes

1. Indeed, in accordance with section 502B of the Foreign Assistance Act of 1961, delivery of U.S. foreign assistance is subject to approval based on a recipient country's human rights record. As such, three principles condition delivery of U.S. foreign assistance: first, aid must serve to increase the observance of internationally recognized human rights; second, no security assistance will be provided to any country that engages in a consistent pattern of gross violations of internationally recognized human rights; and third, the United States will fund only international security assistance programs that promote and advance human rights, thereby avoiding identification of the United States with governments that deny internationally recognized human rights and fundamental freedoms to their people. An annual review process headed by the secretary of state, with assistance from the coordinator of human rights affairs and nongovernmental organizations, identifies countries that meet the three conditions.

2. Bruce M. Bagley, "Colombia and the War on Drugs," *Foreign Affairs* (fall 1988): 78.

3. Russell Crandall, *Driven by Drugs: U.S. Policy toward Colombia* (Boulder, Colo.: Lynne Rienner Publishers, 2002), 26.

4. Stephen J. Randall, *Colombia and the United States: Hegemony and Interdependence* (Athens: University of Georgia Press, 1992), 247.

5. Bagley, "Colombia and the War on Drugs," 79–80.

6. Crandall, *Driven by Drugs*, 28.

7. Ibid., 27.

8. Ibid.; Bagley, "Colombia and the War on Drugs," 79.

9. Francisco Leal Buitrago, *Estado y Política en Colombia* (Bogotá: Siglo Veintiuno de Colombia, 1984), 266.

10. Human Rights Watch, *Colombia's Killer Networks* (New York: Human Rights Watch, 1996), 16.

11. Leal Buitrago, *Estado y Política en Colombia*, 270.

12. President Jimmy Carter, inaugural address, January 20, 1977.

13. Bagley, "Colombia and the War on Drugs," 80.

14. Ibid.

15. Human Rights Watch, *Colombia's Killer Networks*, 17.

16. Ibid., 17–18.

17. Juanita Darling and Ruth Morris, "Colombia: Concerns Grow about U.S. Military Aid to Colombia," *Los Angeles Times*, August 17, 1999.

18. Human Rights Watch, *Colombia's Killer Networks*, 18–19.

19. Randall, *Colombia and the United States*, 252–253.

20. Ibid., 253.

21. Bagley, "Colombia and the War on Drugs," 81.

22. Ibid.

23. Ibid., 83.

24. Crandall, *Driven by Drugs*, 29.

25. Bagley, "Colombia and the War on Drugs," 83.

26. Human Rights Watch, *Colombia's Killer Networks*, 20.

27. Crandall, *Driven by Drugs*, 33.

28. Human Rights Watch, *Colombia's Killer Networks*, 23–24.

29. Human Rights Watch, *The "Drug War" in Colombia* (New York: Human Rights Watch, 1990), 13–14.

30. Human Rights Watch, *Colombia's Killer Networks*, 25.

31. John P. Sweeney, *Tread Cautiously in Colombia's Civil War*, Backgrounder #1264 (Washington, D.C.: Heritage Foundation, March 25, 1999), appendix.

32. María Margarita Malagón, "Los Derechos Humanos en las Relaciones Estados Unidos-Colombia (1977–1997)," in *Estados Unidos, Potencia y Prepotencia,* ed. Luis Alberto Restrepo (Bogotá: Tercer Mundo, 1998), 123.

33. Sweeney, *Tread Cautiously in Colombia's Civil War*, appendix.

34. Ibid.

35. President George Bush, statement on U.S. Emergency Antidrug Assistance for Colombia (August 25, 1989).

36. Ibid.

37. Crandall, *Driven by Drugs*, 34.

38. Human Rights Watch, *State of War: Political Violence and Counterinsurgency in Colombia* (New York: Human Rights Watch, 1993), 131.

39. Ibid.

40. Peter Zirnite, "Militarization of the U.S. Drug Control Program," *In Focus* 3, no. 27 (September 1998).

41. "The Drug War: Colombia Is Implementing Antidrug Efforts, but Impact Is Uncertain," statement of Joseph E. Kelley, director-in-charge, international affairs issues, National Security and International Affairs Division, GAO/T-NSIAD-94-53 (October 5, 1993).

42. Human Rights Watch, *Colombia's Killer Networks*, 27.

43. Ibid., 28.

44. Ibid., 29.

45. Ibid., 3. In 1991 the United States increased its arms shipments to Colombia. The United States provided the Colombian military with 10,000 M-14 rifles; 700 M-16 rifles; 623 M-79 grenade launchers; 325 M-60 machine guns; 26,000 60 mm rifle grenades; 20,000 40 mm rifle grenades; 37,000 hand grenades; 3,000 Claymore mines; and approximately fifteen million rounds of rifle ammunition. Ibid., 4.

46. U.S. General Accounting Office, quoted in Human Rights Watch, *State of War*, 133.

47. Ibid., 134.

48. Ibid., 132.

49. Thomas McNamara, quoted in Washington Office on Latin America, *Clear and Present Dangers: The U.S. Military and the War on Drugs in the Andes* (Washington, D.C.: Washington Office on Latin America, October 1991), 52–53, and in Human Rights Watch, *State of War*, 132.

50. Human Rights Watch, *Colombia's Killer Networks*, 90. Weapons sales by U.S. firms included AR-15 rifles built by Colt Manufacturing Company in West Hartford, Connecticut. According to Human Rights Watch, those rifles had been used on a regular basis by paramilitary units in Colombia, even though the Colombian government had declared their use by civilians illegal.

51. U.S. General Accounting Office, *The Drug War: Colombia Is Undertaking Antidrug Programs, but Impact Is Uncertain* (Washington, D.C.: General Accounting Office, August 1993), 6.

52. Thomas P. Hamilton, counselor for political affairs, letter to *Americas Watch*, September 27, 1993, quoted in Human Rights Watch, *State of War*, 138.

53. Human Rights Watch, *State of War*, 138.

54. Lawyers Committee for Human Rights, *Colombia: Public Order, Private Injustice* (Washington, D.C.: Lawyers Committee for Human Rights, February 1994).

55. Human Rights Watch, *State of War*, 131.

56. Ibid., 138.

57. These included Mobile Brigade One and the Fourth Division in Meta; Third Brigade in Cali; Fourth Brigade in Medellín; Sixth Brigade in Ibagué; Eighth Brigade in Armenia, Valle; Ninth Brigade in Neiva; Eleventh Brigade in Antioquia; Sixteenth Brigade in Yopal and Arauca; and three Special Forces units. Human Rights Watch, *Colombia's Killer Networks*, 88.

58. Andrew Borowiec, "U.S. Called Partner in Colombian Murders," *Washington Times*, March 16, 1994, A1.

59. Washington Office on Latin America, *Losing Ground: Human Rights Advocates under Attack in Colombia* (Washington, D.C.: Washington Office on Latin America, October 1997), 34, 38.

60. Human Rights Watch, *Colombia's Killer Networks*, 76–77.

61. Ibid., 45.

62. Ibid., 46.

63. Ibid., 44.

64. Human Rights Watch, *War without Quarter* (New York: Human Rights Watch, 1998), 88.

65. Dana Priest, "U.S. May Boost Military Aid to Colombia's Anti-Drug Effort," *Washington Post*, March 28, 1998.

66. Douglas Farah, "U.S. to Aid Colombian Military; Drug-Dealing Rebels Take Toll on Army," *Washington Post*, December 27, 1998.

67. Diane Jean Shemo, "Congress Steps Up Aid for Colombians to Combat Drugs," *New York Times*, December 1, 1999.

68. Douglas Farah, "Pact Near on Aid to Colombia: Hill, White House Want $1 Billion-Plus for Anti-Drug Effort," *Washington Post*, October 9, 1999.

69. David Passage, *The United States and Colombia: Untying the Gordian Knot* (Carlisle Barracks, Pa.: U.S. Army War College, Strategic Studies Institute, 2000), 19–20.

70. General Accounting Office, *Drug Control: U.S. Assistance to Colombia Will Take Years to Produce Results* (Washington, D.C.: General Accounting Office, October 2000), 33.

71. Ibid.

72. Douglas Farah, "Colombian Rebels Tap E. Europe for Arms; Guerrillas' Firepower Superior to Army's," *Washington Post*, November 4, 1999.

73. General Accounting Office, *Drug Control: Narcotics Threat from Colombia Continues to Grow* (Washington, D.C.: General Accounting Office, June 1999), 21.

74. Harold Hongju Koh, assistant secretary for democracy, human rights, and labor, "Colombia: Bringing Human Rights at Home" (remarks made at the Conference on Human Rights in Colombia, Medellín, Colombia, April 10, 1999), discussed in Winifred Tate, *U.S. Human Rights Policy toward Colombia Advances* (Washington, D.C.: Washington Office on Latin America, 1999).

75. Ibid.

76. U.S. Department of State, *Human Rights Report for 1999—Colombia* (Washington, D.C.: Department of State, Bureau of Democracy, Human Rights and Labor, February 25, 2000).

77. U.S. Committee for Refugees, *Weekly Update: The Growing Threat for Civilians in Colombia,* December 31, 1999.

78. U.S. Central Intelligence, Crime and Narcotics Center, *Latin American Narcotics Cultivation and Production, Estimates 2001* (Washington, D.C.: U.S. Central Intelligence, Crime and Narcotics Center, March 2002).

79. Larry Rohter, "Colombia Tries, yet Cocaine Thrives" *New York Times,* November 20, 1999.

80. U.S. Department of State, Report to Congress, July 27, 2000; available online at www.ciponline.org/colombia.

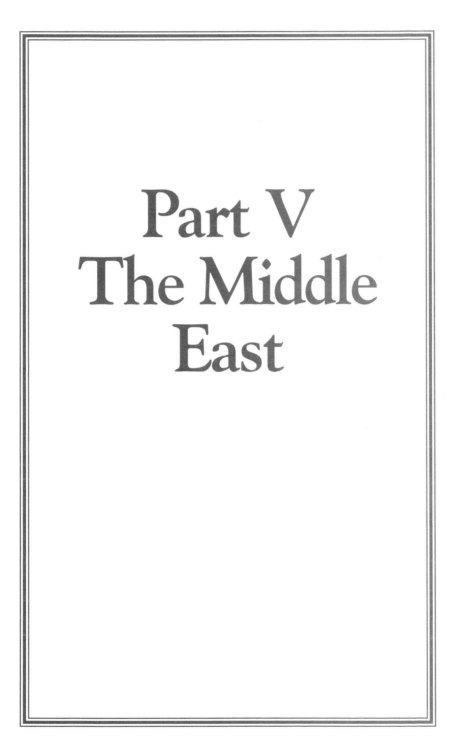

Part V
The Middle East

12

The United States, Turkey, and Human Rights Policy

Henri J. Barkey

MONG COUNTRIES WITH TROUBLESOME HUMAN RIGHTS and democratization records, Turkey occupies a unique place for U.S. policymakers. This is a close ally, a long-standing member of the NATO alliance, and a country whose relative strategic location and importance have increased considerably since the Soviet Union's demise. Perhaps perversely, Turkey's enhanced import has prevented the United States from constructing a policy with Turkey at its core. On any given day, U.S. diplomats confront challenges, often only indirectly related to Turkey proper, necessitating close interactions with their Turkish counterparts. In this context, these diplomats can perceive issues of democratization and human rights as "unwelcome" intrusions and even counterproductive to their essential mission: maintenance of the strategic relationship. Yet, in part because of the heightened sensitivity to such human rights–related issues in the post–Cold War environment, the Turkish record on human rights tends to cast a shadow over U.S.-Turkish relations. The overwhelming amount of evidence of abuses, compiled by the State Department in its own annual human rights reports, domestic pressures coming from the NGO community and others, and the perception that a U.S. official ought not remain unconcerned about such abuses by an ally have forced Washington to frequently express disquiet and offer criticisms. Because such criticisms often elicit negative responses from Ankara, creating a dynamic of their own, Turkey's human rights record directly intrudes into the making of U.S. foreign policy.

In general, though allowing for stylistic differences, U.S. administrations have preferred to pursue "quiet diplomacy," arguing that confrontations with Turkish officialdom do not advance the cause of human rights and, to the contrary, force the Turks to "circle the wagons" and ignore U.S. requests. The overall focus, therefore, has been on creating a workable balance between the advocacy of democratization and the pursuit of fundamental "strategic interests." Included in this policy are the encouragement of civil society groups to push for democratization and the strengthening of institutional structures and mechanisms capable of improving human rights monitoring. Similarly, the United States has supported Turkish efforts at becoming a candidate for membership in the European Union while being fully cognizant that fulfilling accession requirements would fundamentally alter the nature of Turkey. Nonetheless, as will be demonstrated later, this policy approach has not impeded the emergence of high-profile disagreements between the two countries.

Despite the closeness of the U.S.-Turkish relationship, successive governments in Ankara have always harbored deep suspicions of U.S. intentions. This is due in part to the general misgivings Turks have held over the role foreign powers are said to have played in the dissolution of the Ottoman Empire and more recently over actions such as the U.S. Congress's decision to impose an arms embargo in 1975 after Turkey's invasion of Cyprus a year earlier. Although the embargo was never supported by Republican or Democratic administrations and was lifted in 1978, the damage was done. Since then, congressional and administration scrutiny of U.S. arms exports because of the Aegean conflict or human rights considerations has further contributed to Ankara's unease.

From a human rights perspective, the 1990s were a particularly trying period. Two domestic challenges, which Ankara clearly perceived as existential ones to the regime—namely, the Kurdish insurrection and Islamic revivalism—gave rise to significant human rights abuses and restrictions on basic individual freedoms, especially that of thought. Precisely because the threat was defined as existential, the Turkish state became impervious to external criticisms and was mostly unwilling to heed the advice of anyone.

This chapter focuses primarily on the Clinton administration's tenure and assesses U.S. intentions, objectives, tactics, and achievements from the narrow perspective of human rights. This narrow perspective cannot, of course, be accomplished without a discussion of the setting of U.S.-Turkish relations and the interplay of other policy concerns and objectives. The aim of this chapter, however, is not to offer a detailed analysis of the broader setting but rather to provide an overview.[1]

THE STRATEGIC CONTEXT

During the Cold War, Turkey's relationship with the United States was framed by the NATO alliance and the confrontation with the USSR.[2] The 1979 Islamic revolution in Iran and the Soviet invasion of Afghanistan further enhanced Turkey's strategic importance. Such concerns led the United States to mute its criticisms of the Turkish generals' September 1980 overthrow of the government. The coup was a reaction to a protracted period of domestic political impasse, economic paralysis, and internecine and sectarian violence that caused serious concerns regarding the very stability of the regime in Ankara. Outsiders perceived the 1980 military coup, the third in a series of interventions, as necessary if order was to be reestablished. The generals' rule gave way to a controlled and tutelary democratic process. While the military continued to have an important and even a determining voice, Turkey under Turgut Özal, who became prime minister in 1983 and president in 1989, took strides toward opening up first the economic and then the political systems. In addition to economic liberalization, perhaps Özal's other most important accomplishment was to begin a short-lived process of civilianizing the military. On the foreign policy side, Özal's decision to back the U.S.-led alliance against Iraq in 1990, despite opposition at home, including from the military, earned him and Turkey a great deal of praise and appreciation from Washington.

The Post–Cold War Era

The demise of the Soviet Union unambiguously altered basic U.S. calculations regarding the purposes of the NATO alliance, the importance of military bases, and the United States as a frontline state. In the absence of an enemy, the United States and indeed Western policy in the 1990s became primarily reactive, extinguishing regional fires and challenges while searching for an overarching purpose to foreign policy. The Clinton administration's initial and perhaps most enduring focus was on managing globalization, largely defined as ensuring political stability to integrate newly independent countries and others into the international market. In this mixed strategic environment, Ankara's strategic location abutting on the unstable Caucasus, the Middle East, the Balkans, and especially Iraq and Iran, together with its potential influence in Central Asia, increased its *relative* importance. In comparison, Greece, Turkey's traditional nemesis, could offer a stabilizing role only in the Balkans.

Washington's reliance on Ankara increased, as seen in its willingness to support the construction of oil and gas pipelines from the Caspian Sea basin through Turkey to the Mediterranean, an endeavor with a triple purpose: to create alternative routes to Iran and Russia for the export of hydrocarbons, to enhance Turkey's role as a conduit for oil while providing it with foreign exchange, and to give support to the newly independent states of Central Asia and the Caucasus. Özal's economic reforms in the 1980s had transformed Turkey into a potential regional power and serious market for U.S. goods and investments.

U.S. policy toward Turkey, reflecting the uncertainties of the post–Cold War era and regional concerns over Iraq, the rest of the Middle East, the Balkans, the Caucasus, and Central Asia, was pulled in many different directions. In addition, Washington continued to be apprehensive of domestic problems in Turkey, especially after President Özal's death in 1993, when Turkish policies at home became increasingly erratic. Weak governments, civil-military strife, and a violent Kurdish insurrection accentuated economic difficulties. Faced with this plethora of issues, U.S. diplomats struggled to support Turkey while ensuring that it remained on course with U.S. initiatives and concerns. To encourage increased bilateral trade and commercial relations, Turkey was included in the list of the ten Big Emerging Markets (BEMs), which included the likes of South Korea, Brazil, Mexico, Indonesia, and India. As the decade of the 1990s came to a close, the United States became even more proactive in these efforts. Perhaps the most important policy initiative was to support Turkey's candidacy for membership in the European Union. In 1997 at their Luxembourg Summit, EU members refused even to admit Turkey into the waiting room, while many other countries, ranging from Cyprus to Malta and Slovenia, were given the green light. This led to a serious crisis in Turkish-EU relations, and the Clinton administration spared no effort to get the Europeans to reverse their decision. The crowning achievement for many U.S. diplomats was the European Union's 1999 Helsinki Summit decision, which, after an intense administration-led lobbying effort, opened the way for Turkey's candidacy.

Iraq and Operation Northern Watch

Throughout the 1990s Turkey's most important contribution to U.S. policy interests was in Iraq, the scene of the first major post–Cold War confrontation. By maintaining a no-fly zone over northern Iraq, U.S. and British planes based at the Incirlik air force base near Adana, as part of what was called Operation Northern Watch (ONW), provided the U.S. administration with one of its most effective tools for containing the regime in Baghdad. ONW and its southern counterpart, Operation Southern Watch, put continuous real and psychological pressure on Saddam Hussein's regime. More important, ONW ensured that the Kurds in northern Iraq could continue to live in a de facto autonomous and protected zone. The operation represented both a U.S. commitment to the Kurds and Washington's way of making amends for having abandoned them in the aftermath of the Persian Gulf War, when Saddam Hussein's troops, taking advantage of U.S. inaction, severely dealt with the rebellious Kurds. It would not be an exaggeration to argue that without ONW, Washington's Iraq policy could have collapsed. The waning popularity of the U.S.-led sanctions policy at the end of the 1990s helped further enhance Turkey's relative importance in preserving the containment policy.

ONW and its predecessor, Operation Provide Comfort (OPC), were never popular in Turkey. The 1990–91 Gulf War coincided with the most explosive stage of an insurrection by Turkey's own Kurds in the southeastern provinces adjacent to northern Iraq. Even before the Gulf War, and with Baghdad's consent, the Turkish military regularly crossed the border into Iraq to conduct hot-pursuit operations to capture Kurdish insurgents seeking refuge there. The failure of the Iraqi Kurdish insurrection in 1991 created a humanitarian nightmare—close to five hundred thousand Kurds sought refuge on the Turkish border and another million did so on the Iranian side. This crisis was relieved only when OPC came into existence. Ankara was uneasy about the demonstration effect on its own Kurdish minority of the autonomous Iraqi Kurdish entity that formed on Turkey's borders and was receiving direct support from the United States. As a result, until the mid-1990s the renewal of OPC was a difficult process that required parliamentary approval in Turkey and often necessitated voluminous U.S. lobbying.[3]

To be sure, this has not been a one-sided relationship. Although the United States relied heavily on Turkey for its Iraq policy, did Turkey really have an alternative? What would have been the cost to Turkey in Washington had Ankara pulled the plug on OPC and ONW? Ankara was also well aware that Washington's predicament in Iraq made the United States dependent on Ankara and, therefore, that it had been dealt a very rich hand. Yet this was a double-edged sword: if Ankara had not approved OPC and ONW, a return of Saddam to northern Iraq could have resulted in a repeat of the 1991 refugee crisis and the backlash against Turkey in Washington could have had a debilitating effect on the bilateral relationship.[4]

Fear of Instability in Turkey

Given Turkey's geostrategic location, the maintenance of domestic stability in Turkey has been a critical goal for Washington. An economically and politically unstable Turkey can either export its own problems or exacerbate existing ones among its neighbors. Turkey has served as an anchor among the many troublesome regions it straddles, and a weak unstable regime in Ankara potentially can have a deleterious impact on U.S. interests.

In the 1990s, Özal's wide-ranging economic reforms of the previous decade notwithstanding, years of mismanaging Turkish politics gave rise to the emergence of two significant problems that would have a bearing on human rights and democratization questions in Turkey. These were the Kurdish insurrection in the southeast and the rise of the Islamist Welfare Party. They raised serious concerns about Ankara's ability to manage significant challenges to its rule through peaceful and constitutional means. The Kurdish insurrection, led by the Kurdish Workers Party (PKK), almost took the form of a civil war, forcing Ankara to dispatch well over two hundred thousand troops to the region, causing large numbers of casualties, and creating a terrible financial burden. In addition, the insurrection threatened regional relations in view of Syria's and Iran's support for the PKK and domestic stability, with violence potentially spreading from the southeast throughout Turkey.

The other important development, the rise to power of the Islamist-led coalition government in 1996, provoked a crisis that pitted more conservative and religious forces against an array of secularist counterparts and their military allies dead set against any compromise with forces of "reaction." The ensuing confrontation culminated with the forcible resignation of the government in 1997 in what many observers called a "stealth" or "postmodern" coup d'état. The military working with the new "secularist" government and the judiciary imposed a series of tough restrictions on freedom of speech and political activity.

U.S. officials, while unsympathetic to the demands of Kurdish and Islamist extremists, were alarmed by the means the state employed to deal with the threats the extremists posed. Many in the United States felt that these means, including the use of massive force, extra-constitutional measures, and the suppression of free speech, not only put into question the ability of Turkey's leadership to manage change and challenges but also seemed to exacerbate the problems rather than resolve them. Thus, instability in Turkey undermined other aspects of the U.S.-Turkish relationship, including arms sales. Strobe Talbott, then deputy secretary of state, articulated this worry when he argued that "we believe that limiting avenues for legitimate political activity—whether by putting people on trial or in jail for what they write or say or by banning political parties or by shutting down NGOs —carries with it the risk of an unintended consequence: It may turn moderates into extremists, who will then provoke further curtailment of freedom and undermine the health of democracy itself."[5]

The Human Rights Environment in Turkey

In the late 1980s and early 1990s, the human rights environment deteriorated rapidly, first with the advent of the Kurdish insurgency and then with Islamist revivalism. These events challenged Turkey's very organization as a secular, ethnically homogenous, and territorially united entity. The Turkish state's reaction was uncompromising. As Kenan Evren, leader of the 1980 military coup and president of the republic until 1989, once told his prime minister, Özal, the army was unlikely to get involved in overthrowing governments except as a result of "either the Islamic or Kurdish questions."[6]

A great deal of the state's reaction to the Kurdish insurrection was conditioned by age-old policies and attitudes to the Kurds and the southeast, which, in turn, caused it to mismanage the conflict from the outset. The Kurds, an estimated 20 percent of the Turkish population, had historically chosen different routes to integration into the majority Turkish republic.[7] While some willingly assimilated, others chose the pathway of minimum resistance by maintaining a sense of inner identity and others simply resisted, peacefully or violently over the years.

As far as the state was concerned, the Kurds had been relegated to a nonexistent status. The Turkish establishment—civilian, bureaucratic, and military—viewed the primarily Kurdish southeast and east as a backwater worthy only for exiled officials, be they teachers, policemen, or any other type of civil servant. With few attachments or links to the southeast, those officials appointed by the central government to these regions perceived the resident Kurds as a potential threat, an attitude that would prepare the groundwork for the massive abuses of human rights to come later. When the PKK began its operations in the southeast in 1984, first by attacking other Kurds, local villagers often were the first to seek protection and support from security officials against the terrorists' activities. Within a few years the tables would be turned on the same security forces: abuses of the region's inhabitants through the use of torture and village evacuations alienated the population from the state while the PKK won more adherents. This involvement of Turkish officials, whether local administrators, special police squads, the gendarmerie, or the local judiciary as well as their higher-ups in Ankara, in the Kurdish issue made it difficult for the United States not to criticize Ankara publicly and privately. What made matters worse was the determination of Turkish authorities to make peaceful political protest and organization also illegal. As a result, pro-Kurdish political parties are to this day routinely harassed and banned and parliamentarians imprisoned.

As far as human rights abuses in the southeast were concerned, there was a marked improvement after the capture of the PKK leader Abdullah Öcalan in February 1999 and his subsequent call for his fighters to leave Turkey and put an end to the "armed struggle." This capped a successful Turkish counterinsurgency campaign that had also worn down the people of the southeast, who experienced a decade and a half of upheaval in their daily lives, rapidly declining economic conditions, and internal migration that overwhelmed the local cities.

Turkey's Islamist problem has its roots in the creation of the republic, when the new leaders decided to impose a strict secular system that aimed at putting religion under the control of the state. While the secular state never attempted to deny access to religion, it did try to enforce rules and regulations regarding dress codes, membership in secretive religious orders that had prevailed since A.D. 1000, and political speech. In its current form, Islamism is not only a reaction to these restrictions but also a by-product of the inability of traditional mainstream political parties to address the day-to-day concerns of ordinary citizens laboring under difficult, if not sometimes impossible, economic conditions.

Ever since the 1970s an Islamist party had operated on the Turkish political scene, even taking part in governing coalitions. The shock for the authorities came when the latest incarnation, the Welfare Party, won a plurality of the votes and hence the largest block of parliamentarians in the December 1995 elections. This success was followed by the creation of a coalition government with a center-right secular party that allowed for the assumption of the prime ministry by the bête noire of Turkish politics, Necmettin Erbakan.[8] What ensued was a period of protracted conflict between state institutions, including the military and the judiciary, in alliance with secular civil society organizations and a variety of culturally conservative and/or Islamic groups

and parties and their allies. In a February 28, 1997, showdown
between the government and the military members of the National
Security Council, the officers imposed a series of onerous conditions
on the government coalition that eventually ended with its dissolution.
The Welfare Party was banned (as was its successor in 2001) and many
Islamist writers, journalists, politicians, and even businessmen faced
prosecution for speech-related crimes. Among the most celebrated was
the then popular mayor of Istanbul, Recep Tayyip Erdogan, who was
forced to resign and later imprisoned. The state, often prodded by the
military or others, pursued a policy of harassing its opponents through
the use of the judicial system.

The Domestic Institutional Framework

Turkey's human rights performance has been determined by two sets
of institutional influences. The first is the legal system. Turkey is a
country of laws, where magistrates and prosecutors routinely apply
laws that impede the right to free speech and political opposition. At
the root of the legal system is the military-inspired 1982 constitution,
which narrowly defines what is acceptable and what is not. Turkish
prosecutors have selectively and liberally applied loosely worded provisions in the law to prosecute journalists, politicians, political parties, NGOs, and political activists for "thought" crimes.[9] This has had
a chilling effect on the media as well as on political activity. Many
journalists, academics, and political activists have been deterred by
the constant legal harassment they and their colleagues have been
subjected to over the years. In effect, the state has created a multitude
of institutional structures, such as State Security Courts, to protect
itself from its citizens. The second institutional development has
been the growing role and influence of the military establishment in
the political process, with the lines of authority between the military
and the civilian government becoming increasingly blurred in the
1990s. Two reasons account for this development. First, ever since the
first military coup in 1960, the possibility of another coup has haunted
the Turkish political scene and its politicians. The 1960 coup opened
a Pandora's box of sorts by creating the expectation that political
stalemates could always be resolved through a military intervention.
This subtle psychological influence has helped the military keep its

traditional immunity from parliamentary oversight and severely curtail its accountability. The 1971 and 1980 coups have only reinforced this perception. Moreover, the Turkish military, unlike its counterparts in the Western world, has a specific ideological mission. It perceives itself as the defender of the legacy of modern-day Turkey's founder, Mustafa Kemal Ataturk, a legacy often referred to as Kemalism. This provides the military with an added element of coherence, corporate unity, and source of strength. The long Kurdish insurgency, by necessitating a military campaign, has also contributed to the growing influence of the officer corps.

The second reason is that the officer corps has institutionalized its power through constitutional means. The 1960 constitution and its 1982 successor have enshrined the role of the military through the creation of the National Security Council (NSC), a body composed of acting senior officers and members of the government. The NSC acts as an institutionalized conveyor belt for the senior officers' preferences who make up the Turkish General Staff. In fact, the crises over the Kurdish question and the Islamists demonstrated that military influence does not emanate solely from the NSC but rather from all echelons of its General Staff. It was the deputy chief of staff who orchestrated the campaign against the Islamist-led coalition government in 1997. In effect, the generals have stepped into a vacuum created by a weak and ineffective political leadership accustomed to deferring to the Turkish General Staff's wishes. The resulting real and de facto prominence of the military hierarchy has created an added layer of impediments to both reform efforts and attempts at influencing developments in Turkey from abroad.

U.S. POLICY TOWARD TURKEY

The Decision-Making Environment in Washington

As with every other policy issue in any administration, U.S. human rights policy reflects a balance between and within external and internal actors and forces. On the external side the most prominent are the U.S. Congress and its committees, ethnic- and issue-based lobbies and NGOs, and other interested groups, such as individual companies or business associations. Internally, pressure originates from the interplay of the bureaucratic politics within the administration, which pits bureaus and agencies with differing agendas against one another. In the case of Turkey, the very complexity of the geostrategic concerns as well as the multiplicity of areas of interaction between the United States and Turkish governments has had a direct impact on the saliency of the human rights agenda.

Ever since the 1975 arms embargo on Turkey, Congress has taken a great deal of interest in all matters Turkish. Responding to different constituencies, individual lawmakers have championed a wide variety of causes, often to the great annoyance of Ankara, although the latter has engaged lobbying firms to do its bidding and respond to what it perceives as hostility in Congress.[10] As the amount of aid provided to Turkey has dwindled with time, Congress's only source of influence has been its oversight of arms sales to Turkey. Over the years, the administration has come under fire for acquiescing to numerous Turkish arms requests. Occasionally, the prospect of intense opposition from Congress, as well as from within the administration itself, has forced the U.S. government to deny certain types of ammunition. In 1996 congressional opposition even forced Ankara to rescind its request for Cobra attack helicopters. Similarly, Ankara turned down a modest aid package in 1998 because of human rights conditions attached by Congress. Other provisions, unrelated to Turkey, enacted into law have also allowed Congress to indirectly exercise a certain degree of control. For instance, the Leahy Amendment to a 1996 law, which prohibits funding units of the security forces involved in human rights violations, became a major stumbling block in the sale of armored personnel vehicles to Turkey in 1999. Although the State Department had issued an export license, the Leahy Amendment prohibited the use of U.S. loan guarantees, which proved almost to be a deal breaker.[11]

Two ethnic lobbies of Armenian and Greek Americans have been particularly effective in militating against Turkey. Both lobbies and their constituencies try to maintain pressure on Ankara either to seek Turkish recognition of the Armenian massacres at the beginning of the twentieth century or to redress the results of the 1974 Turkish invasion of Cyprus.[12] On the surface, these lobbies are motivated by interests that have little to do with the current state of human rights in

Turkey. Armenian Americans are also interested in pursuing policies supporting Armenia's territorial dispute with its Turkey-supported neighbor, Azerbaijan. In addition to Cyprus, Greek Americans are concerned about demarcation of the Aegean Sea and claims between Greece and Turkey over the continental shelf. Turkey's poor human rights record, Ankara's general reluctance to address it, and the general perception that generals play an inordinately important role in the governance of Turkish affairs have helped these lobbies make their case for their own interests.[13]

The concentration of Greek and Armenian Americans in critical electoral states such as New York, New Jersey, and California is what gives them clout. The nascent Turkish American community pales in comparison to the other two in sheer number, organizational skills, and, therefore, clout. Turkey, with its burgeoning military and economic ties to Israel, has countered by attempting to gain the support of the pro-Israeli organizations and lobbies in Washington. This has been partially successful, although American Jewish organizations are unlikely to completely run afoul of other ethnic-based interest groups with which they have closely collaborated over many years. By the end of the Clinton administration, the tide had shifted in Washington. Miscues by the Greek government, especially on combating terrorism, greater appreciation of Turkey's strategic importance, beginning reforms in Turkey, rapprochement between Greece and Turkey, and heavy administration lobbying in this regard have all helped Turkey's image in Congress.

With the end of the Cold War, the protection that the U.S. struggle against the Soviet Union provided Turkey has disappeared. This in turn has encouraged NGOs working to improve human rights —ranging from Human Rights Watch to Amnesty International—to direct more of their energies toward Turkey. Not only have they helped local Turkish NGOs work under difficult circumstances, but they also have been a major source of information for both the U.S. government and Congress. NGOs have mobilized significant resources, employed professional staffs, and conducted studies that either brought new information to the public debate or buttressed evidence collected by other sources. Their influence has been noted by the likes of the State Department, which felt the need to include them, together with manufacturers, in its deliberations on Turkish plans to purchase attack helicopters. It is easy to overestimate the importance of the NGOs, but different administrations have forged ties with different segments of the human rights NGO community. Whereas Republican lawmakers and administrations may be more inclined to listen to NGOs critical of traditional foes of the United States such as Cuba, Sudan, and China, their Democratic counterparts are generally more sensitive to a wider range of cases, including those of close allies such as Turkey.[14] This is why for these NGOs, the proposed $3.5 billion sale of 145 attack helicopters became a litmus test of the Clinton administration's willingness to pursue a human rights agenda not just with respect to Turkey but also beyond. In the end, the Clinton administration decided to pursue the sale. The Turkish government, ironically, was not sufficiently convinced of the administration's commitment and decided to delay its decision until after the 2000 presidential election.

Turkey, despite its impressive economic reforms in the 1980s, has yet to attract significant quantities of U.S. foreign investment. Much of this inability can be attributed to protectionist investment laws, most of which are in the process of being modified, and chronically high rates of inflation. To date, the exception has been the energy services companies and arms manufacturers. Until 2000, the growing economy and population base had made an attractive market for U.S. energy companies seeking to build power plants and other forms of energy infrastructure. Also, at a time when worldwide defense expenditures were declining in the 1990s, Turkey embarked on an ambitious military modernization drive that promised to cost as much as $31 billion in the short run and almost $150 billion over a thirty-year window. In effect, Turkey transformed itself overnight into potentially one of the most lucrative markets for armaments exporters, and one that no U.S. policymaker could ignore. Some of the anticipated near-term contracts included attack helicopters ($3.5 billion), tanks ($7 billion), and AWACS ($1 billion). Not surprisingly, U.S. military contractors extensively lobbied the administration to ease up on the conditions attached to the granting of export licenses, especially those conditions related to human rights. However, faced with two severe economic crises in November 2000 and February 2001, Turkey has had to immediately put much of its arms purchases on hold, as much as

$19 billion, according to some reports. Unlike the Chinese, who c
count on blue-chip U.S. firms to support them in Congress at critical
junctures, there is no U.S. manufacturing or other industry support
group willing to mobilize to support Turkey in the U.S. Congress.

Still, Turkey is not without its defenders. Although it does not
have a large and well-established ethnic community in the United
States to provide it with the equivalent electoral clout some of its principal and traditional detractors or adversaries have had, Ankara can
rely on the U.S. government to act as its foremost supporter. Despite
the absence of electoral considerations and the difficulties often posed
by Turkish diplomacy, the strategic attributes of Turkey, its geopolitical
environment, and the accumulated memories of past cooperation have
contributed to the emergence of a pro-Turkish bias within successive
administrations. Perhaps the most emblematic event of the Clinton
years occurred during the president's trip to Greece and Turkey in
November 1999. He not only spent five days among the Turks and at
the OSCE Summit and was well received in Turkey but also had to curtail his subsequent trip to Athens, where he was met by violent demonstrators angry at the U.S. role during the Kosovo crisis.

The pro-Turkish bias had been strongest, as expected, within the
Department of Defense, where the connections between officers have
been of long standing. Similarly, elsewhere in the government a great
deal of familiarity and ease comes with having worked together. For
many diplomats, Turkey is a prized post; it is an important and active
account in ways in which Spain or Portugal and many other "desirable
posts" are not. Moreover, U.S. officials have never made a secret of
their preference for the Turkish secular and Western-oriented model
as one to be emulated by Muslim countries, especially Arab ones,
even though the Arab world has always chafed at this comparison.

Within the Turkish government, the very existence of the annual
human rights reports prepared by the State Department's Bureau of
Democracy, Human Rights, and Labor (DRL) creates a dynamic that
is difficult to ignore. The human rights reports, prepared with great
diligence and often after protracted bureaucratic battles between U.S.
embassies, regional bureaus, and DRL, have become a reference source
for NGOs, Congress, lobbies, and officials. When the evidence appears
to be damning and incontrovertible, it can potentially embarrass the

U.S. government and undermine the implementation of related policies. But DRL's influence, especially in cases involving U.S. allies, is relatively weak.

Bureaucratically speaking, it is the geographically organized regional bureaus that are entrusted with the day-to-day implementation of policy.[15] Unlike with cases such as China, where most of the U.S. bureaucracy and public opinion are unsympathetic to the Beijing government, U.S. desk officers, regional bureau directors, and embassy personnel have a great deal to gain from smooth relations with their allies, even problematic ones. Understandably, human rights reports or requests to deliver démarches to countries for behaving poorly against their own citizens upset this relationship and, therefore, are resisted by the diplomats. For the individual Foreign Service officer, a tour in DRL is not seen as a career-enhancing prospect. Complicating matters also is the fact that, unlike the DRL officer, for whom there is one primary concern, the regional desk or embassy officer has to balance a series of concerns, relationships, and demands. Human rights are rarely the issue that makes the top of the list. Often, DRL officials find that promises made to them regarding the implementation of specific policies are undercut by their counterparts in the regional bureaus who have so many more levers to play with. Finally, as former U.S. ambassador to Turkey Morton Abramowitz admits, Turkey is one of the few countries where the U.S. ambassador exerts "real and a continued influence in Washington" in large measure because of the complexity of the country's internal politics and the general lack of knowledge among senior U.S. officials of that country.[16] Ambassadors not only communicate extensively with Washington but also have the ability to shape the kind of information their embassies produce, highlight, or simply report.

U.S. Policy Objectives

How important are democratization and improved human rights in Turkey as policy objectives for the United States? There are countries with much worse human rights records than Turkey's, but the fact remains that in Turkey, a long-standing NATO ally, abuses have had a different kind of resonance, amplified perhaps by the end of the Cold War. The abuses clash with the democratization image and policies the United States had tried to project around the world during the Clinton years.[17] Although questions of democratization and human rights abuses in Turkey, an ally, do not engender the same passion that guides policymakers in their approach to countries with which the United States has an adversarial relationship, these issues cannot be ignored either. In addition to responding to purely U.S. domestic interests, U.S. policymakers are spurred on in their concern for developments in Turkey by their own calculations of U.S. self-interest. What do problems of democratization and human rights implementation say about the country's economic and political stability, the functioning of its institutions, its future reliability as a partner of the United States, the possible demonstration effect on the remainder of the region, and its ability to achieve its own goals?

Washington's primary objective has been to foster stability, democratic governance, and prosperity in its ally. It has not, however, viewed this goal as a mission to single-handedly transform the country and its institutions. The overall strategy can be distilled into a two-prong process: a push on domestic issues, primarily to address Ankara's democratic deficit and its inadequate economic policies and structures, and help for Turkey in improving its external security environment. In this context, human rights considerations are part of a pragmatic calculation. The more democratic and respectful of human rights Ankara is, the less problematic its relationship with Washington will likely be. Clearly, a democratic Turkey respectful of its citizens' rights can facilitate closer collaboration, avoid protracted battles for arms sales, and limit the influence of the different lobbies operating in Congress and the public. Moreover, such a Turkey is also viewed to stand a greater chance at gaining admission into the European Union. This policy can best be summarized as "helping Turks help themselves."

Ironically, the strong support the United States offered Turkey in its quest to become a candidate for EU admission marked, at least indirectly, a shift in the policy that the United States should avoid trying to rearrange Turkey's internal institutions. Support for the European Union's stringent qualifying conditions immediately meant that the United States wanted to see a wholesale transformation of Turkey, and quickly. Adhering to the candidacy process also meant that, in exchange for a more prosperous future, any candidate country had to adhere to the strict Copenhagen criteria, which laid out definite rules regarding democracy and respect for human rights. In short, a Turkey deserving of admission into the European Union would naturally have to be very different from today's Turkey. All of its institutions, the constitution, the roles of the military and the judiciary, and the relationship between the state and the individual would have to be redefined to fit the European mold. The process envisaged for Turkey is not different from the one that helped Greece, Spain, and Portugal make their transition from being authoritarian regimes to being democratic and economically sound societies. It has never been clear whether Turkey will be able to institute all the changes Europe requires or, for that matter, whether the Europeans will be ready to incorporate the most populous candidate nation. The result of encouraging EU membership is that a significant share of the burden for improving economic, political, and human rights conditions has been transferred onto the shoulders of the Europeans.

Policy Implementation

The modus operandi of the Clinton administration was engagement.[18] Even if improving human rights in Turkey was not a priority, but rather an attempt to eliminate or reduce an irritant in bilateral relations, Washington sought different avenues to accomplish this goal. The policy outcome was necessarily complex, fractured, contradictory, and prone to misunderstandings.

Human rights–related policy actions took four different forms: (1) public diplomacy, (2) quiet diplomacy, (3) carrots and sticks, and (4) support for institution building. These, of course, are not mutually exclusive categories, and a significant degree of natural overlap exists between them.

PUBLIC DIPLOMACY. Public diplomacy, or rhetoric, is probably the most common method of attracting attention to problems of democratization and human rights violations. Washington's public rhetoric has gained in importance commensurately with its enhanced stature in the era of globalization. When public rhetoric is sometimes accompanied by concrete and symbolic actions, it further focuses the attention, making the message difficult to ignore. With Turkey and other countries, the most commonly used public means to relay messages are the daily briefings of the State Department spokesperson, the annual human rights reports, and statements by administration principals. Public statements, just like policy, reflect compromises struck by different parts of the bureaucracy and, especially in such highly visible cases as the closing down of a party or imprisonment of a noted dissident, there is tremendous pressure to be consistent. In other words, the State Department cannot ignore the banning of a party in one country and not in another because U.S. public discourse faces intense scrutiny by an army of journalists. Even when the State Department would rather not comment on a specific event or decision, it is forced to prepare itself for questioning by journalists. The process of preparing "press guidance" is an arduous task on its own that often chews up, especially in controversial cases, many man hours and literally is not resolved until the spokesperson steps onto the podium.

The United States has frequently made use of the different forms of public diplomacy to criticize or congratulate the Turkish authorities on specific actions. Although the Turkish government may downplay such public statements if it finds them inconvenient, the fact of the matter is that they are rarely ignored. Statements tend to be dissected and analyzed not just by the government but also by those who view themselves as the victims.

Strong U.S. criticism of the closure of the Welfare Party, for instance, struck a chord among that party's supporters, primarily because Washington and a few European capitals denounced the move, whereas most Muslim countries remained silent.[19] At other times, the United States has chosen to stress its displeasure with a symbolic action. When Recep Tayyip Erdogan was sentenced to prison and a lifetime ban from participation in politics for reading a poem by a nationalist Turkish poet of the early Republican period, the U.S. consul general in Istanbul visited the popular mayor in his office. The visit caused an uproar; the United States was accused of interfering in the domestic affairs of the country.

The State Department's annual human rights reports remain Washington's primary weapon in seeking improved observance of human rights because, as suggested earlier, the reports serve as a reference point for anyone who wants to look into abuses in a specific place. With close allies such as Turkey, U.S. criticisms in the human rights report tend to have significantly more impact, perhaps because many assume that Washington would naturally want to go easier on a friend than on a foe.

Other forms of public rhetoric have included speeches by leading members of the administration or by United States diplomats stationed in Turkey. The frequency with which they make such speeches varies from individual to individual. For instance, when he was ambassador to Ankara, Marc Grossman, while stressing all aspects of the U.S.-Turkish relationship, made a point of reiterating often that most of Turkey's problems "would be resolved by the expansion of democracy" and not by imposing new limits on speech. This formulation was later incorporated into the State Department's press guidance regarding human rights concerns. Grossman's successor, Mark Parris, in contrast, focused on a five-point U.S.-Turkish agenda, which emphasized energy needs and distribution networks and more traditional concerns such as security. As part of the engagement strategy with Turkey, assistant secretaries for democracy, human rights, and labor undertook visible missions to Turkey. Of these, Harold Koh's August 1999 trip, especially because of the tumultuous reception he received in the Kurdish southeast, attracted the most attention.[20] Deputy Secretary Strobe Talbott spoke in a variety of settings, emphasizing Turkey's importance to the West and the need for Europeans to include it while also criticizing Ankara's shortcomings in human rights and free speech. In the most comprehensive speech delivered in recent times by an incumbent high-ranking U.S. official, he detailed the reasons for U.S. anxieties over Turkish human rights practices.[21] Secretary of State Madeleine Albright also took up the case of free speech and protection of journalists when she singled out a Turkish journalist, Nadire Mater, who was being prosecuted for publishing a book of interviews with soldiers who served in the southeast conflict with the PKK.[22] Finally, President Clinton in his November 1999 trip to Turkey, in an unprecedented speech in the Turkish parliament, which was full of praise for his hosts, took on the sensitive subject of Turkey's Kurdish minority. His speech outlined the administration's vision:

The future we want to build together begins with Turkish progress in deepening democracy at home. Nobody wants this more than the people of Turkey. You have created momentum and edicts against torture in a new law that protects the rights of political parties, in the achievements and vitality of this assembly. Avenues are opening for Kurdish citizens of Turkey to reclaim that most basic of birth rights—a normal life.[23]

Although the United States has been critical of Turkish efforts to resolve the Kurdish problem exclusively through military means, it was unforgiving of the Kurdish rebel group's activities. The PKK was included on the terrorism list and Washington spared no effort in trying to prevent this organization's activities. Washington's unabashedly anti-PKK discourse provided it with some credibility,[24] although its criticism of Turkish behavior was always open to deliberate misinterpretation by Ankara. For instance, when Ambassador Parris in spring 2000 tried to open a liaison office in the southeast primarily to encourage U.S. businesses to invest, he was turned down.

QUIET DIPLOMACY. Quiet diplomacy, by its very nature, is the first preference of diplomats. Diplomats believe that quiet diplomacy, which avoids publicly embarrassing the other party, in this case Ankara, is therefore more likely to produce the desired results. Quiet diplomacy has the added benefit of avoiding nationalistic backlashes and public displays of indignation at foreign pressure. Thus, it strengthens the hand of those already inclined to change policy in the "right direction" and does not force them to side with hard-liners.

The close nature of the U.S.-Turkish dialogue and the high frequency of bilateral visits offer many occasions for communicating discreet messages. Over the years U.S. diplomats have delivered numerous messages from U.S. administrations to their counterparts, asking the Turkish authorities there to improve their record on human rights. In private meetings U.S. officials have advocated decriminalizing freedom of expression; releasing journalists, parliamentarians, and human rights workers; meaningfully ending the state of emergency in the southeastern provinces; and calling for the reopening of offices belonging to human rights NGOs. Occasionally, officials have delivered these messages in a rather blunt fashion.

The preeminent role of the military in Turkish society and the fact that many human rights problems can be laid at the door of the officer corps naturally transformed the existing intimate military-to-military channels into a convenient method of communicating sensitive messages. Often the White House and the State Department sought to enlist the Department of Defense, specifically the uniformed officers, to convey messages to Turkey and influence its behavior. The special relationship between the deputy chief of the Joint Chiefs of Staff, General Joseph W. Ralston, and his counterpart, General Çevik Bir, was particularly conducive to these endeavors. However, U.S. military officers in general resisted such efforts; they did not like to mix political issues with their already overloaded and tense dialogue with their Turkish counterparts.[25] Moreover, it is not clear how much the Ralston-Bir channel was effective, especially considering that Bir was very much part of the problem in that he had spearheaded many of the campaigns that displeased the United States.[26]

While quiet diplomacy can often produce results, it cannot become the single policy tool. Its effectiveness is ultimately influenced by an administration's willingness to go public as well. Similarly, public diplomacy will not produce intended benefits unless it is coordinated with its quiet counterpart.

CARROTS AND STICKS. To influence policy in Ankara, Washington has also tried to offer rewards or withhold them. With the decline in U.S. foreign aid to Turkey, the United States has few concrete carrots left to dangle except for military sales. Other rewards, such as support in international institutions or trade agreements, are less tangible and not always conducive to conditionality. Using arms sales for conditionality is an untidy method of influencing policy. Manufacturers are well aware of the economic incentives available to them to influence U.S. policymakers. More important is that often U.S. administrations have wanted Turkey to modernize its equipment, preferably with U.S. merchandise, in order for Ankara to better fulfill its NATO obligations. Hence, the White House, the State Department, and certainly the Pentagon have resisted arms conditionality. In contrast, Congress has played the bad cop to the administration's good cop.

The best-known case of a carrot-and-stick approach occurred during Prime Minister Mesut Yilmaz's Washington trip in December 1997. At issue was the Turkish government's desire to purchase a large quantity of attack helicopters. A year after its decision not to buy the Cobra attack helicopters, Turkey was particularly sensitive to U.S. criticisms.[27] A month before Yilmaz's visit, the deputy chief of staff of the Turkish General Staff, Çevik Bir, was in Washington as part of a delegation to discuss defense matters. He reportedly told journalists that "human rights issues were discussed in detail during my meetings here in Washington [and] regarding human rights, we told our counterparts that the Turkish Armed Forces are far ahead compared to many European nations. Unfortunately we are facing double standards in human rights."[28]

General Bir's complaints aside, the State Department, facing intense congressional pressure, compiled a list of seven criteria by which it would judge Turkish progress on the human rights front. The list was shared with the NGO community and consists of the following: "1) Decriminalization of free speech; 2) release of journalists and parliamentarians who have been imprisoned for political reasons; 3) an end to torture and police impunity; 4) reopening of non-governmental organizations that have been shut down by Turkish authorities; 5) democratization and expansion of political participation; 6) the lifting of the state of emergency in southeastern Turkey; and 7) the resettlement of internal refugees displaced by the civil war."[29] The pending helicopter decision had provided the Clinton administration with an ideal opportunity to explicitly state its preferences—to draw up a road map. Then by briefing the NGO community and the manufacturers, it sought to make the process transparent and satisfy both critics and partisans of the arms sales. Realistically speaking, the administration could not have expected complete (or perhaps even partial) progress along every dimension of the State Department's list. In fact, it can be argued that the net cast was wide enough to provide the administration with enough flexibility to argue at an opportune moment that some progress had been achieved. It was a clever maneuver: the list as a road map could be used to pressure the government in Ankara at a time when the perception in the United States was that Turkey's human rights violations had reached a peak. The list was designed to let

Ankara know that should it usher in reforms, the bar would not be raised at a later date. The list could potentially generate concerted attention by those on both sides of the debate to convince the Turks that movement along these lines would be rewarded. On the other hand, a detailed checklist risked mobilizing opponents of the sale, who could argue that if Turkey did not comply fully, then the helicopters ought not receive an export license. The attack helicopter sale, because of its sheer size (potentially $3.5 billion for 145 units), was destined to become a litmus test for the administration's overall record on human rights, not just on human rights in Turkey. Hence, it required special handling by the administration. But if the strategy's success was based on the assumption that the Turkish authorities would cooperate, Washington was quickly disappointed, as Turkey's Constitutional Court banned the Welfare Party soon after the understanding with Yilmaz had been achieved, thereby undermining the first of the conditions. Still, this did not deter the administration from attempting to achieve moderate improvements, and the process dragged on.

Arms sales are clearly the most visible carrot and stick available to U.S. policymakers who want to influence the human rights policy, and the United States has a commanding lead in both sheer market size and technology. Nonetheless, the intense competition among industrialized states for military equipment has somewhat blunted the usefulness of this carrot and stick. This plus the size of some of the pending contracts, in fact, provides the purchaser significant leverage. Continuous concerns expressed over the possibility of sales have elicited criticisms from the Turkish side about the unreliability of the United States as an arms exporter.[30] Part of the Turkish concern over arms supplies was inspired not only by holds on human rights–related equipment but also by U.S. efforts at maintaining a balance in the Aegean between Greece and Turkey. In reality, very few arms shipments were put on hold subject to human rights concerns.

Complicating matters for policymakers were Turkey's NATO connection and participation in critical events such as the Kosovo conflict. Denying arms sales to a NATO ally could have a corrosive effect on the alliance relationship and the basic premises on which that relationship was based. The mammoth helicopter deal in the end languished, but not because of direct U.S. action. Turkish officials, unsure of the State Department's reaction in view of the 1997 criteria, delayed the decision, perhaps calculating that a more sympathetic administration led by a Republican president after 2001 would not be so diligent in applying the 1997 criteria.[31]

SUPPORT FOR INSTITUTION BUILDING. The U.S. government has supported initiatives designed to bolster civil society groups in Turkey and institution building in general. This approach also fits well with the strategy of "helping Turks help themselves." Such initiatives have taken two forms. The first consisted of direct U.S. government–initiated activities, such as sending U.S. prosecutors or judges to Turkey for training and information exchange missions or inviting their Turkish counterparts to the United States for training. The second was support for the activities of U.S. and international NGOs in Turkey. These two forms, while political in nature, did not carry the visible opprobrium associated with either public diplomacy or hassle over arms sales and helped the difficult and slow-moving progress toward democratization. They also communicated to both the Turkish government and the Turkish public the degree of U.S. commitment to improving in human rights. For the United States, the challenge was always that resources devoted to such activities were meager and, in fact, were overshadowed by the European Union's more generous allocations.

While the work of U.S. and other NGOs has been significant, even critical in the case of torture victims, institution building is a slow process. Programs aimed at making the Turkish parliament more responsive to its constituents and more attentive to human rights were unlikely to succeed if parliamentarians feared the entrenched establishment and were, by and large, powerless. One institution that needed help was the press, which with few notable exceptions was reluctant to challenge the state. The proliferation of programs helped the U.S. government politically make its case that progress was around the corner and that Turkey was making a genuine effort at improving its record.

The Success and Failure of U.S. Policy in Turkey

The U.S. strategy on Turkey's human rights has been a difficult balancing act: while helping Turkey better integrate into Western institutions, and not just the military ones, the United States has had to evaluate the cost of pushing for an improved human rights environment against "strategic concerns." Ankara clearly has not always welcomed U.S. engagement. As Alan Makovsky argues, human rights conditionality, especially regarding arms sales, "offends Turkish pride."[32] Turkish officials have also bristled at the State Department human rights reports, criticizing both the content and the methods employed to document the reports. During the Clinton administration they put limits on consultations with U.S. authorities. After Assistant Secretary Koh's "controversial" visit to Turkey, Ankara refused to allow him to return on the grounds that protocol dictated that the Turkish minister for human rights visit the United States first. Yet Ankara turned down repeated invitations for him to come to the United States.[33]

Given this difficult environment, can the United States claim credit for improvements? Similarly, can it be blamed for the absence of amelioration or even deterioration? Should the seven-point criteria established in 1997, perhaps one of the few times that an explicit set of goals was written down on paper, be considered the yardstick by which U.S. policy ought to be judged?

By the time the Clinton administration left office, the situation in Turkey had taken a turn for the better. The number of mysterious disappearances, incidents of torture, village evacuations, and politically motivated prosecutions had significantly declined. This was directly attributable to the end of the PKK-led insurrection in the southeast. The years of repression and conflict had taken an enormous toll on the people of the southeast, sapping their political strength, and with the military gaining the upper hand and the PKK leader in jail, the threat was not as severe as it had appeared in the early part of the 1990s. The U.S. government could claim a certain degree of credit for the improvement: it played a critical role in the capture of Abdullah Öcalan, the PKK leader who had escaped to Kenya, and was instrumental in convincing the European Union to open the door of candidacy to Turkey. In the latter case, a 1997 Luxembourg Summit decision that excluded Turkey even from the candidacy status was reversed, with help from the United States, at the 1999 Helsinki Summit. Both of these events have contributed to a lessening of political tensions and a relaxation of certain, mostly self-imposed, restrictions, primarily on the mainstream media. In turn, there has been a great deal more discussion on issues previously considered taboo, and amendments have been made to the military-inspired 1982 constitution.

Initially, the Ecevit-led government undertook measures indicating that it was interested in improving human rights conditions. It passed a constitutional amendment removing the military judge from the three-member state security courts (SSCs), passed a law suspending for three years the sentences of writers and journalists convicted of crimes related to freedom of expression, made it more difficult to close down political parties, and increased the penalties for people convicted of torture. While the United States heralded these developments, they have had at best a marginal impact, if any. The military judge was not at the root of the problem with the SSCs; the rules of evidence and the right to a fair trial were. The three-year suspension for journalists did lead to the release of some authors, but the suspension carried the threat that if an author was convicted again of a similar crime, he or she would have to serve both sentences consecutively. This has had a chilling effect on authors and journalists. In addition, the prosecutions of journalists for "thought crimes" have continued unabated. Turkish media often exercise self-censorship either because they are afraid or because they tend to share the objectives of the state.[34] The change in the political party law is perhaps the most ironic. It resulted from horse trading in parliament between the governing coalition and the opposition, specifically the Virtue Party, the Welfare Party's successor, which demanded this change as a quid pro quo for supporting a constitutional change easing restrictions on privatization of state assets. Still, this was not enough to save the Virtue Party from closure. The end of the insurgency has not led to a relaxation of the ban on Kurdish linguistic rights, and pro-Kurdish parties have continued to be harassed or closed down (as are Islamist parties and politicians). The scope of the state of emergency has been reduced but not completely eliminated either.

The State Department's 1999 and 2000 human rights reports show that limits on freedom of speech and freedom of the press continue. Books and newspapers are routinely banned; prominent politicians and activists have been prosecuted and convicted. Human rights associations have been closed down at will. The most common accusation is collaboration with the PKK. In February 2000 three mayors from the southeast were summarily arrested, summoned in front of a state security court, and dismissed from their jobs overnight for supposedly having had contact with PKK representatives while in Europe. They were released pending their trial and eventually returned to their jobs following an international uproar, including a strongly worded public denunciation by Assistant Secretary Koh.

In summary, institutional improvements have not buttressed the practical improvements. Why so few results? Three reasons come to mind. First, the issues at hand pose an existential threat to the Turkish elite and especially its bureaucratic-military component. This has intensified resistance to U.S. criticisms. Moreover, the state has erected a legal wall to protect itself from society. Take, for instance, Article 159 of the Penal Code, which deems any statement that discredits the moral character of "Turkishness, the Republic, its institutions such as the government, parliament, the ministers, justice system and military" is punishable with up to six years in prison. Hence, the law provides judges with significant flexibility in finding someone guilty while not prosecuting others. Given the weakness of Turkey's political institutions, the United States has had difficulty finding institutional partners to work with in order to advance its human rights agenda. The military has made the job of "regime survival," as defined by officers, its own and can, therefore, dominate the public agenda. In effect, the military establishment has become a political actor just like any other. This makes the role of civilian institutions Sisyphean: they often face insurmountable difficulties in trying to shift the agenda or even change laws. Devoid of any serious responsibility, these institutions have become careless, thus completing a vicious cycle. The weakness of civilian political institutions, especially of parliament, is therefore a major handicap for a U.S. administration trying to influence and induce change. When a politician dares to challenge the military, as the admittedly highly erratic and inconsistent former prime minister Mesut Yilmaz did in March 1998, he is likely to find himself alone. Abandoned, Yilmaz then had to beat a humiliating retreat.

Paradoxically, the politicians' weakness and the primacy of the national security apparatus in Turkey have occasionally been helpful to U.S. interests. During the Operation Provide Comfort/Operation

Northern Watch debates, the military was quite helpful; the U.S. Department of Defense, although reticent to carry political messages, by virtue of its "good dialogue" with its military counterparts in Ankara has made use of the military channel to get things done.

The second reason for the paucity of results has to do with the U.S. ability to sustain a long and focused campaign for human rights. Agenda overcrowding prevented the administration from staying on message. One event worth noting occurred during a 1998 public dispute between Prime Minister Yilmaz and the Turkish General Staff. The State Department issued a carefully worded statement implying support for the civilian authority. Turkish politicians immediately noticed the language and responded positively. Yet the State Department never again employed similar language, perhaps for fear of upsetting the powerful military. The helicopter sale, which many in the administration wanted to realize, provided a focus. Clearly, without some improvements the sale was unlikely to pass Congress even if it did pass through the administration's internal reviews. However, with the end of the PKK insurgency and resulting improvement, attention to this issue began to wane; when the Constitutional Court, for example, closed down the Virtue Party, Washington, unlike earlier, remained fairly quiet. This was attributable not solely to waning interest but also to a transition in U.S. administration.

Finally, there is the EU reason. Having succeeded in convincing the Europeans to open the door, however slightly, to Turkey, the United States can pass the buck on this issue to its partners across the Atlantic. If Turkey is to have any chance of entering the European Union, it will have to amend its laws and alter its practices. This has as much to do with the Copenhagen criteria as it has to do with the general reluctance of the Europeans to admit Turkey. Therefore, they will insist that Ankara implement every minutia of these agreements with the hope of delaying the accession as long as possible. The danger for the United States will come in the future when Turkish officials, frustrated or unwilling to implement critical criteria, will once again rely on Washington to pry open European doors. Until the advent to power of the Justice and Development Party in November 2002, Turkish officials, including elected ones, have tried to get away with doing the absolute minimum on EU-required reforms.

LESSONS LEARNED

Turkey matters to the United States. The more developed and institutionalized Turkish democracy is, the stronger the alliance with the
United States will become. Hence, it is in the U.S. self-interest to push
for reforms in Turkey. For this reason alone, U.S.-Turkish relations will
exhibit elements of both friction and cooperation. The recent economic
crisis befalling Turkey is very much the result of an archaic, inflexible,
opaque, and corrupt political system. Hence, the cost of a poorly
developed democratic system can now be seen in expensive bailout
packages by the International Monetary Fund.

Even though Turkey's eventual fate lies in closer cooperation with
Europe, the United States will continue to play an inordinate role in
this country's future. EU accession is unlikely to happen for another fifteen to twenty years. The U.S. global role and U.S. willingness to discuss issues of human rights and democracy will continue to mean that
the Turkish government, its opposition, and Turkish society at large
will analyze and reanalyze every utterance by a U.S. official.

In short, public diplomacy, if consistent, can work. It will not
always achieve its desired result, such as getting people out of jail or
reversing decisions that are clearly violations of individual rights.
Consistency and coordination with other policy options can make public diplomacy work. Moreover, public diplomacy is important in winning friends and strengthening the hands of reformers. Diplomats,
because they are accustomed to dealing with state officials, often tend
to equate public or official pronouncements with what the public
wants. The weakening of political institutions in Turkey and the inability to implement reform are a result and a reflection of a public's diminished faith in the country's ossified governing class.

Perhaps the most important decision any U.S. administration
must make about human rights policy is how to integrate it into an
overall policy toward Turkey. It is unrealistic to expect that this consideration will lead the list. The main challenge is to address the issue
not on an ad hoc basis but as part of a coherent whole. Although
Strobe Talbott's speech was the most important made by a senior
Clinton administration official, the negative reaction in Turkey forced
—mistakenly—the State Department to backtrack from it. Any

strategy on human rights must include nonstate actors, be they NGOs or others. Diplomats admittedly have institutional difficulties in integrating nongovernmental actors into their inner sanctums. Yet the information revolution and the proliferation of actors on the international scene increasingly mean that these forces cannot be ignored. In an era of diminished budgets, foundations, NGOs, and others can provide critical financial help unavailable from the U.S. government.

Washington can also facilitate a great deal more dialogue between critics and supporters of Turkey in the United States as a means of harnessing their energy to push the democracy agenda. Because bargaining is inherently part of the process, no one group can hope to achieve all of its aims, but compromises advance the agenda just as much. This bargaining also requires greater transparency on the part of the government. The State Department took a first step when it initiated a separate dialogue with NGOs and military contractors about the pending helicopter decision.

Did carrots and sticks work? If the 1997 criteria developed in conjunction with the impending helicopter purchase request is any indication, the answer ought to be no. At the end of the Clinton administration and three years after their promulgation, few, if any, of the items on that list had been acted upon. This is despite a much improved domestic situation in Turkey, especially after Öcalan's arrest and conviction. The irony, of course, is that the United States eased up on its pressure for reform just when it could have been most effective, that is, after the end of the conflict and the decline in violence that Ankara claimed was the reason for not moving ahead with improvements. In effect, the tools to use have to be calibrated with the influence Washington exercises at a given point.

Clearly, the future is linked to the EU accession process, as it represents the most important goal for Turkey and, therefore, the point of greatest influence. The United States, having worked hard to convince the reluctant Europeans to clear a path, can help this process along by pushing Turkey to accede to the Copenhagen criteria. What Washington cannot do is to echo Turkish arguments that Turkey is a special case that deserves special status on issues of democracy, rule of law, and the role of the military. On the contrary, the United States needs to develop a collaborative approach with the Europeans to speed up the process of Turkey's European Union accession.

POSTSCRIPT

The Bush administration's early emphasis on security issues, especially its preoccupation with Saddam Hussein's regime, signaled that human rights and democratization would be a much lower priority for Washington when dealing with allies such as Turkey. And with the attacks of September 2001, Turkey was propelled to the front lines of Washington's "war on terrorism." Two of the three countries that President Bush said formed the "axis of evil," Iraq and Iran, border Turkey, thereby emphasizing its geostrategic importance.[35] For Ankara, the U.S. war on terrorism validated two long-held beliefs: that the terrorism from which Turkey had suffered during the years of the PKK insurgency was a common enemy, as was fundamentalist Islam. Turkish civilian and military leaders expected that henceforth the United States would show greater understanding when Ankara took measures that otherwise would have been deemed too harsh against Kurdish and Islamist groups.

The State Department, however, has continued to criticize Turkey in its annual human rights reports, and congressionally mandated initiatives such as the annual *International Religious Freedom Report* and the *Trafficking in Persons (TIP) Report* have created further resentment in Ankara. In fact, the 2002 TIP report, which was highly critical of Turkey, elicited strong and indignant reactions from Ankara at a time when the Bush administration was constantly showcasing Turkey as a role model for Islamic nations. The first crisis in Turkey with which Washington had to contend was not political but economic: a fight between the Turkish president and the prime minister caused the Turkish currency to collapse and sent the economy into a tailspin. Washington reacted quickly and engineered a large IMF-led package of measures to bolster the Turkish economy.

The worsening economic conditions helped bring a pro-Islamist government to power. Ironically, the authorities' decision to ban the Virtue Party enabled the charismatic former mayor of Istanbul, Recep Tayyip Erdogan, to break away from the religiously traditionalist and conservative elements of the Virtue Party to form his own, more moderate, political movement, the Justice and Development Party (AKP). In the November 2002 elections, his party captured almost two-thirds of the seats in parliament. The new majority party soon found a way to invalidate the ban on their leader's involvement in politics and to get him elected to parliament.

The new party, unlike its predecessors, had based its campaign on a promise to make Turkey a member of the European Union and on furthering the democratization process. The AKP's insistence on improving ties to the European Union and furthering democratization was influenced by the realization that after the February 28, 1997, military memorandum it could survive as a conservative and religiously minded political movement only if, under the guise of pursuing reforms required by the European Union, Turkey civilized its political life. Hence, the AKP's discourse is a welcome development for Washington because Turkey's EU aspirations represent the shortest route to long-term stability based on a functioning democracy and economic prosperity. The AKP faces great difficulties in reshaping a state structure that still criminalizes many forms of political behavior. In fact, irrespective of the promises of the new government, the Turkish state apparatus continued to push for restrictive policies. In March 2003, for instance, it closed down the pro-Kurdish party HADEP, which had been under considerable pressure for many years.

If the AKP is going to succeed in this endeavor, it must push through reforms quickly, despite the opposition of establishment forces for whom the liberalization of language restrictions on broadcasting and the gradual elimination of the military's influence in domestic politics are anathema. The Iraq war may ironically have helped the AKP government. First, even before Erdogan won a special election that enabled him to become a member of parliament and, therefore, become eligible to assume the office of the prime minister, the Bush administration decided to invite him to the White House for a meeting with the president This invitation immensely increased his stature as a leader and was designed to send a message to the Turkish establishment that the United States recognized him as the rightful leader of Turkey irrespective of the ban on his political participation. More important, the protracted negotiations with the Turks over the basing of U.S. troops on Turkish soil to open a second front on Saddam's regime tested the patience of both sides. The Turkish military's lukewarm support for the United States—inspired mainly by its desire to pin the blame for an unpopular war on a government it did not favor—angered Washington. The Bush administration and especially the Pentagon put the blame on the Turkish military for the surprise failure of the government's motion in parliament to allow U.S. troops to be based in Turkey. The reticence of the military to provide support when asked to do so during the war against Iraq further infuriated the Pentagon. In a much-discussed interview with a Turkish television network, Deputy Secretary of Defense Paul Wolfowitz signaled that for the first time in decades, the most important supporter within the U.S. government of Turkey and its military, the Department of Defense, felt betrayed by its longtime ally.[36]

The Wolfowitz warning was unexpected given the importance the United States and especially the George W. Bush administration had attached to the strategic location of Turkey. U.S. admonishments to the military have come at a time when the Turkish military is under intense pressure to approve—or at least not obstruct—EU-required reforms. Similarly, it is under intense pressure by the secular establishment to rein in the pro-Islam AKP. The unintended consequence of the war and the U.S.-Turkish dispute has been to strengthen the hand of the civilian politicians at the expense of the military. Although the ball is in the Turkish government's court, how Washington reacts to what is likely to be an immense struggle over the next few years will significantly influence the outcome.

NOTES

1. For a detailed analysis of U.S.-Turkish relations, see Morton Abramowitz, ed., *The United States and Turkey: Allies in Need* (New York: Century Foundation, 2003); Morton Abramowitz, ed., *Turkey's Transformation and American Policy* (New York: Century Foundation, 2000); and F. Stephen Larrabee and Ian O. Lesser, *Turkish Foreign Policy in an Age of Uncertainty* (Santa Monica, Calif.: RAND, 2003).

2. Heinz Kramer, *A Changing Turkey* (Washington, D.C.: Brookings Institution, 2000), 223–231.

3. Many in Turkey portrayed OPC and ONW as a disguised U.S. project aimed at creating a Kurdish state in northern Iraq. For most of the 1990s, Bülent Ecevit, who would become prime minister at the end of the decade, was perhaps the most strident critic of OPC and ONW, often portraying them as part of this deliberate plot to create an irredentist Kurdish state.

4. Yalim Eralp recounts how Suleyman Demirel, the main opposition leader to President Turgut Özal in the early 1990s, had also promised to do away with OPC. But once in office, Demirel, when reminded of his unfulfilled promise, was supposed to have said, "[W]hat was I to do, damage the relationship with the United States?" Yalim Eralp, "An Insider's View of Turkey's Foreign Policy and Its American Connection," in *The United States and Turkey*, ed. Abramowitz, 115.

5. Strobe Talbott, "U.S.-Turkish Relations in an Age of Interdependence" (Second Turgut Özal Memorial Lecture presented at the Washington Institute for Near East Policy, Washington, D.C., October 14, 1998). For the complete text, see www.washingtoninstitute.org/media/talbott.htm.

6. *Milliyet*, June 13, 2000.

7. The Kurds, who with approximately 20 percent of the population form the single largest minority group, have been disenchanted for decades with the government's policies that denied their existence and cultural rights. Periodically, this dissatisfaction has turned into armed rebellion, heightened political activity, and civil disobedience. The Turkish state has always been wary of Kurdish activity on its soil, fearing that the Kurds may seek to secede, and, therefore, has often employed harsh means to prevent Kurdish political activity. See Henri J. Barkey and Graham E. Fuller, *Turkey's Kurdish Question* (Lanham, Md.: Rowman and Littlefield, 1998); and Kemal Kirişçi and Gareth M. Winrow, *The Kurdish Question and Turkey* (London: Frank Cass, 1997).

8. Erbakan, who single-handedly introduced Islamist politics into Turkey in the 1970s, made his reputation with a virulent anti-U.S., anti-EU, and anti-Semitic discourse. He constantly criticized the secular institutions of the Turkish state and became a source of concern for the establishment.

9. For a critique of the laws and regulations restricting the freedom of thought, see TÜSIAD (Turkish Businessmen and Industrialists Association), *Türkiye'de Demokratiklesme Perspektifleri* (Istanbul: TÜSIAD, 1997); and Human Rights Watch, *Violations of Free Expression in Turkey* (New York: Human Rights Watch, 1999). The annual human rights reports published by the State Department also detail the prosecution of individuals for similar crimes.

10. "Turkish policymakers . . . tend to regard congressional scrutiny of arms transfers as a de facto embargo and have taken steps to diversify the country's defense-industrial relationships." Ian Lesser, *NATO Looks South* (Santa Monica, Calif.: RAND, 2000), 41.

11. Dana Priest, "New Human Rights Law Triggers Policy Debate," *Washington Post*, December 31, 1998, A34. In the end, the issue was resolved through a compromise that allowed the Export-Import Bank to provide loan guarantees for vehicles going to Turkish provinces where there was no discernible evidence of human rights violations and that denied such guarantees where there was such evidence.

12. For a detailed analysis of the role of different ethnic and other interest groups in U.S. foreign policy making on Turkey, see Morton Abramowitz, "The Complexities of American Policy Making on Turkey," in *Turkey's Transformation and American Policy*, 160–171.

13. For a good example, see American Hellenic Institute president Eugene Rossides's uncompromising letter of August 5, 1999, to Assistant Secretary Harold Koh regarding human rights abuses in Turkey; accessed at www.ahiworld.com/koh.html.

14. The human rights NGOs were also very critical of the PKK and its gross abuses during the conduct of the insurgency. In fact, during Öcalan's search for a home in Europe, the primary U.S.-based organization, Human Rights Watch, called on the European governments to bring the PKK leader to justice and prevent his escape. In general, NGOs directed most of their efforts at mobilizing criticism of government authorities, over which they had some degree of influence through lobbying U.S. and EU governments.

15. Even in the bureaucratic pecking order, regional bureaus report to the undersecretary for political affairs, the third-highest person in the State Department, whereas DRL falls under the purview of the undersecretary for global affairs.

16. Abramowitz, "The Complexities of American Policy Making on Turkey," 176.

17. U.S. officials would often be confronted by poignant questions, such as during the Kosovo war when they were asked why the Kurds in Turkey were viewed differently from the Albanians in Yugoslavia, for whom presumably the United States had engaged in combat operations.

18. For a concise statement of the issue, see former ambassador to Turkey Marc Grossman's statement as director general of the Foreign Service to House International Relations Subcommittee on International Organizations and Human Rights, September 14, 2000 (accessed at www.usemb-ankara.org.tr/Press/Archive/armenia.htm): "Turks know that they have more to do in this area. There are still unacceptable limits on freedom of expression and the media. Torture must stop. . . . We continue to believe the best way to push for improvement is through engagement. Anything that might diminish our standing in Turkey will set back our efforts."

19. In contrast, when in June 2001 the Turkish authorities banned the Welfare Party's successor, the Virtue Party, the State Department was considerably more circumspect in its criticism.

20. For a bitter critique of Koh's trip, see Mehmet Ali Kislali, "A US Gaffe," *Radikal*, August 6, 1999.

21. Talbott, "U.S.-Turkish Relations in an Age of Interdependence."

22. Albright's reference to Mater made the front-page headline in the daily *Milliyet*, taking the Turkish establishment by surprise and drawing attention to her book, *Mehmedin Kitabi*, which the authorities had banned. *Milliyet*, October 15, 1999; and *Sabah*, October 18, 1999.

23. http://clinton4.nara.gov/textonly/WH/New/html/19991115.html.

24. PKK leader Öcalan's capture in February 1999 represents the most important instance of U.S.-Turkish cooperation, although the U.S. role in the affair is still shrouded in mystery.

25. Operation Northern Watch was the one issue that gave rise to most of these tensions.

26. For instance, Bir was later discovered to have been the primary mover in getting two extremely well respected journalists critical of the establishment, Mehmet Ali Birand and Cengiz Çandar, fired from their newspaper, *Sabah*, in a blatant attempt at silencing and punishing them.

27. Turkey pulled back its request in the face of stiff opposition in Congress and among the NGO community.

28. Ugur Akinci, "General Bir: 'We Are Ahead of Europe in Human Rights,'" *Turkish Daily News*, November 27, 1997.

29. Tamar Gabelnick, William D. Hartung, and Jennifer Washburn, *Arming Repression: U.S. Arms Sales during the Clinton Administration* (Washington, D.C.: World Policy Institute and Federation of American Scientists, October 1999), 6.

30. See, for instance, the comments of Lt. General Batmaz Dandin, chief of the planning and principles division of the Turkish General Staff, who argued that "the United States was becoming 'an unreliable defense source for Turkey day by day.' He warned that U.S. weapons contractors will not be able to win Turkish tenders if that attitude continues." *Turkish Daily News*, May 15, 1999.

31. Turkey did announce that it would buy U.S. helicopters, but the Clinton administration had not signed a formal contract as negotiations between the manufacturer, Textron, and Turkey had not been completed. Since then the severe economic crisis befalling Turkey has forced the military authorities to defer this purchase.

32. Alan Makovsky, "U.S. Policy towards Turkey: Progress and Problems," in *Turkey's Transformation and American Policy*, 254.

33. Turkish officials have not hidden their displeasure of Koh, and their reticence to continue the dialogue may have more to do with their desire to exclude him. Koh, however, did participate in the U.S. presidential trip to Turkey in November 1999.

34. For an analysis of the Turkish press, see Andrew Finkel, "Who Guards the Turkish Press? A Perspective on Press Corruption in Turkey," *International Affairs* 54, no. 1 (fall 2000): 147–166.

35. See Henri J. Barkey, "The Endless Pursuit: Improving U.S.-Turkish Relations," in *The United States and Turkey: Allies in Need*, ed. Morton Abramowitz (New York: Century Foundation, 2003).

36. Deputy Secretary of Defense Paul Wolfowitz in his interview with CNN-Turk publicly criticized the TGS for failing to show leadership in the Iraq conflict. Ironically, in the same interview he went out of his way to say that the government, in contrast, had submitted a resolution on the deployment of U.S. troops with the intention of getting it passed. For a transcript see http://dod.mil/transcripts/2003/tr20030506-depsecdef0156.html.

13

The U.S.-Egypt Partnership

Are Human Rights Included?

Denis J. Sullivan

Evolution of a Strategic Partnership

For more than a quarter century, the United States and the Arab Republic of Egypt have been committed to maintaining a solid bilateral relationship. This relationship, indeed this partnership, was established firmly in 1974 as a result of President Anwar Sadat's willingness to make peace with Israel; he accomplished this task after signing the Camp David Accords in 1978 and the peace treaty with Israel in 1979. Sadat's primary objective was not to reach a peace with Israel as much as it was to achieve a partnership with the United States, which could help return the Israeli-occupied Sinai Peninsula back to Egypt as well as deliver much-needed military and development assistance. Peace with Israel was the price Sadat would pay for both: an improved relationship with the United States and a return of the Sinai. But while they received enormous benefits from this peace, Sadat and Egypt paid a high price for it—political turmoil at home, expulsion from Arab and Islamic organizations, boycotts, and reduction in Arab aid. Even so, Egypt's strategic role in the region is undisputed, and in the 1980s the

401

Arab world welcomed Egypt back into the fold after it supported Iraq
during the Iran-Iraq War. Egypt continues the delicate balancing act
of nonbelligerence with Israel, close and "warm" ties with the United
States, and patient but strong leadership among Arab states. To that
end, and in part owing to Israel's policies toward Palestinians, the
Egypt-Israel relationship has been a "cold peace" for years.[1]

Nearly thirty years of partnership is no small achievement; still,
Egyptian and U.S. officials would prefer to be celebrating an even
greater milestone. Indeed, had the United States not committed what
President Richard M. Nixon said was "one of the greatest mistakes
that we made," when the Eisenhower administration rescinded an
offer in 1956 to finance construction of the Aswan Dam, the two
countries would likely be approaching the fiftieth anniversary of their
partnership.[2]

Even though the Cold War rationale for the partnership has now
disappeared, the United States continues to value its relationship
with Egypt for various (and obvious) reasons:

- Egypt's geography, demography, and political and military leadership within the Arab world combine to make it a strategic asset
  from the U.S. point of view, helping to protect the security of oil
  supplies to the United States.

- Egypt was the first (as well as the most significant and strongest)
  Arab state to make peace with Israel and remains key to securing
  Palestinian-Israeli coexistence (none dare yet call it peace).

- Egypt is thus central to U.S. interests in the Arab-Israeli conflict, the Persian Gulf, and the region in general.

Egypt values its relationship with the United States for its own
various (and obvious) reasons—all of which can be boiled down to U.S.
support for Egypt's military and thus for its political regime, and
U.S. support, in the form of both aid and trade, for Egypt's economy.
Outside the political, or state-to-state, relationship, there is an equally
solid people-to-people relationship between Egyptians and Americans.
Americans remain fascinated by Egypt, even if they tend to focus on
the pharaonic past and tradition; the U.S. educational system helps to
maintain that focus on and appreciation of Egypt. Egyptians also are

fascinated by the United States and generally effusive toward Americans living in or touring Egypt. There is very little anti-Americanism in Egypt—and when such sentiments are expressed in demonstrations or in the media, they are clearly aimed at U.S. foreign policy (not at "America" writ large) and occur primarily when Israel is seen as acting aggressively against Palestinians, Lebanese, or other Arabs. Large-scale demonstrations did occur in the first week of the U.S. invasion of Iraq in March 2003, perhaps the most anti-American spectacle witnessed in Egypt in decades. But those demonstrations also quickly took on an anti-Mubarak as well as an anti-American tone, and the Egyptian security forces crushed them within a matter of days.

The still-evolving U.S.-Egypt partnership has weathered many storms and challenges. In the 1980s U.S.-Egypt relations were strained owing to Israel's 1982 invasion of Lebanon and siege of Beirut and the hijacking of the *Achille Lauro* in 1985.[3] Although Egypt was indispensable to the U.S.-led coalition against Iraq in 1990–91, the two countries later differed strongly over Iraq and Libya. This challenged Egypt to develop a "delicate balancing act between its US and Arab interests," with one analyst predicting that Egypt would favor its Arab ties.[4] The balance was tested yet again when the United States, in 1996, vetoed a second term as UN secretary-general for Boutros Boutros-Ghali, Egypt's former foreign minister. And across the years, Washington's constant and unflinching support of Israel remains a constant challenge to the relationship. Despite such differences, both countries see their national and international interests as firmly linked.

In the aftermath of September 11, 2001, and the Bush administration's declaration of a global "war on terrorism," Egypt has not been able to refrain from displaying a somber "I told you so" attitude. Throughout the 1990s the Egyptian government led its own internal "war on terrorism" yet faced severe criticism from the United States and others. Much of that criticism was appropriate, given Egypt's failure to distinguish between militant Islamist opponents (the Islamic Group [Gama al-Islamiyya] and Islamic Jihad [al-Jihad]) and nonviolent groups (the Muslim Brotherhood [al-Ikhwan] and non-Islamists such as women's rights groups) that happen to voice a similar message but use very different methods. Since the attacks on the World Trade Center and the Pentagon, Egypt feels its actions are better understood in

U.S. government circles, especially given the fact that Osama bin Laden and al Qaeda, America's "Enemy No. 1" (until Saddam Hussein edged them out in 2003), owe much of their success to Egyptian militant Islamists who serve in leadership roles in that terror network. In fact, the United States has even adopted some of Egypt's techniques. For example, Egypt regularly violates the rule of law by using military trials for civilians suspected of terrorist activities.[5] The U.S. Department of State's annual human rights report for 2001 (released in March 2002) eased up on Egypt after several years of criticism. There was a "diminished American voice of condemnation toward the use of military courts in Egypt" as a result of the U.S. decision to use military tribunals in its own war on terrorism.[6] The human rights report for 2002 (released on March 31, 2003) "moved from condemning state security courts two years ago, to last year changing the language to make such courts seem less bad. This year, the report says that Egypt is bringing inappropriate cases in those courts—but does not take issue with the courts themselves."[7] And in March and April 2003, when U.S. forces were toppling Saddam Hussein, there were no official U.S. condemnations of human rights abuses committed by the Egyptian government in a crackdown on opponents of the regime, human rights workers, students, and demonstrators.[8]

President Hosni Mubarak's regime has not suddenly become so repressive; for years it has stifled freedoms of speech, assembly, and association and has used laws effectively to thwart political opposition. Mubarak keeps Egypt an authoritarian system, far from the "democracy" that it pretends to be. Mubarak's primary target in all these efforts is the Muslim Brotherhood, the oldest (it was founded in 1928) and most popular opposition movement in Egypt. But Mubarak also has his sights on other Islamists, including militant groups. And his government and the parliament he controls have introduced laws on a wide variety of issues to prevent human rights organizations, women's rights groups, and other nongovernmental organizations (NGOs) from organizing, fund raising, and providing social welfare services that seek to treat symptoms born of poverty and political exclusion. Alongside these laws are an array of procedures and policies—especially Emergency Law, which effectively suspends Egypt's constitution—as well as torture, political imprisonment, and military courts that expedite convictions of civilians, allow the government to accelerate executions, and deny the accused any recourse to judicial review. And whenever there is an upcoming election for parliament, the government of Egypt rounds up scores—and sometimes hundreds—of Muslim Brothers who are candidates for office. All of these methods serve as the foundation of an authoritarian system that has changed little since its establishment by Gamal Abdel Nasser in the early 1950s.

And yet Egypt has a vibrant civil society and a variety of political institutions that would promote democracy—if only Mubarak would abide by his own promise, made repeatedly since he came to power in 1981, to allow democracy to function. Egyptian politics thus remains both restricted and promising.

This chapter on Egypt examines the role that human rights play in the formulation of U.S. foreign policy in Egypt, the impact (if any) of U.S. policy on human rights practices there, the challenges to implementation of U.S. policy, and the instruments and agencies that the United States relies on to advance a human rights agenda in Egypt.

EQUAL PARTNERS?

William Quandt saw "the structure of U.S.-Egypt relations" in 1990 as one with an enormous power imbalance, making "a relationship of real equality almost impossible."[9] The second aspect of that relationship —Israel—has made the U.S.-Egypt partnership more of a triangular than a bilateral arrangement. Egypt and the United States have struggled either to ignore these realities or to overcome them. They have sought to make their relationship permanent and to expand it beyond the Middle East peace process: while Egypt is central to U.S. foreign policy regarding the Arab-Israeli conflict, both states agree that economic and military objectives are as essential to their partnership as is diplomatic interdependence.

Since the mid-1970s, the U.S.-Egypt partnership has been measured in dollars, primarily the amount transferred to Egypt in the form of U.S. economic and military assistance. Egypt currently receives about $2 billion annually in both forms (about $600 million in economic grants and $1.3 billion in military aid). Egypt has received around $25 billion in economic aid since the late 1970s and more than $30 billion in military aid.[10] After Egypt joined the Gulf War coalition against Iraq in 1990, the United States gave Egypt another significant gift: forgiving nearly $7 billion in debt.

In 1994, in an effort to move the partnership from one based on aid to one based on trade, Egypt and the United States established the U.S.-Egypt Partnership for Economic Growth and Development. Focusing on commercial ties, the U.S.-Egypt Partnership has functioned to "initiate public-private sector dialogue on policies aimed at expanding economic growth and job opportunities in Egypt, and at building mutually beneficial economic and commercial ties between the two countries."[11] By 1998 Egyptian officials had begun using their controlled media to publicize their dissatisfaction with their U.S. partners, especially Vice President Al Gore, for taking Egypt for granted and generally neglecting the U.S.-Egypt Partnership, for which Gore was largely responsible.[12] Frustrated by this "neglect" and always seeking to be treated equally with Israel, Egyptian officials launched their own initiative to enhance ties to the United States. According to the government of Egypt, its then foreign minister, Amr Moussa, presented the Egyptian-U.S. Strategic Dialogue Draft Project to Secretary of State Madeleine Albright in November 1997. Both foreign ministers officially inaugurated the dialogue on July 10, 1998.[13]

Three years after its launch, a new U.S. ambassador to Egypt, David Welch, discussed the dialogue with Egypt's leading daily newspaper, *al-Ahram*. He suggested that such a relationship had actually existed for many years: "I have always thought we had a strategic dialogue with Egypt and its leadership. Our work as diplomats is to package those dialogues in some manner and find an institutional framework for their conduct. [Of course,] more can be done in this area, though. And you will see in the coming weeks and months very strong evidence of a dialogue at a strategic level between our nations."[14]

ISRAEL, AID, COUNTERTERRORISM— BUT NOT HUMAN RIGHTS

While the U.S.-Egypt partnership has evolved and been tested and threatened since the 1970s, it has remained strong and likely will continue to be strengthened. Few of the tests or threats to the partnership have involved human rights abuses on the part of the government of Egypt; the case of Saad Eddin Ibrahim is the most glaring exception to this rule (as is discussed below). This is not to say that Egypt is a model of respect for human rights, nor is it to say that the United States does not care about human rights abuses in Egypt. Rather, the United States has not sought to confront Egypt publicly, or to use strong-arm tactics privately, on Egypt's myriad human rights abuses.

As policymakers, activists, and academics explore *which* tools and mechanisms the United States has used to improve respect for human rights abroad, the case of Egypt begs the question of *whether* the United States has sought to implement human rights in a consistent and meaningful fashion. This chapter argues that Washington's close relationship with Egypt has actually inhibited the U.S. ability to maneuver. "Friendship" has prevented a clear U.S. sense of purpose on human rights, democratization, and the rule of law. The overriding U.S. concern for stability—a topic that Egyptian officials consistently raise—means that other U.S. interests are virtually ignored. Thus, the United States "is hamstrung in its relationship with Egypt. Short-term interests in stability appear to conflict with longer-term interests in economic and political liberalization that would promote long-term stability."[15] The tools with which the United States has sought to promote human rights have been limited to

- quiet diplomacy,
- the State Department's annual *Country Reports on Human Rights Practices*,
- congressional inquiries (focused especially on Coptic Christians),
- Federal Immigration Court rulings on individual cases, and
- NGO/human rights organizations' public campaigns against torture as well as criticism of Egyptian measures, including legislation, to restrict freedom of speech and assembly.

HUMAN RIGHTS AND THE FORMULATION OF U.S. POLICY TOWARD EGYPT

"What role do human rights issues play in the formulation of U.S. foreign policy?" In the case of Egypt, the answer to this question is:

almost certainly none. Human rights are not central or significant to U.S. foreign policy toward Egypt, especially in its formative stage, when fundamental principles are established and "strategic objectives" are set. What *is* central to U.S. foreign policy is the Middle East peace process, aid and trade, a strong and stable Egypt, and the U.S.-Egypt partnership in the region as a whole.

The United States does not focus on human rights in its relationship with Egypt. On the contrary, Washington often will ignore human rights abuses. It does this especially under the rubric of "counterterrorism," which was a fundamental U.S. objective long before September 11, 2001, and has only attained greater importance. Largely unchecked by U.S. criticism, Egyptian military, internal security officials, and police engage in significant human rights abuses against both militant and nonviolent groups, which are rarely discouraged or punished by Egypt's political leaders. Indeed, the political leadership justifies such abuses by saying that the abusive actions are aimed against terrorism, a justification that resonates with the United States' own preoccupation with fighting terrorism.[16] In other words, *counterterrorism trumps human rights concerns.*

Human rights *do* play a part in the U.S.-Egypt relationship, but it is an issue that both governments work hard to avoid discussing. When human rights abuses surface through press reports of heavy-handed police tactics (e.g., the detention and torture of family members of suspected terrorists, the ill treatment of Coptic Christians by the Egyptian police), the two governments seek ways to justify the abuses or explain them away as "isolated" incidents.

According to one U.S. official who contributes to the State Department reports on human rights practices in Egypt and elsewhere, "[O]ur human rights officers *do care* about human rights, getting the facts right, and being bold."[17] This official acknowledged that once the State Department gets "the facts" from its human rights officers in the field, "we massage the report but keep it honest. We also talk to Amnesty International, Human Rights Watch, and other NGOs and include their comments." Massaging facts is important, according to this official, because even when "we just establish the facts, it's difficult to get all these [into the report] because we need to certify countries on human rights practices and *we can't help countries with gross human rights violations,*"[18] even when they are U.S. allies. This raises questions:

- Is Egypt in gross violation of human rights?
- If so, does the United States choose not to acknowledge these violations?
- If so, does the State Department massage facts to maintain Egypt's reputation on Capitol Hill and in the White House so that Egypt can maintain its military and economic aid package from the United States?

Whatever the answers to these questions, the State Department is clearly engaged in a delicate balancing act: getting the facts right, reporting them without analysis, but also "massaging" reports for the purpose of maintaining strong bilateral relations with friends such as Egypt. State Department officials are indeed proud of their *Country Reports* and see them collectively as "one of the most used documents from State in terms of U.S. policymaking."[19]

One State Department official responsible for Egypt suggests that "in private, Egypt is beat up a lot. But we don't pillory Egypt in public. Then again, we tend not to pillory any important country in public. We talk to Egyptians in private. The [U.S.] ambassador has to deliver the message but we can't cross the line from advice to badgering. If we do, the GOE [government of Egypt] gets mad, backs off, but they don't tell us to get lost."[20]

SAAD EDDIN IBRAHIM: THE EXCEPTION THAT PROVES THE RULE

When human rights improve in Egypt it is rarely, if ever, due to U.S. or other foreign pressure but rather is due to Egypt's willingness to improve them—for example, when Egyptian officials see that they have "won" against Islamists or recognize that their tactics are counterproductive. And Egypt is very good at resisting U.S. pressure, including in high-profile cases of human rights violations against U.S. citizens.

The most prominent case in recent years involved U.S. citizen and Egyptian national Saad Eddin Ibrahim. Ibrahim, a respected professor of sociology at the American University in Cairo, founded the

Ibn Khaldun Center for Development Studies in the late 1980s to address, as the center's website proclaims, "social, economic, political and cultural dimensions [of development]. The center's conception of development aims at freedom, democracy, justice and creativity."[21] In June 2000 Ibrahim was arrested and detained without charges. Later, the government charged him, along with several colleagues from his Ibn Khaldun Center, with jeopardizing his "country's stability and sow[ing] the seeds of disunity."[22] The charges were subsequently changed over the succeeding months to "defaming Egypt's image" and accepting foreign funding without government permission. On May 21, 2001, the State Security Court convicted Ibrahim and twenty-seven codefendants, who were staff members and contractors from the Ibn Khaldun Center, of violating military Decree No. 4 (of 1992), which prohibits the receipt of funds from abroad. For "accepting foreign funds without government authorisation" and "making false statements about the country's internal situation,"[23] Ibrahim received a sentence of seven years' hard labor; his codefendants received sentences ranging up to five years' hard labor.

In February 2002 Egypt's highest appeals court, the Court of Cassation, overturned the conviction, called for a retrial, and released Ibrahim, but only temporarily. One significant question remained unanswered: whether the temporary release was due to repeated (albeit quiet) U.S. pressure. Ibrahim's lead defense lawyer, Ibrahim Saleh, "denied claims that the ruling was due to international pressure. 'Egypt's judicial system does not respond to pressures of any kind and is completely independent.' . . . [He cited the February 2002] verdict as 'the best example of that.'"[24] This is almost certainly the case, given that the courts do enjoy a reputation for relative independence from the executive branch. Still, Ambassador Welch "welcomed" the decision by the court to overturn the conviction of Ibrahim and the twenty-seven others. To make sure there was no doubt about the U.S. position, Welch added: "We have repeatedly expressed our concern about the fairness of the process with the Egyptian government, and hope that the case against Dr. Ibrahim will now be dropped."[25]

But the charges were not dropped. The State Security Court, under Emergency Law, retried Ibrahim, and in July 2002 he and several colleagues were sentenced to prison terms; Ibrahim's sentence was again seven years with hard labor.[26] The following month, the Bush administration announced at a press conference that Egypt would "not be welcome" to a potential additional $38 million in aid in the coming year because of the detention of Ibrahim. It should be noted that the administration was under pressure from journalists and democracy and human rights advocates at the time, and it should be emphasized that the administration said only that it would oppose *additional* foreign assistance to Egypt. Even so, this was a major new development in the efforts to free Ibrahim and to promote democracy in Egypt. The White House action marked the first time that any administration has linked the human rights record of a Middle Eastern country to its eligibility to receive foreign assistance.

Fortunately for U.S. interests—and of course for Ibrahim—but almost certainly independent of U.S. interest in the case, in December 2002 the Court of Cassation again overturned the conviction, and a new trial was scheduled for February 2003. On March 18, 2003, the court finally acquitted the human rights defender and the codefendants on all charges.[27]

THE STATE VERSUS IBRAHIM: BACKGROUND AND IMPACT

Charges similar to those against Ibrahim were brought against the general secretary of the Egyptian Organization for Human Rights in December 1998. The charges against Hafez Abu Sa'ada were connected to a report he issued on human rights violations in a predominantly Coptic Christian village. Hafez Abu Sa'ada was released on bail following widespread protests by human rights organizations in Egypt and abroad.[28]

Ibrahim believes he was arrested for similar reasons because "authorities were unhappy with his involvement in a planned NGO project to monitor the [2000] parliamentary elections and by reports he issued on the status of Coptic Christians."[29] One U.S. State Department official expressed confusion over Egypt's motives: "I still don't understand the logic of this case—why the GOE undertook to stop Ibrahim and his group. Perhaps they had reasons; perhaps good reasons; or perhaps no legitimate concerns at all—other than he is an annoyance to the government. Regardless, we are concerned about this. He is a U.S. citizen after all."[30]

Despite strong pressure on the government, including public awareness that former U.S. ambassador Daniel Kurtzer had raised Ibrahim's case directly with Prime Minister Atef Ebeid and Foreign Minister Amr Moussa, Egypt brought Ibrahim and the twenty-seven others to trial, condemning Kurtzer's interference. The trial was held not in civilian court but in the military State Security Court, as allowed for under Egypt's ongoing Emergency Law. The only way to commute sentences from this court is by presidential decree (the Court of Cassation can *overturn* convictions but not *commute* sentences).

What may be as chilling as the government's reaction to Ibrahim's research work and activism were the division, confusion, and general ambivalence this case prompted among Egyptian NGO leaders, academics, and journalists. Their lack of unity and support stemmed in part from their differing opinions on whether to protest Ibrahim's arrest and Security Court trial, accept "outside" intervention,[31] or put trust in the rule of law and judicial process in Egypt.[32] U.S. embassy officials in Cairo and State Department officials in Washington expressed frustration over the lack of attention that Egyptian citizens gave to the case: "When we went to Saad Eddin's trial to show our public support, Egyptian human rights organizations [HROs] were nowhere to be seen. Was their neglect due to jealousy? Was it due to these HROs being co-opted by the government of Egypt? Or were they simply kowtowed and intimidated by their government? All are plausible, although I fear that 'jealousy' is the more likely answer."[33]

When U.S. officials do stand up for human rights yet fail to find any domestic players standing with them, they become even more reticent about doing so in the future. "If Egyptian civil society organizations—especially HROs—are not with us on human rights, on what grounds do we the United States stand?"[34] But the injustices done to Ibrahim and his colleagues should not be the test case on whether the United States supports human rights in Egypt, for Ibrahim's case was sufficiently widely reported in the United States as to virtually ensure that U.S. officials would voice, privately and publicly, their concern. The real test cases are those in which human rights abuses for which the Egyptian government is responsible are committed against individuals who have no advocates, internationally or at home. U.S. officials, it may be noted, were taken to task by Egyptian, U.S., and other human rights advocates for supporting Ibrahim but ignoring his codefendants. Only Ibrahim received special treatment from U.S. officials, and "only because of his U.S. passport did we care."[35]

Under the cover of antiterrorism, Egypt continues to stifle freedoms of association, speech, and expression. In another infamous case (but one involving no Americans), fifty-two men were arrested and tried between May and November 2001 for "debauchery" (i.e., homosexuality). Amnesty International and several European Union governments condemned aspects of these trials, especially the use of Emergency Law and State Security Courts to render "justice" in such a case. However, the United States was never vocal publicly. Was this silence due to the differences of opinion between Presidents Clinton and Bush on the question of gay rights? Did the trials become lost in the horrors of September 11 and Washington's inward focus? Perhaps—but the most important reason for U.S. silence seems to have been that, unlike the Ibrahim case, the trial of the gay men involved no Americans.

STATE-SOCIETY CONFLICT IN EGYPT

Terrorism has for years been a part of the conflict in Egypt between state and society. The 1997 murder of fifty-eight tourists and four Egyptians by militants in Luxor, and the several assassination attempts on President Mubarak are the best known of many incidents. Such attacks notwithstanding, the government has not had to face a *serious threat* to its existence, although the Islamist *challenge* has been active for decades. It is not to downplay the impact on Egyptian life of violence by militant Islamist groups in the 1990s to note that the conflictual atmosphere in state-society relations in Egypt is often exacerbated not by opposition groups but by the policies, attitudes, and actions of Egyptian government officials.[36]

Early on in the state's crackdown during the 1990s on militant as well as nonviolent Islamists, it was predicted that such heavy-handed methods of dealing with Islamist opponents "will prove counter-productive in the long run—and even in the short run. . . . [Mubarak's] regime spares no effort to antagonize the masses and alienate the elite. Ordinary Egyptians already endure economic crisis and structural adjustment. They require no further harassment in the form of increasing police brutality."[37] And yet further harassment was exactly what the state provided, in the form not only of police brutality and torture against various groups but also a string of laws and other actions to limit personal freedoms and otherwise strengthen government control over Egyptian society. These repressive measures include

- Law 32 of 1964, a restrictive "law of associations" and the government's attempts to replace it, beginning with Law 153 of 1999 aimed at limiting NGO activity[38] and then the even more restrictive Law of Associations, Law 84, passed by parliament in June 2002.[39]
- Emergency Law, in effect since 1981 (indeed, first implemented in 1967), which effectively suspends the 1971 constitution.
- The Anti-Terrorism Law of 1992, which gives the government sweeping powers in determining who is a "terrorist" (and allows execution for the crime of simply *belonging* to a "terrorist organization").
- The 1992 executive order (and subsequent policies) aimed at "nationalizing" private mosques, attempting to forge a single, government-controlled voice of Islam across Egypt.
- The Syndicates Law of 1993, which gives the government power to appoint Governing Boards to unions and syndicates.
- The manipulation of elections (local and national) in 1990, 1995, and 2000.
- Turning a blind eye to police use of excessive force and extrajudicial killings.
- The use of military courts for civilian crimes (which expedite trials and executions and prevent judicial review and appeals).
- Law 93, the Press Law of 1995, which curtails freedom of the press.

Together with increased physical repression and torture, these measures have diminished what little popular support the political system previously enjoyed. Still, this government is not in danger of losing power to a society resurgent: Islamist revolution is unlikely in

Egypt, and the secular opposition is unable to transform the political system. The regime has long had the ability to thwart any competition or threat to its existence—whether Islamist violence, foreign invasion, economic crises, social unrest, or internal division and drift—thanks to the continued strength and general loyalty of the armed forces, central security forces (al-Aman al-Markazy), and secret police (Mukhabaraat).

The foiled assassination attempt on Mubarak in Addis Ababa in June 1995 gave the government a rationale to demonstrate the effectiveness of its security forces, the indispensability of Mubarak to stability in Egypt, and the necessity of continued vigilance against terrorism.[40] The Addis Ababa incident, continuing violence between Islamist militants and police, and unchallenged electoral irregularities have emboldened the government in its efforts to crush nonviolent opponents of the regime as well as violent groups—a battle that also prevents the development of a more free and open civil society.

Perhaps it is no coincidence that after the popular show of support for Mubarak upon his safe return to Cairo from Ethiopia in 1995 and as parliamentary elections approached, the government accelerated a massive campaign against the previously tolerated Muslim Brotherhood, which espouses nonviolence and a willingness to play within the rules of Egypt's political game.[41] The government claimed to have found a "paper trail" linking the Brotherhood with the outlawed Islamic militant groups Jihad and Jama'aat Islamiyya. It imprisoned more than two hundred mainly young members of the Brotherhood in July 1995. A similar pattern of government intimidation of political candidates from Islamist groups occurred in the 2000 parliamentary elections.[42] Fahmy Howaidy, a prominent Islamist columnist for the semiofficial *al-Ahram* Arabic daily, compared such moves with the mistakes that Algeria's government made when it cracked down on the Islamic Salvation Front in January 1992, sending the country into military dictatorship and chaos.[43] While Egypt is far from falling into such chaos, the fear among many Egyptians is that without any limits on government dictates, the country could head in the same direction as Algeria.

Many analysts inside Egypt place blame for the continuing instability on the government. Muhammad Hassanein Heikal, a close confidant of the late president Nasser, criticized the massive government assault on the Cairo slum district of Imbaba in December 1992, an act that gave the militants a "bonus of strength" they did not really have. It frightened away would-be visitors to Egypt and "killed" tourism.[44] Six months before this government assault, in June, the security forces were sent into another poor Cairo suburb after the assassination of Farag Fouda, a liberal Muslim intellectual, a leader in the human rights and democracy movement, and strong critic of Islamic fundamentalists and militants. His murderers, one of whom was caught immediately, were said to be from the outlawed Jihad organization, the group associated with the assassination of Anwar Sadat in 1981. In the aftermath of Fouda's murder, pro-government journalists were warning of the dangers should the government overreact. Hasan Ragab, of the daily newspaper *al-Akhbar,* said that these militants/terrorists "love to be martyrs and they want to move the government toward confrontation. And the more repressive the government becomes, the more unstable it becomes. If the government takes away civil liberties, the extremists have succeeded." The highly respected columnist Mustapha Amin similarly warned that the extremists "are strong when you hit them—weak when you argue with them."[45]

The government, however, did not heed this advice and instead has consistently taken the opposite tack. It strikes hard. It avoids accommodation. The Egyptian Organization for Human Rights, Amnesty International, Human Rights Watch/Middle East, and other groups have documented hundreds of cases of torture by government officers, primarily against Islamists.[46]

It took some time for the U.S. government to acknowledge that its most important ally in the Arab world has a consistent record of human rights abuses. In 1993 the U.S. Department of State acknowledged that "there is convincing evidence that police and security forces systematically practice torture. . . . Most torture is perpetrated by officers of the Interior Ministry's GDSSI [General Directorate for State Security Investigations]."[47] By 1995 the State Department was even more direct: "There continued to be widespread human rights violations in 1994. . . . Security forces committed human rights abuses in their campaign against terrorist groups, but frequently victimized noncombatants as well."[48] In its 1999 report the State Department noted that

> torture and abuse of detainees by police, security personnel, and prison guards is common. . . . Torture takes place in SSIS [State Security Investigations Sector] offices, including its headquarters in Cairo, and at Central Security Force camps. Torture victims usually are taken to an SSIS office where they are handcuffed, blindfolded, and questioned about their associations, religious beliefs, and political views. Torture is used to extract information, coerce the victims to end their antigovernment activities, and deter others from such activities.
>
> Egyptian human rights groups and victims reported a number of torture methods that are employed by state security personnel and the police. Detainees frequently are stripped; hung by their wrists with their feet just touching the floor or forced to stand for prolonged periods; doused with hot or cold water; beaten; forced to stand outdoors in cold weather; and subjected to electrical shocks. Some victims, including female detainees, report that they have been threatened with rape.[49]

And torture is not limited to suspected militants. It extends to family members and legal counsel as well.[50] Egyptian and international human rights reports document not only the abuse of human rights but the failure of the government of Egypt "to punish those responsible for torture."[51]

The strength of Egypt's security and police apparatuses and their combined disregard for human rights and civil liberties means that the government can indeed control Egyptian society, but the methods it uses weaken its legitimacy to govern. Egyptians have long tolerated the authoritarian rule that Nasser established, but only while their basic economic needs have been met and their personal and social liberties have remained relatively "unencumbered" by political processes such as free and fair elections, rights of association and expression, and other aspects of democracy. This was the "social contract" established under Nasser and maintained, albeit with some major violations, by his successors.

Increasing domestic instability and Islamic militancy—attacks on police and other government officials, on Coptic Christians, on tourists, and on other innocent bystanders—are arguably manifestations of severe economic dislocation and government repression. Such dislocation includes consistently high inflation and unemployment, overpopulation (mainly in urban areas), bank failures (primarily Islamic Investment companies), and inadequacy of transportation, housing, education, and health services.[52] Authoritarian politics of exclusion is an equally important factor explaining the continuing conflict between state and society in Egypt. Such exclusion limits the outlets of expression of dissatisfaction, anger, and frustration. In these circumstances, the growing popularity of Islamic groups is not surprising.[53]

The Muslim Brotherhood is popular among the middle and working classes. It frequently wins contested elections in the syndicates (unions) of professional workers as well as in independent races for parliament. Still, there is no way to gauge the full extent of this popularity and whether it translates into a desire to place these mainstream, nonviolent Islamists in control of the state and its police, military, and intelligence apparatus.

From the perspective of U.S. policymakers, given the choice between a nondemocratic but friendly government and the prospect of the coming to power of a movement with an untested respect for the values that the United States preaches, the former option seems the more attractive. If the United States gives too much support for democracy, human rights, and the rule of law in Egypt, then it might help to bring to power the Muslim Brotherhood, a notion that makes many in Washington uncomfortable, given the experiences of Algeria and Afghanistan, even though the case of Egypt and its nonviolent Muslim opposition is quite different

THE U.S. RESPONSE?

When circumstances have allowed it no other option but to express concern (never "outrage") over human rights practices in Egypt, the U.S. government has relied almost exclusively on quiet diplomacy. One State Department official suggested that it "falls to the U.S. ambassador to Egypt to whisper in Mubarak's ear that we have a concern" about a particular human rights issue.[54] In addition, Egypt appears in the State Department's annual reports on human rights practices.

During the 1990s the language in those reports evolved from caution and uncertainty over how to acknowledge or even criticize a U.S. "friend," to increasing honesty about human rights abuses, to a more bureaucratic and formulaic recital of the facts. The formula is such that one official in the State Department's Bureau of Democracy, Human Rights, and Labor acknowledges that people "skip to paragraph four" (or thereabouts) of nearly any *Country Report* to see what the U.S. assessment of the situation is: whether, for instance, it is "good," "improving," "worsening," or "poor."[55]

The State Department's annual reports on human rights could be an important tool for makers of U.S. foreign policy. While mandated by Congress, these reports are not designed specifically to be *the* U.S. government response or reaction to human rights practices in any given country. Still, they have become institutionalized and are vital to both Congress and the White House during the formulation of foreign policy. However, Congress and the White House can also ignore the reports. At a minimum, the reports put governments on notice that the United States takes human rights practices into consideration on bilateral issues. They also may provide recognition, if not full protection, to local human rights activists and monitoring groups.

In the case of Egypt, the report for 1999 observed that the Egyptian government continues "to commit numerous serious human rights abuses" but also acknowledged that "its record again improved somewhat."[56] The February 2001 State Department report recorded that Egypt "generally respected the human rights of its citizens in some areas, and its record improved somewhat over the previous year, primarily due to a decrease in terrorist activity by Islamic extremists; however, the Government's record was poor with respect to freedom of expression and its treatment of detainees, among other areas." The report also criticized "the arrests of thousands of members of the Muslim Brotherhood in the months before [parliamentary] elections."[57]

The U.S. Agency for International Development (USAID) also is poised to address human rights in Egypt, the largest recipient of USAID-managed funds in the world. One might expect that, because USAID is a development organization, it would not make a point of promoting human rights in Egypt. But given that USAID is in reality an arm of the U.S. State Department and given that the United States claims to respect human rights in its foreign policy, USAID and State should in fact work more closely together in promoting such rights.[58] And, indeed, the State Department's Bureau of Democracy, Human Rights, and Labor defines part of its mission as working bilaterally—through USAID—and multilaterally to link assistance to foreign governments with performance in the areas of democracy and human rights. However, according to one official, communication between the bureau and USAID is "terrible. We don't coordinate in fact; and when we try to meet to discuss priorities or plan activities, turf and politics get in the way. We need approval from the Assistant Secretary of State and his counterpart at AID—just to hold a meeting."[59]

At a minimum, USAID may address human rights problems *indirectly* through specific programs aimed at developing democratic institutions: for example, programs in the administration of justice, participatory rural governance, private voluntary organizations, and a partnership project for girls and young women, among others. These have as objectives the strengthening of rights, liberties, and opportunities of Egyptian citizens.

Stating such objectives and realizing them are two different things, however. At USAID/Egypt during the Clinton administration, for example, the United States targeted four areas: economic growth, population and health, protecting the environment, and promoting democracy. But at the end of the Clinton administration, it was admitted in USAID's FY 2000 *Performance Report* that efforts in the last of these areas—a program aimed at encouraging "more transparent and accountable government institutions"—had "failed to meet expectations."

Other U.S. agencies hoping to have an impact on human rights have had similar experiences. Take, for instance, the U.S. Department of Justice's International Criminal Investigative Training Assistance Program (ICITAP), which attempted to initiate training on human dignity and civil disorder management for police forces in Egypt in 1999. The project aimed "to provide professional law enforcement services based on democratic principles, respect for human rights and the rule of law."[60] By 2001 this project had been suspended. One official involved in this effort recognized that the police and military establishments are under little or no political pressure to reform in general or to respect human rights in particular. ICITAP is not presently involved with the government of Egypt, and officials at ICITAP have little expectation of future engagement.[61]

Beyond the executive branch, several other elements of the U.S. government play a role in promoting (or at least in raising concerns about) human rights in Egypt. These include Congress, independent commissions (e.g., the Commission on International Religious Freedom), and the judicial branch (e.g., the Federal Immigration Court). Immigration judges regularly hear complaints from Egyptians seeking political asylum in the United States. Some asylum seekers from Egypt, especially Copts, fear that they will be persecuted by militant groups or individuals if they are forced to return; others fear that they will be imprisoned on their return by a government that tortured them in the past; still others fear that their daughters will be forced to undergo genital mutilation. The judges' decisions, as often as not, do offer protection to individuals and their families (in the case of minor children) from the persecution and torture they would otherwise expect at home.[62]

U.S. constituents and interest groups regularly lobby Congress to investigate human rights abuses, especially those related to restrictions on religious freedom and to government-tolerated anti-Semitism in the Egyptian media. For the executive branch and Congress, the primary leverage available to the United States is its annual aid package to Egypt. As an aide to the Senate Committee on Foreign Relations explains, a typical scenario for congressional action runs as follows: first, Congress holds hearings on religious freedom or anti-Semitism abroad; second, Egypt's name is introduced as a "country of concern" on these topics; third, members of Congress question whether the United States should be spending so much money in Egypt, given that it tolerates acts that violate U.S. values; and fourth, the Egyptian government responds either by rejecting U.S. pressure or by reassuring members of Congress that Egypt does indeed share those same values.[63]

Congress also reproaches Egypt directly when it comes to renewing the $2 billion annual aid package. In a June 27, 2000, meeting of the House Appropriations Committee to consider the Foreign Operations, Export Financing, and Related Programs Appropriations bill for fiscal year 2001, Representative Robert B. Aderholt (R-Ala.)

added the following text to the paragraph about U.S. financial aid to Egypt: "Nevertheless, the Committee is concerned about ongoing violence experienced by the Christian minority in Egypt. The Committee urges Egypt to expedite the investigations of the murders of 2000 and 1998 in Al-Kosheh, and of the 1998 interrogations."[64] The representative acknowledged that "Egypt is a valuable ally and has greatly helped U.S. efforts to advance peace in the Middle East." But he also drew attention to the

> fact that Christians in Egypt, especially Coptic Christians, face ongoing violence and are in need of full protection of the Egyptian Judicial system. The worst of these outbreaks is the murder of 21 persons in January, 2000 in the town of Al-Kosheh. . . . My report language expresses the concern of the Committee about this violence and urges Egypt to expedite investigations regarding this incident but also of events in 1998 in the same small town. There were two murders [of Copts] in 1998 and allegations of brutal interrogations by the Police; 1014 Christians were arrested and interrogated. . . . When tourists were killed in Luxor [in 1997], the reaction of Cairo was swift and decisive, including the appointment of a new Minister of the Interior, who oversees the police. That sent a powerful message throughout the country, and Egypt is currently a very safe country to visit. The great majority of Muslim citizens of Egypt are law-abiding and desire peace. I am afraid that because of concerns about possibly energizing extremist Muslim groups to the point of violence, Cairo is reluctant to prosecute Muslims when there are incidents of violence against Christians.[65]

(Aderholt's primary focus on Coptic Christians is understandable, and his concern for their protection is very laudable. At the same time, Congress should note explicitly that *all* Egyptians deserve full protection of the law and full respect for their civil and human rights.)

Despite such reproaches, it remains unclear whether Congress actually has any influence over the Egyptian government's record on human rights. It sometimes seems that the public warnings that Congress issues (while still authorizing billions of dollars in aid to Egypt each year) are merely a move in a political game played out by two partners who would prefer not to deal with this sensitive topic. Furthermore, even if Congress were to step outside the rules of the game and press for reductions in U.S. aid to, or even for sanctions against, Egypt, it might only harden the resolve of the Egyptian government to resist U.S. demands to reform its human rights practices. Punishing Egypt is not feasible, given that Egypt will more likely "get mad . . . get more nationalistic, defensive, and unresponsive," even if "they hear us."[66]

CONCLUSIONS

Three Key Challenges

The first challenge for the United States in implementing its human rights agenda in Egypt is the closeness of the relationship between the two countries. For decades, the United States has lacked the political will to encourage Egypt to adhere to human rights conventions or standards. The White House and Congress have yet to agree on whether the United States could, should, or would press Egypt on human rights. When such issues are addressed in general terms, discussion can be fruitful, but when discussion centers on a specific strategic partner, such as Egypt, it tends to falter.

The second challenge, which is also tied to the question of political will, may be the overriding one: the inherent complexity of implementing human rights programs in Egypt. As discussed at the beginning of this chapter, the U.S.-Egypt partnership since the 1970s has been a delicate one; it demands a sensitive approach from the United States but also an understanding from Egypt that sometimes the United States has to be more direct and less nuanced in discussing national interests such as human rights promotion. Because of U.S. support for Israel—especially when Palestinians are being killed in large numbers by Israeli forces—and other U.S. policies that are unpopular within Egypt, an occasional resurgence of anti-American sentiment in Egypt and the region as a whole is to be expected; pushing Egypt on human rights at such times would certainly be counterproductive. Furthermore, while the United States should promote respect for human rights in Egypt, in doing so it must maintain some public distance between itself and Egyptian human rights activists if those activists are not to be discredited in the eyes of many Egyptians by being seen as the servants of U.S. interests.

The third challenge is posed by perceived double standards in
U.S. foreign policy in the Middle East. Egyptians regularly condemn
U.S. interference in Egypt's internal affairs, especially on issues related
to human rights, and point to the U.S. refusal to apply similar pressure on Israel for its abuses of human rights. The fact that Washington's
primary concern is for Egypt's Coptic Christians, not for Egypt's Muslim majority, is also taken as evidence of U.S. double standards. If
U.S. policymakers were to explicitly encompass the Muslim majority
in their calls for an end to abuses, and if they were to ask more of
allies such as Israel, Turkey, and Saudi Arabia in terms of respecting
human rights, Egypt would find it harder to deflect U.S. criticism of
its human rights policies.

Multilateral versus Bilateral Channels

A multilateral approach to human rights implementation in Egypt
may prove even less effective than the existing bilateral approach.
The World Bank, for example, manages billions of dollars in projects
in Egypt (e.g., the Social Fund for Development) in areas related to
civil society, democratization, local governance, and so on. However,
the World Bank has not even considered linking aid to Egypt's respect
for human rights.[67] And because Egypt, although it has little respect for
human rights, does not commit large-scale atrocities, its behavior does
not warrant UN intervention. Sanctions against Egypt—multilateral
as well as bilateral—are not an option.

Engaging the Police

Egypt, as the United States needs to acknowledge, is a combination
of a police state and a military regime. To have a significant impact
on Egyptian human rights policies, therefore, the United States must
work directly with Egypt's police force and armed forces. Concrete,
albeit minimal, steps by U.S. policymakers might include a stronger
commitment to engaging in discussions with Egyptian police and, especially, the internal security services. Police training programs, particularly those that focus on methods of interrogating prisoners and suspects, could be implemented through the democracy programs at
USAID and perhaps through professional exchange programs. Such

training might also promote the idea that suspects have rights and should be treated as innocent until proven guilty.

Some programs already exist to promote discussion of freedom of expression and assembly, to foster the rule of law, and to strengthen civil society. These programs should be expanded and carefully reviewed to ensure that they are not perceived by Egyptians as examples of U.S. condescension or self-righteousness. In addition, the vast existing network of Egyptian, Palestinian, Lebanese, Jordanian, and other Arab civil society organizations should be enlisted to spearhead such initiatives. Persuading the Egyptian government to agree to such involvement of nongovernmental organizations will be difficult at best; nevertheless, the case should be made and pushed by the United States.

Strengthening the Strategic Partnership

Although there is little evidence to suggest that the United States has been successful in promoting human rights in Egypt, it should not abandon the attempt. On the contrary, it should seek to engage the government of Egypt more forthrightly in this cause by further strengthening the strategic partnership it claims to have with Egypt. By embracing the government of Egypt more closely, and in particular by improving strategic military, intelligence, and other security relations, the United States will be in a stronger position to work with the Egyptian police and military—and perhaps the legislature and the courts—in pressing for much greater respect for human rights.

NOTES

1. For reasons behind Egypt's increasingly cold stance toward Israel, see Dina Ezzat, "The Big Freeze," *al-Ahram Weekly*, no. 505, October 26–November 1, 2000, www.ahram.org.eg/weekly/2000/505/pal3k.htm.

2. For the context of Nixon's 1974 remark, see Ambassador Hermann Frederick Eilts, foreword to William J. Burns, *Economic Aid and American Policy toward Egypt, 1955–81* (Albany: State University of New York, 1985), xiv.

3. Palestinian hijackers seized the *Achille Lauro* in October 1985 off Port Said, Egypt, killed American Leon Klinghoffer, and held more than four hundred hostages for two days before surrendering to Egyptian authorities. Egypt promised safe passage to the terrorists, but the U.S. Navy intercepted Egyptian jets attempting to fly the hijackers to safety. U.S.-Egypt relations were seriously threatened.

4. Gregory L. Aftandilian, *Egypt's Bid for Arab Leadership: Implications for U.S. Policy* (New York: Council on Foreign Relations Press, 1993), 65.

5. In mid-November 2001, President George Bush signed an executive order allowing the trial of noncitizens suspected of terrorist activities, the trials to be held in military rather than civilian courts. "Terror Suspects Face US Military Trials," *BBC News, World: Americas*, November 14, 2001, http://news.bbc. co.uk/hi/english/world/americas/newsid_1655000.1655169.stm. That same week, President Hosni Mubarak charged ninety-four people with forming an underground terrorist group and propagating "anti-government literature"; it was the first military trial in Egypt in nearly two years. The defendants' families cried foul: "These people have done nothing," said one angry mother. "We are paying the price for America's so-called war against terrorism, and the government wants to show that it is being cooperative." "Islamists Face Military Trial," *al-Ahram Weekly*, no. 561, November 22–28, 2001, weekly.ahram.org.eg/2001/561/eg7.htm.

6. U.S. State Department official instrumental in developing the human rights report for Egypt, interview by author, Washington, D.C., April 4, 2002.

7. Elissa Massimino, Lawyers Committee for Human Rights, "Statement on 2002 Department of State Human Rights Country Reports," March 31, 2003, www.lchr.org/media/2003_alerts/0331.htm.

8. According to the Lawyers Committee for Human Rights in New York, "The Egyptian government may be taking advantage of the international attention focused on the war in Iraq to take further steps to intimidate independent activists and government critics. The government's harsh crackdown, that has followed a major anti-war demonstration in Cairo on March 20, has greatly exceeded in its scope and intensity restrictions on the right to freedom of peaceful assembly that are permitted in international law. Scores of activists remain in detention, and many report beatings and torture." Reported on the Democracy-Egypt website, March 27, 2003, www.democracy-egypt.org/files/NGO/2003/03-2703LawyersCommittee.htm.

9. William B. Quandt, *The United States and Egypt: An Essay on Policy for the 1990s*, Brookings Institution Report (Cairo: American University in Cairo Press, 1990), 5.

10. Twenty-five years of U.S. economic aid to Egypt includes $5.8 billion in commodity imports, $5.7 billion in infrastructure development (water, wastewater, sanitation, and power), $5.1 billion in health care, family planning, education, agriculture, and environmental protection, $3.9 billion in food aid, and $3.6 billion in cash transfers. U.S. Department of State, USAID-Egypt Desk office (mimeograph, January 2001).

11. See the U.S.-Egypt Partnership page on the website of the U.S. embassy in Egypt (as of February 2001), usembassy.egnet.net/usegypt/usegmain.htm.

12. "The slow development of the Egyptian-U.S. partnership in the past year has alerted authorities in both capitals to the political problems that may obstruct the partnership initiative. Diplomatic circles in Egypt and the United States did not conceal that Vice President Al Gore, President Mubarak's partner in the initiative, had postponed his visit to Egypt three times in the last year for political reasons." Abdel Azim Hammad, "Letter from Cairo," *al-Ahram Weekly*, April 30–May 2, 1998. See the website of the Egyptian Ministry of Information, www.sis.gov.eg/public/letter/html/text190.htm.

13. Given their steadfast commitment to the pursuit of a comprehensive and just peace, regional stability and welfare, and security for all, "the United States and Egypt have found it incumbent upon them to engage more closely through the mechanism of the Strategic Dialogue, to further promote these shared objectives in the Middle East and to exchange assessments on how best to realize them." James Rubin, State Department spokesman, July 15, 1998, www.usembassy-israel.org.il/publish/peace/archives/1998/july/me0715a.shtml.

14. Ambassador David Welch, interview by Thomas Gorguissian, *al-Ahram Weekly*, no. 547, August 16–22, 2001, weekly.ahram.org.eg/2001/547.

15. Jon B. Alterman, "Egypt: Stable, but for How Long?" *Washington Quarterly* (fall 2000): 116.

16. See Amnesty International, "Egypt: In the Name of Fighting Terrorism, Indefinite Detention and Torture Become Systematic," December 16, 1996, online at www.amnesty.it/news/1996/51201696.htm. The report states that "[h]uman rights violations in Egypt are continuing—and in many cases increasing—in the name of fighting terrorism." The report focuses on "administrative detention without charge or trial, systematic torture of known or suspected members of armed Islamist opposition groups, the death penalty, as well as on killings and other abuses committed by armed opposition groups."

17. U.S. Department of State official, Bureau of Democracy, Human Rights, and Labor, interview by author, Washington, D.C., February 13, 2001.

18. Ibid., emphasis added.

19. Ibid.

20. Ibid.

21. See www.ibnkhaldun.org/index.html.

22. Ibrahim was formally charged with receiving $240,000 from the European Union without government permission to fund two projects for promoting political awareness and participation in national elections. Khaled Dawoud,

"The State versus Ibrahim," *al-Ahram Weekly*, February 22–28, 2001, www.ahram. org.eg/weekly/2001/522/egb.htm.

23. Jailan Halawi, "Prosecution Case under Fire," *al-Ahram Weekly*, January 18–24, 2001, www.ahram.org.eg/weekly/2001/517/eg5.htm.

24. Jailan Halawi, "Going Home," *al-Ahram Weekly*, February 7–13, 2002, weekly.ahram.org.eg/2002/572/fr3.htm.

25. Ibid.

26. Four other defendants also received prison terms: Magda al-Bey, three years; Mohammed Hassanain, three years; Nadia Abdel Nour, two years; and Marwa Zaki, two years (in absentia).

27. For extensive background on this case, see Lawyers Committee for Human Rights, www.lchr.org/defenders/hrd_middle_east/hrd_Egypt/hrd_ibrahim/ hrd_ibrahim_old.htm.

28. See www.amnestyusa.org/action/special/ibrahim.html.

29. Dawoud, "The State versus Ibrahim." The Coptic Christians make up between 6 and 10 percent of Egypt's population.

30. U.S. Department of State official, interview by author, Washington, D.C., February 14, 2001.

31. Saad Eddin Ibrahim's wife, Barbara, expressed this concern to me in e-mail correspondence. The Egyptian media have also expressed this concern. While Ibrahim and his family and friends are right to want to avoid the appearance of heavy-handed U.S. pressure on the government of Egypt, they must also not allow Ibrahim's *alleged* crimes to go unchallenged. Thus, such U.S. intervention is understandable and desirable, given that Ibrahim is a U.S. citizen; it is also necessary for Egyptians themselves to pressure their own government to respect and abide by the rule of law. However, that is not a standard for which Egypt is known.

32. Egyptian academics and journalists, interviews by author, Washington, D.C., April 4, 2001.

33. U.S. Department of State official, Bureau of Democracy, Human Rights, and Labor, Washington, D.C., August 2, 2001.

34. Ibid.

35. U.S. Department of State official, Bureau of Democracy, Human Rights, and Labor, Washington, D.C., April 4, 2002.

36. For "liberal Islamist" criticism of militant Islam, see Judge Muhammad Said Al-Ashmawi, *al-Islam al-Siyasi* (Cairo, 1987). For "liberal Muslim" criticism, see many of the works by Farag Fouda, including *al-Haqiqa al-Gha'iba* (The absent reality) (Cairo, 1987) and *al-Irhab* (The terror) (Cairo, 1988).

37. Ahmed Abdalla," Egypt's Islamists and the State: From Complicity to Confrontation," *Middle East Report* (July-August 1993): 29.

38. Egypt's Supreme Constitutional Court declared Law 153 unconstitutional in June 2000.

39. See www.lchr.org/media/2002_alerts/0605.htm.

40. For example, in its first issue after the attack on Mubarak, Egypt's *al-Ahram Weekly* newspaper celebrated his survival with the following headlines: "Towards Greater Reforms: No Fear for Democracy," "Confronting Terrorism beyond Egypt's Borders," "United We Stand," "Egypt Able to Oust Bashir" (Bashir was the military leader of Sudan, accused by Egypt of encouraging or planning the attempt), and "Marchers Celebrate Mubarak's Safety," June 29– July 5, 1995, 1–3.

41. See Denis J. Sullivan and Sana Abed-Kotob, *Islam in Contemporary Egypt: Civil Society vs. the State* (Boulder, Colo.: Lynne Rienner, 1999). See also Abed-Kotob, "The Accommodationists Speak: Goals and Strategies of the Muslim Brotherhood of Egypt," *International Journal of Middle East Studies* 27, no. 3 (August 1995): 321–339.

42. Jailan Halawi, "A Running Clampdown," *al-Ahram Weekly*, October 12–18, 2000, weekly.ahram.org.eg/2000/503/eg2.htm.

43. James Whittington, "Egypt's Islamists: Proscribed or Provoked?" *Financial Times*, August 9, 1995, 4.

44. As reported in James Napoli, *Washington Report on Middle East Affairs* (December 1992–January 1993): 41.

45. Ibid.

46. The following are all from Human Rights Watch/ Middle East Watch, *Behind Closed Doors: Torture and Detention in Egypt* (July 1992); *Egypt: Hostage-Taking and Intimidation by Security Forces* (January 1995); *Egypt: Trials of Civilians in Military Courts Violate International Law* (July 1993); and *Egyptian Authorities Clamp Down on Dissent* (February 13, 1991).

47. U.S. Department of State, *Country Report on Human Rights Practices for 1992*, report submitted to Senate Committee on Foreign Relations and House Committee on Foreign Affairs (Washington, D.C.: Government Printing Office, February 1993), 991.

48. U.S. Department of State, *Country Report on Human Rights Practices for 1994*, report submitted to Senate Committee on Foreign Relations and House Committee on Foreign Affairs (Washington, D.C.: Government Printing Office, February 1995). The quotation is from page 1 of a document acquired directly from the State Department.

49. U.S. Department of State, Bureau of Democracy, Human Rights, and Labor, *1999 Country Reports on Human Rights Practices*, released February 25, 2000, www.state.gov/www/global/human_rights/1999_hrp_report/egypt.html.

50. On April 30, 1994, Abdel-Harith Madani, a lawyer defending Islamists charged with terrorism, was reported by the Egyptian Bar Association to have been tortured to death in police custody. The government, calling him a "terrorist," said he died of asthma.

51. U.S. Department of State, *Country Report on Human Rights Practices for 1994*.

52. See Hala Mustafa, *al-Islam al-Siyasi fi Misr: min harakat al-islah ila jama 'at al-c unf* (Political Islam in Egypt: From the movement of reform to associations of violence) (Cairo: al-Ahram Center for Strategic Studies, 1992). See also Raouf Abbas Hamed, "Factors behind the Political Islamic Movement in Egypt" (paper presented at Middle East Studies Association annual meeting, San Antonio, Texas, November 1990).

53. One of the earlier works describing the popularity of Islamist organizations on Egyptian campuses is Gilles Kepel, *Muslim Extremism in Egypt: The Prophet and the Pharaoh* (Berkeley: University of California Press, 1986).

54. U.S. Department of State official, interview by author, Washington, D.C., February 13, 2001.

55. Ibid.

56. U.S. Department of State, *1999 Country Reports on Human Rights Practices: Egypt*.

57. U.S. Department of State, *Egypt: Country Reports on Human Rights Practices, 2000*, report submitted to Senate Committee on Foreign Relations and House Committee on Foreign Affairs (Washington, D.C.: Government Printing Office, February 2001).

58. Officially, "USAID is an independent federal government agency that receives overall foreign policy guidance from the Secretary of State." "This Is USAID," www.usaid.gov/about.

59. U.S. State Department official, Bureau of Democracy, Human Rights, and Labor, interview by author, Washington, D.C., April 4, 2002.

60. "ICITAP's mission is to help achieve U.S. criminal justice and foreign policy goals by assisting foreign governments in developing the capacity to provide professional law enforcement services based on democratic principles, respect for human rights and the rule of law." From U.S. Department of Justice, International Criminal Investigative Training Assistance Program, "The Experience of ICITAP in Assisting the Institutional Development of Foreign Police Forces," n.d.

61. ICITAP official, interview by author, August 2, 2001.

62. Attorney, interview by author, Boston, Mass., March 5, 2001. This Boston attorney has argued the cases of scores of Egyptians (Copts especially) seeking political asylum through the Federal Immigration Court system.

63. Senate Committee on Foreign Relations aide, interview by author, Washington, D.C., February 13, 2001.

64. *Congressional Record,* "Investigation of Murders in Al-Kosheh, Egypt—Hon. Robert B. Aderholt" (Washington, D.C.: Government Printing Office, June 28, 2000), E1137.

65. Ibid.

66. Senate Committee on Foreign Relations aide, interview by author.

67. World Bank official responsible for Egypt and Social Fund for Development, interview by author, Washington, D.C., April 1998.

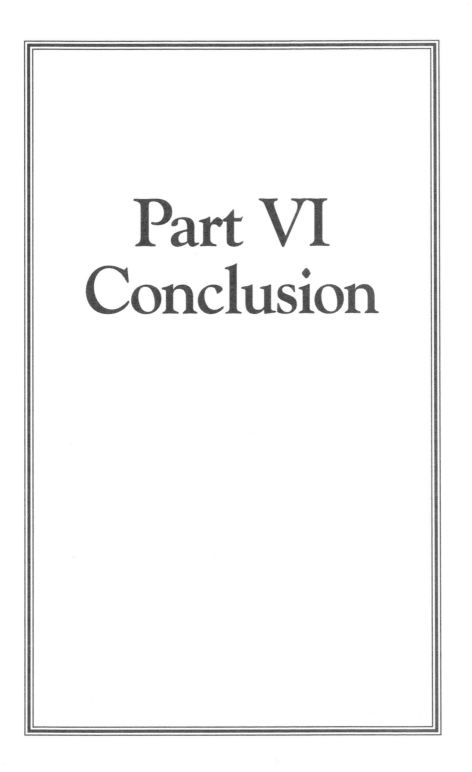

Part VI
Conclusion

Conclusion

What Works?

DEBRA LIANG-FENTON

T HIS BOOK WAS INSPIRED by a deceptively simple question about the implementation of U.S. human rights policy: What works? As the preceding case studies of fourteen countries have amply demonstrated, there are no easy answers. First, it is not always clear whether a particular policy has in fact worked; we may be able to point to a change in a state's respect for human rights, but it can be difficult to be sure of the extent to which that change was prompted by action taken by the United States. Second, understanding what works obliges us not only to judge the success or failure of a policy but also to assess why and how that policy was implemented. In other words, we need to examine not only the outcomes but also the factors that shaped the formulation of a particular policy and the tools used to conduct it. Third, we must also take into account the context within which implementation occurred. In fact, we should more accurately speak in the plural, of the contexts, for the fate of a policy is determined not only in the target country but also in the United States and indeed in the broader international arena.

Given these myriad contexts and the great range of influences that shape the making of policy and the numerous and varied tools used to implement it, the task of providing neat and tidy answers to the question What works? is Herculean, if not Sisyphean.

Fortunately, however, while we cannot determine the precise formula that worked in the past or predict exactly what will work in the future, we can draw some more general but no less useful conclusions. This chapter organizes these conclusions into two categories: tools and lessons. The first category identifies the set of tools most commonly used by U.S. policymakers and assesses the conditions under which they are most likely to be effective. The second distills from the case studies a series of guidelines that should be of practical help to those who craft and execute U.S. human rights policy.

TOOLS FOR IMPLEMENTING U.S. HUMAN RIGHTS POLICY

The case studies have identified nine tools commonly employed by those who make and implement U.S. human rights policy:

- private diplomacy,
- public diplomacy,
- the annual *Country Reports on Human Rights Practices* issued by the U.S. Department of State,
- congressional action,
- cultural, scholarly, and other exchanges,
- sanctions and incentives,
- democracy building,
- symbolic actions, and
- the media.

Each of these tools has its own strengths and weaknesses, and each is more appropriate to some circumstances than to others. Which tools can be used in a given situation, and to what extent, is determined not least by the nature of the bilateral relationship that the United States has with the target state; as U.S. objectives toward a given country vary, so too will U.S. behavior vary—and with it, the methods U.S. policymakers use.

Invariably, these tools are used not in isolation from one another but in some combination. Deciding what combination will best achieve a particular outcome is a complex calculation that involves a host of variables ranging from the character of the target regime to the character of the human rights abuses being committed, to the economic and political resources at hand in Washington. The case studies have shown that tools should be selected based on a solid understanding of the situation and carefully calibrated to the prevailing circumstances; they must also be recalibrated as situations and actors change and as new opportunities emerge for the promotion of human rights.

Private Diplomacy

Private diplomacy (or "quiet diplomacy") is a representation of concern communicated within the confines of a private discussion. It does not raise the stakes in a way that public diplomacy, with its attendant media coverage and subsequent political fallout, can. It also has the advantage of creating few painful side effects if a request goes unmet.

Private diplomacy is often used by U.S. policymakers seeking to bring about a change in human rights practices—indeed, it has featured in most of the cases examined in this volume—and is the tool of choice among diplomats, who typically prefer to have friendly relations with their host country and thus seek not to embarrass the local regime.

The reasons for using private diplomacy are primarily twofold: to avoid publicly humiliating another government in order to maintain good relations, and to avoid provoking, through public criticism of the target state, a nationalistic backlash against U.S. "interference," which might force a regime to side with local hard-liners. Once Mikhail Gorbachev introduced measures that set the former Soviet Union on the path toward democracy, for example, the United States expressed its criticisms quietly behind closed doors so as not to weaken his domestic position or force him to "grandstand" against the United States. Sometimes the quiet threat of a public complaint can elicit a desired outcome. In the case of South Korea, then U.S. assistant secretary of state for East Asian and Pacific affairs Gaston Sigur told the Chun Doo Hwan government quietly in 1987 that the U.S. government would publicly complain if the regime cracked down on demonstrators.

Wishing to avoid this public humiliation, the Chun government refrained from cracking down.

Private diplomacy has its shortcomings, however. In Rwanda, for instance, the application of private diplomacy in the events leading up to the 1994 genocide seems only to have given legitimacy to the Habyarimana regime. Another significant shortcoming is that a quiet request may be quietly ignored. In the case of China, the United States used private diplomacy for six months to win the release of scholar Song Yongyi. When it became evident that these efforts were not producing a desired outcome, his case went public. One month later, Song was released.

Public Diplomacy

Policymakers and diplomats use public diplomacy to attract attention to human rights abuses and breaches in the observance of democratic principles. Public pronouncements may take such forms as speeches, statements, or testimonies before Congress and are almost invariably intended to elicit media coverage—indeed, the effectiveness of public diplomacy is directly related to the importance of media attention in prompting greater respect for human rights in a given case.

The United States has used public diplomacy in a wide variety of instances: when prominent political dissidents or individuals have been imprisoned without due process (in China, for example); when a political party has been banned and its supporters have been jailed on speech- or assembly-related offenses (such as the Islamist Welfare Party in Turkey); and when the credibility of an important strategic alliance has been jeopardized (such as in the case of Bosnia, when the United States came to see the growing crisis there as threatening to U.S. interests in NATO and the United Nations).

Public diplomacy can also have the positive consequence—albeit sometimes unintended and often indirect—of bolstering the work of indigenous NGOs in target states. According to Merle Goldman, for example, public accusations of human rights abuses have helped to call into being a growing body of human rights experts in China. External condemnations of abuses may not have much overt impact on the Chinese government, but they have altered international expectations, encouraged domestic human rights advocates, and even prodded the Chinese leadership into using the language of rights.

In Kenya, "rogue ambassador" Smith Hempstone articulated dissatisfaction with the Moi regime's record on human rights. Hempstone's outspoken style emboldened local human rights groups and even other foreign ambassadors.

Generally, U.S. public diplomacy serves to enhance U.S. credibility among other governments and human rights constituencies. By the same token, however, U.S. actions that do not support U.S. rhetoric can undermine public diplomacy efforts. In 1976 in Santiago, Chile, Secretary of State Henry Kissinger delivered his first major speech on human rights before the Organization of American States. The impact of this significant event was undermined by Kissinger's meeting with General Augusto Pinochet just before the speech, during which the secretary of state mentioned that he had agreed to give the speech only in response to congressional pressure at home, and he assuaged any doubts Pinochet might have had about the U.S. commitment to continue helping Chile.[1]

The possible drawbacks of public diplomacy may go beyond discrediting the seriousness of U.S. leaders whose deeds do not match their words. Public diplomacy may prompt a rights-disregarding regime to adopt a defensive posture toward the United States and become even more resistant to change, or to take specific counter-actions to indicate that the pressure has not been successful. It can also hurt an otherwise strong relationship with an ally.

Country Reports on Human Rights Practices

In 1977 President Jimmy Carter initiated a program of reporting designed to shine a brighter spotlight on human rights abuses around the world. Every year since, the State Department has issued its *Country Reports on Human Rights Practices*, which seek to detail and catalogue deficiencies in human rights adherence in countries around the world. Over the years, these reports have become more candid, have included more countries, and have grown more dispassionate in tone. Unlike other forms of U.S. public diplomacy, they do not attempt to serve as a platform for U.S. government policy. Rather, they signal to foreign governments that their practices are under scrutiny and that poor human rights practices have the potential to cost them in political or economic terms insofar as Congress, for example, may take information from these reports to justify imposing sanctions. The reports also in-advertently make it difficult for the executive branch of the U.S. gov-ernment, for Congress, and for NGOs to claim ignorance as a basis for inaction, and they make it easier for policymakers and diplomats to formulate a well-informed human rights policy.

The White House relied on the State Department reports to de-termine whether to certify El Salvador for further U.S. military assis-tance. Human rights organizations provided policymakers with infor-mation linking the Salvadoran government and military to human rights violations, and this information appeared in the reports. While this process did not directly produce improvements in El Salvador's respect for human rights, it did give the State Department an oppor-tunity to press its Salvadoran allies to adhere more closely to interna-tional human rights norms.

The *Country Reports on Human Rights Practices* have had an indi-rect impact in China. In response to its appearance in the reports, China has published its own annual report on human rights abuses in the United States, which quotes organizations such as Amnesty Inter-national and Human Rights Watch. On the one hand, this report serves to heighten animosity that ordinary Chinese citizens feel against the United States for its perceived unwillingness to practice what it preaches. On the other hand, the Chinese government is now citing documents prepared by the two largest international human rights organizations in the world, which have been highly critical of China's own human rights record in the past. By citing these organizations, China acknowledges that the information they put forward is credible, and, by extension, any criticism they may have about China's human rights abuses is legitimate. Human rights achievements, however modest, are important because of the difficulty in encouraging abu-sive governments to adhere to internationally recognized norms.

The main shortcoming of the country reports is that the impact on a target country is indirect. It is quite easy for a target government to disregard and remain indifferent to its appearance in the document.

Congressional Action

By proposing or enacting legislation that restricts U.S. economic or military support given to countries with poor human rights records, the U.S. Congress can prod the White House into action on issues that it may be reluctant to address and send a strong signal to foreign governments about the seriousness with which the United States regards particular human rights issues. Reluctantly or otherwise, the White House in turn can use such legislation to apply pressure to other governments. The results can be significant. For example, the Jackson-Vanik Amendment to the Trade Act of 1974 succeeded in pressing the Soviet Union on emigration reform. The Leahy Amendment prohibits U.S. military assistance to foreign military units that violate human rights with impunity and has helped temper human rights abuses by government forces in countries such as Colombia. Other legislation *not* directly aimed at spurring human rights reforms has also given Congress an opportunity to air its concern over the record of particular countries, as in the case of the protracted debate on granting Most Favored Nation trading status to China.

The Comprehensive Anti-Apartheid Act (CAAA) of 1986, the provisions of which included terminating direct air flights from the United States to South Africa, prohibiting new U.S. investments in South African businesses (except in black-owned firms), requiring the application of the Sullivan Principles, and limiting imports from South Africa, put human rights concerns above strategic interests. Passed by Congress despite the objections of the Reagan administration, the CAAA pressured the South African regime to abandon apartheid while laying out a clear path by which Pretoria could normalize its relations with Washington.

The Leahy Amendment was used in 1998 to help bring about the dismantling of the Colombian army's 20th Intelligence Brigade, which had been charged with committing egregious human rights abuses. But with respect to Plan Colombia (an aid package that was linked to efforts to advance the peace process), President Clinton waived the requirement that the Colombian government meet certain human rights conditions before funding could be released by declaring the situation in Colombia a U.S. national security interest. Some observers have noted that that decision undermined the strength of human rights conditionality as an effective policy tool in Colombia. Yet cutting off U.S. security aid would almost certainly have made human rights conditions worse. This dilemma underscores the challenge facing policymakers when they deal with a case as complex as that of Colombia.

Cultural, Scholarly, and Other Exchanges

The U.S. government has engaged in a wide variety of exchange programs with a vast number of countries. These programs bring together members from universities, civic groups, and sporting associations to exchange ideas and be exposed to different academic, professional, and social environments. Exchanges also may take the form of social gatherings in the homes of diplomats, as well as State Department–facilitated meetings among academics and activists. All such activities have the potential to foster a new understanding of the nature, role, and extent of human rights.

David Steinberg notes that many young people from South Korea's social elite study in U.S. graduate schools. While these South Korean students are in the United States, they are exposed to U.S. media and academic concepts that reinforce notions of political transparency and human rights and can change their outlook about rights. Similarly, the growing Korean American community is helping to export U.S. conceptions of human rights into South Korea by promoting a sharing of viewpoints among families and friends. Greater political awareness—and consequently openness—has likewise been encouraged by South Korea's hosting of the Olympic Games in 1988 and the soccer World Cup in 2002.

U.S. prosecutors and judges have been sent on training and information-exchange missions to Turkey, which has reciprocated by sending members of its judiciary to the United States. In the Soviet Union, Ambassador Jack Matlock would invite members of the Soviet parliament to his official residence, Spaso House, where they could meet with U.S. constitutional experts to discuss such topics as freedom of speech and federal-state relations. Often, ideas exchanged in this venue would sooner or later be voiced on the floor of the Soviet parliament.

One controversial form of exchange is military human rights training. The International Military Education and Training program (IMET) is the U.S. government's largest military-to-military program that has a formal human rights objective as part of its overall mandate. According to Section 541 of the Foreign Assistance Act, IMET-funded training is intended not only to improve mutual understanding and military effectiveness but also "to increase the awareness of nationals of foreign countries participating in such activities of basic issues involving internationally recognized human rights." In 1989 Colombia became Latin America's top beneficiary of the IMET program. According to Michael Shifter and Jennifer Stillerman, more than two thousand Colombian military and police officers received training in U.S. schools in the early 1990s. It is unclear, however, how significant an impact this training has had on human rights adherence by military and police personnel in Colombia. Because a collegial relationship between on-the-ground personnel and U.S. officers is developed during the IMET training sessions, it can be difficult for U.S. personnel to monitor effectively their Colombian counterparts for possible abusive practices except in cases in which particularly egregious human rights abuses occur.

Sanctions and Incentives

Various U.S. actors—from the president to Congress to private corporations—have used sanctions and incentives to try to encourage greater respect for human rights in many countries. The types of carrots and sticks that have been used vary widely, from offering or denying economic trade benefits to providing or withholding military training, to scheduling or canceling a visit by a high-ranking U.S. official. Sanctions and incentives provide muscle to back up human rights rhetoric, and when used appropriately they can be a key component of an effective human rights implementation strategy. However, they are by no means always successful and sometimes hurt the very groups they are intended to help. For example, withholding food aid to punish abusive regimes is often argued to have little impact on government behavior, because withholding such aid adds to the misery of a society's most oppressed citizens and enables the regime to portray the United States as indifferent or hostile to their suffering.

Sometimes a single violent act can trigger the imposition of a sanction. For example, in El Salvador in 1989 the murder of six Jesuit scholars generated outrage in Congress and motivated it to reevaluate military spending in that country. In 1990 Congress issued a report implicating the Salvadoran military in the murders, and soon thereafter U.S. military support for El Salvador was cut in half, with human rights–related conditions placed on the remaining half.

El Salvador and Guatemala provide an interesting example of how U.S. military training affected state behavior with respect to human rights adherence. According to Susan Burgerman, because El Salvador's armed forces were dependent on U.S. financing and training, the threat of losing that assistance helped persuade the military to submit to control by civilian government. In Guatemala, official U.S. military assistance helped build the armed forces into a modern, well-equipped, well-organized institution during the 1960s and 1970s, but such assistance was cut off under President Carter. By the time it was resumed in 1986, the Guatemalan military had established other sources of arms, such as Taiwan and Israel, and had found other enterprises, such as banking and real estate, to finance its operations. Burgerman states that the Guatemalan military's strong sense of nationalism was fostered and accentuated by a desire not to rely on U.S. assistance. In this case, less reliance on U.S. military assistance meant less leverage for the U.S. government in trying to modify the behavior of the Guatemalan government.

In the former Soviet Union, U.S. sanctions grew out of growing concern in Congress over Soviet restrictions on the right of Soviet Jews to emigrate. The Jackson-Vanik Amendment prohibited giving MFN status to non-market-economy countries that did not already enjoy MFN status unless the president could certify that these countries had no restrictions on the right to emigrate. Another piece of legislation, the Stevenson Amendment, restricted the size of loans the Export-Import Bank made for U.S.-Soviet trade. In the Soviet Union, these sanctions experienced both successes and failures linked to the overall state of U.S.-Soviet relations.

The most prominent cases of sanctioning concern China and South Africa. In the 1980s China's MFN status was hotly debated in Congress. In 1991–92 Congress voted to place conditions on trade status renewal for China, but the Bush administration vetoed those conditions on the grounds that the U.S. relationship with China was too important to jeopardize. The Bush administration also believed that MFN renewal was not the right tool with which to exert pressure, because it would serve only to isolate China. President Clinton came into office committed to emphasizing the need for China to improve its human rights record and linked China's MFN renewal with improved human rights practices. In 1994, however, Clinton delinked MFN status from China's human rights record in a shift toward emphasizing improved economic relations. According to Merle Goldman, linking MFN to human rights improvements in China did little to change China's behavior.

In South Africa, the CAAA incorporated a number of well-calibrated sanctions that made an important contribution to the collapse of the apartheid regime. As Pauline Baker notes, an important feature of the CAAA was that it provided South Africa with a road map for lifting the sanctions, thereby keeping the door open on the bilateral relationship. (Sanctions were eventually lifted in 1991, once the five conditions spelled out in the law had been satisfied.) The effectiveness of the CAAA was enhanced by other measures, notably, adoption of the Sullivan Principles and deepening engagement with the South African black population, which provided blacks with economic and educational support, which strengthened civil society and black leadership. At the same time, the United States maintained diplomatic ties with South Africa and scholarly exchanges continued between the two countries.

Democracy Building

The promotion of democracy has been a central part of U.S. foreign policy since the presidency of Woodrow Wilson, and after the end of the Cold War the link between efforts to build democracy and those to protect human rights grew stronger. As Harold Hongju Koh, former assistant secretary of state for democracy, human rights, and labor, has noted, democracy building and the promotion of human rights are typically mutually reinforcing:

> Democracy and respect for human rights have long been central
> components of U.S. foreign policy. Supporting democracy not only
> promotes such fundamental American values as religious freedom
> and worker rights, but also helps create a more secure, stable, and

prosperous global arena in which the United States can advance its
national interests. . . . [D]emocracy is the one national interest that
helps to secure all the others.[2]

Through agencies such as the U.S. Agency for International
Development (USAID) and nongovernmental organizations such as
the National Endowment for Democracy (NED), the United States
has supported a plethora of local NGOs around the world that focus
on grassroots initiatives that strengthen civil society.

In the 1990s USAID funded modest programs in Kenya that
were designed to strengthen the local legislature and promote electoral
reform. As Joel Barkan notes, the U.S. government supported several
civil society organizations, including the Human Rights Commission of
Kenya and the Law Society of Kenya, and eventually expanded its programs by providing support to the electoral process from the African
Regional Election Assistance Fund. This support included grants
totaling more than $100,000 to the National Election Monitoring
Unit, a consortium of Kenyan NGOs that ultimately trained and posted
observers to roughly half of the nine thousand polling stations established for the 1992 elections. Such efforts, together with calls for the
introduction of a multiparty political system by Ambassador Smith
Hempstone, former cabinet ministers from the government of President Daniel arap Moi, and the international donor community, contributed to a gradual shift in the character of the regime, culminating
in Moi's legalization of multiparty politics in 1991. These democracy-
building efforts have had a positive impact on human rights conditions
within Kenya and constitute the first steps in a long path toward a
rights-based regime.

As for Turkey, Henri Barkey notes that the issues of human rights
and democracy promotion have engendered lower-key responses from
U.S. policymakers. That said, the United States has supported programs that have helped to strengthen civil society in Turkey, including
judicial exchanges and support for NGO activities. Neither of these
programs inflames sensitivities in the way that public U.S. condemnations of human rights abuses would, and they have helped to move
Turkey closer to democracy. They also demonstrate a commitment by
the U.S. government to improving respect for human rights.

Symbolic Actions

U.S. diplomats have found that symbolic actions can be of great value when not only the target government but also the media are paying attention. For example, when, in the late 1990s, the mayor of Istanbul (and later the prime minister), Recep Tayyip Erdogan, was imprisoned and barred for life from politics for reading a poem, the U.S. consul general in Istanbul was instructed to visit Erdogan in his office. The visit caused uproar in Turkey and sent a strong message to the Turkish regime that the U.S. government disapproved of this infringement on freedom of speech. In Kenya, Smith Hempstone would invite members of the dissident community to parties at the U.S. ambassador's residence. This gesture was intended to convey to the Moi regime that while the U.S. government was prepared to engage with the regime, it also intended to remain engaged with the grassroots opposition groups. Such examples underscore one of the strengths of symbolic actions: because their meaning tends to be implicit rather than explicit, the target state finds it harder to complain of U.S. interference in its internal affairs. For instance, a regime would be loath to admit that it would want to exert control over the U.S. ambassador's choice of personal guests at a social function.

On occasion, the failure to make a symbolic gesture can also send a powerful—if unintended and unfortunate—message to a regime about the level of U.S. concern with its human rights record. For instance, the failure of Jeane Kirkpatrick, the U.S. ambassador to the United Nations, to visit any leading human rights advocates during her 1981 visit to Chile attracted much attention in that country and elsewhere. Perhaps not coincidentally, one of those leading advocates was exiled by the Pinochet regime just a few days after Kirkpatrick's departure from the country.

The Media

The media offer policymakers a means to communicate a message to a vast audience, both within the United States and abroad. Policymakers must usually compete, however, with other actors, such as NGOs, for media attention. Moreover, the U.S. media have a tradition of prizing their editorial independence and are careful not to be seen as mouthpieces for the government in Washington, and foreign media are often skeptical of U.S. motives and claims. But while U.S. officials must accept that the media may air the concerns of groups critical of the U.S. government's human rights policy or may question Washington's assertions, they can take comfort in the fact that the appearance in the media of stories supporting the government's position can greatly enhance the government's credibility with the public.

Different elements of the U.S. government bureaucracy sometimes use the media to fight their internal battles. For instance, in an effort to apply public and political pressure on the executive to pay more attention to the crisis in Yugoslavia, the State Department deliberately leaked to the *New York Times* a draft of a highly sensitive intelligence document that predicted the breakup of federated Yugoslavia.

More often, however, the U.S. government must respond to the impact of news coverage rather than shape that impact. For instance, television images of South African security forces brutalizing anti-apartheid activists fueled the debate in the United States and helped to mobilize a U.S. constituency against the apartheid regime.

Problems generated by the media's independence do not, of course, occur with those media that the U.S. government itself funds and operates, such as the Voice of America. These give the government an opportunity to transmit the range of American thought directly to people in other countries, including views on human rights. In the Soviet Union, to cite one example, Radio Liberty would broadcast book-length productions of samizdat material at dictation speed so that listeners in that country could transcribe the broadcasts.

LESSONS FOR HUMAN RIGHTS POLICYMAKERS

The following six lessons are intended as guidelines for those entrusted with crafting and executing U.S. human rights policies. Together, they may serve as a useful frame of reference as policymakers pilot policies through an increasingly complex international arena. A number of the lessons may seem self-evident, but they nevertheless seem to have been forgotten or overlooked by U.S. officials on various occasions.

Each recommendation has emerged in at least two of the case studies explored in this volume, which offers some assurance that the lessons may be transferable to other situations. Even so, the lessons are not intended to be used as a universally applicable checklist of do's and don'ts. Sometimes it may be impossible to follow the advice given in the following pages. Always it will be necessary to interpret and apply the recommendations (which have deliberately been kept general) in light of situation-specific objectives, resources, and constraints.

Adopt a Long-Term Perspective and a Sustained Approach

Establishing, nurturing, and reinforcing conditions that ensure human rights protections require perseverance and commitment from U.S. policymakers. Maintaining a long-term vision is crucial if the goal of a rights-protective environment in any specific country is to be accomplished. This is not to say that short-term objectives should be neglected; rather, the challenge confronting policymakers is to balance short- and long-term goals. Too often, however, the long-term vision necessary to bring about profound change in the respect accorded human rights is superseded by immediate-term objectives. While short-term policy responses are necessary to end immediate human rights abuses, short-term goals are best achieved within the framework of a long-term strategy for respecting and protecting all human rights. Action to promote long-term objectives (such as creating and sustaining a political environment that protects freedom of speech, allows room for dissenting opinion, and fosters an independent judicial system) can also help to promote short-term objectives (such as securing the release of political prisoners, clamping down on torture, and ending the use of child soldiers). Sustaining a long-range human rights policy objective while addressing immediate human rights violations will have lasting impact on the target country.

The case of Bosnia illustrates that policies of ignoring human rights abuses become increasingly hard to sustain over time and can allow those abuses to evolve into broader, much more significant U.S. foreign policy concerns. Jon Western argues that early preventive diplomacy by the United States could have forestalled the surge of violence in Bosnia. He notes that when the United States and other NATO members finally issued strong and unambiguous condemnations of Serb atrocities in Bosnia, Serb behavior changed.

Joel Barkan contends that the most important lesson from the experience of Kenya in the 1990s is that the path to democracy and human rights adherence is long and arduous. With this in mind, policymakers must remember that a single election does not indicate that democratic principles have been established or will be sustained. Keeping a long-term perspective on human rights goals will help to avoid a tendency to abandon a policy prematurely because officials mistakenly view a short-term achievement as the final outcome of a policy goal.

Just as elections do not mean that democracy has necessarily taken root in a given country, the end of a dictatorship does not necessarily mean that human rights will henceforth enjoy protection. For this reason, it is essential that the United States not abandon human rights and democratization efforts just as a transition to democracy gets under way.

The challenge of adopting a long-term perspective is compounded by the nature of the U.S. government bureaucracy. U.S. human rights policy must be constructed and implemented within the unwieldy structure of a bureaucracy that fosters competing interests within itself. The interagency policy process requires that policymakers spend much of their time coordinating their agendas with, or advancing their agendas over the objections of, other U.S. government agencies. Typically, too, influential policymakers tend to spend at most a few years in one post, which gives them precious little time to oversee the adoption, still less the implementation, of a particular policy, and which encourages the tendency to favor short-term over long-term objectives. Furthermore, the department charged with protecting human rights and promoting democracy does not have the same prestige and authority within the U.S. bureaucratic apparatus that other regional bureaus do, which not only makes it harder to promote human rights concerns but also illustrates the lower importance accorded to human rights within the overall scheme of U.S. foreign policy making.

Choosing which human rights problems to address extends beyond the Bureau of Democracy, Human Rights, and Labor to encompass the U.S. government as a whole. With limited resources, all policymakers must designate human rights priorities, and typically these priorities are self-selecting: those countries in the midst of crisis, especially if the crisis is being widely covered in the media, tend to elbow their way onto the U.S. agenda, pushing aside longer-term problems with lower media visibility. As policymakers lurch inconsistently from crisis to crisis, their credibility inevitably suffers.

Long-term human rights objectives are worth pursuing because they bring about incremental changes that provide the foundation for meaningful and enduring improvement in human rights adherence. As Susan Burgerman notes in her chapter on El Salvador and Guatemala, benefits that can result from a foreign policy that incorporates a human rights component include domestic and international credibility, the delegitimization of abusive governments, and the empowering of indigenous human rights organizations and other marginalized groups in civil society. One of the main lessons of U.S. human rights policy toward Latin America is that quick fixes seldom eradicate the problem. Indeed, rather than expecting immediate and tangible results from its human rights policies in Latin America, the United States should measure success in systemic terms: strengthening the rule of law, consolidating civil societies, encouraging greater policy coherence in the U.S. government, increasing effectiveness of multilateral institutions, and heightening perceptions of U.S. support for human rights in the region.

Include Human Rights in Democracy Building

Developing democratic institutions is critical to sustaining advances in the protection of human rights. The mechanisms and institutional infrastructure that make up a democratic system of government also protect the rights of its citizens. Furthermore, when the United States does little to encourage authoritarian governments with which it is allied to introduce democracy and respect human rights, it risks the overthrow of those governments and their replacement with equally authoritarian but unfriendly regimes.[3]

Democracy-building initiatives seek to develop, for example, informed public opinion, an independent judiciary and legal system, fair trials, and a political system that depends on open debate and permits considerable individual freedom. The long-term success of democracy building is essential for the protection of human rights, though tensions sometimes develop between democracy building and human rights objectives in the short-term because they are not always identical. Democracy building without human rights promotion risks opening the door to what Fareed Zakaria has called illiberal democracy—a system of government that allows elected officials to carry out rights-abusing practices.[4]

Evidence from Rwanda in the late 1980s to early 1990s demonstrates the dangers of allowing human rights violations to continue while pursuing broader efforts in democracy building. Alison Des Forges notes that the U.S. government provided democratization assistance and support for human rights organizations. President Juvénal Habyarimana gave the appearance of respecting human rights by speaking publicly in support of them, hosting conferences on the subject, and declaring his support for political openness. In reality, however, the regime was discriminating against the Tutsi minority by excluding Tutsi from schools and government jobs and using a system of population registration and identity cards that specified ethnic affiliation. The United States, encouraged by Habyarimana's effective administrative style and rhetoric, failed to directly challenge the regime on egregious human rights violations, thereby allowing the violence to escalate.

Paula Newberg draws similar conclusions in a critique of U.S. policy toward Pakistan in the late 1990s. The U.S. attitude toward Pakistan's human rights record ignored lessons learned in promoting democracy elsewhere. Newberg notes that democracy can be achieved only with systemic rights guarantees. "When rights are separated from politics, rights cannot be guaranteed . . . When external powers accede to the diminution or disregard for rights in order to achieve other objectives, their complicity in denying rights dramatically limits any capacity to realize those other goals."

The Soviet Union in the 1980s is an example of how democracy-building efforts and human rights promotion can work together and reinforce other important policy objectives. U.S. government efforts to promote both human rights and democracy were generally successful in the Soviet Union in the 1980s. President Reagan's 1985 four-point policy plan toward the Soviet Union made human rights goals a part of other important aspects of the U.S.-Soviet relationship—reduced nuclear weapons, an end to superpower military involvement in regional conflicts, greater respect for human rights and greater political openness, and improved communications. According to Jack Matlock, Reagan indicated that no single area would see improvement unless all areas saw improvement. By 1991 citizens of Moscow and surrounding areas enjoyed basic rights such as free speech, a free press, and the right to assemble. Matlock reminds us, however, that while the United States set the conditions for the end of the Cold War, internal forces were ultimately responsible for the end of communism in the Soviet Union.

Support Local NGOs in Target Countries

Since the 1960s the number of human rights–oriented NGOs has grown substantially, as has their ability to shape public opinion and affect government decision making. NGOs such as the Kenya Human Rights Commission and the Egyptian Center for Women's Rights play vital roles in, for example, monitoring and evaluating governments' compliance with human rights standards, publicizing abuses, demanding the prosecution of those responsible, campaigning for greater observance of international norms, and educating the general public about their rights. Through such activities, NGOs have improved the human rights performance not only of governments but also of many prominent transnational corporations. Indeed, efforts by the NGOs to promote corporate responsibility have compelled many firms to establish policies and programs to address the possible negative effects of their operations on human rights; this trend, in turn, is helping to ensure that human rights policies will not become subordinated to commercial interests in U.S. policymaking.

Recognizing the crucial role the NGO community plays, since the 1980s the U.S. government has increased its involvement with and support of local NGOs working to improve human rights conditions in many different countries. Support can take different forms, including direct financial assistance, technical assistance and training, and public endorsements and statements of support. Benefits to U.S. objectives may include tangible improvements in human rights conditions and better insight into local issues, thus helping to develop more effective policies.

As Harry Barnes comments, although the key developments enabling the transition to democracy were undoubtedly indigenous to

Chile, U.S. policies and actions invigorated the pro-democracy movement. USAID channeled assistance through the Organization of American States for voter registration. Meanwhile, the U.S. embassy promoted the sharing of ideas with opposition leaders and NGOs working in the areas of voter registration and civic education—and with members of the junta, human rights NGOs, the church, and the media. While the opposition movement and the intra-junta divisions can be credited with driving the transition in Chile, various U.S. actors—Congress, USAID, NGOs, and the White House—furthered the cause through their work with the NGO community. While both advantages and problems flow from the partly adversarial, partly collaborative relationship between the U.S. government and the NGO community, as the case of Chile illustrates, the overall impact of this collaboration on human rights has been positive.

The case of China demonstrates the importance of working with local actors to encourage domestic reform. As Merle Goldman indicates in her chapter, the development of a core of human rights experts in China has led to the slow but necessary process needed to bring about a shift in Chinese views on human rights and to move China to narrow the gap between its domestic policies and internationally accepted norms regarding human rights.

The promotion of human rights also depends on engagement with a wide array of local actors other than NGOs: businesses, religious communities and leaders, media, teachers, and so forth. These groups and individuals—together with international actors such as intergovernmental organizations and lending institutions[5]—help to broaden the U.S. government's base of knowledge, which is necessary to create an informed, effective policy. The advent of new technologies such as the Internet and cell phones has made communication with this varied group easier.

The United States cannot impose its own style of democracy and particular conception of human rights on any country, but it can help foster an environment of increased openness that can lead to an improved human rights situation. Given that the pressure for profound societal changes must come from within the society itself, it is critical for the United States to help local actors find a foothold, especially in environments where repressive regimes continually frustrate reform efforts. Support for local NGOs was important to the collapse of communism in the former Soviet Union and the fall of the apartheid regime in South Africa; it also helped ensure that the transitions to democracy in both those countries were relatively peaceful.

Work Multilaterally, Whenever Possible

The United States should use the potential of multilateral action to the fullest. As many of the case studies have shown, working multilaterally or supporting multilateral efforts through intergovernmental institutions such as the United Nations tends to be more productive in influencing the behavior of a target government than are unilateral initiatives. Unilateral initiatives are also likely to be controversial and more costly. Multilateral action can take a wide variety of forms, ranging from imposing economic sanctions through international lending institutions, to joining with coalition partners in military action against an abusive regime, to banding together with like-minded member-states in a diplomatic setting to criticize another country's poor human rights record. In a limited number of circumstances, unilateral action may be desirable—for example, in situations in which time is of critical importance, such as cases involving the release of political prisoners. But the danger of acting unilaterally is that U.S. motivations may be questioned and U.S. credibility on human rights issues imperiled.

In China, pressure has proved more effective when the United States and Western nations have been united on tactics and goals. Merle Goldman argues that the most effective means for dealing with China's abuses have been through multilateral institutions such as the UN Human Rights Commission (UNHRC). Rising nationalism and increased resentment toward the United States has resulted in Chinese leaders giving more weight to criticisms from the international community, particularly those voiced through the UNHRC. Multilateral efforts in the UNHRC helped prompt China to sign the International Covenants on Economic, Social and Cultural Rights and on Civil and Political Rights in the late 1990s. The fact that their government has acknowledged the validity of these human rights documents has emboldened Chinese citizens to secure greater freedom. In 1998, for example, China's first opposition party, the China Democracy Party, was formed.

In Bosnia, despite U.S. unresponsiveness in the initial phases of the war, combined U.S. and NATO forces waged an air campaign that deterred further abuses.

In Kenya, the United States has had a greater impact in promoting respect for human rights and democracy when it has joined forces with other international actors.

Another example of successful multilateral efforts is the Helsinki Final Act of 1975, a document that, although nonbinding, articulated unprecedented consensus among thirty-five countries on a broad range of international issues, among them human rights. The Helsinki Final Act had two immediate positive benefits vis-à-vis the Soviet Union: it allowed Soviet officials to discuss specific human rights problems, even in cases in which U.S. citizens were not involved (at that time, Soviet authorities refused to discuss human rights concerns other than those with a direct U.S.-citizen interest); and it gave dissidents a legitimate reason to organize to monitor how Soviet authorities observe an international document signed by the Soviet leader. While being a signatory to the Helsinki Final Act did not prevent the Soviet regime from trying to suppress the dissident movement, such action only discredited and weakened the Soviet regime at home.

Avoid Double Standards

A theme that has resonated throughout this evaluation has been the need to balance competing interests in order to achieve a more effective human rights policy—striking this balance involves recognizing that trade-offs must be made to advance a multilayered and complex U.S. foreign policy. According to State Department officials, U.S. foreign policy rests on a foundation of interests, the top tier of which is national security, economic stability, and respect for human rights. (Secondary interests include public health and the environment.) While these interests complement one another, they also compete for resources and attention in the policy sphere.

Policymakers must weigh human rights concerns against strategic and economic considerations as they formulate foreign policy. Where human rights falls in the pecking order depends on the bilateral relationship between the United States and any given country. China is of particular importance to the United States, and so while the issue of human rights is now a frequent point of contention between the two countries, it is also not an issue that ranks above such concerns as combating terrorism, maintaining stability in East Asia, preventing nuclear proliferation, and expanding U.S. trade and investment in the region. Conversely, in Burma, where no other first-tier U.S. interests are involved, observance of human rights is the stated top concern of the U.S. government. This is not to say that human rights will figure prominently only where no other interests are at stake, but it is to underline the fact that human rights must always compete for the attention of policymakers.

The aftermath of the attacks of September 11, 2001, and the onset of the "war on terrorism" have shed a particularly stark light on the struggle to balance competing objectives. Consider the case of Pakistan. After General Pervez Musharraf took power in the 1999 coup, Pakistan was shunned by the Western world. It was a country that fell abysmally short of internationally recognized human rights standards even before Musharraf assumed power, and under his leadership the situation has arguably grown worse. Musharraf has abrogated the constitution, handpicked supreme court judges and military officials, arrested politicians without charge or trial, and given himself the ability to dissolve parliament at will. Immediately after September 11, Pakistan acquired frontline status in the U.S.-led war on terrorism, and to secure its vital cooperation the United States lifted sanctions and restored economic and military assistance. Human rights concerns now haunt the sidelines of U.S. policy toward Pakistan.

In this instance, the United States' immediate strategic interests outweigh its long-term interests in democracy and human rights. The problem is that short- or indefinite-term support for antidemocratic regimes may breed more terrorism in the long run, given that terrorism thrives in the shadow of tyranny. It may be recalled that after the 1979 Soviet invasion of Afghanistan, the United States rewarded an earlier Pakistani strongman, General Zia ul-Haq, with billions of dollars of assistance, much of which Pakistan's secret police and military-intelligence apparatus channeled to Islamic extremists and their allies.

In South Korea, according to David Steinberg, no U.S. administration (with the possible exception of the Carter administration) put human rights concerns above those of security on the Korean peninsula. During the Cold War, the United States saw the Korean peninsula as an area where a local conflict could threaten the security of the entire region. One way in which the United States sought to counter this threat was to encourage the development of an independent and democratic South Korea. However, because the United States mostly worked through quiet diplomacy, the perception among South Koreans was that the United States was condoning Seoul's authoritarian government.

Be Public about Condemning Abuses and Honest about Human Rights Goals

When serious human rights abuses exist, the first priority should be to stop them. Sometimes quiet initiatives can achieve success in this regard. But in the absence of a clear and public condemnation of ongoing abuses, tools such as private diplomacy can give the impression of U.S. complicity in or indifference toward the abuses.

In Rwanda, the U.S. government had some success in halting abuses by using quiet diplomacy—protecting Jehovah's Witnesses from arbitrary arrest in 1986 and saving Tutsi from targeted killings in 1990, for example. But as Alison Des Forges notes, without a clear, firm, and public condemnation of the abuses, those efforts did not produce long-term reform. The regime returned to harassing Jehovah's Witnesses after their release from prison and began to slaughter Tutsi again after halting one massacre. Des Forges goes on to note that the absence of public condemnation served to strengthen the extremists and weaken the moderates in the regime, thereby discouraging those who might have resisted the brutal killing campaign.

Together with public condemnations, a consistent articulation of the place of human rights goals within the broad framework of other policy goals helps to communicate to both a domestic and an international audience the rationale for seemingly inconsistent behavior. As long as policies continue to be pursued in an ad hoc fashion, policymakers will continue to be criticized for double standards. An honest account of policy action can serve to lessen these accusations. If the United States is giving aid to Pakistan because Pakistan is essential to the prosecution of the U.S. war on terrorism, the United States should explicitly state as much. It is damaging to the credibility of the United

States to pretend that nondemocratic nations have better human rights records than they do or practice democratic reforms when they don't. Paula Newberg contends that both the United States and Pakistan "act and speak as if rights-disregarding regimes were simply alternative forms of government"; "rights and democracy have become dispensable in Pakistan because they have been treated as if they were disposable."

In looking at South Korea, David Steinberg concludes that "a policy of transparency related to rights and regime support will prove more effective over the long term." He also notes that, to judge from the South Korean experience, abusive governments will hold up U.S. silence on human rights abuses or undemocratic practices as an example of support for abusive policies and practices. Such silence diminishes U.S. credibility in the eyes of many South Koreans.

Denis Sullivan argues that because Egypt is seen as a critical ally in maintaining the fragile stability in the Middle East, it has escaped U.S. public censure for its human rights abuses. The lack of an immediate forceful and public condemnation of the lengthy prison sentence handed down to Saad Eddin Ibrahim illustrates the absence of a long-term U.S. strategy for stability in the region. In response to the audible protests from NGOs and U.S. and international media over the failure of the United States to react in any forceful way to Ibrahim's sentencing, the U.S. government for the first time publicly threatened an aid freeze and linked economic aid to Egypt's treatment of Ibrahim and of pro-democracy organizations in that country. When the United States fails consistently to give vocal support to democratic institutions in other countries, it undermines strategies to dampen extremist forces in those countries and endangers its integrity and credibility in the world community.

• • •

Since the presidency of Jimmy Carter, the promotion of human rights has been one of the stated organizing principles of U.S. foreign policy-making. The events of September 11, 2001, however, have shifted the foreign policy paradigm dramatically. Protecting the nation from the threat of terrorist attacks now dominates the framework within which human rights objectives are pursued. Despite this change in focus, however, the lessons distilled from the case studies in this volume continue to apply. Indeed, given that states that ignore the human rights of their citizens are more likely to harbor and export terrorism than are rights-respecting nations, those lessons have yet greater importance and relevance than before.

Some critics of U.S. human rights policy have advocated much greater consistency in its application. Such a goal, however, will always be thwarted by the fact that making and implementing U.S. policy toward a particular country is shaped by the inevitably unique bilateral relationship that the United States has with that country and by the unique and constantly shifting local and regional context. Even so, if U.S. policy implementation cannot be perfectly consistent, it can be a good deal less inconsistent if policymakers and diplomats heed the lessons presented in this chapter. Greater consistency in the U.S. response to human rights violations abroad will enhance U.S. credibility with other nations, as well as with individuals and groups seeking improvements in human rights conditions. Improved consistency may also contribute to a more effective overall policy.

In most cases, the U.S. government's ability to encourage greater respect for human rights in a given country depends on the extent of U.S. influence over local actors. A coherent, consistent, and articulated approach to human rights causes is critical to the U.S. government's ability to exercise such influence. Policy positions articulated and advocated at the highest levels of government leave an impression of serious intent, associate the United States directly and clearly with the defense of human rights, and ensure that all the relevant actors know where the United States stands. The global preeminence that the United States holds at the outset of the twenty-first century makes it all the more important for the United States to set an example of strong leadership in the field of human rights. This preeminence is its historical fate; such leadership is its historical responsibility.

NOTES

1. Kissinger saw to it that the United States concluded new military contracts with Chile before Congress could impose restrictions, abstained in a

vote at the United Nations on a resolution critical of Pinochet, and voted to support loans to Chile from the leading international financial institutions.

2. U.S. Department of State, *Bureau Performance Plan, Fiscal Years 1999, 2000, 2001* (Washington, D.C.: Department of State, Bureau of Democracy, Human Rights, Labor, June 1999).

3. In a similar vein, Thomas Friedman has argued in reference to the Muslim world that if the alternative to violent expression of dissent is democracy and if democratic alternatives are not available, "the only route left in many countries for expressing discontent is religious fundamentalism." Thomas Friedman, "Bush's Shame," *New York Times,* August 4, 2002.

4. See Fareed Zakaria, "The Rise of Illiberal Democracy," *Foreign Affairs* 76, no. 6 (November-December 1997).

5. Joel Barkan points out in his chapter that the World Bank does not determine lending based on human rights criteria. But if it and other international lending institutions continue to support repressive regimes, democratization efforts will be more difficult to pursue successfully.

Selected Bibliography

The following works have helped to inform the Human Rights Implementation Project during the course of its study.

An-Na'im, Abdullahi Ahmed, and Francis M. Deng, eds. *Human Rights in Africa: Cross-Cultural Perspectives*. Washington, D.C.: Brookings Institution, 1990.

Brown, Peter G., and Douglas MacLean, eds. *Human Rights and U.S. Foreign Policy: Principles and Applications*. Lexington, Mass.: D. C. Heath, Lexington Books, 1980.

Carothers, Thomas. *Aiding Democracy Abroad: The Learning Curve*. Washington, D.C.: Carnegie Endowment for International Peace, 2000.

Chase, Robert, Emily Hill, and Paul Kennedy, eds. *The Pivotal States: A New Framework for U.S. Policy in the Developing World*. New York: W. W. Norton, 1999.

Cortright, David, and George A. Lopez. *Sanctions and the Search for Security: Challenges to UN Action*. Boulder, Colo.: Lynne Rienner, 2002.

Dalacoura, Katerina. *Islam, Liberalism and Human Rights*. London: I. B. Tauris, 1998.

Diamond, Larry. *Promoting Democracy in the 1990s: Actors and Instruments, Issues and Imperatives*. New York: Carnegie Commission on Preventing Deadly Conflict, Carnegie Corporation of New York, 1995.

Donnelly, Jack. *International Human Rights*. Boulder, Colo.: Westview Press, 1998.

———. *Universal Human Rights in Theory and Practice*. Ithaca, N.Y.: Cornell University Press, 1989.

Forsythe, David P. *Human Rights and U.S. Foreign Policy*. Gainesville, Fla.: University of Florida Press, 1988.

———. *Human Rights in International Relations*. Cambridge: Cambridge University Press, 2000.

Forsythe, David P., and Barbara Ann J. Rieffer. "U.S. Foreign Policy and Enlarging the Democratic Community." *Human Rights Quarterly* 22, no. 4 (November 2000): 988–1010.

Hesse, Carla, and Robert Post, eds. *Human Rights in Political Transitions: Gettysburg to Bosnia*. New York: Zone Books, 1999.

Ignatieff, Michael. *Human Rights as Politics and Idolatry*. Princeton, N.J.: Princeton University Press, 2003.

Ignatieff, Michael. "Is the Human Rights Era Ending?" *New York Times*, February 5, 2002.

Korey, William. *NGOs and the Universal Declaration of Human Rights: A Curious Grapevine*. New York: Palgrave Macmillan, 1998.

Lawyers Committee for Human Rights. *In the National Interest 2001: Human Rights Policies for the Bush Administration*. New York: Lawyers Committee for Human Rights, 2001.

Mayer, Ann Elizabeth. *Islam and Human Rights: Tradition and Politics*. Boulder, Colo.: Westview Press, 1999.

Müllerson, Rein. *Human Rights Diplomacy*. London: Routledge, 1997.

Newsom, David D., ed. *The Diplomacy of Human Rights*. Washington, D.C.: Institute for the Study of Diplomacy, Georgetown University, and University Press of America, 1986.

Nolan, Cathal J. *Principled Diplomacy: Security and Rights in U.S. Foreign Policy*. Westport, Conn.: Greenwood Press, 1993.

Ottaway, Marina, and Thomas Carothers, eds. *Funding Virtue: Civil Society Aid and Democracy Promotion*. Washington, D.C.: Carnegie Endowment for International Peace, 2000.

Plattner, Marc F., and João Carlos Espada, eds. *The Democratic Invention*. Baltimore, Md.: Johns Hopkins University Press and the National Endowment for Democracy, 2000.

Power, Samantha. *"A Problem from Hell": America and the Age of Genocide*. New York: Perennial Press, 2003.

Renteln, Alison Dundes. *International Human Rights: Universalism versus Relativism*. Newbury Park, Calif.: Sage, 1990.

Schulz, William F. *In Our Own Best Interests: How Defending Human Rights Benefits Us All*. Boston: Beacon Press, 2002.

Shue, Henry. *Basic Rights: Subsistence, Affluence, and U.S. Foreign Policy*. Princeton, N.J.: Princeton University Press, 1980.

Steinmetz, Sara. *Democratic Transition and Human Rights: Perspectives on U.S. Foreign Policy*. Albany, N.Y.: State University of New York Press, 1994.

Van Ness, Peter, ed. *Debating Human Rights: Critical Essays from the United States and Asia*. New York: Routledge, 1999.

Vogelgesang, Sandy. *American Dream, Global Nightmare: The Dilemma of U.S. Human Rights Policy*. New York: Council on Foreign Relations, W. W. Norton, 1980.

Weiss, Thomas G., David Cortright, George A. Lopez, and Larry Minear. *Political Gain and Civilian Pain: Humanitarian Impacts of Economic Sanctions*. Lanham, Md.: Rowman and Littlefield, 1997.

Index

467

IMPLEMENTING U.S. HUMAN RIGHTS POLICY

This book is set in Goudy; the display type is Goudy Bold. The Creative Shop designed the book's cover; Mike Chase designed the interior. Helene Y. Redmond made up the pages. David Sweet copyedited the text, which was proofread by Karen Stough. The index was prepared by Sonsie Conroy. The book's editor was Nigel Quinney.